LATE
NIGHTS
ON
**A WOMAN'S
GUIDE TO
VIDEO
AND FILM**
VENUS

COMPILED AND REVIEWED BY JEAN WARMBOLD

A Larkdale Press Book

LATE NIGHTS ON VENUS

A Larkdale Press Book
Published by Larkdale Press
2014 Larkdale Avenue
Glenview, Illinois 60025-4210

First edition: Januaary 2000
Copyright © 1999 by Larkdale Press

Library of Congress Cataloging-in-Publication Data:
Late Nights on Venus: A Woman's Guide to Video and Film
compiled by Jean Warmbold. Includes index.

Design: Carol Gerhardt

ISBN 0-9675292-0-4

I. Motion Pictures... Reviews.
II. Video Recordings... Reviews.
III. Feminism and Motion Pictures.

Printed in the United States of America.

CONTENTS

INTRODUCTION

*"Men and women disagree
about what's sexy on screen."*
Guy Garcia,
THE NEW YORK TIMES

Precisely. There are also times when we disagree about
what is funny, romantic, adventurous, and clearly too violent on screen. Which should come as no surprise. As the
saying goes, women are from Venus, men are from Mars.

Now in your hands is the first unabashedly female-attuned
guide to video and film, conceived *by* a woman *for* women.
The author—a lifelong movie buff—has spent close to four
years viewing and re-viewing thousands of videos, ultimately whittling down her selection to 550 eminently
entertaining films. It's blood relations over blood baths,
apt wit over slapstick, mindful deed over mindless speed,
and strong female characters who are no longer trapped
inside a male's imagination or fantasies.

It is not only gender perspective which sets LATE NIGHTS apart from other video guides, but format. Mood is the operative word here—your mood.

Longing for some old-fashioned romance, where in spite of all obstacles the woman gets her man? Chapter One—**THAT CRAZY THING CALLED LOVE**—will amply fill the bill.

Or vice versa, fancy a film where the woman is duking it out solo? We suggest any of the choices under **ON OUR OWN**.

Had a downer with your boss/boyfriend/girlfriend/Mom/ ad infinitum? Then **COMEDY WITH A HEART** is guaranteed to give you that needed lift.

Or would you rather cry than laugh with a cathartic five-hankie weeper? Check into **HEARTBREAK HOTEL**.

For straightforward drama see **TIMELESS TALES WELL TOLD**.

And when looking for a mystery or live-wire thriller which both you and your Significant Other can enjoy, refer to **WHODUNIT?** and **NAIL-BITERS**.

A final bonus chapter suggests a number of video festivals for those rainy weekends on the lam.

It should be noted that all the films included in this guide *are* available on video cassette. If your local outlet doesn't stock certain desired selections, do not hesitate asking them to consider adding the movies to their inventory. (We found independent video stores in our area to be happily willing to cater to customer requests.)

Another option is to buy the films outright from bargain basement distributers found on the internet. With that in mind, we have provided you with an extended list of web site video superstores, many which will sell you new and used videos for as low as $3.95. (We celebrated completing this guide by purchasing thirty-five gems at prices between $6 and $9 a piece.) Why buy when you can rent, one may well ask. Our answer: for the simple reason that many of those special, heartfelt films get even better with the passage of time.

Now get out that bowl of popcorn, kick back, and enjoy!

OUR WEB SITE MAIL-ORDERING GUIDE...

Surf and you shall find!

abbyroad.com

amazon.com

bestvideo.com

blowoutvideo.com

buyvideos.com

bigstar.com

blockbuster.com

borders.com

brainplay.com

cdworld.com

dvdexpress.com

formovies.com

moviesunlimited.com

net.flix.com

newreleasesvideo.com

picpal.com

reel.com

secondspin.com

spree.com

starguideweb.com

totale.com

usedvideo.com

videoflicks.com

video express.com

videoserve.com

the video station.com

videovault.com

video@yesteryear.com

THAT CRAZY THING CALLED LOVE

"As my old friend Zannebaum used to say: women make the best psychoanalysts until they fall in love. Then they make the best patients."
Michael Chekhov to Ingrid Bergman,
SPELLBOUND

"I just met the most wonderful man. He's fictional, but you can't have everything."
Mia Farrow commenting on the new love in her life,
THE PURPLE ROSE OF CAIRO

ABOUT LAST NIGHT...

opens with a sexy one-night stand which catches co-stars Demi Moore and Rob Lowe off-guard by turning into a serious relationship. The two soon move in together, much to the distress of their best friends Elizabeth Perkins and James Belushi, and an exceptionally genuine love story unfolds. But it doesn't take long for the predictable polarities to kick into action, driving the increasingly restless and all-too-handsome Lowe to greener pastures elsewhere. If the only enjoyment you derive from this film stems from the abundance of erotic scenes between our two principals, it's still worth the price of admission. But there are plenty of fringe benefits to this seriocomic look at the mating rituals of the 80s, not the least which are the solid contributions from Perkins and Belushi as the love-struck couple's increasingly possessive confidantes. (Belushi has the macho blowhard down to an exact science.) Direction by Edward Zwick, the man who brought us 'thirtysomething,' and a piquant screenplay co-written by a woman, reinforce the film's fair-minded approach to the age-old battle of the sexes. Special mention is due Moore's unusually sympathetic performance, and for a few well-positioned love tunes, including 'She's Living Inside My Heart Now,' and 'When You Love Someone.'
1986. 113m. DIR: Edward Zwick. WRIT: Denise DeClue, Tim Kazurinsky. CAST: Demi Moore, Rob Lowe, James Belushi, Elizabeth Perkins, George DiCenzo.

THE AFRICAN QUEEN...

shot on location in the former Belgian Congo, is a delightful mix of unpredictable adventure and offbeat romance. Katharine Hepburn co-stars as the prim and proper spinster sister of Methodist missionary Robert Morley. When Morley is murdered in German East Africa after the outbreak of WWI, the stranded Hepburn has no choice but to accept an offer of safe passage from gin-guzzling steamer captain Humphrey Bogart. At the onset, these two lost souls appear to be utterly ill-matched. (Bogie to his new charge: "I asked you on board 'cause I was sorry for you on account of losing your brother and all. Well, I ain't sorry no more, you crazy, psalm-singing, skinny old maid!") Which is all the more reason to savor how credibly their original distrust, nigh aversion, gradually transmutes into a love for the ages. It is a moving story, playful, humorous, and thrilling by turn, as our wayfarers meet increasing dangers down the river, both from beast and—in a rousing finale—from man.

1951. 105m. DIR: John Huston. WRIT: James Agee, John Huston. CAST: Katharine Hepburn, Humphrey Bogart, Robert Morley.

THE AMERICAN PRESIDENT...

is a politically savvy and sweet-natured love story made all the more refreshing by treating the office of the Presidency with respect, sympathy, and humor. Michael Douglas stars as a widowed Democratic president who—after a long romantic dormancy—finds himself attracted to outspoken environmental lobbyist Annette Bening. Choosing to ignore the political fallout such a liaison might portend for an upcoming election year, Douglas pursues the appealing Bening, and a roller-coaster romance plays out against the drama of behind-the-scenes political deals, factional infighting, and presidential protocol. Cheers for Martin Sheen and Michael J. Fox's supporting contributions, and director Rob Reiner's moxie in giving carte blanche to the humanistic, liberal slant of the script.

1995. 112m. DIR: Rob Reiner. WRIT: Aaron Sorkin. CAST: Michael Douglas, Annette Bening, Richard Dreyfuss, Martin Sheen, Michael J. Fox.

ANGELS AND INSECTS...

co-written by a woman, is a period piece deeply entrenched in the mores of Victorian England. Mark Rylance stars as a lowly-born entomologist who lands a position at an upper-class English manor tutoring his employer's children, while cataloguing the man's collection of zoological specimens. Before long, Rylance falls in love with his boss' coldly beautiful daughter Patsy Kensit and can scarcely believe his good fortune when she appears to return his affections in kind. An engagement is announced and a marriage quickly takes place, which doesn't prevent affinities from springing up between Rylance and the family's well-educated niece Kristin Scott Thomas as they collaborate on a naturalist text. On still a *third* front, murky family secrets are destined to see the light of day, before the film's somewhat arcane denouement. It's a twisted tapestry of psycho-sexual relationships, with Rylance's still and powerful performance anchoring nearly every scene.

1995. 117m. DIR: Philip Haas. WRIT: Belinda & Philip Haas. CAST: Mark Rylance, Kristin Scott Thomas, Patsy Kensit, Jeremy Kemp, Douglas Henshall.

AVANTI...

Italian for Enter!—ushers us into a delightful screen experience and sleeper of the first order. For over ten years American business mogul Walter Armbruster Sr. has been spending the month of August at the Grand Hotel Excelsior in gorgeous Ischia, Italy, taking advantage of radioactive mud baths to alleviate his arthritis. But when our story opens, he has just been killed in a car accident, his Fiat falling 200 meters into an Italian vineyard. Enter Jack Lemmon as Walter Armbruster Jr., the uptight Baltimore executive who flies to Ischia to pick up his father's body. In the process, he discovers that Pop had been trysting with a secret paramour on the island all these years, that in fact the lady in question also died in the car crash, and the woman's daughter has arrived to pick up her mother's body, as well. What follows are many wild and crazy misadventures with Lemmon and Juliet Mills equally fine as two very different people who find themselves falling in love. Special mention is due Clive Revill as the worldly-wise and accommodating hotel manager whose sly machinations come close to stealing the show.

1972. 144m. DIR: Billy Wilder. WRIT: I.A.L. Diamond, Billy Wilder. CAST: Jack Lemmon, Juliet Mills, Clive Revill, Edward Andrews, Gianfranco Barra.

BABY, IT'S YOU...

based on a story by co-producer Amy Robinson, is director John Sayles' cannily observed tale of two high school seniors who fall in love in 1960s Trenton, New Jersey. Roseanna Arquette is the college-bound, ambitious one and Vincent Spano's the semi-greaser, Sinatra wanna-be who manages to get himself expelled. Despite the differences between this mismatched pair, their mutual attraction is genuine. Then comes high school graduation—hers. In trouble with the law, Spano takes a hike to Miami. Arquette heads to Sarah Lawrence College, where her provincial roots make adjustment a difficult one. Out of need and loneliness, she visits Spano in Miami at semester break and the trip quickly degenerates into disaster, the young man who had appeared so sexy and mysterious back in high school now seeming even more hapless than she. (The scene where she learns how Spano obtained his nickname 'The Sheik' says it all.) Arquette returns to college convinced that Spano is out of her life. Not so fast, Roseanna...Watch for early appearances from Robert Downey Jr. and Matthew Modine.

1982. 105m. DIR&WRIT: John Sayles. CAST: Roseanna Arquette, Vincent Spano, Jack Davidson, Joanna Merlin, Nick Ferrari, Dolores Messina, Tracy Pollen.

BACHELOR MOTHER...

Ginger Rogers' first solo effort after splitting up with Astaire, stars Rogers as a single salesclerk, working at a department store owned by Charles Coburn and run by son David Niven. When Rogers discovers an abandoned baby on the doorsteps of an adoption agency, both the institution's directors and Roger's boss Niven assume the child to be Rogers' own, and no amount of protest on her part can persuade them otherwise. Niven proceeds to instruct our reluctant 'mother' on the responsibilities of parenting, and a sprightly, remarkably non-judgmental comedy unfurls. Special mention is due Charles Coburn's felicitous contribution as the man so crazy about the idea of becoming a grandfather, he makes the whole thing come true. ("I don't care who's the father—*I'm* the grandfather!")

1939. 82m. B&W. DIR&WRIT: Garson Kanin. CAST: Ginger Rogers, David Niven, Charles Coburn, Frank Albertson.

BAREFOOT IN THE PARK...

slightly dated around the edges, stays afloat on the efforts of its congenial cast. Jane Fonda and Robert Redford co-star as newlyweds making the tough adjustment to everyday life, back in the days when folks married first and *then* found out what it was like to live together. Among the myriad challenges they face is an unheated, fifth floor walk-up apartment in Greenwich Village, an ever-present if most congenial mother-in-law Mildred Natwick, and the widely divergent temperaments these two young people bring to their marriage. Fonda is the free spirit, and Redford is the straight-laced attorney who finds his wife's relentless yen for new people and experiences increasingly exasperating. Adding salt to Redford's wounds is bohemian upstairs neighbor Charles Boyer's habit of encouraging Fonda's unconventional ways, in the process becoming as smitten by Mom Natwick as the rest of us. Among highlights is our four principals' night on the town at a Staten Island Albanian restaurant, back in the days when Ouzo was still relative exotica. A glass of that anise-flavored aperitif might well be in order!

1967. 106m. DIR: Gene Saks. WRIT: Neil Simon. CAST: Jane Fonda, Robert Redford, Mildred Natwick, Charles Boyer.

BEFORE SUNRISE...

follows Frenchwoman Julie Delpy and American Ethan Hawke as they meet sweet on a trans-European rail journey and spend 24 hours together exploring the streets of Vienna. As revealed in the palm-reader's sequence, it would appear we have a believer and a non-believer, an optimist and a cynic falling in love. Or is it that simple? Among many deftly-handled scenes, there's the moment in a music store's listening booth when mutual feelings are wordlessly articulated, and the imaginary phone call each makes to a distant friend attempting to explain their burgeoning attraction for one another. Two beguiling actors, an unusually thoughtful script which revels in the art of conversation, and the muted hues of Vienna are the winning mix in this twenty-something romance. Of note: for those who have ever been on one of those adventurous train trips across Europe, the opening scene brings it home with sumptuous immediacy.

1995. 100m. DIR: Richard Linklater. WRIT: Richard Linklater, Kim Krizan. CAST: Julie Delpy, Ethan Hawke, Andrea Eckert, Hanno Poschi, Erni Mangold.

THE BEST YEARS OF OUR LIVES...

offers five-star romance while also being one of the great masterpieces of American film. The year is 1945, and three WWII veterans from divergent backgrounds are returning to 'Boone City' USA. A trio of love stories effectively interweave and merge as we watch the soldiers and their families struggle with the realities—emotional, psychological, and economic—of postwar America, a country which has indeed moved on while her fighting men were overseas. Fredric March is coming home to a bank job he detests, Dana Andrews to a wife who no longer loves him, and Harold Russell to the huge adjustments of life without the arms he lost in the war. The ensemble cast does a superb job, highlighted by an indelible performance from March. Among a plethora of poignant scenes, there's the reunion between March and wife Myrna Loy, and a later moment where the two set straight naive daughter Teresa Wright vis-a-vis the complexities of their marriage. (Loy to her husband, in front of daughter Wright: "How many times have I told you that I hated you and believed it in my heart? How many times have you said you were sick and tired of me, that we were all washed up? How many times have we had to fall in love all over again?") Then there is the bedtime vignette between Russell and girlfriend Cathy O'Donnell, surely one of the tenderest sequences on celluloid. Special mention is due Robert E. Sherwood's excellent screenplay, Gregg Toland's vivid black-and-white cinematography, and Hugo Fried-hofer's affecting musical score.

1946. 170m. B&W. DIR: William Wyler. WRIT: Robert E. Sherwood. CAST: Fredric March, Dana Andrews, Harold Russell, Myrna Loy, Teresa Wright, Cathy O'Donnell, Virginia Mayo, Hoagy Carmichael.

THE BISHOP'S WIFE...

is an old-fashioned romantic fantasy featuring Cary Grant as the guardian angel who comes down to Earth to answer belea-guered Bishop David Niven's prayers for a new cathedral. Or so Niven believes. But the bishop is so obsessed with finding the necessary funds to build his fashionable and imposing church that he gives short shrift to other parish problems, including his relationship with his own wife and daughter. The man is clearly in need of a celestial nudge in more com-passionate directions, and Grant is just the spirit for the job. He most willingly takes up Niven's slack, in particular by spending countless enchanting hours with the lonely Young and falling in love in the process. Among many pleasures, there's the manner in which the entire cast blossoms under angel Grant's gracious attentions, Monty Woolley's endearing supporting contribution as an elderly writer who has never managed to finish 'that book,' and the splendid Christmas Eve sermon at film's finale.

1947. 109m. B&W. DIR: Henry Koster. WRIT: Robert E. Sherwood, Leonardo Bercovici. CAST: David Niven, Loretta Young, Cary Grant, Monty Woolley, Elsa Lancaster.

BLISS...

opens on co-stars Craig Sheffer and Sherl Lee's wedding day, with Craig still harboring serious doubts about his fiancée's many compulsive quirks, including her need to thoroughly clean the apartment two times every day. But as he freely con-fesses to his best friend: "God, I love her." Six months later, they're going through counseling, wherein Sherl admits to faking her orgasms and, on a more essential level, having no real identity or inner strength. On the sly, she begins seeking guidance of a different nature from Tantric sex therapist Terence Stamp. When Craig discovers this 'betrayal,' he angrily confronts the therapist, whereupon Stamp persuades him to become a client as well. Over a series of visits, the young man learns subtle and tender techniques of lovemaking—ways to sensitize his wife's body and awaken her responses—which he takes home and uses to great advantage. Bottom line, Craig has never stopped loving his wife, and his willingness to work on his own sensibilities transforms a flailing relationship into a deeply caring one. The film may be a little too touchy-feely for some, but it isn't afraid to laugh at itself while taking a non-exploitive and knowledgeable approach to eroticism.

1996. 103m. DIR&WRIT: Lance Young. CAST: Craig Sheffer, Sherl Lee, Terence Stamp, Casey Siemaszko, Spalding Gray, Lois Chiles

BREATHING LESSONS...

based on Anne Tyler's novel, is a marvelous, seriocomic portrait of one day in the life of a long-married couple, their excursion to an old friend's funeral serving as a catalyst for rebirth and discovery anew. The couple's drive from Baltimore to Pennsylvania provides many small scale adventures, culminating in a stopover at their daughter-in-law's house to visit their only grandchild. Not willing to let well-enough alone, Grandma convinces her daughter-in-law to accompany them back to Baltimore, in hopes of engineering a reconciliation between the young woman and their roustabout son. Co-stars Joanne Woodward, as the flighty, well-meaning, ever-meddling wife, and James Garner, as her pragmatic, ever-suffering husband are picture-perfect in the leading roles. Among highlights, there is Woodward trying to repair a dent she caused in their newly-overhauled automobile, her vocal turn at the funeral, a playful moment at the post-internment gathering which suggests the sexual spark between this pair is still operative, and the film's final scene, which encapsulates the acceptance and affection that under-score any successful long-term relationship. *1994. 98m. DIR: John Erman. WRIT: Robert W. Lenski. CAST: Joanne Woodward, James Garner, Paul Winfield, Kathryn Erbe, Joyce Van Patten, Eileen Heckart, Tim Gulnee, Henry Jones, Stephi Lineburg, Jean Louise Kelly, John Considine.*

THE BUTCHER'S WIFE...

co-scripted by a woman, features Demi Moore as your friendly neighborhood psychic in the fairy tale setting of Greenwich Village, N.Y. She is a woman not unlike many of us gals, great at straightening out everybody's life but her own. Jeff Daniels co-stars as the smug psychiatrist who loses his patients one by one to Moore's extrasensory counseling. (Daniels to one of his patients: "Someone as intelligent as you doesn't need a clairvoyant telling you how to lead your life. That's what *I'm* here for!") Moore's husband George Dzundza, the butcher whom she has mistakenly assumed was her des-tiny, hires Daniels to convince his 'crazy' wife there's no such animal as ESP. But we can imagine who winds up converting whom in this congenial little love story. The supporting cast shines, particularly Mary Steenburgen as the timid church choir director who dreams of singing the blues. (Catch her rendition of Lil Green's 'In the Dark.') *1991. 107m. DIR: Terry Hughes. WRIT: Marjorie Schwartz, Ezra Litwack. CAST: Demi Moore, Jeff Daniels, George Dzundza, Mary Steenburgen, Frances McDormand, Margaret Colin, Max Perlich.*

CASABLANCA...

possibly America's most cherished film, skillfully juggles its love-triangle plotline with a variety of themes—selfishness and sacrifice, friendship and betrayal, duty and desire, war and intrigue—and seamlessly fuses all these elements into a screenplay so inspired that hundreds of lines remain etched on our collective memory. ("Did you abscond with the church funds or run off with a senator's wife? I'd like to think you killed a man. It's the romantic in me.") ("I'm shocked, *shocked* to find that gambling is going on in here!") ("If that plane leaves the ground and you're not with him, you'll regret it. Maybe not today, and maybe not tomorrow, but soon and for the rest of your life.") ("Louis, I think this is the beginning of a beautiful friendship.") When one considers that the beleaguered screenwriters were scribbling and re-scribbling their masterpiece throughout production, their feat seems doubly miraculous. The entire cast gives outstanding performances, with Ingrid Bergman and Humphrey Bogart's scenes together nothing short of magical. Director Michael Curtiz deserves a special nod, as well, for taking the complex storyline and pacing it so expertly, there is never a moment's slack. (i.e. Notice how fluidly we are introduced to the exotic French Moroccan locale, its political and moral ambiguities, and our leading man, all within the first two minutes of film.) Further applause is due Max Steiner's musical score, Arthur Edeson's dazzling black-and-white cinematography, and Dooley Wilson's classic rendition of 'As Time Goes By.'

1942. 102m. B&W. DIR: Michael Curtiz. WRIT: Julius & Philip Epstein, Howard Kock. CAST: Humphrey Bogart, Ingrid Bergman, Claude Rains, Paul Henreid, Sydney Greenstreet, Peter Lorre, Conrad Veilt, Dooley Wilson, S.Z. Sakall, Marcel Dalio.

ÇESAR AND ROSALIE...

a French comedy/drama about the evolution of a love triangle over ten years' time, stars Romy Schneider as the disarming divorcée whom Yves Montand and Sami Frey both wish to call their own. When Romy is with her aging live-in companion, scrap-metal tycoon Montand—a man who adores her as much as life itself—his coarse temperament pushes her into former love Frey's more refined, if decidedly melancholy arms. At which point the exuberant Montand starts growing on her, all over again. And so it goes throughout the years, until our two leading men work out a sublime, oh-so-French solution to Romy's indecisive predicament. It's a charming film which never takes its characters too seriously, with Montand's performance the enduring highlight.

1972. 110m. In French w/English Subtitles. DIR&WRIT: Claude Sautet. CAST: Romy Schneider, Yves Montand, Sami Frey, Umberto Orsini, Isabelle Huppert.

CHILDREN OF A LESSER GOD...

directed and scripted by women, stars Marlee Maitlin as the profoundly angry young deaf woman who long ago gave up the challenge of learning to talk because of the cruel teasing her efforts evoked from childhood friends. Enter William Hurt as the new teacher at the school for the hearing-impaired where Maitlin is janitor, and a passionate romance takes wing. But the troubles set in when Hurt makes the mistake of trying to change the new woman in his life, first by encouraging her to quit her job, then by insisting that she start trying to speak. Among highlights, there's Maitlin in that swimming pool, Hurt's interaction with his young and irrepressible students, and a curiously silent dinner party where everyone 'talks' in sign-language. It's a singular love story, one which brings us a little closer to that 'middle ground between silence and sound' where both the hearing and the deaf can meet.

1986. 119m. DIR: Randa Haines. WRIT: Hesper Anderson. CAST: Marlee Maitlin, William Hurt, Piper Laurie, Philip Bosco, Alison Gompf.

CIRCLE OF FRIENDS...

involves two seemingly mismatched Irish university students who surprise themselves by falling deeply in love. Coed Minnie Driver is large-boned, tall, and distinctly non-anorexic, which makes her an unlikely romantic interest for the bland but handsome soccer star Chris O'Donnell. But it doesn't take long for our two principals to realize that they are, in fact, ideal for one another. O'Donnell is more compassionate and reflective than first appearances might suggest, while Driver, despite her intellectual prowess, has an endearing earthiness which intrigues O'Donnell from the onset. The road to true love rarely runs smooth, of course, and complications will include the influences of a strict Catholic upbringing, and a doomed love affair between Minnie's best friend and the more sophisticated Colin Firth. Picturesque atmosphere enhances this nostalgic 1950s scenario.

1995. 114m. DIR: Pat O'Connell. WRIT: Andrew Davies. CAST: Minnie Driver, Chris O'Donnell, Geraldine O'Rawe, Saffron Burrows, Colin Firth, Alan Cumming, Aidan Gillen.

COMING HOME...

co-scripted by a woman, provides Jane Fonda and Jon Voight with two of the best dramatic roles of their respective careers. The year is 1968, and Fonda is the politically naive, loyal wife of gung-ho Vietnam-bound marine Bruce Dern. After Dern is shipped overseas, she is on her own for the first time in her life. Much to her surprise, she revels in her independence, buying a used sports car, renting a cottage on the beach, and most importantly, volunteering at a nearby Veterans' Hospital. It is at this medical center that she befriends disabled war-vet Voight, and his cynical, worldly temperament is destined to bring about many changes in Fonda's outlook on life. In effect, their relationship parries an exceptional love story into one woman's coming-of-age drama, all set within the context of the most polemic era in recent American history. In spite of Fonda's thoroughly credible contribution as our heroine in transition, highest honors go to Voight's powerhouse performance as a man struggling to come to terms with a permanent disability without falling into the trap of self-pity and directionless rage. Among highlights is the opening sequence where several paraplegic war vets are taking a second look at their experience in Vietnam, as well as Voight's masterful handling of his wheelchair, and the unusually erotic love scenes between him and Fonda.

1978. 130m. DIR: Hal Ashby. WRIT: Nancy Dowd, Robert C. Jones, Waldo Salt. CAST: Jane Fonda, Jon Voight, Bruce Dern, Penelope Milford, Robert Carradine, Robert Ginty.

THE COMPETITION...

co-stars Amy Irving and Richard Dreyuss as two concert pianists entering the same international round-robin. Romance would seem in the offing, but Dreyfuss—the older of the two virtuosos—is convinced this particular musical sweepstakes represents his last chance for fame and fortune before surrendering to the distinctly less exciting prospect of a teaching career. He is therefore determined to keep his killer instinct intact by temporarily suppressing all inclinations toward the fairer sex. But will Irving's sweetness prevail? It's an occasionally self-conscious, but touching love story set to Tchaikovsky, Sibelius, and Brahms, with the added bonus of offering us an insider's look at the competitive recital circuit. Special mention is due the extensive practice which our two co-stars underwent, making it appear that they are truly playing those magnificent piano concertos. Lee Remick deserves kudos, as well, for giving another in a long string of on-target performances as Irving's musical mentor. (The film's last line, Remick offering Irving a little womanly advice: "You've got a century to wait before evolution produces the man you have in mind. So in the meantime, get out there and dance with what there is.")

1980. 125m. DIR&WRIT: Joel Oliansky. CAST: Richard Dreyfuss, Amy Irving, Lee Remick, Sam Wanamaker, Joseph Cali, Ty Henderson, Priscilla Pointer, James B. Sikking.

COUSINS...

a remake of the French film *Cousin, Cousine*, improves on its precursor, which is no easy feat when considering the high quality of the original. Ted Danson and an incandescent Isabelle Rossellini co-star as two unhappily married people whose respective mates, Sean Young and William Petersen, meet at a wedding reception and strike up a none-too-furtive affair. Left to their own devices, Danson and Rossellini pay back their spouses by feigning a dalliance of their own. Pretense quickly slips into reality, and a jubilant love story unfolds. There are excellent contributions from our two leads, their champagne chemistry sparkling every scene they're in together. But this is essentially an ensemble effort, highlighted by Lloyd Bridges' portrayal of Danson's ne'er-do-well dad, and Sean Young as Danson's second wife, a woman essentially clueless about what she should be doing with her life.

Special mention is due Gina DeAngelis as the hilariously muttering widow observing this passing parade. (Among many of her acerbic comments to Danson's son, this one concerning Bridges' bride-to-be Norma Aleandro: "Your grandfather is about to marry the Bermuda Triangle.")

1989. 110m. DIR: Joel Schumaker. WRIT: Stephen Metcalfe. CAST: Ted Danson, Isabelle Rossellini, Sean Young, William Petersen, Lloyd Bridges, Norma Aleandro, Keith Cooper, Gina DeAngelis.

CRAZY FROM THE HEART...

scripted by a woman, chronicles an unorthodox and touching romance between small-town high school principal Christine Lahti and the school's Mexican-American janitor Ruben Blades. When the film opens, Lahti is stagnating within a long-term relationship with couch-potato/football coach William Russ. But upon learning that best friend Mary Kay Place is about to become a grandmother, Lahti's biological clock starts ticking big time, and she confronts Russ with an ultimatum—marriage or else. His response to her 'brainless tantrum' is less than underwhelming, and out of spite and frustration Lahti finds herself responding to the attentions of the congenial Blades. A rollicking night on the town together segues into a fling south of the border, where Lahti is seduced by the tequila, the dancing, and Blades' warm-hearted spirit. The rest is history, or could be, if Lahti can surmount judgmental peer prejudice when her unusual liaison becomes the talk of the town. Of note: director Schlamme is Lahti's real-life husband, which might account for her delightfully freewheeling performance.

1991. 104m. DIR: Thomas Schlamme. WRIT: Linda Voorhees. CAST: Christine Lahti, Ruben Blades, Mary Kay Place, Brent Spinner, William Russ, Louise Lolham, Tommy Muniz, Kamala Lopez.

CROSSING DELANCEY...

directed and scripted by women, stars Amy Irving as a happily single, thirty-something working girl, crazy for her job as the manager of a landmark Manhattan bookstore. But life gets more complicated when her Jewish grandmother starts playing matchmaker, arranging a meeting between Irving and Lower East Side pickle merchant Peter Riegert. Due to misplaced aspirations elsewhere, our quasi-elitist heroine turns her back on this charming fellow and spends the remainder of the film paying the price. *We* know that pompous, skirt-chasing author Jeroen Krabbé is going to spell unmitigated disaster for Irving, but will she wake up and smell the coffee before it's too late? Among highlights, there is the 'Enchanted Evening' vignette in a New York deli, the supermarket singles salad bar scene, Reizl Bozyk's contribution as Irving's beloved 'Bubbie' in her belated film debut, and director Joan Silver's cinematic flair with the Big Apple. *1988. 97m. DIR: Joan Silver. WRIT: Susan Sandler. CAST: Amy Irving, Peter Riegert, Reizl Bozyk, Jeroen Krabbé, Sylvia Miles, Suzzy Roche, George Martin, John Bedford.*

THE CUTTING EDGE...

plunks romance down on ice with affable, comic panache. D.B. Sweeney co-stars as a professional hockey player forced into early retirement due to an eye injury. Enter Roy Dotrice as a Russian-American skating coach who arm-twists Sweeney into becoming the figure-skating partner of ice queen Moira Kelly, a woman as spoiled and demanding as she is talented and smart. (Her difficult temperament made mince meat of eight partners in the last two years.) It's hostility at first sight for these two strong-willed characters, but we can surmise what is going to transpire as they go through the grueling training necessary for the 1990 Olympics. There's great chemistry between our two leads, both on and off the rink, with the magic of high-level, competitive figure-skating serving as the icing, as it were, on the cake. *1992. DIR: Paul Michael Glaser. WRIT: Tony Gilroy. CAST: D.B. Sweeney, Moira Kelly, Roy Dotrice, Dwier Brown, Terry O'Quinn.*

DESPERATELY SEEKING SUSAN...

written and directed by women, was only director Seidelman's second effort. But whether it be the result of uncanny casting, excellent stewardship, a deliciously screwy script, or an artful convergence of all three, every actor in this low-budget marvel gives a perfectly attuned, low-keyed comic performance. Even Madonna comes up a winner, which is not much of a stretch since she is basically playing herself. Roseanna Arquette stars as the bored New Jersey housewife, vaguely aware that her husband is philandering on the side. To mainline a little excitement into her days, she lives vicariously through the personals, in particular by following the adventures of two lovers—the mysterious Susan and her beau Jimmy—as they arrange a series of rendezvous via ads in the paper. One afternoon our heroine commutes into Manhattan to spy on her idol, has an accident, wakes up with amnesia, and begins to suspect that she herself is the wild and crazy Susan. Enter danger, magic, and sweet romance. For this New Jersey housewife, neither life nor love will ever be the same! Highlights include Laurie Metcalf's hilarious contribution as Roseanna's sister-in-law, the growing vibes between Roseanna and the new man in her life—Aidan Quinn, at his sexiest and most endearing—and the zany finale at the 'Magic Club.'
1985. 91m. DIR: Susan Seidelman. WRIT: Leora Garish. CAST: Roseanna Arquette, Madonna, Aidan Quinn, Mark Blum, Laurie Metcalf, Robert Joy, Richard Hell, Annie Golden, John Turturro, Ann Magnuson.

DOGFIGHT...

directed by Nancy Savoca, is the term given to a crude 'competition' played by a group of young Army recruits their last night in San Francisco, before shipping out to Vietnam. The scheme is to divide and conquer, scouring the town for the ugliest girl available, then bringing her back to a party being thrown at a designated bar. The guy with the homeliest entry wins. Birdlace, artfully played by the late River Phoenix, picks up a plain-Jane waitress who turns out to be the sweetest, smartest young woman he's ever spent time with. It does not take long for our waitress/folksinging poet to realize what kind of mean-spirited game is being played on her and all the other women at the party. Indignant and turned off, she wants out of the picture just when Phoenix wants in. A night of tender love follows, our heroine helping a confused young man come to know his better self. Lili Taylor's performance stands at the center of this film, as she blossoms into knowing radiance before our very eyes.

1992. 94m. DIR: Nancy Savoca. WRIT: Bob Comfort. CAST: River Phoenix, Lili Taylor, Richard Panebianco, Anthony Clark, Mitchell Whitfield, Brendan Fraser.

DON JUAN DEMARCO...

invites us into the fantasy world of an original lost soul who long ago escaped the pathetic trappings of his 'real' life by transforming himself, mask and all, into the great mythic lover Don Juan. When our dreamer is brought to a mental clinic for treatment, attending psychiatrist Marlon Brando strikes a deal: his patient does not have to take the hated psychotropic drugs for the next ten days, in which time he must convince Brando he is truly who he claims to be. Johnny Depp throws himself with panache into the role of Don Juan. But Brando is the surprise here, charming and droll as the aging cynic who comes to recognize his patient's soaring romanticism as a door into a new lease on life, his marriage to the ravishing Faye Dunaway prospering accordingly.

1994. 97m. DIR&WRIT: Jeremy Leven. CAST: Johnny Depp, Marlon Brando, Faye Dunaway. Geraldine Pailhas, Bob Dishy, Rachel Ticotin.

84 CHARING CROSS ROAD...

is the true-life account of a twenty-year correspondence between single New York scriptwriter Helen Hanff and married London antiquarian bookstore proprietor Frank Doel. She adores old books ("I love second-hand books that fall open to the favorite page of its previous owner."), and after discovering Doel's shop in an advertisement, sends him an order.

What begins as a business association gradually evolves into a lasting and profound friendship, energized not only by Doel's uncanny ability to ferret out our bibliophile's challenging requests, but by the natural affinities springing up between two kindred spirits. This is a most unusual love story in that these two 'pen pals' never meet face to face. But if this appears to be a dramatic obstacle, not to worry. It is the growing intimacy and understated sensuality of protracted letterwriting which is the focus of this surprisingly cinematic scenario. The well-honed talents of Anne Bancroft and Anthony Hopkins are eminently suited to the film's delicate tones.

1986. 100m. DIR: David Jones. WRIT: Hugh Whitmore. CAST: Anne Bancroft, Anthony Hopkins, Judi Dench, Maurice Denham, Jean De Baer, Mercedes Ruehl.

EVERY TIME WE SAY GOODBYE...

co-written by a woman, features Tom Hanks in a nice change of pace as a WWII pilot temporarily grounded in Jerusalem with a broken leg. When his buddy fixes him up with an eighteen-year-old Jewish woman—played with understated intensity by Israeli actress Cristina Marsillach—the attraction is powerful and instantaneous. But the girl's desire for this particular gentile is totally unacceptable for her archly conservative Sephardic family. Although we empathize with Hanks' deepening frustration over Cristina's continual attempts to break off the relationship, the young woman's dilemma is indeed a profound one. Her father, for one, does not mince any words: "If you marry this boy, you will be outside the law and outside the family. You will no longer be my daughter." There are genuine sparks flying between our two leads, and an endearing contribution from Monny Moshonov as the cousin who has loved Cristina since the day she was born. The movie's haunting theme song, 'The Nightingale Sang in Barkley Square,' adroitly places our scenario in its proper time and place.

1987. 97m. DIR: Moshe Mizrahi. WRIT: Moshe Mizrahi, Leah Appet. CAST: Tom Hanks, Cristina Marsillach, Benedict Taylor, Monny Moshonov, Anat Atzman, Gila Almagar.

THE FABULOUS BAKER BOYS...

stars real-life siblings Jeff and Beau Bridges in a convincing and well-crafted character study of two piano-playing brothers. Jeff is the restless, talented one, a quintessential loner whose only friends are his aging Black Labrador and the little girl from upstairs. Beau is the embodiment of the family man who has been handling their increasingly pedestrian club act for the last fifteen years. In the interest of revitalizing their gig, he decides to bring a female vocalist on board, and Michelle Pfeiffer's dauntless, seductive presence serves as the catalyst for long-simmering resentments between these two brothers. The rocky love story between J. Bridges and Pfeiffer is far from an afterthought; it heats up the entire film. Jeff and Michelle are at their sexiest, with our sultry chanteuse deserving a few extra points for never resorting to lip-synch. That is her own lovely voice throughout. Accolades are also due David Grusin's musical score, and some nifty piano duets dubbed by Grusin and John Hammond.

1989. 113m. DIR&WRIT: Steven Kloves. CAST: Jeff Bridges, Beau Bridges, Michelle Pfeiffer, Elie Raab, Jennifer Tilly.

FOR THE MOMENT...

another achingly beautiful love story from north of the border, is rightfully dedicated to the 250,000 men and women from various parts of the British Commonwealth who came to Canada for flight training during WWII. Russell Crowe co-stars as an Australian pilot stationed in Manitoba with best mate Peter Outerbridge circa 1942. Soon enough Russell meets his buddy's Canadian fiancée and her family, which includes married sister Christianne Hirt. Hirt's husband is already fighting overseas, and she does her loyal best to resist the overtures of this winsome Aussie lad. But it's a losing battle, with a teasing flirtation soon evolving into a profoundly intense love affair. A second story line follows the travails of war widow Wanda Cannon, as she attempts to hold family and farm together while falling in love with flying instructor

Scott Kraft. The film's occasional slow pacing is more than compensated for by its evocative script and superb acting. Among highlights is Crowe's heartfelt recitation of John Gillespie McKee's ode to flight—"the long, delirious, burning blue"—and the painterly on-location cinematography. *1994. 120m. DIR&WRIT: Aaron Kim Johnston. CAST: Russell Crowe, Christianne Hirt, Wanda Cannon, Scott Kraft, Peter Outerbridge, Sara McMillan.*

FORGET PARIS...

is unique for concentrating on the nuts and bolts of making a marriage work *after* the whirlwind courtship has run its course. Billy Crystal and Debra Winger co-star as the couple who meet in the City of Light and spend an idyllic few days together before Crystal returns to his job as a professional basketball referee. Distance makes Winger's heart grow fonder, and she chucks her great airline job in Paris to marry Crystal, only to crash land at dead-end employment in Texas while hubby is on the road two weeks out of every three. To placate Winger's growing desperation, Crystal reluctantly gives up his officiating career to become a used car salesman, and bad goes to worse when Winger's senile dad moves onto the premises. The story is told in a series of flashbacks around a restaurant table, where a group of Crystal and Winger's common friends—Joe Mantegna, Julie Kavner, Richard Masur, and Cathy Moriarty—gather to celebrate Mantegna's upcoming nuptials to newcomer Cynthia Stevenson. It's an entertaining, if slightly disheartening perspective on the trials and tribulations of the married state, i.e. *real life*. Forget Paris! Special mention is due Cathy Moriarty's typically droll performance and Robert Costanzo's contribution as the restaurant waiter whose asides keep this party zipping along. *1995. 101m. DIR: Billy Crystal. WRIT: Billy Crystal, Lowell Ganz, Babaloo Mandel. CAST: Billy Crystal, Debra Winger, Joe Mantegna, Cynthia Stevenson, Julie Kavner, Richard Masur, Cathy Moriarty, Robert Costanzo.*

FOUR WEDDINGS AND A FUNERAL...

a romantic comedy with a delightfully sardonic edge, serves up an excellent ensemble effort—Hugh Grant, Kristin Scott Thomas, John Hannah, James Fleet, and Simon Callow—who portray a close-knit group of Englishmen and women attending the proceedings of our title. Andie MacDowell, the sole American who shows up at the various celebrations, initiates a roller-coaster flirtation with the charming Grant. But our confirmed bachelor blows his opportunity, and MacDowell marries somebody else. Will a happy ending prevail? A running ruse which sparks this wonderfully life-affirming scenario is the fact that each wedding serves as the catalyst for a love affair which in turn inspires the ensuing nuptial event. *1994. 118m. DIR: Mike Newell. WRIT: Richard Curtis. CAST: Hugh Grant, Andie MacDowell, Simon Callow, Kristin Scott Thomas, James Fleet, John Hannah, Charlotte Coleman, David Bower, Corin Redgrave.*

FRENCH KISS...

features comedienne Meg Ryan in top form as a thirty-something school teacher with an intense dread of airplanes and the French. But she is soon obliged to overcome both phobias in order to fly to Paris and confront wandering fiancé Timothy Hutton and his new 'god*dess*.' In transit, she crosses paths with smarmy French con-man Kevin Kline, who— unbeknownst to Ryan—avoids customs officers by hiding a stolen diamond necklace in her bag. In order to retrieve said necklace, Kline sticks close to Ryan's side, ultimately accompanying her to the Cote D'Azur, where he promises to help her win back Hutton. En route, in the best of romantic-comedy traditions, our two principals fall hopelessly in love. The panoramas, both in and out of Paris, are as splendid as the rest of this cinematic outing, and that includes the soundtrack. So be advised to keep the VCR rolling through the final credits for Kline's vocals on 'La Mer' and Van Morrison's on 'Someone Like You.' Extra kudos are due the French cast, uniformly excellent, and for Ryan's smarts in co-producing this gem. *1995. 103m. DIR: Lawrence Kasdan. WRIT: Adam Brooks. CAST: Meg Ryan, Kevin Kline, Jean Reno, Susan Anbeh, François Cluzet.*

THE FRENCH LIEUTENANT'S WOMAN...

posits a film within a film, presenting us parallel love stories set in two different centuries. The scenario opens in the 1800s on the coast of England, where we meet a mysterious young woman—Sarah Woodward—obsessed with the army officer who abandoned her the year before. She in turn becomes the fixation of a wealthy scientist who is visiting the area, Charles Smithson. Cut! And the scenario shifts to modern-day England, where we meet the sophisticated actress and actor who are playing the leading roles, Anna and Mike. Not so coincidentally, these two happen to be carrying on their own love affair while the movie is being made. No sooner do we make their acquaintance and settle into contemporary life, then we are plunged back into Victorian England once again. Either story could stand on its own, but their continual jux-taposition is cinema at its most inventive, dramatizing how sex roles and attitudes have changed over the years, as well as providing insights into the art of movie-making itself—in particular, the difficulty actors have in drawing lines between their 'reel' and real lives. Jeremy Irons and Meryl Streep are equally splendid as our star-crossed, time-traveling paramours, and screenwriter Harold Pinter deserves special mention for his seasoned treatment of time and perspective. *1981. 123m. DIR: Karel Reisz. WRIT: Harold Pinter. CAST: Meryl Streep, Jeremy Irons, Leo McKern, Hilton McRae, Emily Morgan.*

THE GHOST AND MRS. MUIR...

stars Gene Tierney as an independent-minded widow who takes advantage of her newly single status by moving into a remote and lovely cottage on the English coast. Enter Rex Harrison as a long-dead sea captain, a crabby, sharp-tongued curmudgeon of a ghost who has successfully bullied a series of previous residents into abandoning 'his abode.' But Tierney refuses to be intimidated, and over time the sea captain finds himself falling in love with this strong-willed and beautiful lady. Financial difficulties eventually force Tierney to con-template remarriage, whereupon our increasingly possessive

sea captain redeems the situation by dictating his salty sea adventures to her—memoirs which she parleys into a best-selling novel. It's an artful, gentle love story, with Bernard Herrmann's musical score mixing the right amount of lyricism and whimsy to bring it all home with feeling.
1947. 104m. B&W. DIR: Joseph Mankiewiez. WRIT: Philip Dunne. CAST: Gene Tierney, Rex Harrison, George Sanders, Edna Best, Anna Lee, Vanessa Brown, Robert Coats, Natalie Wood.

GIGI...

based on Colette's novella of a girl's coming-of-age in turn-of-the-century Paris, is a fine vehicle for Leslie Caron's fresh and alluring talents. First and foremost, however, this film is a showcase for the delightful Louis Jourdan. The French actor gives his most savvy screen performance as the world-weary aristocrat Gaston Lachaille, a man serenely unaware he is falling in love with his young confidante. When our story opens, Gigi is being groomed for her future as a courtesan by Aunt Isabel Jeans. Both Jeans and Grandmother Hermione Gingold are privately hoping that given time, Gigi will naturally become the mistress of her super-wealthy pal Gaston. But when our young gamin blossoms into dazzling womanhood, seemingly overnight, unexpected consequences ensue. Among highlights, there's Maurice Chevalier and the inimitable Gingold reminiscing about their long-ago love affair, 'Ah Yes, I Remember It Well' (he, of course, remembers little at all), and Jourdan's poignant rendition of 'Gigi.' Filmed on location, director Vincente Minnelli uses the Parisian backdrop to great advantage.
1958. 119m. DIR: Vincente Minnelli. WRIT: Alan Jay Lerner. COMP: Alan Jay Lerner, Frederick Loewe. CAST: Leslie Caron, Louis Jourdan, Maurice Chevalier, Hermione Gingold, Isabel Jeans, Eva Gabor.

THE GOODBYE GIRL...

stands as one of playwright Neil Simon's most successful film adaptations due to the comic flair which Marsha Mason and Richard Dreyfuss bring to their respective roles, adopting Simon's wisecracking, witty dialogue as their own. Mason

plays the single mom who has just been unceremoniously dumped by yet another all-too-handsome and chauvinist boyfriend. To add injustice to indignity, the cad surreptitiously sublet their apartment and ran off with the three month down-payment, leaving Mason with little choice but to allow the new tenant, aspiring actor Elliot Garfield (Dreyfuss) to temporarily share her digs. Antipathy slowly de-escalates into a guarded truce, which eventually blossoms into the real thing, aided and abetted by the natural affinities between Dreyfuss and Mason's precocious nine-year-old daughter Quinn Cummings. An amusing subplot involves our thespian's humiliating efforts to adapt to his director's wacked-out conception of Richard III. (A *New York Times* theater review, after the first and only performance: "Elliot Garfield researched Richard III and discovered him to be England's first badly-dressed interior decorator.")
1977. 100m. DIR: Herbert Ross. WRIT: Neil Simon. CAST: Marsha Mason, Richard Dreyfuss, Quinn Cummings, Paul Benedict, Barbara Rhoades.

HE SAID, SHE SAID...

co-directed by a woman, is a romantic comedy which developed out of a real-life incident. When married journalists Marisa Silver and Ken Kwapis were asked by friends to describe the manner in which the two got together, they were amazed at their divergent renditions of the chain of events. Hence the title of this movie—his segment directed by Kwapis, hers by Silver—on how two Baltimore journalists meet, fall in love, and begin grappling with the kinks of a long-term relationship. The merriment comes in seeing many of the same episodes from two distinct and gender-orientated perspectives. There is also great chemistry between leads Elizabeth Perkins and Kevin Bacon, a memorable comic contribution from Nathan Lane as their frantic TV producer, and a sizzling Sharon Stone as the ex-girlfriend from hell.
1991. 115m. DIR: Marisa Silver, Ken Kwapis. WRIT: Brian Holfield. CAST: Elizabeth Perkins, Kevin Bacon, Nathan Lane, Sharon Stone, Anthony LaPaglia.

HOLIDAY...

stars Cary Grant as a non-conforming yet successful business-man who is engaged to snobbish rich girl Doris Nolan. Our would-be vagabond is not yet aware that his fiancée and her upper crust parents are not going to tolerate his plan to take a few years vacation from the work-a-day world for a voyage of self-discovery. Enter Katharine Hepburn as Nolan's spunky, unconventional older sister, and it becomes immediately apparent that she and Grant are genuine soul mates. They take a while longer than we do to discover the obvious, which is all part of the fun, of course. Despite being a breezy comedy of manners and romance, the movie offers an earnest subtext. Risk over riches, and adventure over assets, is our two principals' trumpet call; 'holiday' as a metaphor for living life at its highest denominator. Yes!

1938. 93m. B&W. DIR: George Cukor. WRIT: Donald Odgen Stuart, Sidney Buckman. CAST: Cary Grant, Katharine Hepburn, Doris Nolan, Edward Everett Horton, Ruth Donnelly, Lew Ayres, Binnie Barnes.

INDISCREET...

stars a luminous Ingrid Bergman as a successful, albeit lonely forty-something British stage actress whose world gets turned upside down upon meeting debonair American diplomat Cary Grant. The fly in the ointment is that Grant is already married, if unhappily so, and divorce is out of the question. Unable to resist his considerable charms, Bergman invites Grant to dinner, whereupon our 'indiscreet' courtship is launched, with Bergman's older sister and brother-in-law, the equally marvelous Phyllis Calvert and Cecil Parker, chafing nervously in the wings. Unexpected, oft-hilarious entanglements ensue. Our two leads flaunt their magnetic vibes—they're a truly great cinematic team—making one wonder why more of these 'August' love affairs don't make it to the silver screen. Ditto for the excellent supporting cast, right down to David Kossoff as the flustered butler, forced to play decidedly against type in Bergman's little revenge scheme at film's finale. Among highlights is Grant's improvised

Scottish jig at a genteel London club, as well as Michael Rodney Bennett's memorable musical motif.
1958. 100m. DIR: Stanley Donan. WRIT: Norman Krasna. CAST: Ingrid Bergman, Cary Grant, Phyllis Calvert, Cecil Parker, David Kossoff, Megs Jenkins.

I.Q...

is an engaging comedy-romance starring Walter Matthau as the sixty-something irascible Albert Einstein. When the story opens, Matthau/Einstein is increasingly unhappy with brainy niece Meg Ryan's choice of boyfriends—stuffy lab scientist Stephen Fry. To remedy the situation, he engineers a meeting between Ryan and the lovable local garage mechanic Tim Robbins. Robbins is immediately taken with the comely young lady, but Ryan, convinced that she has an obligation to marry a brilliant man, is going to need more nudging in Robbins' direction. And so Matthau and three of his eccentric cronies attempt a miracle by transforming the artless Robbins into a physics genius overnight. Credibility is not this film's strong suit, nor is it meant to be. It's a sweet, old-fashioned romance, revved into high gear by Matthau's delectable performance. Lou Jacobi, Gene Saks, and Joseph Maher deserve special mention for the comic flair they bring to the scenario as Matthau's querulous, yet good-hearted friends.
1994. 107m. DIR: Fred Schepisi. WRIT: Michael Lesson, Andy Breckman. CAST: Walter Matthau, Meg Ryan, Tim Robbins, Stephen Fry, Lou Jacobi, Gene Saks, Joseph Maher, Charles Durning, Frank Whaley.

IT HAPPENED ONE NIGHT...

the prototype for the countless screwball comedies to follow, is quite arguably the one which began it all. In one corner we have Clark Gable as the heavy-drinking, hard-talking, recently-fired newspaper reporter; in the other corner sits high society heiress Claudette Colbert, on the lam from her parents, who have just annulled her ill-advised marriage to playboy Roscoe Karns. When our two principals wind up on the same bus together, a deal is struck: Gable won't turn

Colbert in, in fact he agrees to help her journey from Florida to her fiancé in New York, as long as he gets an exclusive on her story, thereby earning himself back his job on his paper. A classic battle of the sexes is the delightful end result, as these two make their way across country, predictably falling in love in the process. Of note: Gable and his T-shirt were both unknown assets before the release of this landmark film! *1934. 104m. B&W. DIR: Frank Capra. WRIT: Robert Riskin. CAST: Clark Gable, Claudette Colbert, Roscoe Karns, Walter Connolly, Alan Hale.*

JANE EYRE...

the 1983 British mini-series, stands as the superior version of the celebrated Charlotte Bronte novel, with Zelah Clarke sublime as the stalwart Jane. She may be 'plain' in the conventional sense of the word, but her guts, honesty, and intelligence shine through in every scene. Which explains why Mr. Rochester, here played with a wonderfully caustic edge by Timothy Dalton, cannot stop himself from falling under her fiery spell. The art of conversation takes center stage in this production, as Rochester insists on Jane's company for many a nightly colloquy. The early scenes in the orphanage are difficult viewing—God forbid to have been an orphan in Victorian England—but Jane is the ultimate survivor, and the latter half is a transcendent love story, with our two principals endowing the scenario with heartrending immediacy. *1983. 239m. DIR: Julian Amyes. WRIT: Alexander Baron. CAST: Zelah Clarke, Timothy Dalton, Sian Patterson, Judy Cornwell, Robert James, Kate David.*

LADY AND THE TRAMP...

one of Disney's finest animated features, might seem an odd selection for the romance category. But we challenge anyone to find a more amorous and heartwarming scene than our young canine couple being serenaded 'Bella Nolte' at Tony's Italian restaurant. Mama Mia! Then there's Peggy Lee's sizzling vocals, making the most out of 'He's A Tramp.' And catch that oh-so-catty pair of Siamese. For our beloved cocker spaniel Lady, the trouble begins when her mistress and master, 'Darling' and 'Jim Dear,' become increasingly distracted by their newborn baby girl. Bad goes to worse when they take a short holiday, leaving the new arrival and Lady in the charge of Aunt Sarah. To Lady's great distress, Auntie insists upon keeping her strapped in a muzzle. Tramp—'foot loose and collar free'—comes to her rescue, liberating her from the wretched muzzle. The rest is history, as Lady proceeds to have the adventure of a lifetime with our wild and roguish mongrel stray. (The film's opening invocation: "In the whole history of the world, there is but one thing that money cannot buy: to wit, the wag of a dog's tail." Amen!)

1955. 76m. DIR: Hamilton Luske, Clyde Geronimi, Wilfred Jackson. WRIT: Erdman Penner, Joe Rinaldi, Ralph Wright, Don DaGradi. VOICES: Peggy Lee, Barbara Luddy, Larry Roberts, Bill Thompson, Bill Baucon, Verna Felton, Sonny Burke, Stan Freberg, Alan Reed, George Givot.

LOVE AFFAIR/AN AFFAIR TO REMEMBER...

both the 1937 original and the 1959 remake, are unique for boasting not only the same screenwriters, but the same director, Leo McCarey. For those unfamiliar with the story, it concerns two beautiful, charming, and ever-so-witty people falling in love while traveling on a luxurious trans-Atlantic ocean liner. Unfortunately, each is romantically committed to someone else. They resolve this complication by agreeing to meet at the top of the Empire State Building in six months' time, in order to see if their feelings for one another have held true. Although both adaptations come recommended, the earlier version—starring Irene Dunne and Charles Boyer—is superior to its more famous follow-up, chiefly because the key middle segment works like it should, showing us two people who are discovering they are truly meant for one another. In large part, this is due to the multileveled talents which the great actress Maria Ouspenskaya brings to the all-important role of the grandmother. In the remake, in spite of Deborah Kerr and Cary Grant's excellent contributions, the 'grandmother sequence' rings contrived. That said, both scenarios offer a nimble mix of humor, pathos, and passion, with heart-tugging, five-hankie finales.

1939. 87m. B&W. DIR: Leo McCarey. WRIT: Delmer Daves, Leo McCarey. CAST: Irene Dunne, Charles Boyer, Maria Ouspenskaya, Lee Bowman, Astrid Allwyn.

1957. 115m. DIR: Leo McCarey. WRIT: Delmer Daves, Leo McCarey. CAST: Deborah Kerr, Cary Grant, Richard Denning, Neva Patterson, Cathleen Nesbitt, Robert Q. Lewis.

MAKING MR. RIGHT...

co-scripted and directed by women, features fine performances from co-stars John Malkovich and Ann Magnuson, and a scenario which flaunts a witty feminist twist. Malkovich plays an uptight, if dedicated scientist who invents a lifelike android in his own image. Posthaste he hires hotshot PR consultant Magnuson to groom the robot into perfect talk-show material, in hopes that the publicity will provide his corporation needed funds for continued research. But on her way towards teaching 'Ulysses' how to become 'Mr. Right,' Magnuson falls for the increasingly congenial android and vice versa. Among highlights of this offbeat romantic comedy is Malkovich's accomplished tightrope act as both the dour scientist and the disarming android, the pithy points which are made on the occasions when other characters mistake scientist and android for one another, Robert Trebor's memorable cameo as a tuxedo salesman, and the audaciously happy finale. Credit is due director Seidelman for consistently aiming for the satirical high road, preferring the knowing chuckle over the more customary cliché.

1987. 95m. DIR: Susan Seidelman. WRIT: Laurie Frank, Floyd Byars. CAST: John Malkovich, Ann Magnuson, Glenne Headly, Ben Masters, Laurie Metcalf, Polly Bergen, Robert Trebor.

MAMA, THERE'S A MAN IN YOUR BED...

scripted and directed by a woman, is an ingenious tale of class and race disparities in contemporary Paris. The fine French actor Daniel Auteuil stars as a harassed CEO at a big-time yogurt company. He's a workaholic who gives wife and children short shrift and is about to pay the price when he's framed for an insider trading deal by jealous co-workers. Enter Firmine Richard as the company's black, financially-strapped after-hours cleaning-lady and mother of five. She is the only witness to the crime, and knows who set up Auteuil and why. Together they plot revenge and a counter-takeover in her tiny flat, where our CEO is obliged to hide out from the police. Soon enough he wins back his former position, but seems to have forgotten the essential help Firmine provided him along the way. All that's about to change, of course, and an improbable yet credible love story unfolds. Among highlights, there's the opportunity of witnessing Firmine's five ex-husbands, her five children, and Auteuil's son and daughter all attending the same gala.

1989. 111m. In French w/English Subtitles. DIR&WRIT: Coline Serreau. CAST: Daniel Auteuil, Firmine Richard, Pierre Vernier, Maxime Le Roux, Gilles Privat, Muriel Combeau.

A MAN AND A WOMAN...

the very embodiment of romance, co-stars Anouk Aimee and Jean-Louis Trintignant as a widow and widower who meet at their children's boarding school and strike up a mutual infatuation. But this promising love affair between two seemingly kindred spirits is quickly imperiled by the anguishing memories both harbor for the recent and sudden deaths of their respective spouses. In particular, script woman Aimee continues to be heartsick at the passing of her beloved stunt man/husband Pierre Barouh, and her haunting flashbacks while on location with him in the Pampas of Argentina become integral to our film. Among highlights of this visually eye-catching scenario (orbiting cameras, slow motion takes, shifts from color to black-and-white), there is Aimee revving up the nerve to send race-car driver Trintignant a three-word telegram after the finale of the Monte Carlo 500, and his impassioned response. Should we all have it so good!

1966. 102m. In French w/English Subtitles. DIR: Claude Lelouch. WRIT: Claude Lelouch, Pierre Uytterhoeven. CAST: Anouk Aimee, Jean-Louis Trintignant, Pierre Barouh, Valerie Lagrange.

MEDICINE RIVER...

co-scripted by a woman, tells the story of a Toronto-based photojournalist, played to droll perfection by Graham Greene, who returns to his Blackfoot Indian Reservation after a twenty-year hiatus to attend his mother's funeral. Unbeknownst to this hotshot globe-trotter, he's about to have his life turned upside down by a most persuasive fellow Blackfoot, Tom Jackson. Jackson convinces Greene to stick around the reservation a few more weeks, ostensibly to help them put together a photo-calendar of the tribe's elders. But with this canny trickster there is always more cooking than meets the eye. It's a comical, heartfelt tale of rediscovering one's roots, with a tender love story thrown in for good measure. Among highlights, there's Greene and Jackson's visit to elder Martha Old Crane, Jackson's charming contribution as our fast-talking wheeler-dealer, and a wonderful closing sequence. Of note: with one exception, it is an entirely Native American cast.

1992. 96m. DIR: Stuart Margolin. WRIT: Thomas King, Ann MacNaughtin. CAST: Graham Greene, Tom Jackson, Sheila Tousey, Byron Chief Moon, Janet-Laine Green.

MEMORIES OF A MARRIAGE...

opens in the present with our middle-aged couple preparing to host their annual summer garden party, on the very day that one of them has been diagnosed with a terminal disease. As the party proceeds, various moments trigger the husband's memory bank, sending him reeling through flashbacks of his marriage. It is not the prosaic, daily flow of their years together which we are privy to, but the high points and crises—how they first meet, an overly flirtatious young wife, confrontations with the mother-in-law, a never-to-be-forgotten Christmas dinner—every sequence presenting generous insight into life with an occasionally difficult woman who is deeply loved by her spouse.

1990. 90m. In Danish w/English Subtitles. DIR: Kaspar Rostrup. CAST: Ghita Norby, Frits Helmuth, Rikke Bendson, Henning Moritzen.

MISSISSIPPI MASALA...

written and directed by women, is a voluptuous tale of inter-
racial courtship. Denzel Washington and Indian actress Sarita
Choudhury co-star as the young couple whose blossoming
passion sets off similarly escalating tensions within the small
southern community where they work and live. 'Masala,' as
Sarita explains to Denzel one afternoon, is an Indian season-
ing which blends many different-colored and tasting spices.
The same could be said of the film itself, an arresting amalgam of comedy, romance, and social commentary which offers
a fascinating insight into the Indian emigre´ community in
the United States. A subplot concerning our heroine's father's
ongoing lawsuit with the government of Uganda—the country from which he and thousands of other Indians were unceremoniously expelled by Idi Amin some twenty years before—
fittingly opens and closes the movie's ongoing themes.
1992. 118m. DIR: Mira Nair. WRIT: Sooni Taraporevala. CAST:
Denzel Washington, Sarita Choudhury, Roshan Seth, Shamila Tagore,
Charles Dutton, Joe Seneca, Ranjit Chowdhry.

THE MORE THE MERRIER...

is an old-fashioned romantic gem co-starring Jean Arthur and
Joel McCrea as our prospective lovebirds, and Charles Coburn
as the matchmaker who uses every ingenious strategy known
to man to bring them together. The story is set in
Washington D.C. during WWII, where overcrowded housing conditions convince Arthur, who is presently engaged to
Richard Gaines, that it's her patriotic duty to lease the extra
room in her apartment. New tenant Coburn promptly rents
out half of his room to architect McCrea, and in spite of herself, Arthur becomes attracted to her newest tenant, while
falling out of love with her fiancé. ("Don't shush me! You've
been shushing me for the last twenty-two months. You just
shushed your last shush!") Among highlights is a sexy front-
stoop snuggle which allows Arthur to show what's on her
mind, and the sweetest across-the-wall marriage proposal on

celluloid. The few corny moments at film's onset will be long forgotten by final curtain.

1943. 104m. B&W. DIR: George Stevens. WRIT: Robert Russell, Frank Ross. CAST: Charles Coburn, Jean Arthur, Joel McCrea, Richard Gaines, Bruce Bennett, Ann Savage.

MR. AND MRS. LOVING...

based on a true story, opens circa 1960 in Carolina County, Virginia, where we meet high school sweethearts Timothy Hutton and Lela Rochon. Although Hutton is white and Rochon is black, their respective families have dealt reasonably well with the relationship, and the couple decide to get married. Unfortunately, the local sheriff abides by the racist anti-miscegenation laws still on the books in Virginia and hauls the 'illegally married' couple off to jail. Bad goes to worse when the district judge orders them to leave the state, forcing the young couple to build an already difficult marriage without the support of community and friends. The problems proliferate for these two, racial and otherwise, and they ultimately decide to fight the courts for the right to bring up their family in their own hometown. This is the case which led to the landmark 1967 Supreme Court ruling on the equal protection clause of the 14th amendment. Hutton and Rochon generate heartfelt sympathy as the working-class couple whose pursuit of decency and justice changed the very fabric of our judicial system.

1995. 95m. DIR&WRIT: Richard Friedenberg. CAST: Timothy Hutton, Lela Rochon, Ruby Dee, Bill Nunn, Corey Parker, Israel Washington.

MR. WONDERFUL...

scripted by women, is a bittersweet romantic comedy starring Matt Dillon and Annabella Sciorra as the young couple who divorced two years earlier for all the right reasons. Sciorra, desperate to leave her Italian-American background far behind her, is now attending graduate school and carrying on an affair with married English professor William Hurt. In the meantime, Con Ed man Dillon continues to be happily ensconced in the old Italian neighborhood, while dating devoted girlfriend Mary-Louise Parker. The problems set in when Dillon and his buddies decide to renovate a neighborhood bowling alley. Dillon's monthly alimony payments to Sciorra make it impossible for him to ante up his share of the investment, so he decides to find her a new husband, thereby canceling out the need for the monthly remunerations. But in the process of seeking a 'Mr. Wonderful' for his ex-wife, he finds himself falling in love with her all over again. Among memorable scenes, there's Sciorra helping Dillon put his convertible-top back up and the palpable nostalgia for their former life together which this simple act evokes.

1983. 99m. DIR: Anthony Minghella. WRIT: Amy Schor, Vicki Polon. CAST: Matt Dillon, Annabella Sciorra, Mary-Louise Parker, William Hurt, Luis Guzman, Dan Hedaya, Vincent D'Onofrio.

MUCH ADO ABOUT NOTHING...

filmed on location at a 14th century villa in the lush Tuscan countryside, celebrates the sensual edges to life with sunlit abandon. Sequence after sequence—in particular, the opening home-from-the-war bathing scene—is dedicated to all that is verdant, lusty, and good. The only evil in this Shakespearean outing, aside from the obligatory if ineffectual villain, is the hasty judgment of men toward their better halves. The storyline dances around two evolving romances, Hero and Claudio's courtship easily bested by the continual war of wits between the bantering Beatrice and Benedick, characters brought vividly to life by Kenneth Branagh and Emma Thompson. It's a high-spirited ado about the vagaries of love from a Shakespearean perspective. Or as Beatrice advises us gals in the opening prologue:

> The fraud of men was ever so
> Since summer first was leafy,
> So sigh no more, but let them go
> And you be blithe and bonny,

Converting all your sounds of woe
Into hey, nonny, nonny.
1993. 110m. DIR: Kenneth Branagh. WRIT: The Bard, as adapted by Branagh. CAST: Emma Thompson, Kenneth Branagh, Denzel Washington, Keanu Reeves, Michael Keaton, Robert Sean Leonard, Kate Bechinsale.

MURPHY'S ROMANCE...

co-scripted by a woman, takes the bygone innocence of small-town Mayberry and shifts it west to Arizona, where our divorced heroine has moved with her young son to begin life anew. Sally Field is predictably on target as the horse-training single mom struggling to make ends meet. And James Garner, as the local pharmacist whose support and friendship enhances Field's transition to new environs, gives one of the most memorable performances of his career. He brings this lovable, independent character to life with such savvy flair, we have no trouble understanding how the thirty-something Field finds herself falling for a fellow veering on sixty. It's the embodiment of an affirmative flick, one which even allows the hopelessly unreliable ex-hubby Brian Kerwin to have his particular charm. The final scene, where Garner tells Field just what kind of a man she can expect if she opts for this relationship, is as choice as they come. Special mention is due Carole King's evocative theme song 'Running Lonely.'
1985. 107m. DIR: Martin Ritt. WRIT: Harriet Frank, Jr., Irving Ravetch. CAST: Sally Field, James Garner, Brian Kerwin, Corey Haim, Dennis Burkley, Charles Lane, Georgann Johnson.

THE MUSIC TEACHER...

tells the tale of a venerable 19th century opera star who retires from the stage to devote himself to inculcating a young female soprano with greatness. The teacher and his worshipful student retreat to his sumptuous country estate, where his wife rues fatalistically that her celebrated husband is bound to fall in love with his young protégée. We feel likewise, but the actual romance in this story comes from an unexpected direction when our voice coach brings a second operatic neophyte under his tutelage. As played by Phillipe Volter, this pick-pocket-turned-brilliant-tenor becomes increasingly attractive as the film progresses. Musical instruction and romantic complications intensify, climaxing with a singing duel to be savored by opera and non-opera fans alike. Lush cinematography and period art direction make the movie look as good as it sounds.

1988. 95m. In French w/English Subtitles. DIR: Gerard Corbiau. CAST: Jose Van Dam, Patrick Bauchau, Sylvie Fennec, Phillipe Volter.

THE NIGHT WE NEVER MET...

builds on the premise that about-to-be-married sleazebag Kevin Anderson, loathe to give up his rent-controlled apartment, opts for the perfect compromise: he will use the flat two nights a week for stag parties with the guys, and sublease it the remaining days to anyone in need of an occasional pied-a-terre. Enter Annabella Sciorra as the bored young wife looking for a part-time art studio, and Matthew Broderick as a recent 'dumpee' in need of peace from the chaotic flat he now calls home. With our three principals in place—sharing the same dwelling, but never knowingly crossing paths—an elusive love triangle takes wing. Sciorra is repulsed by the fellow who is always leaving beer bottles and cigarette butts in his wake, and equally intrigued by the one who bequeaths her gourmet suppers and new window boxes for her plants. Ultimately, she decides to meet this prince of a man, with romantic possibilities in mind. But unbeknownst to Sciorra, Party Boy switched nights with our epicurean plant-lover, and she's about to come-a-courtin' the very wrong chap.

1993. 98m. DIR&WRIT: Warren Leight. CAST: Matthew Broderick, Annabella Sciorra, Kevin Anderson, Justine Bateman, Jeanne Tripplehorn.

AN OFFICER AND A GENTLEMAN...

gives us two parallel and equally involving plotlines, the grueling training which recruits undergo at a Washington State Navel Academy serving as an effective counterpoint to the rocky love story between co-stars Richard Gere and Deborah

Winger. Gere is a Naval pilot wanna-be who continues to harbor any number of hurts from his embittered past, including his mother's suicide when he was only eleven, and the non-existent parenting he received from alcoholic dad Robert Loggia. Winger is a working girl living across Puget Sound—on the other side of the tracks as it were—who, like many other young women in her neighborhood, sees this Academy as her ticket to the happily-ever-after by becoming an officer's wife. They meet at the school's Regimental Ball, after which a series of motel rooms serve as points of rendezvous between the two lovers. Back at the base, tensions mount between the rebellious Gere and tough drill sergeant Lou Gossett Jr., climaxing in a visceral karate match. Among highlights are those sequences which commit us to the recruits, Gere's moving 'confession' when Gossett is about to oust him from the Academy, and a standout performance by Gossett. Unfortunately, the oh-so-Hollywood finale cuts into the credibility of all that precedes it.

1982. 126m. DIR: Taylor Hackford. WRIT: Douglas Day Stewart. CAST: Richard Gere, Debra Winger, Lou Gossett Jr., David Keith, Lisa Blount, Robert Loggia.

ON GOLDEN POND...

stands as quiet testimony to the joys of a long and loving marriage. Katharine Hepburn and Henry Fonda co-star as the elderly couple arriving for their annual summer holiday at their bucolic lakeside cottage. In due time, their daughter Jane Fonda shows up with fiancé Dabney Coleman and his twelve-year-old son Doug McKeon. When Jane expresses her desire to leave Doug behind with Mom and Pop so she and Dabney can enjoy a month-long European vacation, Hepburn talks her curmudgeon of a hubby into going along with the idea. Fonda and Coleman take off, leaving young Doug bristling for being 'ditched.' But as the weeks go by, a tender camaraderie springs up between the old man and young boy, which may or may not portend a reconciliation with Henry and estranged daughter Jane later that same summer. Among

highlights, there's Henry Fonda's superb final film performance, the indomitable Hepburn's sympathetic contribution, and a most majestic setting.
1981. 108m. DIR: Mark Rydell. WRIT: Ernest Thompson. CAST: Katharine Hepburn, Henry Fonda, Doug McKeon, Jane Fonda, Dabney Coleman.

ONLY YOU...

scripted by a woman, is a romantic comedy which comes highly recommended for the Robert Downey Jr. fans among us. A congenial Marisa Tomei co-stars as 'Faith,' who at eleven years of age is told by a Ouija board that she's destined to marry a man named Damon Bradley. At fourteen, a fortune-teller stuns her by delivering the identical prediction. Cut to the present, fourteen years later, where that prophecy is about to be negated by our heroine's impending marriage to Dwayne the Podiatrist. But when Dwayne's friend telephones to inform them he won't be attending their wedding because he's flying off to Italy, and identifies himself to Faith as none other than *the* Damon Bradley, she rushes to the airport to meet her destiny. His plane takes off before she gets there, and without a second thought she hops on the next flight to Venice with best friend Bonnie Hunt in tow, determined to track Damon down. Truly breathless scenery courtesy of ace cinematographer Sven Nykvist, highlighting Venice, Rome, and the exquisite mountain town of Positano, and fine comic performances from Tomei, Hunt, and the ever-reliable Downey add up to a winsome cinematic outing.
1996. 109m. DIR: Norman Jewison. WRIT: Diane Drake. CAST: Marisa Tomei, Robert Downey Jr., Bonnie Hunt, Joaquim de Almeida, Fisher Stevens, Billy Zane.

THE PHILADELPHIA STORY...

stars a positively glowing Katharine Hepburn as a Philadelphia socialite, recently divorced from Cary Grant and now engaged to coal company executive John Howard. What she sees in fuddy-duddy Howard is apparently everything her first husband, an ex-alcoholic, was not. Enter James Stewart and Ruth Hussey as the scandal-sheet reporter and photographer assigned to cover their upcoming high society nuptials. Hepburn and her upper crust clan detest media exposure, but are being blackmailed into cooperating with *Spy* magazine in order to prevent the release of a story concerning Hepburn's father's adulterous affair. As last minute preparations for the wedding collide with impending crisis, a romantic triangle unfolds, the returned Grant still in love with his ex-wife, while newcomer Stewart finds himself likewise enamored. All three principals give top-notch performances, but it's a particular treat watching Stewart and Grant work off each other, the only film in which they ever appeared together. The dated script is less noteworthy for offering us some mighty dubious musings, including the philandering Papa getting away with blaming his sexual excesses on his daughter! *1940. 112m. B&W. DIR: George Cukor. WRIT: Donald Odgen Stewart. CAST: Katharine Hepburn, Cary Grant, James Stewart, Ruth Hussey, Roland Young, John Howard, Virginia Weidler, Mary Nash.*

PRIDE AND PREJUDICE...

follows a contingent of society's elite and would-be elite as they play the socially charged game of courtship and marriage in the gorgeous countryside of 19th century England. The ongoing motif—one pervading all of Jane Austen's masterworks—concerns a contemporaneous law which forbids women from inheriting their fathers' estates. Marriage, suitable or otherwise, is the five Bennett daughters' only bulwark against relative destitution. Ergo Mrs. Bennett's all-consuming ambition to find her daughters wealthy mates. The romantic intrigues of the two eldest daughters take center stage, in particular the burgeoning attraction between our two principals, the prideful Elizabeth and the decidedly prejudiced Darcy, 'whose good opinion once lost, is lost forever.' Their natural affinity for one another is continually sabotaged by differences in background and circumstance. The 1940 black-and-white original of this Austen classic co-stars the inimitable Greer Garson and Laurence Olivier. Their divine leading performances are further enhanced by an incisive script and a uniformly topnotch supporting cast, with special mention due Mary Boland as Mrs. Bennett and Edna May Oliver as the oh-so-haughty Catherine de Bourgh. Incredibly enough, as entertaining and accomplished as is this earlier version, the fleshed out six-part 1995 Masterpiece Theater remake surpasses it. (In this case, more *is* better.) Boasting excellent production values and magnificent cinematography, this scenario showcases the talents and white-hot chemistry of co-stars Jennifer Ehle and Colin Firth. Rarely have smoldering looks taken us so far!

1940. 118m. B&W. DIR: Robert Z. Leonard. WRIT: Aldous Huxley. CAST: Greer Garson, Laurence Olivier, Edna May Oliver, Edmund Gwenn, Mary Boland, Maureen O'Sullivan.

1995. 300m. DIR: Simon Langton. WRIT: Andrew Davies. CAST: Jennifer Ehle, Colin Firth, Alison Steadman, Benjamin Withrow, Susannah Harker.

REALITY BITES...

scripted by a woman, looks at life, love, and the pursuit of meaningful employment through the eyes of Generation X. Winona Ryder stars as the college valedictorian now biding her time as production assistant for obnoxious TV show host John Mahoney, while spending her after-hours documenting the '90s perspectives of her buddies on an ever-present video camera. The cast of characters include comedienne Janeane Garofalo, treading water as a manager at The Gap, and the brooding Ethan Hawke as an aspiring musician, hawking newspapers to help make ends meet. (He claims life is "a series of misses and meaningless tragedies" which can only be savored in the details, such as "the sky ten minutes before it rains.") Enter Ben Stiller as the ambitious TV exec who finds a kindred spirit in the comely Ryder. But will self-proclaimed bench-warmer Hawke decide life is more than the sum of its parts and fight for Winona's heart? You make the call.

1995. 99m. DIR: Ben Stiller. WRIT: Helen Childress. CAST: Winona Ryder, Janeane Garofalo, Ethan Hawke, Ben Stiller, Steve Zahn, Swoosie Kurtz, John Mahoney.

REGARDING HENRY...

stars Harrison Ford as a career-driven, cold-hearted attorney who is cheating on his wife with a beautiful colleague in his law firm. But a bullet to the head is going to change all of that. Henry awakes from a coma unable to walk or talk, and having no memory of his previous existence. As he slowly regains his motor skills, his wife Annette Bening, eleven-year-old daughter Mikki Allen, and former law partners are all confounded to find a child-like, compassionate human being emerging from where that ruthless workaholic once lived. The real joy in this film, aside from the friendship which springs up between Ford and physical therapist Bill Nunn, is in seeing a loving family materialize, where once there had been none. The relationship between Henry and his daughter, as they get to know each other for the first time, serves as the movie's emotional and artistic centerpiece.
1991. 107m. DIR: Mike Nichols. WRIT: Jeffrey Abrahm. CAST: Harrison Ford, Annette Bening, Bill Nunn, Mikki Allen, Donald Moffat, Nancy Marchand.

ROMAN HOLIDAY...

is a whimsical romance starring Audrey Hepburn as a sheltered European princess who craves a taste of the real world. On impulse, she escapes her royal trappings to roam the city of Rome for one precious day, incognito and free. Enter Gregory Peck as the not-so-hard-boiled reporter who becomes wise to our heroine's true identity. Angling for an exclusive on the princess, he takes her on an extended sightseeing tour of the Eternal City, in the process falling hopelessly in love. It's an enchanting, if occasionally dated scenario, with the kind of heart-tugging finale that reflects the essence of the entire film. Hepburn is at her most fetching, while Peck brings quiet yearning to the role of a man who has no choice but to walk away from the love of his life. Of note: although Ian McLellan Hunter is credited, blacklisted Dalton Trumbo penned the script.
1953. 118m. B&W. DIR: William Wyler. WRIT: Dalton Trumbo. CAST: Audrey Hepburn, Gregory Peck, Eddie Albert, Tullio Carminati.

ROOM WITH A VIEW...

scripted by Ruth Prawer Jhabvala, is Merchant-Ivory's finest collaboration to date, a gracefully etched romantic ballad set in the lush landscapes of Tuscany and the English countryside. Helena Bonham Carter stars as the young woman who travels to Italy with aunt Maggie Smith, where she finds herself falling in love with enigmatic British compatriot Julian Sands. This is a three-tiered story that begins with our group of English tourists hitting the highlights of Florence. Then Bonham Carter returns to her family's country home in Surrey and acquiesces to engagement to a most supercilious Daniel Day-Lewis. But when Sands and father Denholm Elliot turn up in the neighborhood the following summer, the passion between Sands and our heroine re-ignites. With the exception of Day-Lewis, who gives a surprisingly broad interpretation of an English prig, the performances are uniformly marvelous—comic, poignant, and passionate by turn. Among delicious moments, there's a classic screen kiss shared by our hero and heroine, the spirited romp three of the principals take in an idyllic country pond, and Smith reading a letter from her niece at film's finale. Special mention is due the sumptuous Puccini score.

1986. 117m. DIR: James Ivory. WRIT: Ruth Prawer Jhabvala. CAST: Helena Bonham Carter, Julian Sands, Maggie Smith, Simon Callow, Denholm Elliot, Judi Dench, Rupert Graves, Daniel Day-Lewis, Rosemary Leach.

SABRINA...

both the original and the 1996 remake, are romantic fairy tales—'Once upon a time on the north shore of Long Island'—about a chauffeur's daughter who is headlong in love with the handsome if prodigal younger son of her father's wealthy boss. But the rogue doesn't give her a second glance until she returns from a sojourn in Paris sophisticated and gorgeous, at which point the infatuation becomes mutual. This is bad news for the button-down older brother, who has been engineering his profligate sibling's engagement to the daughter of a business tycoon, for the profitable corporate merger which will result. So he keeps Sabrina out of his younger brother's sight by pretending to court her himself, falling in love with the lovely lady in the process. Both versions of this story come recommended, although the original has the major shortcoming of providing little chemistry between Humphrey Bogart and Audrey Hepburn. On the other hand, there *is* the winsome Hepburn. In the update, we see much more of Paris, which is surely a plus in anyone's book. And all the female characters are smarter and more credible, no doubt due to a script which is co-written by a woman. Julia Ormand makes a lovely and knowing Sabrina. Nancy Marchand is a hoot as our two brothers' outspoken Mom. (Catch that wardrobe!) And Greg Kinnegar is sweet and comically on-target as the not-so-caddish man about town. Special mention is due Richard Crenna and Angie Dickenson's comic contributions as the future in-laws.

1954. 113m. B&W. DIR: Billy Wilder. WRIT: Ernest Lehman, Billy Wilder, Samuel Taylor. CAST: Audrey Hepburn, Humphrey Bogart, William Holden, Walter Hampden, John Williams.

1995. 127m. DIR: Sydney Pollack. WRIT: Barbara Benedeck, David Rayfield. CAST: Julia Ormand, Harrison Ford, Greg Kinnegar, Nancy Marchand, John Wood, Lauren Holly, Richard Crenna, Angie Dickenson.

SAME TIME, NEXT YEAR...

co-stars a fresh-faced Ellen Burstyn and Alan Alda as two happily married people, albeit not to one another, who meet at a Northern California resort in the innocence of the fifties and surprise themselves by slipping into a one-night tryst. By following morning, the two realize that they truly care for one another and decide to maintain their adulterous relationship, at a distance as it were, by rendezvous-ing one weekend every year. Henceforth, we witness these annual encounters at five-year intervals for the next twenty-five years—reunions which uncannily reflect not only the shifting circumstances of our part-time lovers, but the changing times and fortunes of our country, as well. Among many excellent features of this affectionately entertaining script is the fact that we come to know each of their off-screen spouses almost as much as we come to know the two leads. Otherwise said, this movie is as much about marriage as it is about adultery. Special mention is due Burstyn and Alda's sympathetic performances, and Marvin Hamlisch's theme song 'The Last Time I Felt Like This'—crooned by Johnny Mathis and Jane Olivor—which serves as a most mellifluous link between the five installments.

1978. 119m. DIR: Robert Mulligan. WRIT: Bernard Slade. CAST: Ellen Burstyn, Alan Alda.

SAY ANYTHING...

stars John Cusak at his most endearing, as a high school graduate with one goal in life, which is to win the heart of the class valedictorian, the accomplished and hardworking Ione Skye. Competition comes in the form of Skye's doting father John Mahoney, who feels an 'idle' character such as Cusak—a young man who has already decided he doesn't want to "sell, buy, or process anything as a career"—is surely going to stand in the way of his daughter's high-road journey toward success. But nothing is quite as it seems, and there will be more than one crisis of conscience before this love story runs its course. Special mention is due the sweet supporting contributions from Lili Taylor and Amy Brooks as Cusak's devoted best friends. (The movie's last lines: "Nobody thinks this is going to work, do they?" "No—but you just described every great success story." Yes!)

1989. 100m. DIR&WRIT: Cameron Crowe. CAST: John Cusak, Ione Skye, John Mahoney, Joan Cusak, Lili Taylor, Amy Brooks, Jason Gould.

SENSE AND SENSIBILITY...

scripted by Emma Thompson and based on another of Jane Austen's classics, takes us back to early 19th century England, when women were not only denied an inheritance, but were not even allowed to work for a living. Thompson and Kate Winslet co-star as the loving, if dissimilar sisters, the former reticent and reserved, the latter outspoken and vivacious. (Or, as Winslet exclaims in a fit of pique: "We have nothing in common. You, because you conceal everything. I, because I conceal nothing!") When their father is obliged by law to leave his estate to their greedy half-brother, the two sisters and their mother are left at the mercy of a generous second cousin—gleefully portrayed by Robert Hardy—who offers them the use of a cottage on his property. Once settled in their small but cozy abode, our two sisters tussle with the vagaries of romance in the persons of previously engaged Hugh Grant and dashing gad-about Greg Wise, with solitary aristocrat Alan Rickman waiting in the wings. Among highlights, there's the splendid English countryside, a wry and literate script, and first-class period art direction.

1995. 135m. DIR: Ang Lee. WRIT: Emma Thompson. CAST: Emma Thompson, Kate Winslet, Emile François, Hugh Grant, Alan Rickman, Greg Wise, Harriet Watler, Robert Hardy.

THE SHOP AROUND THE CORNER...

is an old-fashioned delight about two people falling in love through the mail, without realizing that they are the very same feuding clerks who work together in a Budapest leather-goods shop. "Modern girl wishes to correspond on cultural subjects anonymously with intelligent, sympathetic young man," writes Margaret Sullavan in her lonely hearts ad. The 'sympathetic young man' who eagerly responds is contentious officemate James Stewart. "My heart was trembling as I walked into the post office. And there you were, lying in box 237. I took you out of your envelope and read you. Read you right there. Ah, my dear friend." Such is the tenor of their postal romance. In the shop it is more like: "It's true we're in the same room! But we're definitely *not* on the same planet!" You will recognize Mr. Matrischek of Matrischek and Company as Frank Morgan of *Wizard of Oz* fame. Sullavan's comic performance, as evoked by ace director Lubitsch, is surely her finest.

1940. 99m. B&W. DIR: Ernst Lubitsch. WRIT: Samson Raphaelson. CAST: Margaret Sullavan, James Stewart, Frank Morgan, Sara Hadeur, Joseph Schilaut, Felix Bressard, William Tracy, Charles Halton.

SINGLES...

stars a most fetching Kyra Sedgwick as a twenty-something ecologist who falls in love with transportation consultant Campbell Scott. It's a seemingly idyllic pairing until Sedgwick becomes pregnant and the complications set in. Couple number two is Matt Dillon, as the hilariously narcissistic leader of a grunge-metal band Citizen Dick ("Touch me, I'm Dick."), and Bridget Fonda as the misguided young lady who is so smitten with this loser she's considering 'enhancement surgery' to gratify his Amazon-breast fetish. Couple number three is Sheila Kelley and whomever she manages to connect with via her video-dating service. Which brings us to an amusing cameo by Peter Horton of 'thirtysomething' fame, still riding that bike and as flakingly charming as ever. It's a well-observed and entertaining slice of life from Seattle's Generation-X.
1992. 100m. DIR&WRIT: Cameron Crowe. CAST: Kyra Sedgwick, Campbell Scott, Bridget Fonda, Matt Dillon, Sheila Kelley, Peter Horton.

SLEEPLESS IN SEATTLE...

directed and co-written by Nora Ephron, revels in the romantic tradition of our cinematic past, in particular by playing on our collective memories of *An Affair To Remember*. Tom Hanks stars as a grieving widower haunted by memories of his dead wife. His increasingly desperate son Jonas contrives to get his Pop to speak to a psychologist on a national radio talk show, at which point newspaper reporter Meg Ryan, languishing across the continent in Baltimore, hears Hanks' voice over the wires and falls instantly in love. The remainder of the film focuses on our two principals' complicated attempts to connect in person, in order to see if those initial vibes will transmute into the real thing. Ryan and Hanks give satisfactory, if uninspired performances, their problem—and one endemic to the film—being a script which allows them so little screen time together. Among highlights is a very humorous argument between the guys and gals concerning what makes for poignant cinema. It's a scene which crystallizes just why this film guide *Late Nights* was originally conceived.

1993. 100m. DIR: Nora Ephron. WRIT: Nora Ephron, David S. Ward, Jeffrey Arch. CAST: Tom Hanks, Meg Ryan, Rosie O'Donnell, Bill Pullman, Rob Reiner, Rita Wilson.

SLIDING DOORS...

features Gwyneth Paltrow's most sprightly performance to date, in an imaginative romantic comedy which has her living in parallel universes. After a revealing prelude, Paltrow arrives at her publicist job only to be fired for trivial embezzlement. When she heads to the London underground to catch a homebound commuter train, the scenario serves up a momentous split second which takes our heroine's life down two diverging paths. In one development, she misses the train, gets mugged, is taken to the hospital, and upon release returns to her apartment only moments after her boyfriend's secret paramour has split the scene. In the second storyline, she catches that train and arrives on the home front in time to find her lover still in bed with his former girlfriend. These two narratives continue to shift effortlessly back and forth, eventually overlap, then converge quite cleverly by film's finale. Without giving away anymore of the plot, suffice it to say that it's far better to know the truth about a faithless spouse, suffer through the emotional consequences, and then move on with one's life. Otherwise, how would you ever meet someone as adorable as John Hannah? John Lynch, on the other hand, is hang-dog and hopeless as our spineless "shagging wanker," whose confessional bar-room chats with best mate Douglas McFerran prove to be some of the film's hilarious highlights. Rent this one and treat yourself to a witty, touching, and surprisingly feminist gem.

1997. 110m. DIR&WRIT: Peter Howitt. CAST: Gwyneth Paltrow, John Hannah, John Lynch, Zora Turner, Jeanne Tripplehorn.

THE SOUND OF MUSIC...

boasts one of the most glorious opening sequences on film, with co-star Julie Andrews singing our title song while dancing across the majestic highlands of Austria. Based on the true story of the singing von Trapp family, Andrews portrays the young governess whom the recently widowed Christopher Plummer hires to care for his unruly brood of seven. Andrews quickly tames her young charges by way of their common passion for music, while she and Plummer fall inexorably in love. Then come the Nazis and the need for escape via a musical festival in Salzburg. Among highlights, there's Mother Superior's heartfelt rendition of 'Climb Every Mountain,' the nuns demanding 'How Do You Solve A Problem Like Maria?' and Andrews and Plummer's lovely duet, 'Something Good.' We would concur with Andrews, who in a recent interview graciously acknowledged that it is Plummer's solid performance which gives this film its enduring quality.

1965. 174m. DIR: Robert Wise. WRIT: Ernest Lehman. COMP: Richard Rodgers, Oscar Hammerstein. CAST: Julie Andrews, Christopher Plummer, Eleanor Parker, Peggy Wood, Charmian Carr, Marni Nixon.

STARMAN...

is a love story which easily doubles as a sci-fi flick, even a bit of a heartbreaker, while managing to give us a twist on the Messiah myth in the bargain. Jeff Bridges stars as the alien whose spaceship is zapped by our military, forcing him to crash-land in the woods of northern Wisconsin. He finds shelter in a nearby farmhouse, and while widow Karen Allen sleeps, takes advantage of a lock of her dead husband's hair to clone the husband's body as his own. When Allen awakes, he abducts her, hoping to recruit her help in eluding the Army, while racing to a crater in Arizona where fellow aliens will be meeting him in three days' time. Many clever plot devices work successfully at once, among them Allen's initial dismay at keeping company with an extra-terrestrial who's a carbon copy of her beloved late husband, the opportunity of viewing

the pluses and minuses of Planet Earth from the ultimate outsider's perspective, and Bridges' remarkable portrayal of an alien struggling to adopt to humanoid behavior. (Which scene, from which 1953 Hollywood film, helps our Starman to grasp the erotic allure of lovemaking?)
1984. 115m. DIR: John Carpenter. WRIT: Bruce A. Evans, Raynold Gideon. CAST: Jeff Bridges, Karen Allen, Charles Martin Smith, Richard Jaeckel.

THE STATION...

part romantic comedy, part truly heart-palpitating thriller, is a marvelously original film from Italian director/writer Sergio Rubini. Ennio Fantastichini stars as a sweet and unassuming stationmaster living in a southern Italian town with his invalid mother. After a brief prologue, the young man heads off to cover his usual all-night shift at the local train station, unaware that by morning he will have lived through an experience bound to be remembered, and savored, for the remainder of his days. It all begins when beautiful heiress Margherita Buy—realizing that her fiancé is only interested in her money—ditches her cad of a boyfriend at a nearby party and arrives at the station to catch a train to her family's home in Rome. But it's almost midnight, and the next scheduled coach north won't be passing through until early the following morning. This leaves the young beauty with no choice but to remain at the small railway depot overnight. And now a truly refreshing love story unfolds, as two very different people are gradually drawn to one another via a series of quixotic episodes taking place in and around this station. Then the tenor of the scenario shifts dramatically when the spurned fiancé shows up, in danger of losing a very important deal and determined to drag his girlfriend back to the party. Margherita is just as determined to stay put, and our stationmaster, having no honorable choice but to help this lady in distress, initiates an escalating battle of wits and physical acumen with the increasingly violent intruder. It's a well-crafted, involving story, with special mention due Fantastichini's appealing leading performance.

1992. 92m. In Italian w/English Subtitles. DIR&WRIT Sergio Rubini. CAST: Ennio Fastastichini, Margherita Buy.

STRICTLY BALLROOM...

stars real-life ballet dancer Paul Mercurio as the dedicated hoofer who continues to scandalize the powers-that-be at his Australian dance club by insisting on bringing original material to his routines. When his longtime partner quits in disgust, gypsy Tara Morice enters the scene as the plain-Jane beginner with creative choreographic ideas of her own. A most unlikely partnership and romance ensue. There are wonderful dance sequences—among them Mercurio stepping out to 'Time after Time' and our two leads' finale flamenco—as well as terrific comic contributions from the supporting cast. But more than a musical novelty, the movie is a celebration of the creative powers of the human spirit.

1992. 94m. DIR: Baz Luhrmann. WRIT: Craig Pearce, Baz Luhrmann. CAST: Paul Mercurio, Tara Morice, Bill Hunter, Pat Thomsen, Barry Otto, Gia Carides.

THE SURE THING...

might sound like a total loser upon hearing its premise: horny Ivy League freshman heads out to California at Christmas vacation to connect up with the beddable blond babe his UCLA buddy has promised him upon arrival. The twist arises when our freshman's rent-a-ride west is shared with the cool and clever non-babe coed on whom he's had a dead-end crush for months. Antagonisms gradually transmute into puppy love with apparently nowhere to go, since he's meeting his 'sure thing,' and she is joining her fiancé Boyd Gaines. But happily for all concerned, romance will not be denied these two. It's a most captivating love story due to co-stars John Cusak and Daphne Zuniga's guileless creation of two characters genuinely falling for one another. Watch for a nigh-unrecognizable Tim Robbins as one of our insufferable cross-country chauffeurs.

1985. 94m. DIR: Rob Reiner. WRIT: Jonathan Roberts, Steven L. Bloom. CAST: John Cusak, Daphne Zuniga, Anthony Edwards, Boyd Gaines, Lisa Jane Persky, Tim Robbins, Nicollette Sheridan.

SWING TIME...

is one of the more charming Ginger Rogers-Fred Astaire vehicles, owing to a great Jerome Kern-Dorothy Fields musical score, and to the bona fide rapport between our two principals. The plot, such as it is, has compulsive gambler Astaire obliged to prove himself to his future father-in-law by earning $25,000, at which point he will be allowed to marry fiancée Betty Furness. Astaire heads to New York to make his fortune, meets Rogers at a dance school, and convinces her to be his new partner, in the process falling in love with the enchanting lady. The feeling is mutual until Rogers learns her new partner is engaged, whereupon she agrees to marry unctuous bandleader George Mextexa. Astaire wakes up and smells the coffee, breaks off with Furness, and gives chase to Rogers. Among highlights, there are two great duets, 'Pick Yourself Up' and 'A Fine Romance,' as well as Astaire's solos on 'Never Going To Dance' and 'The Way You Look Tonight,' and his classic rendition of 'Bojangles of Harlem,' which has him dancing with three giant shadows of himself. Such praise aside, be prepared for a dated and corny opening sequence which finds Astaire and buddy Victor Moore penniless on the streets of the Big Apple.

1936. 105m. B&W. DIR: George Stevens. WRIT: Howard Lindsay, Allan Scott. COMP: Jerome Kern, Dorothy Fields. CAST: Fred Astaire, Ginger Rodgers, Victor Moore, Helen Broderick, Betty Furness, Eric Blore.

TO HAVE AND HAVE NOT...

a *Casablanca* re-tread which enkindled one of the most celebrated and long-term romances in Hollywood history, stars Humphrey Bogart as a hardboiled American expatriot, this time around earning his keep as a charter boat skipper on the island of Martinique. But it's WWII, France has just fallen to Nazi occupation, and Bogart is approached by resistance fighter Marcel Dalio for help in smuggling one of the underground movement's top leaders onto the island. The disaffected Bogart refuses, until the comely Lauren Bacall slinks into his erotic landscapes with transportation problems of her own, at which point our skipper agrees to make the dangerous run for Dalio. The somewhat unsteady story line is more than compensated for by classic dialogue and the fiery chemistry between our two leads. A special nod is due Walter Brennan as Bogart's bemused, alcoholic sidekick.

1944. 100m. B&W. DIR: Howard Hawks. WRIT: Jules Furthman, William Faulkner. CAST: Humphrey Bogart, Lauren Bacall, Walter Brennan, Dolores Moran, Hoagy Carmichael, Walter Molnar, Sheldon Leonard, Marcel Dalio.

THE TRUTH ABOUT CATS AND DOGS...

scripted by a woman, is a female twist on the Cyrano de Bergerac theme, in this case the short-in-stature Janeane Garofalo using quintessential waif Uma Thurman as her romantic stand-in. It all begins when dashing British photographer Ben Chaplin calls up Garofalo's pet-advice talk show about problems he's having with his Great Dane. Immediately infatuated by her radio persona, he makes an impromptu visit to her station, whereupon our panicky disc jockey, insecure about her distinctly non-anorexic looks, persuades Thurman to be her stand-in. Once this masquerade is launched, it continues to ride on its own steam, Chaplin courting Thurman in person, whom he still believes to be Garofalo, while wooing Garofalo over the phone. Matters degenerate to such a degree that Garofalo has phone sex with Chaplin—a surprisingly erotic scene—in order to avoid meeting him face-to-face. It's an exemplary cast, Chaplin charming indeed as the befuddled suitor, Garofalo sweet and funny in her first leading role, and Thurman genuinely ingratiating as the beauty who is just as envious of her friend's sassy intelligence as the latter is covetous of Uma's gamin looks. The fact that the growing friendship between our female leads rarely takes a back seat to the two-pronged romance is an added plus to the scenario. *1996. 97m. DIR: Michael Lehmann. WRIT: Audrey Wells. CAST: Janeane Garofalo, Uma Thurman, Ben Chaplin, Richard Cora, Jamie Fox.*

UNTAMED HEART...

stars Marisa Tomei as the impulsively romantic waitress who repeatedly falls for chauvinistic losers. ("My father was the first guy to walk out of my life, but certainly not the last.") All that is about to change when the shy and introverted Christian Slater becomes a busboy in Tomei's restaurant. His attraction to the bubbly waitress is instantaneous, but he loves her from afar until the evening she is viciously attacked by two would-be rapists. Slater comes to her rescue, and a passionate love story takes wing, one which is soon threatened by the deteriorating condition of Slater's rheumatic heart. It's an affecting tale, given added resonance by Rosie Perez's winning supporting contribution as Tomei's gum-snapping fellow waitress, and by the movie's haunting theme song as vocalized by Nat King Cole. *1993. 102m. DIR: Harold Ramis. WRIT: Tom Sierchio. CAST: Marisa Tomei, Christian Slater, Rosie Perez, Kyle Secor, Willie Garson.*

WHEN HARRY MET SALLY...

features great performances from Meg Ryan and Billy Crystal, an often hilarious Nora Ephron script, and a lively musical score which illuminates every scene. Harry and Sally first meet sharing an eighteen-hour drive from Chicago to New York after college graduation. Although obviously attracted to one another, they part company upon reaching Manhattan, since Sally is not interested in a serious relationship, and Harry has prematurely concluded that it's impossible for men and women to be 'just friends.' Five years later they run into each other again, both in love with other people, then meet again five years after that, when their respective relationships have hit the dust. And it is only now, much to Harry's surprise, that a truly marvelous friendship takes flight, as the two help each other recover from recent heartbreak while sharing midnight calls, walks in the park, shopping trips, holiday cheer, and thoughts on life, love, and each other. (Harry's assessment of Sally: "There are two kinds of women in this world, low maintenance and high maintenance. You're the worst kind. You're high maintenance, but you think you're low maintenance.") Perils and pitfalls, sexual and otherwise, await this thriving camaraderie. Ryan and Crystal work so naturally off each other, it's hard to believe this was their first—and to date—only film together. Ditto for Carrie Fisher and Bruno Kirby, who furnish able comic support as their married confidants and friends.

1989. 96m. DIR: Rob Reiner. WRIT: Nora Ephron. CAST: Meg Ryan, Billy Crystal, Carrie Fisher, Bruno Kirby, Steven Ford, Lisa Jane Persky, Michelle Nicastro, Harley Jane Kozak.

WHILE YOU WERE SLEEPING...

is a life-affirming romantic comedy starring Sandra Bullock as a lonely Chicago transit worker who suddenly inherits a host of relatives via an unusual chain of events. It all begins when handsome subway commuter Peter Gallagher, whom our heroine has been admiring from a distance for weeks on end, is mugged in the station and falls unconscious. Bullock comes to his rescue, then visits the comatose Gallagher in the hospital, giving the attending nurses and Gallagher's family the mistaken impression that the two are engaged. Bullock finds herself perpetuating the misunderstanding, primarily because she is secretly thrilled to have a family to call her own during what would otherwise be a bleak and cheerless holiday season. But complications arise when she begins to suspect that her snoozing 'fiancé' is a bit of a self-centered jerk, while older brother Bill Pullman is pushing all the right buttons. This is Pullman's first shot at a romantic lead, and he proves himself clearly up to the task.

1995. 100m. DIR: John Turteltaub. WRIT: Daniel G. Sullivan, Fredric Lebow. CAST: Sandra Bullock, Bill Pullman, Peter Gallagher, Peter Boyle, Jack Warden, Glynis Johns, Micole Mercurio.

WOMAN OF THE YEAR...

was Katharine Hepburn and Spencer Tracy's pairing debut, and the chemistry between them sizzles in every scene. Our story opens with political commentator Hepburn voicing her conviction that such 'frivolities' as professional baseball should be eliminated until the end of WWII, an opinion which is hearsay for dedicated sports writer Tracy. The two journalists launch an in-print rivalry which, to everybody's amazement, heats into a hot romance when they finally meet face to face. After a whirlwind courtship, they marry, only to discover that they are very different people. Or rather, to discover that they are very much the same kind of people, one just as strong, proud, and stubborn as the other. At this point the screenplay begins tasking our credibility by asking us to believe that Hepburn adopts a Greek war orphan without even informing her husband, and then can't find the time to take care of the young boy. This considerable caveat aside, it's a cinematic outing brimming with wit and style, capped by a hilarious finale which has our repentant heroine trying to make hubby breakfast. Hepburn's comedic timing and Tracy's dead-pan reactions are equally sublime.

1942. 114m. B&W. DIR: George Stevens. WRIT: Ring Lardner, Jr., Michael Kanin. CAST: Katharine Hepburn, Spencer Tracy, Fay Bainter, Dan Tobin, Reginald Owen, Roscoe Karns, William Bendix.

YOUNG AT HEART...

stars Doris Day, Dorothy Malone, and Elizabeth Frasier as three marriageable sisters living with Papa Robert Keith and Aunt Ethel Barrymore. When flirtatious composer Gig Young breezes onto the scene and sets his cap for the luminous Day, it's only to be stood up at the altar when she decides to marry the new man in her life, self-pitying but talented night-club singer Frank Sinatra. Although the movie suffers from more than a few comically dated miscues—among other problems, our three sisters are far too old for their parts—the presence of Sinatra and Day easily compensates. The chemistry between them is so palpable, it is difficult to believe they were not actually falling in love during production. And some of Sinatra's greatest cinematic/musical moments are tucked into this film, including his magical renditions of such classics as 'One For My Baby,' 'Just One of Those Things,' and 'Someone To Watch Over Me.' Day is nearly his equal in her treatment of 'Ready, Willing, and Able' and 'Hold Me In Your Arms.' Special mention goes to Barrymore's superb contribution as the all-knowing Aunt Jessie, and to the haunting 'Now, My Love,' which provides an apt ongoing theme and a downright thrilling finale.

1955. 117m. DIR: Gordon Douglas. WRIT: Liam O'Brien. CAST: Doris Day, Frank Sinatra, Ethel Barrymore, Gig Young, Dorothy Malone, Elizabeth Frasier, Robert Keith.

ON OUR OWN

"If I were only meant to tend the nest
then why does my imagination sail,
across the mountains and the seas
beyond the make-believe of any fairy tale?
And tell me where, where is it written
what I'm meant to be,
that I can't dare to pick the fruit of every tree,
or have my share of every
sweet imagined possibility?"
Barbra Streisand, in song, questioning the
many limits put on women in 1904 Eastern Europe,
YENTL

"Marriage is like the Middle East. There's no solution."
Pauline Collins to her kitchen wall, before taking
a much-needed furlough from said marriage in Greece,
SHIRLEY VALENTINE

AFTERBURN...

scripted by a woman, is based on the experiences of real-life crusader Janet Harduvel. Laura Dern, who plays the gutsy Harduvel to perfection, stars as the young widow hellbent on proving her test pilot husband did not die because of human error, as the Air Force claims, but due to defects in the design of the jet he was flying. It's a twist on the David and Goliath theme, one woman pitted against General Dynamics, determined to force this powerful military-industrial giant to take its faulty F-16 jet off line. The steamy love interest between Dern and husband Vincent Spano early in the film helps to explain all that follows. Although a few moments get mired in technical double-talk, it's a compelling and inspiring tale. *1992. 103m. DIR: Robert Markowitz. WRIT: Elizabeth Chandler. CAST: Laura Dern, Vincent Spano, Robert Loggia, Michael Rooker, Andy Romano.*

ALICE...

stars Mia Farrow as a wealthy Manhattan matron sleepwalking through a loveless marriage and a mind-numbing routine, while ruminating on such monumental decisions as to when her first foray into plastic surgery might take place. For treatment of a chronic backache she visits a Chinatown herbalist who discerns the pain isn't in her back at all, but in her heart. He proceeds to prescribe a series of magical teas which send Mia/Alice on a voyage of self-discovery. One herb gives her the clarity to work through impasses with her sister and mother; a second grants her a seductiveness which kindles a much-needed romance; a third endows her with temporary invisibility, enabling her to discover what people near and dear actually think of her; and a fourth infusion, a love potion, sets up the film's cleverest scene. Over a few days time, Alice's emotional landscape changes so dramatically, she is able to heed that greatest of calls from one of our greatest of poets: "You must change your life!" *1990. 106m. DIR&WRIT: Woody Allen. CAST: Mia Farrow, Joe Mantegna, William Hurt, Keye Luke, Alec Baldwin, Cybill Shepherd, Blythe Danner, Judy Davis, Julie Kavner.*

ALICE DOESN'T LIVE HERE ANYMORE...

was a breakthrough film of the early seventies, portraying the challenges of single motherhood with honesty and conviction. Ellen Burstyn stars as the suddenly widowed New Mexico housewife who must piece together a new life for herself and twelve-year-old son Alfred Lutter in a husband-less Brave New World. They pack up and head for her hometown of Monterey, California, where she hopes to resume the singing career sacrificed to marriage many years before. But circumstances force them into an extended stay in Phoenix, then on to another detour in Tucson, where 'Alice' lands work as a waitress and meets world-weary, soft-spoken rancher Kris Kristofferson. The incipient love interest between Burstyn and Kristofferson, while indeed engaging, is easily bested by the deep and abiding affection shared by Burstyn and her son, due in no small part to the young Lutter's remarkable performance. Although scripted by a man, the story maintains the woman's point of view throughout, no doubt because Burstyn herself produced it and brought on board the considerable talent involved.

1974. 105m. DIR: Martin Scorsese. WRIT: Robert Getchell. CAST: Ellen Burstyn, Alfred Lutter, Diane Ladd, Kris Kristofferson, Harvey Keitel, Jodie Foster.

AN ANGEL AT MY TABLE...

directed and scripted by women, is based on the autobiography of celebrated New Zealand writer Janet Frame. Her reclusive, idiosyncratic behavior leads to an errant diagnosis of schizophrenia and an eight-year confinement in a mental hospital, where she is subjected to 200 electroshock treatments. It's a horrific development, yet only one of many afflictions Frame must surmount en route to becoming one of her country's most successful poets and novelists. Mingling whimsy with anguish, director Jane Campion offers us a disjointed, yet intriguing study of the archetypal outsider, in the world but never quite of it, due to a society unable to understand this most unique of human beings. Because of the story's unusual length—it was originally produced as a three-part TV series—an intermission may well be in order.

1989. 157m. DIR: Jane Campion. WRIT: Laura Jones. CAST: Kerry Fox, Alexia Keogh, Karen Fergusson, Iris Chum

ANTONIA'S LINE...

directed and written by a woman, is part family chronicle, part sublime fairy tale, which rejoices in the love, solidarity, and grit of the female spirit. The stark opening sequence has our ninety-year-old heroine getting out of bed to the groan of bedsprings and floorboards, looking into the mirror, and deciding that this is to be her last day on earth. The film then proceeds to take a backward glance at Antonia's life, beginning just after WWII, when the fiercely independent widow returns to her Dutch hometown in order to bury her mother. She opts to remain in this rural village, tilling the family farm and bringing up three generations of womenfolk—a daughter, granddaughter, and great-granddaughter—without the help of the hypocritical church hierarchy or the misogynist populace in her midst. Along the way, Antonia is aided by a flock of social outcasts who gather around her ever-growing communal dinner table for the support and emotional sustenance she provides one and all. Willeke van Ammelrooy's robust performance in the leading role stands at the heart of this buoyantly feminist scenario.

1996. 105m. In Dutch w/ English Subtitles. DIR&WRIT: Marleen Gorris. CAST: Willeke van Ammelrooy, Els Dottermans, Jan Decleir, Mil Seghers, Marina de Graaf, Jan Steen.

BABETTE'S FEAST...

based on an Isak Dinesen short story, tells the tale of two elderly sisters who dedicate their entire lives to sustaining the austere religious sect their late father founded decades before. Through flashbacks, we learn of loves lost and ambitions thwarted in order for the loyal daughters to fulfill their imposed spiritual duty as 'the right and left hand' of their father. The Babette of our title is a French chef who walks into their lives and stays on as loyal cook and servant for the next fourteen years. When she comes into a small fortune, our chef chooses to spend it on a grand French banquet for the sisters and their spiritual brethren. After extraordinary preparations, we play witness to ten determined ascetics gradually succumbing to the sensual delights of a lavish feast. But the good life is not all food and drink. On the contrary, this film suggests that true goodness lies in a generous spirit. Or, as the elder sister espouses: "All we take with us at our death is what we have already given away." Special mention is due Henning Kristiansen's cinematography, which showcases Denmark's starkly beautiful northern coast.

1987. 102m. In French & Danish w/English Subtitles. DIR&WRIT: Gabriel Axel. CAST: Stephane Audran, Bibi Andersson, Bodil Kjer, Birgitte Federspiel, Jean-Phillippe Lafont, Ebbe Rode, Jarl Kulle, Gudmar Wivesson.

BABY BOOM...

co-scripted by a woman, is one of the few non-Woody Allen vehicles allowing Diane Keaton to flex her comedic flair. She stars as an ambitious business exec known as the 'Tiger Lady' by subordinates in her Manhattan office. ("Ken, I need the P&Ls on Atlantic overseas. I also need the latest ZBPs and PBPs. And Robin, I want you to get me the CEO of IBC ASAP!") When distant cousins dump a baby in her lap, she makes a vain attempt at juggling child care with a high-powered career before fleeing the corporate canyons for the serenity of rural Vermont. Unfortunately, the house she acquires proceeds to break down in every possible way through a very cold winter. But there's light at the end of this tunnel in the form of a successful baby-food enterprise and the love interest of local veterinarian Sam Shepard. (Catch the scene where Keaton, believing Shepard to be a general practitioner, spills out the travails of her non-existent sex life.) However, the real love story in this flick is between Keaton and her inherited baby daughter.

1987. 103m. DIR: Charles Shyer. WRIT: Charles Shyer, Nancy Meyers. CAST: Diane Keaton, Sam Shepard, Harold Ramis, Sam Wanamaker, James Spader, Pat Hingle.

BAGDAD CAFE...

co-scripted by a woman, is a wild and crazy tale of new beginnings. Marianne Sagebrecht stars as a German tourist who
checks out of her marriage after a disastrous trip to Las Vegas
and winds up stranded in the desert town of Bagdad. But this
California hamlet turns out to be nothing more than a dilapidated motel, gas station, and cafe, all managed by put-upon
mother of two, CCH Pounder. Make that mother of three, if
one includes the grandchild she tends to, and four, if her
shiftless hubby is taken into account. The high-strung
Pounder is initially suspicious of the gentle foreigner showing up on her doorstep with nowhere to go, but soon realizes
this mystery woman is the best thing that has ever happened
to her family and Bagdad. Big changes are in store!
*1988. 91m. DIR: Percy Adlon. WRIT: Eleonore & Percy Adlon, Christopher
Doherty. CAST: Marianne Sagebrecht, CCH Pounder, Jack Palance,
Christine Kaufmann, Monica Calhoun, Darron Flagg.*

BELOVED...

is based on Toni Morrison's award winning novel, and we suggest up front that to truly understand and appreciate this
film, *first* read the book upon which it is based. That said, this
cinematic offering is as ferocious as they come, eyes wide open
as it brings home the inhumane tragedy of slavery in our
country; which is an intriguing accomplishment when considering that the balance of the tale takes place in the post
Civil War era. The scenario's main focus is ex-slave 'Sethe'
(Oprah Winfrey), who managed a miraculous excape from her
Kentucky 'Sweet Home' plantation eighteen years earlier,
but—as we eventually learn—paid a crushing price in the
process. It is now 1873, and she is farming a small rural Ohio
homestead with the help of her skittish teenaged daughter
Denver (Kimberley Elise), while being literally haunted by
the ghost of her long dead baby girl. Soon enough fellow ex-
slave 'Paul D.' (Danny Glover) appears on the scene and
becomes both Sethe's lover and helpmate. The future looks

hopeful, if not rosy, and the bygone days dead and buried, until the arrival of a mysterious young women, 'Beloved' (Thandie Newton), whose bizarre, inquisitive presence gradually opens the doors into our two leading characters' tortured pasts. Don't let the confusing first half hour put you off; this is a mystical mystery, various plots converging into one harrowing story, and should be approached as such.

1999. 175m. DIR: Jonathan Demme. WRIT: Akosua Busia, Richard LaGravenese, Adam Brooks. CAST: Oprah Winfrey, Danny Glover, Thandie Newton, Kimberly Elise.

BETWEEN TWO WOMEN...

relies on the gutsy talents of its two co-stars, Farrah Fawcett and Colleen Dewhurst. Told in flashback by narrator Fawcett, we learn of her struggles to make a success out of her marriage to aspiring artist Michael Nouri while dealing with an ultra-dominating mother-in-law. Dewhurst is a woman who is continually crashing the party, both figuratively and literally. And Fawcett, finding herself increasingly alienated from both her intrusive mother-in-law and her 'hands off' preoccupied husband, attempts a trial separation. Then Dewhurst falls prey to a life-threatening stroke, and emotions shift big time, the older woman's extremely vulnerable situation causing the younger woman to answer in kind. Not only does Fawcett insist that they move Dewhurst into their home, but with minimal assistance from hubby Nouri she proceeds to nurse her ailing mother-in-law around the clock, learning to love the dying woman in the process.

1986. 100m. DIR: Jon Avnet. WRIT: Larry Grusin, Jon Avnet. CAST: Farrah Fawcett, Colleen Dewhurst, Michael Nouri, Bridgette Anderson, Danny Corkill, Steven Hill, Terry O'Brian.

BEYOND SILENCE...

directed and scripted by women, focuses on the experiences of a young girl who has dedicated her entire youth to interpreting and redefining the world for her deaf-and-mute parents. (In sign language to her beloved father: "Lightning is silent, like the moon.") This impassioned, interdependent relationship is made decidedly more complex by the ongoing antagonisms between the father and his hearing sister. It's a lifelong hostility—facilely boiled down to the fact that one plays music the other cannot hear—which the childless aunt turns into a challenge by competing for her niece's affections. In particular, she passes her love of the clarinet onto the girl, creating what threatens to be a permanent breach between the eighteen-year-old and her proud and stubborn father. Among highlights of this most unique coming-of-age drama is the scene where Lara is 'signing' a movie for her mother, and the manner in which she meets the first serious love of her life. Special mention is surely due the accomplished, luminous performances from the two actresses who play our heroine-in-transition, Tatjana Trieb and Sylvie Testud. Bottom line, whether it be the peal of a church bell, the trill of a robin, or the simple flapping of sheets drying in the wind, one leaves this lovely film deeply appreciative of the world of sound.

1998. 110m. In German w/English Subtitles. DIR: Caroline Link.
WRIT: Carline Link, Beth Serlin. CAST: Tatjana Trieb, Sylvie Testud,
Howie Seago, Emmanuelle Loborit, Sybelle Canonica, Matthias Hobick,
Hansa Czypionka.

THE BURNING BED...

scripted by a woman and based on a true story, recounts one woman's harrowing fifteen-year struggle to save her children and herself from a relentlessly abusive marriage. It is not only the 'loving' husband's unpredictably violent behavior which sets one's teeth on edge, but the bewildering inability of either of the two extended families or our justice system to deal with the problem. One fateful evening, our heroine engineers the tragic conclusion to her ordeal. The story opens at this extremity and shifts back and forth between the county jail where our self-made widow awaits trial, and the series of events which lead up to this moment. Farrah Fawcett drew well-deserved accolades for her riveting performance in the leading role. And Paul LeMat is equally effective—both pathetic and spooky—as her terrorizng spouse.

1985. 95m. DIR: Robert Greenwald. WRIT: Rose Leiman Goldenberg.
CAST: Farrah Fawcett, Paul LeMat, Penelope Milford, Richard Masur,
Grace Zabriskie.

BYE BYE BLUES...

directed and scripted by a woman, is one of the many fine
independent productions coming out of Canada. As the story
opens, devoted wife and mother Rebecca Jenkins is living
with her husband, military doctor Michael Ontkean, in
Singapore circa 1940. But he is soon captured by the
Japanese, leaving Jenkins no choice but to return with her
newborn son to the family farm in Alberta. To help her folks
make ends meet—and to escape the constraints of her overbearing father—Jenkins auditions as a singer for a local swing
band. Although initially rebuffed, the plucky lady presses on,
and with the help of trombone player Luke Reilly lands a permanent position in the band. With continued coaching from
Reilly, our heroine evolves into a salty, sassy singer, falling in
love with her mentor in the process. Among highlights, there
is Jenkins' touching portrayal of a woman reborn, Reilly's
sexy characterization of a bohemian who is transformed by his
new protégée, and those boundless Canadian plains. Of note:
the opening segment in Singapore is regrettably awkward,
but blessedly brief.

1990. 110m. DIR&WRIT: Anne Wheeler. CAST: Rebecca Jenkins, Luke
Reilly, Stuart Margolin, Michael Ontkean, Kate Reid.

C'EST LA VIE...

an autobiographical coming-of-age tale from French director
Diane Kurys, relates the highs and lows of a young girl's thir-
teenth summer, as she plays witness to the breakup of her parents' marriage. It is in the details that the movie shines: the
special joy the seashore holds for children, including the
games they play with one another on and off the beach; the
young mother who is teaching herself to type for reasons our
adolescent heroine is only beginning to suspect; the little boy
who finally learns how to tie his shoes. There is no villain in
this piece, with the possible exception of the annoying gov-

erness. We understand the restlessness of the wife, and even the brutal anger of the husband. But the inevitability of their breakup does not mitigate the ensuing heartaches for all concerned. (An impromptu ballet recital by little sister is a sublime moment, capturing in everyone's face the heavy price to be paid for this particular divorce.) 'That's Life,' as the French title translates, is not a cavalier toss-away, but a multileveled truism, invoking the beauty and tragedy of every-day life.

1990. 110m. In French w/English Subtitles. DIR: Diane Kurys. WRIT: Diane Kurys, Alain Le Henry. CAST: Nathalie Baye, Julie Bataille, Candice Lefranc, Richard Berry, Jean-Pierre Bacri, Zabou.

CHEATIN' HEARTS...

stars Sally Kirkland in a bravura performance as a forty-something woman trying to come to terms with a life that is swerving way off course. Her hubby of twenty three years has recently flown the coop with the typically younger and, in this case, richer woman, leaving Kirkland to salvage the New Mexico homestead which has been in her family for over 100 years. The same weekend Kirkland is informed that the bank is foreclosing on her ranch, is the very weekend she's hosting her younger daughter's wedding. Bad gets much worse when ex-hubby bursts back on the scene, present girlfriend in tow, and tries to put the financial touch on his put-upon ex-wife. The scenario is comic, poignant, and excruciating by turn, with well-textured contributions all around. And that includes James Brolin's droll effort as the amiable user who manages to lose both women in his life. Special mention is also due the gorgeous New Mexico landscapes.

1993. 88m. DIR&WRIT: Rod McCall. CAST: Sally Kirkland, Laura Johnson, Pamela Gidley, Kris Kristofferson, James Brolin, Renee Estevez.

CHRISTOBEL...

based on Christobel Bielenberg's memoirs *The Past Is Myself*, is the true story of one woman's struggle to save her husband from the Nazi death camps. The movie opens a bit too leisurely on Christobel's wedding day, circa 1934 England. The event is indeed a mixed blessing for her parents, who are having difficulty reconciling the loss of their daughter to a young German husband who chooses to return to his homeland just when Hitler's star is on the ascendent. The scenario now moves to Germany proper, where Christobel and hubby Stephen Dillane begin raising a family, while carrying on an eternal debate about the wisdom of remaining in a country where Nazism flourishes in their midst. For too many years they continue to believe it is their duty to stay and fight, rather than turn their backs on fellow socialists, many of whom are being carted off to the camps. Then fate takes a hand in the situation, and Christobel faces the challenge of a lifetime. The film is unusual for giving us an insider's look at what it was like to live in Germany during the nightmare years, including such uncomfortable details as the Allies' failure to help out German citizens when the opportunity arose to do so, and their relentless bombing of Germany's cities and countryside near the end of the war. Elizabeth Hurley gives a fine starring performance, becoming a steadily more striking presence as the scenario unfolds.

1996. 100m. DIR: Adrian Shergold. WRIT: Dennis Potter. CAST: Elizabeth Hurley, Stephen Dillane.

THE COLOR PURPLE...

based on Alice Walker's highly acclaimed novel, features Whoopi Goldberg's amazing screen debut as the movie's central character Celia, a black southern woman whose story of hardship and ultimate survival we follow over the span of four decades. As the story opens, teenager Celia is giving birth to her own father's child. Having been shamefully mistreated by the brute, she is quickly married off to the equally brutal 'Mister' (Danny Glover), who horrendously torments her, as well. What hurts her even more than his physical violence, is his emotional abuse; in particular, his determination to prevent his isolated wife from making any contact with her beloved sister. But she is gradually helped out of her bondage by the two women who enter her life—Oprah Winfrey as the rebellious town local, and Margaret Avery as her husband's lover and the first person to realize how beautiful Celia really

is. This saga of sisterhood and empowerment showcases Goldberg's stunning leading performance, and grand cinematography from Allen Daviau.
1985. 152m. DIR: Steven Spielberg. WRIT: Menno Meyles. CAST: Whoopi Goldberg, Margaret Avery, Oprah Winfrey, Willard Pugh, Akosua Busia.

DESERT BLOOM...

opens with the adult narrator reflecting on her grandmother's lifelong affection for desert flowers, those remarkable flora capable of growing in the bleakest of environments. And now the film transports us back to 1950 Las Vegas to be introduced to the central character, 13-year-old Annabeth Gish. She is obviously the desert bloom of our title, struggling to survive under the harsh dominion of alcoholic stepfather Jon Voight and ineffectual if loving mother JoBeth Williams. 'Daddy' spends the majority of his time in the back room, sipping booze and wrestling with his short-wave radio. Mom works for the Atomic Energy Commission, then returns home to cook up tuna-and-mushroom-soup casseroles while struggling to keep her dysfunctional brood emotionally afloat on a boundless stream of time-worn homilies. When favorite aunt Ellen Barkin comes for a visit, it is the catalyst for a family crisis, with character-building consequences for our young heroine. The film's searing honesty is due in large measure to the excellent performances from the entire cast. Among highlights is a frighteningly realistic knock-down, drag-out fight between our three adult principals, and the pervasive, nigh-surreal Cold War atmosphere.
1986. 103m. DIR&WRIT: Eugene Corr. CAST: Annabeth Gish, Jon Voight, JoBeth Williams, Ellen Barkin, Allen Garfield, Jay Underwood.

DIM SUM: A LITTLE BIT OF HEART...

a humanistic, character-friendly story, focuses on the cultural differences between generational Chinese-Americans. Widow Mrs. Tam lives in San Francisco's Chinatown with her 30-

year-old daughter Geraldine, and steadfastly refuses to assimilate into this country's culture, choosing to remain loyal to her Chinese heritage. Her daughter, understandably frustrated by her mother's 'old country' ways, is torn between the duty and affection she feels for Mom, and her desire to get on with living a 'normal' American life, in particular by marrying her long-term doctor boyfriend, who is based down in Los Angeles. This appealing, if uneventful film features fine contributions from real-life mother and daughter Kim and Laureen Chew in the principal roles.

1985. 88m. DIR: Wayne Wang. WRIT: Terrel Seltzer. CAST: Kim Chew, Laureen Chew, Victor Wong, Ida F.O. Chung, Cora Miao, John Nishio.

DOUBLE HAPPINESS...

speaks well for the future of first-time writer/director Mina Shum. Sandra Oh stars as a dauntless 22-year-old Chinese-Canadian, still living with her folks while attempting to jumpstart her acting career and to find true love, preferably with a non-oriental prospect. Both of her aspirations threaten her traditional parents, who simply wish for their daughter to do the right thing by finding a nice Chinese man and settling down. Towards that end, they arrange a rendezvous between their daughter and a handsome, cultivated Chinese lawyer who turns out to be gay. But not to worry, since Sandra has already fallen into a promising romance with sweet if slightly nerdy Callum Rennie. Will our heroine play it safe for the sake of familial harmony, or risk being disowned, as her brother was before her, by moving into her own apartment and her own independent life? Sandra's excruciating tear along Vancouver's waterfront near film's finale reminds us that 'double happiness'—the torturous attempt to keep both oneself *and* one's parents pleased with our life decisions—very likely prevents us from evolving into our true selves.

1995. 87m. In English & Chinese w/English Subtitles. DIR&WRIT: Mina Shum. CAST: Sandra Oh, Alannan Ong, Stephen Chang, Callum Rennie, Johnny Mah, Frances You.

EDUCATING RITA...

stars Julie Walters as a young married, working-class hair-dresser resolved to make some salient changes in her life. Towards that end, she renames herself Rita after her favorite novelist Rita Mae Brown and enlists in an Open University literature tutorial at nearby Trinity University. Enter Michael Caine as the burnt-out, bleary-eyed professor who becomes Rita's weekly tutor. ("Of course, I'm drunk. You don't really expect me to teach this when I'm sober, do you?") He's a man who desperately wants to escape from the very intellectual world which she is so keen to enter. The profound friendship which develops between these two lost souls over a long British winter works its alchemy, Caine regaining a sense of direction in his life, and Walters coming to understand what a true education really implies. While Caine gives a typically nuanced performance as the cynical Pygmalion who makes the mistake of falling in love with his creation, this is ultimately Walters' show, her gutsy determination to enrich a second-rate existence serving as an inspiration for us all. *1983. 110m. DIR: Lewis Gilbert. WRIT: Willy Russell. CAST: Julie Walters, Michael Caine, Michael Williams, Maureen Lipman.*

ENCHANTED APRIL...

based on the 1922 novel by Elizabeth von Arnim, tells the affable if somewhat calculated story of four British ladies, all strangers to one another, who agree to share a seaside Tuscan villa for a month's respite from a rainy London winter. But it's more than the gloomy weather which has been dampening these women's spirits. As different as our four principals may be in temperament, they all have the common dilemma of being trapped inside vapid, unfulfilling lives. Josie Lawrence's husband habitually disparages her; Miranda Richardson's mate is a chronic philanderer; Polly Walker is involved with a married man who will never leave his wife; and widow Joan Plowright long ago began turning her back on the sensual possibilities of her world. But over the weeks to come, the gorgeous Italian landscape will work its predictable magic on the four women, opening them up to the possibilities within themselves, within each other, and even within the ostensibly stolid men in their lives. Of note: the scenario is filmed in the actual Portofino villa where von Arnim wrote her novel seventy years earlier.

1991. 104m. DIR: Mike Newell. WRIT: Peter Barnes. CAST: Josie Lawrence, Miranda Richardson, Joan Plowright, Polly Walker, Jim Broadbent, Alfred Molina, Michael Kitchen.

EXPERIENCE PREFERRED... BUT NOT ESSENTIAL...

scripted by a woman, is a sweet, unassuming coming-of-age tale which follows the adventures of a young woman working her first summer job at a Welsh seaside resort, circa 1962. The more seasoned waitresses at the hotel are skeptical of this green, virginal college kid. (Or, as our heroine herself laments: "I'm the only one here without a past.") But distrust and class barriers quickly give way to camaraderie as she becomes part of this congenial gang. Although there's a romantic subplot, the film is essentially the story of one woman's voyage toward self-discovery, with leading lady Elizabeth Edmonds evolving from timid and dowdy to confident and knowing in the span of a single summer, ready to embark on the next stage of her life.

1983. 77m. DIR: Peter Duffell. WRIT: June Roberts. CAST: Elizabeth Edmonds, Sue Wallace, Geraldine Griffith, Karen Meagher, Ron Bain.

FEAST OF JULY...

another in the parade of artful Merchant-Ivory collaborations, stars Embeth Davitz as the pregnant Isabelle, penniless and kinless, wandering the 19th century English countryside in search of the scoundrel who promised to marry her, then promptly disappeared. Her journey is indeed an arduous one, but when exhausted and near death, she is given shelter by a kindly family of farmers. As fate would have it, there are three handsome sons on this farm, each of whom falls in love with the beautiful newcomer, an affection which she discreetly answers in kind. But as the months pass, our heroine comes

to realize which of the three is her soul mate, at which point her cad of a 'fiancé' makes a most untimely return.
1995. 113m. DIR: Christopher Menarel. WRIT: Christopher Neame. CAST: Embeth Davitz, Tim Bell, Ben Chaplin, Guy Wise, Kenneth Anderson.

THE FIRST WIVES' CLUB...

is a jubilant, if occasionally contrived female buddy flick about three former college classmates who reunite 25 years later to mourn a common friend's suicide. Over a hilarious round of drinks, our trio discover they have all-too-much in common with their deceased comrade. Like her, they have also devoted their entire adult lives to establishing their husbands' careers, only to have their spouses return the favor by trading them in for younger models. Three of the finest comediennes in the business—Goldie Hawn, Diane Keaton, and Bette Midler—co-star in this unblushing ode to sisterhood, the defining moment coming when they cast their wedding bands into a glass of champagne, thereby initiating a crusade for justice. Their ex-husbands are now going to suffer the same economic and emotional misery which they so cavalierly inflicted on their first wives. Among many highlights are the perfect bookends to our story: Stockard Channing's moving opening cameo, and the triumphantly spirited finale.
1996. 104m. DIR: Hugh Wilson. WRIT: Robert Harling. CAST: Diane Keaton, Goldie Hawn, Bette Midler, Stockard Channing, Sarah Jessica Parker, Heather Locklear, Victor Garber, Dan Hedaya, Stephen Collins, Maggie Smith, Bronson Pinchot.

FLY AWAY HOME...

based on a real story, charts one young girl's voyage of self-discovery, as she and her dad make a supreme effort to save an orphaned bevy of wild geese. As the story opens, 13-year-old Anna Paquin's mother has just died, and relatives decide to uproot her from New Zealand and send her to Canada to stay with the father she barely even remembers. Dad Jeff Daniels is an eccentric craftsman and inventor who has no idea how to reach out to his grieving daughter. But matters improve for our young heroine when she discovers a nest of goose eggs in a neighboring clear-cut forest and adopts them as her own. When the goslings hatch, they 'imprint' on the first thing they see—Anna—embracing her as their mother, which initiates some of the film's most endearing sequences. The problem is that these goslings have no real mother goose to pass on the art of migration, and if they remain on the farm as domesticated geese, local law dictates they must have their wings clipped. To prevent such a regrettable turn of events, Dad comes up with a most improbable stratagem, one which will allow Anna to inaugurate the young birds into the rites of migration. It's a scenario which truly has to be seen to be believed, taking us soaring southward along with Anna and those gorgeous, courageous geese. Special mention is due director Carroll Ballard's modulated direction and Caleb Deschanel's sensational cinematography.

1996. 110m. DIR: Carroll Ballard. WRIT: Robert Rodat, Vince McKewin. CAST: Anna Paquin, Jeff Daniels, Dana Delany, Terry Kinney, Holter Graham.

FORTUNES OF WAR...

a BBC-produced multipart series based on the autobiographical novels of Olivia Manning, tells the story of a young English bride who returns with her new husband to pre-WWII Romania, where he has a teaching position. After Hitler invades Czechoslovakia, the two are forced to flee with their small band of fellow British expatriates to the relative security of Athens, and from there on to Egypt. It is a lonely existence for our heroine, here played by the ever-reliable Emma Thompson. As she rues to husband Kenneth Branagh: "When we first met, you made me feel like the center of the universe. But now I realize you make everyone feel that way." Or as one of the men courting her aptly sums up her situation: "You married a stranger who brought you to a strange land to live among strangers." She eventually takes a hiatus from her marriage, in order to decide whether the relationship can or even deserves to be saved. Among highlights, there are uniformly excellent performances, convincing

period art direction, and glorious location settings throughout Yugoslavia, Egypt, and Greece.
1987. 160m. DIR: James Cellan Jones. WRIT: Alan Plater. CAST: Emma Thompson, Kenneth Branagh, Ronald Pickup, Rubert Graves, Robert Stephens, Charles Kay, Diana Hardcastle, James Villers.

FRIED GREEN TOMATOES...

co-scripted by women, stars Kathy Bates as a dispirited housewife who dutifully accompanies husband Gailard Sartain on his weekly visits to his infirm aunt. But the despicable in-law won't even allow Bates to step foot in her room, a good thing actually, since it allows Kathy to befriend another resident at the rest home, sprightly octogenarian Jessica Tandy. In the weeks that follow, as hubby passes time with his aunt, Bates has long chats with Tandy, thrilling to the elderly lady's tales of an adventurous 'cousin.' This singular personage—played in flashbacks by Mary Stuart Masterson—has a penchant for skirting the rules of the Depression-era South. Not only does she remain willfully single, but she rescues close friend Mary-Louise Parker from an abusive marriage and teams up with her to establish a thriving 'Whistle Stop' cafe. Via the elderly woman's stories of her maverick past (we come to suspect that Tandy is actually speaking about her own youth), Bates is inspired with a newfound sense of potential.
1991. 130m. DIR: Jon Avnet. WRIT: Fanny Flagg, Carol Sobieski. CAST: Kathy Bates, Jessica Tandy, Mary Stuart Masterson, Mary-Louise Parker, Nick Searcy, Cicely Tyson, Chris O'Donnell, Stan Shaw, Gailard Sartain.

GAS FOOD LODGING...

directed and scripted by a woman, focuses on the travails of a single working mom whose situation is made all the more challenging because the older of two daughters is going through the difficult 'I hate Mother, I love boys' teenage years. Younger sibling Fairuza Balk serves as our narrator: "Mom needs a man so we can do all the dumb, fun stuff most families do." And that becomes Fairuza's raison d'être, finding mother Brooke Adams a mate. As luck would have it, the young matchmaker's choice—a married chap with whom Brooke has just ended a secret affair—is a painfully comic disaster. But despite this setback, Fairuza believes she has finally hit paydirt when she manages to track down the deadbeat dad who deserted them many years before. It's a poignant, realistic story: Brooke is a truck-stop waitress; they live in a trailer camp; older daughter Ione Skye gets pregnant and wants to have the baby; and ex-hubby James Brolin is no knight-in-shining-armor. But this film is not a downer, largely due to the fine cast, spearheaded by Brooke's shining performance as the resilient matriarch.

1992. 101m. DIR&WRIT: Allison Anders. CAST: Brooke Adams, Ione Skye, Fairuza Balk, James Brolin, Robert Knepper, David Lansbury.

GETTING OUT...

based on Marsha Norman's play and co-scripted by a woman, stars Rebecca DeMornay as a convicted felon trying to make good after an eight-year stint in prison. Things are not going to be easy for this young lady. For starters, the baby boy to whom she gave birth at the beginning of her sentence is not in a foster home, as she has been given to believe. Instead, the child was put up for adoption by Rebecca's Mom-from-hell, Ellen Burstyn. And if Rebecca makes any attempt to get back her son, or even to contact him, she stands to forfeit her parole. Then there are the usual prejudices that any ex-con comes up against once back on the outside, as well as the corrupting influences of former comrades-in-crime who hope to see our struggling heroine rejoin their ranks. DeMornay gives an intense contribution as the woman seeking to turn her life around, and aside from Burstyn's harsh characterization, the script is solid and three dimensional. Among highlights, there's the scene where Rebecca finally sets eyes on her eight-year-old son.

1994. 92m. DIR: John Korty. WRIT: Ruth Shapiro, Eugene Corr. CAST: Rebecca DeMornay, Ellen Burstyn, Rob Knepper, Richard Jenkins, Carol Mitchell-Leon, Tandy Cronyn, Norman Skaggs.

GONE WITH THE WIND...

opens with Scarlett setting us straight: "Fiddle-dee-dum! War, war, war! This war talk's spoiling all the fun at every party this spring!" Now many things can be said about this particular southern belle, among them that her selfish, foolish ways probably get two husbands killed, and push a third man—Rhett Butler—right out of her life. But she cannot be accused of passive acquiescence. No matter what adversities come her way, including the ravaging of her beloved plantation and her father's descent into senility, this quintessential survivor not only endures, but flourishes. (The impassioned vow she makes to herself in the ruined fields of Tara, gives us a lucid summation of her character: "If I have to lie, steal, cheat, or kill—as God is my witness, I'll *never* be hungry again!") Vivien Leigh gives an unforgettable leading performance which is ably supported by the fine contributions from the rest of the star-studded cast. The scenario also boasts magnificent cinematography and a grand epic sweep, which all helps to explain why this Civil War saga is just as powerful today as when first released fifty years ago. If there be a caveat, it is the film's tendency to romanticize the slave-owning South, a time and a place which thankfully has long been 'gone with the wind.'

1939. 231m. DIR: George Cukor, Victor Fleming. WRIT: Sidney Howard, Jo Swerling. CAST: Vivien Leigh, Clark Gable, Olivia de Havilland, Leslie Howard, Hattie McDaniel, Butterfly McQueen, Thomas Mitchell, Evelyn Keyes, Harry Davenport, Jane Darwell.

THE GOOD FIGHT...

scripted by a woman, stars Christine Lahti as a divorced attorney and partner in a small law firm, who is asked by her son's best friend to take on a very big case. This 21-year-old is dying of esophagus cancer brought on by his addiction to chewing tobacco. (He got hooked at the age of eight, when a huckster at a baseball stadium passed out free samples of the weed, characterizing it as 'bubble gum.') Lahti's law partner refuses to touch this kind of high-powered and expensive litigation, with the tobacco firms favored by all the legal precedents. But Lahti forges ahead, with unexpected help from a band of energized volunteers and a big-time lawyer who also happens to be her ex-husband, Terry O'Quinn. A tireless crusade unfurls.

1992. 91m. DIR: John David Coles. WRIT: Beth Gutcheon. CAST: Christine Lahti, Terry O'Quinn, Kenneth Welsh, Andrea Roth.

GRACE OF MY HEART...

written and directed by a woman, stars Illeana Douglas in a story with many parallels to the life of ultra-talented singer-composer Carole King. Douglas plays a pampered young woman from a rich Philadelphia family who wins a song contest that sweeps her into Manhattan, where she begins a long, uphill struggle for artistic fulfillment in the cutthroat, sexist music business of the late fifties and sixties. As Douglas' songwriting expertise increasingly echoes her own experience rather than that of her producers, she summons the courage to begin singing her own songs, with most satisfactory results. Along the way, she experiences the requisite romantic liaisons-cum-heartbreaks, until finally hitting her stride both on a professional and personal level. There are fine supporting performances from John Turturro and Eric Stolz, while Matt Dillon's contribution might have been better served by some editing-room shears. Director/writer Allison Anders successfully conveys the look and feel of the changing times, as well as the essence of the creative progress.

1996. 116m. DIR&WRIT: Allison Anders. CAST: Illeana Douglas, John Turturro, Matt Dillon, Eric Stolz, Bruce Davison, Patsy Kensit, Bridget Fonda, Jennifer Leigh Warren, Chris Isaak.

HEART LIKE A WHEEL...

chronicles the life and times of Shirley Muldowney, the first woman to break the National Hot Rod Association's embargo against female drivers. The story is set against the backdrop of our country's viscerally competitive speedways and mirrors the challenges women face whenever attempting to break into a male-dominated field. It's a hard road indeed that Bonnie Bedelia's character travels; for every gain there is a corresponding loss, foremost being the disintegration of her marriage. Yet it is an empowering scenario, as her persistence and passion for her vocation bears out, time and again. If you happen to consider drag racing to be, well, a drag, you will be pleasantly surprised at how sympathetically it comes across with a woman at the wheel. The film stands as one of Bedelia's finest hours.

1983. 113m. DIR: Jonathan Kaplan. WRIT: Ken Friedman. CAST: Bonnie Bedelia, Beau Bridges, Leo Rossi, Bill McKinney, Hoyt Axton.

HEARTBURN...

Nora Ephron's tragicomic rendition of the unraveling of her marriage to journalist Carl Bernstein, is unabashedly skewed toward the female perspective and all the more delightful as a result. The central question which is posited by this scenario: once a woman discovers her husband is afflicted with a roving eye, what can she actually *do* about it? Force a showdown? Take a short hike in the hopes of jarring hubby back to his senses? Attempt normalcy by biting the bullet? Meryl Streep's character experiments with all three options before facing up to the only tenable resolution by film's finale. Among highlights, there's soon-to-be-papa Jack Nicholson's twist on Rodger and Hammerstein's *Carousel*, Streep's priceless epiphany in a beauty parlor, and *Masterpiece Theater's* take on our heroine's predicament. The supporting cast is uniformly excellent, including Jeff Daniels as the editor who is hopelessly in love with the preoccupied Streep, Stockard Channing and Richard Masur as Streep's increasingly loyal confidants, and Steven Hill as Streep's feckless, if knowing Dad. Carly Simon's poignant theme song, one which artfully interweaves her own score and lyrics with that plucky 'Itsy-Bitsy Spider,' gives added resonance throughout.

1986. 108m. DIR: Mike Nichols. WRIT: Nora Ephron. CAST: Meryl Streep, Jack Nicholson, Jeff Daniels, Stockard Channing, Richard Masur, Steven Hill, Maureen Stapleton, Kevin Spacey, Milos Forman.

HIGH TIDE...

stars the inimitable Judy Davis as a bush-league rock-and-roll singer who gets fired from her present gig, which in turn strands her in backwater Australia until her car can be repaired. As fate would have it, the teenaged daughter she gave up to her mother-in-law several years earlier, at the time of her husband's death, is staying in a trailer park with her grandmother in the very same town. This chance encounter gives rise to impassioned emotions among all concerned, not the least of which is the grandmother's panic-stricken fear of losing the child she has come to love as her own. Among scenes to relish is Davis, sorely in need of funds, performing at a strip-tease joint. We never see her on stage, only hear the crowd while the camera remains in the dressing room, lingering on her boyfriend's discomfited face. Surely it takes a woman director, in this case Australia's Gillian Armstrong, to shoot a striptease from such a perspective!

1987. 120m. DIR: Gillian Armstrong. WRIT: Laura Jones. CAST: Judy Davis, Jan Adele, Claudia Garven, Colin Friels, John Clayton, Mark Hembrow.

A HOME OF OUR OWN...

based on screenwriter Patrick Duncan's own childhood experiences, stars Kathy Bates as a widow who gets fired from her job at a potato chip factory for striking back at a sexual harassing foreman. She attempts to turn a proverbial lemon into lemonade by packing up the old jalopy and whisking her kids away from the blighting influences of Los Angeles, hoping for greener pastures elsewhere. Although virtually penniless, she is convinced that serendipity is on her side, and sure enough, in the back roads of Idaho they stumble upon an abandoned half-finished house owned by a lonely Japanese-American who runs the nursery across the street. Bates strikes a deal with the gentleman wherein she is given ownership of the dwelling and surrounding property in exchange for housekeeping and other related chores which she and her children will supply the man. She then gets a job as a waitress at a local bowling alley and sets to work winterizing her new home. Then the real troubles set in. Bates' tough, assured performance stands at the center of this oft-difficult, sentimental, yet ultimately inspirational film.

1993. 104m. DIR: Tony Bill. WRIT: Patrick Duncan. CAST: Kathy Bates, Edward Furlong, Soon-Teck Oh, Amy Sakasitz, Tony Campisi.

HOW TO MAKE AN AMERICAN QUILT...

scripted and directed by women, stars Winona Ryder as a twenty-six-year-old lost soul, working on her third master's thesis four years after graduation and questioning her commitment to live-in boyfriend Delmot Mulroney, after he pops the Big Question. In search of 'space' to mull over her future, Ryder decides to visit grandmother Ellen Burstyn and great-aunt Anne Bancroft in Grass Valley, California. As it happens, a quilting bee comprised of lifelong friends is meeting at Grandma's this summer, as it does every year, and over the next two months Ryder learns of the romantic past and present of each of the eight woman in the Bee, their intimate stories helping our heroine to work through her own tribulations. It's a lovely cast of characters whose disparate life narratives are effectively woven into a satisfying, episodic film.

1995. 109m. DIR: Jocelyn Moorhouse. WRIT: Jane Anderson. CAST: Winona Ryder, Ellen Burstyn, Anne Bancroft, Jean Simmons, Maya Angelo, Kate Nelligan, Samantha Mathis, Alfre Woodard, Lois Smith, Kate Capshaw, Delmot Mulroney.

THE JOY LUCK CLUB...

co-scripted by Amy Tan from her best-selling novel, explores the complex universal issues that spring up between mothers and daughters, as they attempt to understand each other's widely differing attitudes toward life. The emphasis is placed on the older generation, as one by one they reveal in flashback their turbulent personal histories in misogynist 1900 mainland China. Neither the screenwriters nor director Wang spare us any melodrama; we are treated to copious doses of passion, suicide, betrayal, and murder, as each of these intrepid women makes the torturous journey to the United States. After their tales have been told, the action moves into the present to have a look at the more commonplace domestic dramas of their American-born, grown-up daughters. The movie is long and at times overly sentimental, while still managing to be both poignant and compelling.

1993. 135m. DIR: Wayne Wang. WRIT: Amy Tan, Ronald Bass. CAST: Kieu Chinh, Tsai Chin, France Nuyen, Lisa Lu, Tamlyn Tomita, Lauren Tom, Rosalind Chao, Chao-Li Chi, Ming-Na Wing.

JUST BETWEEN FRIENDS...

co-stars Mary Tyler Moore and Christine Lahti as two very different people who become close friends and business partners, without either being aware that one of them is having an affair with the other's beloved husband. When tragedy strikes, the truth is not far behind, and a blossoming friendship is painfully short-circuited until the two women can work through their mutual grievances to rediscover what they mean to one another. Both Ted Danson and Sam Waterston give apt, if slightly broad supporting performances. But this is the ladies' movie, Lahti droll and sexy as an ambitious, single working-girl wistfully aware of something missing in her life, and Moore heartfelt as the deeply-wounded survivor left grappling with a score of unresolved emotions. The genuine sensual undercurrents between our female leads give this film its unexpected edge. Of note: perhaps the best way to countenance a tad too many aerobic sequences is to join right in with them.

1986. 110m. DIR&WRIT: Allan Burns. CAST: Mary Tyler Moore, Christine Lahti, Sam Waterston, Ted Danson, Jane Greer.

THE KING AND I...

Rodgers and Hammerstein's musical classic based on the true-life experiences of one Anna Leonowens, tells the story of a 19th century British widow who sails for Siam—what is now modern-day Thailand—to be the English tutor for the king's many children. (Polygamy being the Siamese fashion, there were many children indeed.) Deborah Kerr and Yul

Brynner are most sympathetic as two very different people who find themselves falling in love. But it is an impossible and never-addressed situation, since they are in constant ideological and emotional combat; Anna is a democratically-bred English schoolteacher, while His Highness, for all his sincere attempts at transforming himself into a 'scientific' modern leader, remains at core an absolute monarch. Among highlights, there is 'The March of the Children,' our two principals' jubilantly suggestive 'Shall We Dance,' Kerr's 'Getting To Know You,' and an affecting musical eulogy at the film's finale. Of note: after a viewing of this film, one cannot but pause and contemplate the unimaginable courage it must have taken the real-life Ms. Leonowens to travel with her son so very far, to a fate so very unknown.

1956. 133m. DIR: Walter Lang. WRIT: Ernest Lehman. COMP: Richard Rodgers, Oscar Hammerstein. CAST: Deborah Kerr, Yul Brynner, Rita Moreno, Martin Benson, Terry Saunders, Rex Thompson.

A LEAGUE OF THEIR OWN...

directed by Penny Marshall with hammer held firmly in hand, is a 'true-to-life' comedy concerning the all-female professional baseball league which was organized when the Majors became depleted during WWII. The story opens in the present, with ex-player Geena Davis traveling to Cooperstown for ceremonies honoring the women's league. Cut to 1943, when insufferable baseball scout Jon Lovitz discovers the 'natural' Davis in small-town Oregon. She agrees to journey to Chicago for the tryouts, where over a hundred wanna-bes are quickly whittled down to fifty-six recruits, all ace athletes who must now suffer the ignominy of short-skirted uniforms and 'Charm & Grace' school. When the season begins in earnest, over-the-hill alcoholic Tom Hanks is hired as their coach. (Defending his present comatose lifestyle to his new boss: "I hurt my knee." Boss: "You fell out a hotel window." "Well, there was a fire." "Which you started.") Hanks' character is incapable of grasping the concept of female professional athletes, emblematic of the rest of our patriarchal countrymen. But all that is about to change, of course, which is part of the fun of this essentially cornball cinematic outing. An additional plus is watching women competing athletically on the silver screen.

1992. 124m. DIR: Penny Marshall. WRIT: Lowell Ganz, Babaloo Mandel. CAST: Geena Davis, Lori Petty, Rosie O'Donnell, Madonna, Tom Hanks, Megan Cavanaugh, Tracy Reiner, Bitty Schram.

LITTLE WOMEN...

both the 1933 original and the 1994 re-make, are based on Louisa May Alcott's enduring autobiographical classic. The story focuses on four independent daughters and their beloved mother, as they wrestle with the travails of everyday existence while Pop is away fighting in the Civil War. The eldest daughter Meg is the pretty, conventional one. The second oldest Jo—an obvious stand-in for Alcott herself—is chafing against Victorian constraints, while envisioning a future literary career. Beth is the shy, retiring musician, and Amy the artistic youngest sibling of this close-knit clan. Although the Marches have seen better days, the gumption and invention of 'Marmee' and her four girls are boundless. Jo soon emerges as the central character, braving loneliness and a diminishing sense of self for an independent life in New York City, where she meets her true love while becoming the bona fide writer that is her obvious calling. The earlier version boasts a thoughtful script co-written by a woman, but many predictably dated moments. The remake, written and directed by women, comes more highly recommended for retaining the compelling humanity of Alcott's novel, while re-fashioning it with contemporary freshness. Kudos are due Winona Ryder's assured performance as Jo, Susan Sarandon's indomitable presence as Marmee, and cinematography which takes us through the four seasons in radiant style.

1933. 117m. B&W. DIR: George Cukor. WRIT: Sarah Mason, Victor Heerman. CAST: Katharine Hepburn, Joan Bennett, Paul Lukas, Spring Byington, Edna May Oliver, Jean Parker, Frances Dee, Henry Stephenson.. 1994. 115m. DIR: Gillian Armstrong. WRIT: Robin Swicord. CAST: Winona Ryder, Susan Sarandon, Gabriel Bryne, Eric Stoltz, Samantha Mathis, Trini Alvarado, Clare Danes, Christian Bale.

THE LONG WALK HOME...

is a forceful meditation on the common bonds between all women; how the affinities of gender easily transcend the barriers of class and race when the opportunity shows its hand. The setting is Montgomery, Alabama, 1954, shortly after Rosa Parks' courageous stand at the front of a public bus triggered a black boycott of public transportation. Sissy Spacek and Whoopi Goldberg co-star, Spacek as the wife of a wealthy, conservative businessman, and Goldberg as their day maid, eking out an existence on the other side of the tracks. When Spacek realizes Goldberg has been respecting the bus boycott by walking the nine miles back and forth to work every day, she offers to begin discreetly chauffeuring her across town. But her husband becomes increasingly upset by Spacek's fraternization with 'the enemy,' and more than one showdown ensues. The wondrous contributions from our two principals, and a most stirring finale, highlight this absorbing drama. (The movie's prescient last line, spoken in narration by Spacek's now grown-up daughter: "It would be years before I understood what standing in that line meant to my mother, and much later, what it meant to me."

1989. 95m. DIR: Richard Pearce. WRIT: John Cork. CAST: Sissy Spacek, Whoopi Goldberg, Dwight Schultz, Ving Rhames, Dylan Baker.

LOVE AFTER LOVE...

co-scripted and directed by Diane Kurys, focuses on a woman with an apparent embarrassment of riches, caught between two lovers, one as sexy and smart as the other. But then we are introduced to the additional facet of each story, becoming acquainted with the other ladies in each of these two men's lives. Isabelle Huppert stars as the free-wheeling novelist living with architect Bernard Girardeau, while indulging in an occasional rendezvous with married rock composer Hippolyte Girondot. Hippolyte is sneak number two, cheating on his wife-manager with Isabelle and loving every passionate minute of it until his wife starts playing the same duplicitous game. Architect Bernard is a bit of a sneak himself, occasionally shacking up with the mother of his two children behind Isabelle's back. It's a turbulent twelve months in the life of our novelist, her thirty-fifth birthday party opening the scenario, her thirty-sixth wrapping it up—a year in which her life is destined to take a momentous turn. Special mention is due a soundtrack which is as erotic as the scenario.

1996. 104m. In French w/English Subtitles. DIR: Diane Kurys. WRIT: Diane Kurys, Antoine Lacomblez. CAST: Isabelle Huppert, Bernard Girardeau, Hippolyte Girondot.

MARIE...

is a powerful political drama based on the true story of one Marie Ragghianti, a woman whose courageous battle against corruption within Tennessee's penal system led to the fall of an entire administration. As our story opens, Marie is forced to escape from an abusive husband by moving herself and her three children into her mother's house. She proceeds to support her brood by waitressing, while simultaneously putting herself through Vanderbilt University. Then the big break comes for this single-working mom when an old friend secures her a job with the state as an extradition director. Before long, she is rising within the state's bureaucracy, eventually becoming a member of the State Board of Pardons and Paroles, and finally its chairperson. The conflicts—and the ensuing trial—are set in motion when Marie confronts the state governor concerning his illegal use of influence and extortion to get a series of very guilty felons out of prison. Sissy Spacek gives a low-key, credible performance as our unlikely heroine, and Jeff Daniels goes successfully against type as her duplicitous, foul-mouthed 'mentor.'

1985. 112m. DIR: Roger Donaldson. WRIT: John Briley. CAST: Sissy Spacek, Jeff Daniels, Fred Thompson, Keith Szarabajka, Morgan Freeman, Lisa Banes, Trey Wilson, John Collum, Don Hood.

LATE NIGHTS ON VENUS

MASK...

scripted by a woman from a true story, portrays the powerful
bond between hard-drinking, hard-playing Mom Rusty
Dennis and her resilient teenaged son Rocky, born with a dis-
figuring calcium disease which forces his face grotesquely out
of shape. These two comrades-in-arms, fortified by each
other's abiding love and support, refuse to be cowed by the
boy's affliction. (When Rocky catches people staring at him,
a not uncommon event, he quips "What's the matter? You've
never seen anyone from the planet Vulcan before?") It's a tale
of humor and courage in the face of adversity, with a subtext
which implies that as long as you think and act as if you are
'normal,' it won't take long for everyone else to fall in line.
One major quibble: in a story championing the ability to
transcend physical imperfection, why does our stout-hearted
teenager do quite the opposite by falling in love with a beautiful, if blind, young blond? Special mention is due Cher for
her distinguished screen performance, playing the complex,
angry, and animated Mom to perfection.

*1985. 120m. DIR: Peter Bogdanovich. WRIT: Anna Hamilton Phelan.
CAST: Cher, Eric Stolz, Sam Elliott, Estelle Getty, Richard Dysart, Laura
Dern.*

MEN DON'T LEAVE...

co-scripted by a woman, tells the story of a happily married
wife and mother who is suddenly faced with the inconceivable
when her husband dies in a freak accident. Heartache is com-
pounded by financial crisis, when widow Jessica Lange learns
she and her two sons are essentially broke. Ultimately, they
are obliged to sell their suburban Baltimore home and move
into the city, where Mom hopes to scrape up employment.
The scenario is decidedly not of the *Unmarried Woman* variety,
where the story takes place against an upper-middle-class
backdrop. This family is just getting by, and we feel it, both
the poverty and the pain of the uprooting which has taken
place. In spite of being Lange's movie, the supporting cast is
fine indeed, including Chris O'Donnell as the rebellious older

son who starts up a relationship with 'older woman' Joan Cusak, Kathy Bates as Lange's hard-driving boss, and Arliss Howard as Lange's budding love interest.

1989. 115m. DIR: Paul Brickman. WRIT: Barbara Benedeck, Paul Brickman. CAST: Jessica Lange, Arliss Howard, Chris O'Donnell, Joan Cusak, Kathy Bates, Corey Carrier.

MIAMI RHAPSODY...

an affectionate ode to Woody Allen—asking us to imagine he as a she—stars Sarah Jessica Parker in her most appealing screen performance to date, as a recently engaged ad-copy-writer whose impending wedding opens her eyes to the assorted marriages self-destructing around her. Older brother has just been kicked out of his house for having an affair with his partner's wife; restless younger sis is already falling out of love with her hubby of two months; and Parker's father has been trysting with his travel agent for over a year. Most inconceivable of all for Parker, is the fact that 'rock solid' Mom Mia Farrow has been enjoying the company of young and charming Cuban nurse Antonio Banderas. Then Parker hits the proverbial glass ceiling at work, losing a big account because her boss assumes kids and hubby are destined to be her priority in life. Will our panic-stricken heroine be capable of overlooking the risks and compromises innate to marriage and walk down that aisle? (The film's last line: "Marriage is a lot like Miami: hot, stormy, and dangerous. But if it's really so awful, why is there so much traffic?")

1995. 95m. DIR&WRIT: David Frankel. CAST: Sarah Jessica Parker, Mia Farrow, Antonio Banderas, Gil Bellows, Kevin Pollack, Carla Guigino.

THE MIRACLE WORKER...

based on Helen Keller's autobiography, is a dual acting tour-de-force, with Patty Duke and Anne Bancroft delivering powerhouse performances as the 10-year-old blind-and-deaf mute and the 26-year-old Irish teacher who rescues her from the void. It's an uphill battle for Annie Sullivan, Helen coming to her as a spoiled, embittered creature, resistant to any influence whatsoever. But Annie's relentless persistence and novel methodologies will eventually prevail. Among innumerable high points is the emotional and physical eight-minute battle of wills between these two equally determined personalities over who will be boss, and the wondrous moment when Helen at long last makes the connection between words her throat is mimicking and the palpable objects they represent. But the film's ultimate triumph is the emotional honesty with which these two actresses work off each other. It is also one of the earliest screen scenarios to concern itself with the essence of sisterhood—how one woman can encourage the potential of another, en route finding her own potential as well. Of note: Helen went on to graduate magna cum laude from Radcliffe, henceforth joining with Clarence Darrow and Jane Addams to form the American Civil Liberties Union and spending the remainder of her life in the service of the handicapped. Surely another great film is waiting to be made about the heroic life this woman led after the original miracle was wrought.

1962. 107m. B&W. DIR: Arthur Penn. WRIT: William Gibson. CAST: Patty Duke, Anne Bancroft, Victor Jory, Inga Swenson, Andrew Prine, Beah Richards.

MISS ROSE WHITE...

scripted by a woman, stars Kyra Sedgwick as a successful young career woman in postwar America, who reverts back to Rayzel Weiss every Friday evening—and only on Friday evenings—to celebrate the Sabbath with her father, uncle, and aunt. These two separate identities, which she has been struggling to maintain her entire adult life, begin to unravel when older sister Luisa, presumed to have perished in a Polish concentration camp, comes to stay with Rose in New York. The haunted Luisa, stirringly portrayed by Amanda Plummer, gradually obliges Rose to come to terms with her Jewish heritage, her childhood, and the mother she barely knew. It's a lovely, quiet gem.

1992. 95m. DIR: Joseph Sargent. WRIT: Anna Sandor. CAST: Kyra Sedgwick, Amanda Plummer, Maximillian Schell, D.B. Sweeney, Maureen Stapleton, Penny Fuller.

MOONLIGHT AND VALENTINO...

penned by Neil Simon's daughter and based on her own real-life tragedy, is hampered by an occasionally hackneyed script. But the scenario ultimately clicks due to the fine contributions from our four female leads. Elizabeth Perkins stars as the young woman who wakes up one morning to find herself a widow, her jogging husband the victim of a hit-and-run driver. The remainder of the film focuses on Perkins' anguished attempts to come to terms with her beloved spouse's precipitous death. The three co-stars are Whoopi Goldberg as Perkins' best friend, Gwyneth Paltrow as her virginal younger sister, and Kathleen Turner as the controlling ex-stepmother they all love to hate until oh-so-sexy house painter Jon Bon Jovi swoops onto the scene.

1995. 104m. DIR: David Anspaugh. WRIT: Ellen Simon. CAST: Elizabeth Perkins, Whoopi Goldberg, Gwyneth Paltrow, Kathleen Turner, Jon Bon Jovi, Peter Coyote.

MOSCOW DOES NOT BELIEVE IN TEARS...

is a Russian drama focusing on the triumphs and tragedies of three young women struggling to carve out personal and professional niches for themselves in 1958 Moscow. When the movie skips forward to 1978, we catch up with their lives to find that circumstances and fortunes have changed substantially. And now we become more involved with the emerging central character, the working single mom who has toughed it out through twenty lonely years only to stumble upon her obvious soul mate in the Moscow subway. A memorable adult love story ensues, involving two endearing, stout-hearted characters. If the viewer can compensate for an occasional illegible subtitle, your patience will be its own reward.

1980. 150m. In Russian w/English Subtitles. DIR: Vladimir Menshov. CAST: Vera Alentova, Irini Muravyova, Raisa Ryazanova, Alexei Batalov.

MY BRILLIANT CAREER...

directed and scripted by women, is based on the true-life experiences of Australian writer Miles Franklin, who was born and raised in the Australian outback in the late 1880s, and penning her first autobiographical novel at the astounding age of sixteen. Rendered into film, this story of the artist as a young woman is galvanized by Judy Davis' remarkable performance. There is no call for didacticism or wordy asides when you have Davis' irreverent, engaging presence at the center of the story. Not that our heroine doesn't have plenty of cause for doubt. In spite of her grand literary aspirations, she's basically a headstrong farm girl, misunderstood by a family totally put off by her determination to put pen to paper with no publishers in sight. Sam Neill co-stars as the local landowner who finds himself strongly attracted to this intelligent, outspoken young woman. But will she be capable of working out the necessary compromise between independence and mutual trust to accept a lifelong partnership with this man? The film boasts magnificent landscapes courtesy of cinematographer Don McAlpine.

1980. 101m. DIR: Gillian Armstrong. WRIT: Eleanor Witcombe. CAST: Judy Davis, Sam Neill, Wendy Hughes, Robert Grubb, Max Cullen, Pat Kennedy.

THE NASTY GIRL...

recounts the true story of Anja Rosmus, a bright young German student who becomes the heroine of her small Bavarian town when she wins an international essay contest. Inspired by this first success, Anja enters another contest, her subject being 'My Hometown During the Third Reich.' Expecting to unearth testimonials of village heroism during Nazi rule, all she gets for her efforts is a series of doors slamming in her face. After increasingly bitter harassment from townspeople who prefer keeping their dirty secrets under the proverbial carpet, our 'nasty girl' is obliged to drop her investigation. But years later, as an adult and mother of two, she relaunches an obsessive search for the truth. Among other disquieting discoveries is the case of the local newspaper editor, long hailed as a hero of the Resistance, who actually wrote pro-Hitler editorials in which he urged his readers to pray for the Fuhrer. The movie is a jagged, slightly surreal comedy about a deadly serious subject: Nazi-era scars which still run deep in the German psyche.

1990. 93m. In German w/English Subtitles. DIR&WRIT: Michael Verhoeven. CAST: Lena Stolze, Monika Baumgartner, Michael Gahr, Fred Stillkrauth, Elizabeth Bertram.

NEW YORK, NEW YORK...

is one of director Martin Scorsese's most underrated efforts. As always, he presents New York in singular fashion, but the only blood spurting from this particular cinematic outing is purely metaphorically, from the broken hearts of two people who can't live with or without one another. It's a variation on *The Star is Born* theme, the twist being that neither of our costars, Robert De Niro nor Liza Minnelli, has made it to the big time when they first meet. They're going to climb up that ladder together, whereupon the story proceeds into familiar territory, with the husband emotionally incapable of playing second fiddle to his successful wife. De Niro, as the taxing but talented saxophone player, has never shown better chemistry with a leading lady than he does with Minnelli in this film. The opening post-WWII party scene on V-J Day, with Tommy Dorsey's band playing familiar standards in the background, deftly sets the stage—De Niro's obnoxious, if hilarious, persistence and Minnelli's increasingly diminished resistance destined to be the ongoing motif of their marriage. Whether you sit through the extended 'Happy-Endings' sequence, edited out on original release, is your call. But the remaining musical numbers feature Liza at her finest.

1977. 163m. DIR: Martin Scorsese. WRIT: Earl Mac Rauch, Mardik Martin. CAST: Liza Minnelli, Robert De Niro, Lionel Stander, Barry Primus, Mary Kay Place, George Auld.

NINE TO FIVE...

scripted by a woman, is that rarity of rarities—an unabashedly feminist, slapstick comedy. Lily Tomlin, Jane Fonda, and Dolly Parton co-star as three put-upon office workers who become comrades-in-arms one night over cocktails as they fantasize about ways to dispatch their ultra-chauvinistic boss. When the fellow winds up in the hospital the following day, a frenetic chain of events transpire, resulting in his being kidnaped and held hostage until a blackmail scheme can be devised. Meanwhile, our trio takes advantage of their boss' absence at the office by transforming the place into a female-friendly paradise, offering workers such novelties as parity salaries, a daycare center, and shared jobs for busy moms. (If only!) By film's finale, everyone will have gotten their just desserts, in particular Dabney Coleman, who gives a hilarious performance as the macho-boss-from-hell. Parton wrote and performed the memorable title tune.
1980. 111m. DIR: Colin Higges. WRIT: Patricia Resnick. CAST: Lily Tomlin, Jane Fonda, Dolly Parton, Dabney Coleman, Elizabeth Wilson, Henry Jones.

NORMA RAE...

co-scripted by a woman, is the true story of a stubbornly independent single mother and textile worker who is becoming increasingly frustrated with the low wages and poor conditions at her small-town southern mill. When crusading New York unionist Rob Leibman comes into this Baptist community, circa 1978, to organize Norma Rae's factory, she joins his ranks, giving him the 'home town' support he needs to make his push for a local union. No one is pleased with her efforts at the out set—not her family, not her suspicious new husband Beau Bridges, certainly not her supervisors at the plant, not even fellow workers who are afraid of losing their jobs in the process. But she and Leibman forge on and, with the help of a few black and female co-workers who are the first to see the light, eventually prevail, bringing us to the visually dramatic turning point of our story. The role of Norma Rae is so tailor-made for actress Sally Field, it's difficult to believe she was a relative unknown when this movie was made. And Leibman's sympathetic contribution, giving us the portrait of a man who refuses to be daunted by seemingly insurmountable odds, is a true inspiration.

1979. 113m. DIR: Martin Ritt. WRIT: Irving Ravetch, Harriet Frank Jr. CAST: Sally Field, Rob Leibman, Beau Bridges, Pat Hingle, Barbara Baxley, Gail Strickland.

OBSESSED...

views the issue of revenge from a woman's perspective. A divorced, thirty-something Montreal mom witnesses a living nightmare when her only son is critically injured by a hit-and-run driver. Deeply frustrated by a legal system which refuses to work for her—the culprit is an American businessman, and hit-and-run is not an extraditable offense—our protagonist spends the remainder of the film tracking down the driver and persuading him, through whatever tactics she can muster, to return to Quebec and turn himself in. ("I'm going to make his life so miserable, going back to Canada is going to seem the easy way out.") The strategies she brings to bear are the very ones any clever and loving mother would employ to ensure justice is done to her child. It's an exceptional tale of grief, responsibility, and redemption, featuring superb performances from Kerrie Keane and Saul Rubinek as the ferocious adversaries. Daniel Pilon deserves special mention for his increasingly tender contribution as the man who finds himself falling in love with his ex-wife all over again.

1989. 100m. DIR: Robin Spry. CAST: Kerrie Keane, Saul Rubineck, Daniel Pilon, Lynne Griffin, Alan Thicke, Colleen Dewhurst.

ONE AGAINST THE WIND...

tells the true story of WWII British socialite-turned-heroine Mary Liddell, who is living in Nazi-occupied Paris with her two teenaged children when the occasion arises to smuggle a downed Allied pilot out of the country. Word of Liddell's resourcefulness spreads, and before long a non-stop procession of downed pilots are knocking at her door for help in their escapes. At the risk of capture, even execution, Liddell soon fashions an entire underground railroad for these aviators, and her own life begins to disintegrate in the process. A stellar leading performance from Judy Davis highlights this often unnervingly tense, if inspiring scenario.

1991. 96m. DIR: Larry Ellkmann. WRIT: Chris Bryant. CAST: Judy Davis, Sam Neill, Denholm Elliot, Anthony Higgins.

OUT OF AFRICA...

based on Isak Dinesen's evocative memoirs, tells her story of starting up a coffee plantation on the slopes of Kilimanjaro in colonial Kenya. The film is a grand celebration of land, love, and the independent spirit starring Meryl Streep as Dinesen, and the marvelous Klaus Maria Brandauer as the man she marries. It's a Faustian bargain if ever there was one. Then again, without this marriage of convenience there would have been no Africa, no plantation, and no opportunity for Dinesen to meet the love of her life, safari hunter Denys Finch-Hattan. (Back in the days when one apparently didn't flinch at an array of elephant tusks!) The occasional awkwardness of Robert Redford's contribution as Finch-Hattan is the only shortcoming of this visually glorious epic, highlighted by David Watkins' cinematography, John Barry's evocative score, and Streep's predictably stellar performance.

1985. 160m. DIR: Sydney Pollack. WRIT: Kurt Luedtke. CAST: Meryl Streep, Robert Redford, Klaus Maria Brandauer, Michael Kitchen, Malick Bowens, Michael Gough.

OUT ON A LIMB...

based on Shirley MacLaine's autobiographical account of her pilgrimage toward spiritual renewal and starring MacLaine herself, is an occasionally self-indulgent and lumbering exercise. It is also an intriguing attempt to dramatize how one woman's belief system gets turned on its ear, forcing her to begin exploring the proverbial crack in the cosmic egg. In MacLaine's own opening words: "I'm going to tell you a story that changed my life. When I passed forty, I began asking myself some serious questions, because I felt something was missing, something I knew was there but couldn't quite touch. These questions came into focus because of a love affair. I did not understand then why I felt so compelled to be with this man. Well, I do now..." Highlights include footage of actual psychics performing spiritual channeling, and the lush on-location cinematography shot in California, Hawaii, Sweden, and Peru. Since this is a very long film, an intermission in those Peruvian highlands comes well-advised.

1987. 160m. DIR: Robert Butler. WRIT: Shirley MacLaine, Colin Higgins. CAST: Shirley MacLaine, Charles Dance, John Heard, Anne Jackson, Jerry Orbach.

PASSION FISH...

tells the story of one woman's struggle toward rebirth after an automobile accident leaves her paralyzed from the waist down. Mary McDonnell stars as the caustic ex-soap opera star, now drowning herself in wine and self-pity—her TV remote as umbilical cord—and working her way through a trail of caretakers who can't tolerate her anymore than she can stand herself. Enter Alfre Woodard as the nurse with serious problems of her own, including a daughter whom the courts have given into her father's custody. Woodard's only hope of getting back her child is to maintain this position at McDonnell's Louisiana home. Through mutual perseverance, including McDonnell's reluctant decision to give up the booze, the two achieve a wary truce which gradually evolves into a profoundly meaningful friendship. By film's finale, we sense not only that McDonnell has come to terms with her altered existence, but that these two women have established a mutually rewarding lifelong bond.

1992. 135m. DIR&WRIT: John Sayles. CAST: Mary McDonnell, Alfre Woodard, David Strathairn, Vondie Curtis-Hall, Angela Bassett.

PEGGY SUE GOT MARRIED...

co-scripted by a woman, stars Kathleen Turner as a forty-three-year-old housewife whose marriage has seen better days. Hubby Nicolas Cage is presently shacked up with a younger woman, and Peggy Sue is bracing to attend her 25th high school reunion on her own. But strange happenings are in the works. At the festivities our heroine is elected 'Queen of the Ball,' faints during the award ceremony, and wakes up twenty five years earlier, apparently being given the opportunity to correct the mistakes of her youth. The script works clever magic with the time-travel conceit, and Turner is letter-perfect as our awe-struck voyager, re-living precious time with family and high school friends with a more mature and appreciative sensibility. The excellent supporting cast includes Jim Carrey before he became—well—Jim Carrey, Richard Norvik as the science whiz destined for greatness, and Kevin O'Connor as the solitary beatnik whom Peggy Sue's older persona seduces one starlit night. (Our ascendant beatnik: "I'm shooting for maximum intensity! Yeah! I'm gonna check out of this bourgeois motel, push myself away from the dinner table, and say—No more Jell-O for me, Mom!") For those of us old enough to remember, the 50s art direction is delightfully convincing.

1986. 103m. DIR: Francis Ford Coppola. WRIT: Jerry Leichtling, Arlene Sarner. CAST: Kathleen Turner, Nicolas Cage, Helen Hunt, Richard Norvik, Catherine Hicks, Maureen O'Sullivan, Barbara Harris, Don Murray.

PICTURE BRIDE...

written and directed by women whose grandmothers went through similar experiences, tells the true story in miniature of hundreds of Japanese women who journeyed to Hawaii in the early 1900s as mail-order brides promised to husbands they only knew through photographs. In this case, a sixteen-year-old girl's parents are contacted by a fortyish man selfish enough to have sent a snapshot of himself taken twenty years earlier. When the young Youki Kudoh travels to Hawaii and meets her new husband, she is dismayed by his advanced age—not to mention his deceit—and refuses to consummate the marriage. Instead, she goes to work in the sugar cane fields in order to earn her passage back home. And that is the opening gambit of a film which could just as easily have been entitled 'picture husband,' since it is *his* portrait which must change over the months to come, as his essentially gentle temperament and capacity for love gradually transform him into a man whom Kudoh can accept as her lifelong mate. The story is personal, but the resonance universal, as it reminds us of the enormous challenges facing all would-be Americans coming from foreign shores.

1995. 110m. In English and Japanese w/English Subtitles. DIR: Kayo Hatta. WRIT: Kayo Hatta, Mari Hatta. CAST: Youki Kudoh, Yoko Sugi, Akira Takayama, Tamlyn Tomita, Cary-Hiroyuki, Toshiro Mifuni.

PLACES IN THE HEART...

based on director Robert Benton's own boyhood experiences, stars Sally Field as a devoted mother of two whose nightmare begins when her husband is shot to death in a freak accident. There is much injustice and hardship our young widow must overcome, including the initial helplessness experienced by any housewife suddenly faced with being the family's only breadwinner in 1935 Texas. Her small southern town is so archly sexist that the local banker is of the opinion that Field should be giving up the farm *and* her children. Field is determined to do neither. Enter John Malkovich as the blind and bitter chair-maker whom Field takes in as a boarder, and Danny Glover as the migrant laborer who convinces Field that the forty acres lying fallow behind her house can be transformed into a successful cotton farm. The stage is set for the stirring scenario to follow, one made all the more rewarding for being grounded on a true story.

1984. 110m. DIR&WRIT: Robert Benton. CAST: Sally Field, John Malkovich, Danny Glover, Lindsay Crouse, Ed Harris, Amy Madigan.

POSTCARDS FROM THE EDGE...

scripted by Carrie Fisher in witty, hilarious fashion, actually improves on her best-selling autobiographical novel, thanks to the tremendous talents involved. Meryl Streep gives a bravura comic performance as a thirtyish Hollywood actress who gets fired from the film-within-the-film when her cocaine habit sabotages her ability to remember her lines. Enter Dennis Quaid as a disastrous one-night-stand, which leads to Streep's overdose and a stint in a drug clinic, whereupon a judge orders her overbearing, competitive show-biz Mom Shirley MacLaine to act as her court-appointed guardian. Among many highlights, there's Streep's rendition of 'You Don't Know Me,' MacLaine preparing her daily 'health drink,' Streep making a down-but-not-out Shirley presentable for reporters, Quaid getting his come-uppance, and an exhilarating finale in which Streep demonstrates her impressive theatrical and musical skills. Annette Bening's brief but savvy walk-on launched her cinematic career.
1990. 101m. DIR: Mike Nichols. WRIT: Carrie Fisher. CAST: Meryl Streep, Shirley MacLaine, Dennis Quaid, Richard Dreyfuss, Gene Hackman, Annette Bening.

PRIVATE BENJAMIN...

co-scripted by a woman, is comedienne Goldie Hawn's magnum opus—she both produced and stars in it—as Jewish princess Judy Benjamin. When new hubby Albert Brooks dies of a heart attack before the honeymoon has even begun, Benjamin panics and monopolizes her favorite radio talk-show therapist for hours on end. ("I have never *not* belonged to somebody. Never. My first boyfriend was in nursery school. I was two. He was three. Did you happen to see *Unmarried Woman*? Well, I didn't get it! I would have been Mrs. Alan Bates so fast, that guy wouldn't have known what hit him.") These phone calls lead to a date with Army recruiter Harry Dean Stanton, who promises her private condos, yachts, and the good life if she joins up with Uncle Sam. Our desperate heroine takes the bait, only to have reality hit home in the person of in-your-face drill sergeant Eileen Brennan. Benjamin wants out of the Army, and almost gets out, then changes her mind when her domineering father comes to 'take her back home where she belongs.' Ever so gradually, our heroine gets into the swing of military life, beginning to enjoy the challenge and camaraderie while growing up in the process. But when she meets sexy Frenchman Armand Assante at a New Orleans bistro and takes a romantic Parisian furlough, her pilgrimage toward liberation is put to the ultimate test.

1980. 110m. DIR: Howard Zeiff. WRIT: Nancy Myers, Charles Shyer. CAST: Goldie Hawn, Eileen Brennan, Armand Assante, Albert Brooks, Mary Kay Place, Sally Kirkland, Harry Dean Stanton.

THE RECTOR'S WIFE...

based on the novel by Joanna Trollope, is an exquisitely wrought tale of one woman's struggle for self-hood. Anna Bouverie has been married to the vicar of a small English parish for the last twenty years, which adds up to two decades of scrimping and pinching to raise her children, run a household, and perform the various church tasks which are expected of the wife of a clergyman. It doesn't help matters that her husband is an unappreciative and bitter man who resents any steps that his wife takes toward independence. When Anna begins working part-time at a nearby supermarket, everyone in the parish heartily disapproves, in particular her husband, who sees it as an insult to his ability to support his family. Various showdowns will be at hand, as well as a goodly portion of romance when two different gentlemen take an interest in the restless and radiant Anna. Lindsey Duncan's leading performance stands at the center of this film, in scene after scene her demeanor a masterful reflection of the internal battle between longstanding familial love and the rage of inhabiting an unlived life. Her final liberation becomes ours, as well.

1994. 208m. DIR: Giles Foster. WRIT: Hugh Whitemore. CAST: Lindsey Duncan, Ronald Pickup, Miles Anderson, Jonathan Coy, Simon Fenton, Lucy Dawson, Stephen Dillane, Joyce Redman, Prunella Scales.

RESURRECTION...

is one of the few films in cinema to deal directly with the 'tunnel' phenomenon millions of people have experienced while skirting the boundaries between life and death. For protagonist Ellen Burstyn, it's a car accident which triggers the near-death experience, a crash from which she emerges with spinal injuries doctors predict will leave her a paraplegic for life. Ignoring this grim medical prognosis, Burstyn moves into a cabin behind her father's farm with her dog as sole companion, and over a number of weeks teaches herself to walk again. Midway toward rehabilitating herself, she discovers she's gained the power to heal others, as well. In spite of her increasing success in the healing domain—and a corresponding popularity in her far-flung community—Burstyn's refusal of orthodox theological explanations for her new-found capabilities is destined to get her into trouble with her more conservative neighbors. The movie serves as a reflective look at the gift of faith-healing, with Burstyn contributing an incandescent performance. Sam Shepard, playing her mercurial love interest, is as irreverently sexy as ever.

1980. 103m. DIR: Daniel Petrie. WRIT: Lewis John Carlino. CAST: Ellen Burstyn, Sam Shepard, Robert Blossom, Eva LaGallienne, Clifford David, Richard Farnsworth.

RICH AND FAMOUS...

augered well for the comic flair Candice Bergen would later bring to the TV sitcom Murphy Brown. Bergen and Jacqueline Bisset co-star as college friends who part ways after graduation, Bergen to find marital bliss on the beaches of Malibu, while Bisset settles in Manhattan and pens a critically acclaimed first novel. Five years later they meet up again. Bisset is now suffering from writers' block, while Bergen has managed to scribble out a 'life in Malibu' potboiler. With Bisset's considerable help, Bergen's novel becomes an instant best-seller, launching her to TV talk-show fame, with her marriage suffering accordingly. And so it goes for the next fifteen years, as we follow the shifting romantic and professional fortunes of two lifelong confidantes who are at constant odds, while forever remaining sisters under the skin. Among highlights is Bisset's double-take in an airliner and its aftermath, as well as the quiet New Year's Eve toast which closes the film. Among caveats is a biased if brief take on 'feminists,' and wayward daughter Meg Ryan's wild and crazy 'Puerto Rican' boyfriend.

1981. 117m. DIR: George Cokor. WRIT: Gerald Ayres. CAST: Jacqueline Bisset, Candice Bergen, David Selby, Hart Bochner, Steven Hill, Meg Ryan.

RUBY IN PARADISE...

leisurely paced yet effective, follows the travails of twenty-something Ashley Judd, who is leaving behind her dead-end life in the mountains of Tennessee for an imagined freedom in Panama City, Florida. She remembers the town for an idyllic summer vacation spent there in her youth, but now it's winter and 'Paradise' isn't looking so idyllic anymore. Judd scratches up work selling souvenirs for no-nonsense gift shop owner Dorothy Lyman, while being secretly courted by Lyman's caddish son. Despite her deteriorating situation, Judd forges on, in the process meeting up with boyfriend number two, Todd Field. Such romantic complications aside, this is less a love story than one woman's odyssey of self-discovery—a realistic chronicle of the adventures and misadventures of striking out on one's own. (Or, as our heroine acknowledges in her ongoing journal: "On the edge of the edge, it's now up to me what to be.") Judd is rock solid in her film debut.

1993. 115m. DIR&WRIT: Victor Nunez. CAST: Ashley Judd, Todd Field, Bentley Mitchum, Allison Dean, Dorothy Lyman.

SARAH, PLAIN & TALL...

based on Patricia MacLachlan's popular children's book and co-scripted by MacLachlan and Carol Sobieski, is eminently suitable for the 'grown-ups' among us. Glenn Close stars as a Maine school teacher who becomes a mail order bride, traveling to 1910 Kansas to take charge of the children of stoic widowed farmer Christopher Walken. It's a heartwarming and satisfying tale as our determined heroine achieves the nigh-impossible, creating a loving home for her new family, adapting to the back-breaking work of Kansas farm life, and turning her impassive new husband into an affectionate helpmate. Highlights include Close acquainting her future adopted children with the life she left behind, and endeavoring to learn about the children's and their father's former life with their beloved 'Mama.'

1991. 91m. DIR: Glenn Jordan. WRIT: Patricia MacLachlan, Carol Sobieski. CAST: Glenn Close, Christopher Walken, Lexi Randall, Margaret Sophia Stein, Jon DeVries, Christopher Bell.

SCENES FROM A MARRIAGE...

follows a Swedish couple through twenty tumultuous years—twelve within their marriage, eight after the divorce—and in so doing gives us the unique opportunity of observing the evolution of a relationship long after the initial split. It is the husband who triggers the original estrangement by having an impassioned fling with a younger woman. But it is the abandoned wife who eventually profits the most from the divorce, shedding the patriarchal dictates of her marriage to begin a voyage of self-discovery. With few exceptions, this film is a two-role character study, intense, probing, and, in its intense naturalism, occasionally claustrophobic. But the heartfelt contributions from co-stars Liv Ullmann and Erland Josephson help make this one of Swedish master Bergman's most personal and accessible films.

1973. 170m. In Swedish w/English Subtitles. DIR&WRIT: Ingmar Bergman. CAST: Liv Ullmann, Erland Josephson, Bibi Andersson, Jan Malmsjo, Anita Wall.

SECRETS & LIES...

is a unique family drama courtesy of maverick British director Mike Leigh. The story opens with young black optometrist Marianne Jean-Baptiste attending her beloved adoptive mother's funeral. Cut! And the scenario takes an extended look at the world of white professional photographer Timothy Spall, a man who doesn't have a clue how to deal with his bitter and childless wife Phyllis Logan. Brenda Blethyn plays Spall's sister, an emotionally fragile middle-aged woman who is stuck with a dead-end, assembly-line factory job, a resentful sister-in-law, and a sullen twenty-year-old daughter who shares nothing with her but the flat they live in. The threads of these two stories begin to interweave in wondrous fashion when our black adoptee discovers that Brenda is her birth mother. Marianne gives her a call, and Brenda reluctantly agrees to a meeting in a London coffee-house, setting up one of the more touching scenes in recent cinema. To both women's surprise, they actually like one another, and a friendship blossoms which puts needed joy into both of their lives. Brenda eventually musters the courage to present Marianne to the rest of the family at her younger daughter's 21st birthday party, which leads up to the film's riotous, cathartic denouement. The acting is superb throughout, spearheaded by Blethyn's strikingly poignant leading performance.

1995. 142m. DIR&WRIT: Mike Leigh. CAST: Brenda Blethyn, Marianne Jean-Baptiste, Timothy Spall, Phyllis Logan, Claire Rushbrook, Elizabeth Berrington, Michele Austin, Lee Ross.

SHIRLEY VALENTINE...

is a vibrant forty-something housewife trapped within a marriage that has lost all sense of communication and spontaneity, matters having deteriorated to such a state that Shirley spends a great portion of her day speaking to the kitchen wall. When an unexpected opportunity arises for her to take a pre-paid trip to Greece without her husband, she grabs at the opportunity 'to get back what she used to be,' and a rewarding coming-of-age comedy is the end result. In spite of a spirited dalliance with roguish Greek cafe owner Tom Conti, Shirley's vacation away from her marriage is not about acquiring another man, but about finding a new lease on life.

Pauline Collins' spirited performance as our solo adventurer gives the scenario its wings.

1989. 108m. DIR: Lewis Gilbert. WRIT: Willy Russell. CAST: Pauline Collins, Tom Conti, Alison Steadman, Bernard Hill, Julia McKenzie, Joanna Lumley.

SHOOT THE MOON...

sets the tone with those desolate opening piano notes; a once-strong, fifteen-year-marriage is in the process of coming undone. Our story examines the pain and havoc intrinsic to such a divorce from several angles: the deserted wife who must begin picking up the pieces of her life; the husband who has turned to the proverbial younger woman before comprehending how much he is giving up in the process; and the four young daughters who struggle to come to grips with a tragedy beyond their comprehension or control. Co-stars Albert Finney and Diane Keaton are well matched as the estranged couple who still care deeply for one another, while no longer capable of nurturing their affection under the same roof. Peter Weller is equally commendable as the distinctly 'working class' new man in Keaton's life, whose vital presence drives the formerly saturnine ex-hubby to mad distraction. But it is the forlorn oldest daughter, fourteen-year-old Dana Hill, in a performance of spellbinding credibility, who gives this picture its singular spark and focus.

1982. 124m. DIR: Alan Parker. WRIT: Bo Goldman. CAST: Diane Keaton, Albert Finney, Dana Hill, Karen Allen, Peter Weller.

SISTER ACT...

is a feel-good comedy starring Whoopi Goldberg as a low-brow Reno lounge singer who inadvertently witnesses a murder orchestrated by mob-connected boyfriend Harvey Keitel. She flees the perpetrators, and with the help of police detective Bill Nunn hides out in a San Francisco convent until the mobsters can be brought to trial. A cloistered life is *not* this particular heroine's cup of tea, but matters improve when Mother Superior Maggie Smith insists Whoopi join their tone-deaf choir. Whoopi does her one better by transforming this singing ensemble into one of the hippest, sassiest choral groups west of the Mississippi. Unfortunately, the choir's growing celebrity status alerts the Mob as to Whoopi's whereabouts, whereupon her fellow nuns are called upon to save the day. Plots don't get much more lightheaded than this, leaving us free to concentrate on all the fun.

1992. 100m. DIR: Emile Ardolino. WRIT: Joseph Howard. CAST: Whoopi Goldberg, Maggie Smith, Kathy Najimy, Wendy Makkena, Harvey Keitel, Bill Nunn.

THE SNAPPER...

starts off in-your-face obnoxious, then proceeds to disarm by leaps and bounds. Set in working-class Dublin, our twenty-year-old protagonist Tina Kellegher has just learned that she's pregnant and is so embarrassed about the circumstances which led to her condition, she refuses to tell anybody the identity of the father. After a see-saw period of adjustment, family and friends rally around her decision to have the child, and we follow this motley entourage through the months leading up to the baby's birth. The film showcases a most affecting performance from Colm Meaney as Tina's ever-supportive Dad—reminding us what 'family values' are really all about—and remains amazingly non-judgmental and non-sexist throughout.

1993. 90m. DIR: Stephen Frears. WRIT: Roddy Doyle. CAST: Tina Kellegher, Colm Meaney, Ruth McCabe, Colm O'Byrne, Pat Laffan, Eanna MacLiam, Clara Duffy.

STEALING BEAUTY...

scripted by a woman, is a coming-of-age drama starring the lovely Liv Tyler. After her mother's suicide, Liv reads through the late poet's private journals and learns she had a brief fling in Italy twenty years earlier. The inquisitive daughter wonders if her mother's Italian one-night-stand might have resulted in her own conception. Now an eager and restless nineteen years old, our young protagonist returns to the 'scene of the crime'—a gorgeous Tuscan villa peopled by a group of English expatriates—in hopes of learning the identity of her biological father. But investigating her heritage is not Liv's only motive for this Italian adventure. Ripe for her first sexual encounter, she hopes to transform fantasy into reality by seducing the young Italian with whom she shared a magical kiss four years earlier. Among the film's highlights, there is Jeremy Irons' wry portrayal of a terminally-ill playwright with an all-too-healthy libido, Sinead Cusak and Donal McCann's convincing rendering of a twenty-year marriage which has remained loving, faithful, and erotic throughout two decades, and not least of all, the sun-drenched, magical Tuscan setting.

1996. 119m. DIR: Bernardo Bertolucci. WRIT: Susan Minot. CAST: Liv Tyler, Sinead Cusak, Jeremy Irons, Donal McCann, Diana Grayson, Carlo Lisca, M. Guillaume, D.W. Moffet, Stefania Sandrelli, Rachel Weisz, Joseph Fiennes.

STEEL MAGNOLIAS...

featuring an all-star female cast, recounts the enduring friendship of six southern women—the titular 'magnolias'—who meet at the beauty salon on a regular basis to dish the local dirt and catch up on each others' lives. Of various ages and temperaments, these women are united by a supportive spirit, an irrepressible good humor, and unwavering grit, all put to the ultimate test when the youngest of the circle, Julia Roberts, suffers complications from childbirth which lead to kidney failure. Sally Field is exceptionally impressive as the grieving Mom, as is Shirley MacLaine as the neighborhood fussbudget, and Olympia Dukakis as the group's smart-ass. ("As somebody once said, if you can't say anything nice about anyone, come sit by me.") But to single out these three actresses is not to slight the other performances in this memorable ensemble effort.

1989. 118m. DIR: Herbert Ross. WRIT: Robert Harling. CAST: Sally Field, Dolly Parton, Shirley MacLaine, Olympia Dukakis, Julia Roberts, Daryl Hannah, Tom Skerritt, Sam Shepard.

STRANGERS IN GOOD COMPANY...

scripted and directed by a woman, is a beautiful, leisurely paced film about a busload of elderly women taking a tour through the countryside of Quebec. When the bus breaks down, these fellow-travelers treat it not as a calamity, but rather as an unexpected pause in life's journey, giving them a chance to get to know one another and the wilderness around them. No professional actresses were used in the cast, which contributes to the charming artlessness of the production. It's a coming-of-age flick for the senior citizens among us; a sterling reminder that it's never too late for adventure and discovery anew.

1991. 101m. DIR&WRIT: Cynthia Scott. CAST: Alice Diabo, Mary Meigs, Cissy Meddings, Beth Weber, Winibred Holden, Constance Garneau, Catherine Roche, Michelle Sweeney.

SURVIVING PICASSO...

as scripted by Ruth Prawer Jhabvala, and based on Françoise Gilot's memoirs of life with the celebrated artist, doesn't pull any punches. Pablo is portrayed as a roving-eyed, egotistical misogynist who treated everyone as pawns in his grand hedonistic design to live life as only the great Picasso could and would. But as Gilot freely admits, she doesn't go into this relationship with her eyes closed. He is in his sixties when the nineteen-year-old catches his eye ("I painted your face before you were born."), and seriously involved with another woman. Gilot eventually moves in with Picasso and bears him two children, only to learn that he maintains intimate contact with three of his previous lovers and has no scruples about initiating several new relationships. Taking all this into account, it is amazing that she not only endures, but ultimately prevails, moving on to a creative and satisfying life lived on her own terms. Alas, as we discover, many of Picasso's other mistresses were not so fortunate.

1996. 129m. DIR: James Ivory. WRIT: Ruth Prawer Jhabvala. CAST: Natasha McElhone, Anthony Hopkins, Jane Lapotaire, Diane Verona, Julianne Moore.

SWEET DREAMS...

is based on the life and times of Patsy Cline, the 'cross-over' queen of country-western music. In the leading role, Jessica Lange gives an exuberant and utterly convincing performance, working the stage like she owns it while lip-synching Patsy's greatest hits to perfection. The story line opens at the infancy of her career, where we find the unhappily married Kline singing once a week at a local Honky Tonk bar. Before the woman can catch her breath, she is being whirled off her feet by the likeable redneck who is destined to become her second husband, Charles Dick. With the charismatic Ed Harris lending able support, the movie now focuses on their marriage, one which turns stormy with Kline's steady rise to stardom. There's more booze, infidelity, and brutality on the home front, and undreamed of success on the work front, before tragedy strikes. Special mention is due Ann Wedgeworth's moving contribution as Lange's supportive Mom, and a musical score which boasts innumerable original Kline recordings, including 'Walking After Midnight,' 'Crazy,' 'Sweet Dreams,' and 'I Fall To Pieces.' Patsy lives!
1985. 115m. DIR: Karel Reisz. WRIT: Robert Getchell. CAST: Jessica Lange, Ed Harris, Ann Wedgeworth, David Clennon, James Staley, Gary Basabara.

SWING SHIFT...

tells the story of the many women who staffed our aircraft factories during WWII—'Rosie the Riveters' as they were colloquially coined—while our fighting men were overseas. The scenario opens in 1941 Santa Monica, where Goldie Hawn and conservative hubby Ed Harris are enjoying a little connubial bliss before his orders come due. Once he takes off, Hawn is employed at the local aircraft plant, and along with hundreds of other new female employees is informed by their foreman that "riveting is real suited to you gals, because women are used to repetitive tasks." Much sisterly camaraderie ensues, in particular a blossoming friendship between Hawn and aspiring dance hall singer Christine Lahti, as the

women find their enforced independence to be both a lonely and heady experience. Hawn makes a stab at being the loyal wife, but ultimately succumbs to the sexy wiles of trumpet player Kurt Russell. Vintage newsreels, the forties' soundtrack, and Lahti's supporting performance are all deserving components of this slight but entertaining film.
1984. 100m. DIR: Jonathan Demme. WRIT: Ron Nyswaner, Bo Goldman. CAST: Goldie Hawn, Christine Lahti, Ed Harris, Kurt Russell, Fred Ward, Holly Hunter, Chris Lemmon, Belinda Carlisle.

THELMA AND LOUISE...

is a fresh and colorful buddy-roadtrip, with screenwriter Callie Khouri's feminist perspectives slightly askew. Susan Sarandon and Geena Davis co-star, Sarandon as a world-weary waitress who convinces unhappily married best friend Davis to take a break from her abusive marriage for a weekend camping trip. En route, the two stop off at a country roadhouse for a few drinks, wherein Geena carries on a light flirtation with an unctuous fellow customer. Once out in the parking lot, the brute tries to rape her, an act which is stopped in progress by Sarandon shooting the fellow dead. The two women panic, decide the police aren't going to buy their version of the story, and flee the scene of the crime. Bad goes to worse when they pick up young cowboy Brad Pitt, who posthaste has a one night stand with Davis and proceeds to steal Sarandon's precious stash of cash the following morning. Now penniless and on the lam, 'Thelma and Louise' turn truly desperado, robbing a nearby convenience store in order to finance their flight over the Mexican border. A series of increasingly hell-raising escapades ensue, in the process our two fugitives discovering the delights of independence and sisterhood. But it's a perilous joy-ride they have undertaken, with no escape route in sight. Our leading ladies' exuberant performances cannot be faulted. Ditto for Michael Madsen's utterly affecting contribution as Sarandon's long-term boyfriend, a man who realizes too late just how much he loves his woman. Special mention is also due cinematographer Adrian Biddle's gorgeous sweeps of our country's western landscapes.

Khouri's script *does* have its share of improbable, even brainless plot twists. But that caveat aside, it's a unique scenario boasting many comic and empowering moments.

1991. 128m. DIR: Ridley Scott. WRIT: Callie Khouri. CAST: Susan Sarandon, Geena Davis, Brad Pitt, Harvey Keitel, Michael Madsen, Christopher McDonald.

A THOUSAND PIECES OF GOLD...

directed and written by a woman, is an independent feature depicting the adversities of a young Chinese woman sold into marriage as a mail-order bride by her poverty-stricken parents. But upon arriving at her destination, an Idaho Gold Rush boom town, Lalu learns her 'betrothed' has no intentions of making her his wife. On the contrary, the scoundrel plans to set her up as a prostitute in the back of his thriving saloon. In the battle of wills that follows, our heroine's steely determination triumphs, and with the aid of various townspeople, including incipient love interest Chris Cooper, she works herself up from virtual slave to laundress, cook, and innkeeper, buying back her liberty in the process. Ironically, her new-found freedom creates a dilemma which gives the film its added tension and depth. Rosalind Chao is spirited and charming in the film's central role.

1991. 195m. DIR&WRIT: Nancy Kelly. CAST: Rosalind Chao, Dennis Dun, Michael Paul Chan, Chris Cooper.

THREE WISHES...

directed and written by women, is fantasy/drama/romance all rolled into one. The story opens in the present, with our thirty-something narrator just learning that he must sell the family home to pay off his failing business. And now the action moves to an extended flashback in which he recalls growing up in a 1950s desert subdivision. Mary Elizabeth Mastrantonio proceeds to take center stage as his single working mom struggling to raise two boys and start a business in conservative fifties suburbia. One afternoon she accidentally crashes her car into homeless drifter Patrick Swayze and invites him and his dog to stay at their home until his broken leg can heal. Over the next month, our mysterious stranger is the catalyst for a lot of positive changes in this family, including the fulfillment of those three wishes near film's finale. It's a script with its heart worn proudly on its sleeve, all perfectly realized in the last minute of film. Special mention is due the realistic 50s setting, as well as Swayze's most charismatic screen performance to date.

1996. 114m. DIR: Martha Coolidge. WRIT: Elizabeth Anderson. CAST: Patrick Swayze, Mary Elizabeth Mastrantonio, Joseph Mazerello, Seth Hunt, David Marshall Grant, D.B. Sweeney.

THE TRIP TO BOUNTIFUL...

a moving tale of grace and deliverance, stars Geraldine Page as a widow living in increasing anguish with her son and daughter-in-law, in large part due to the daughter-in-law's equally increasing unhappiness at having her there. (Or, as Page bemoans to son John Heard: "Fifteen years of constant bickering has turned me into the ugly person Jessie May has always thought I am.") One morning Page succeeds in doing what she's been attempting for years, by getting on that bus for a visit to the small Texas town where she was born and raised. Among memorable moments, there are the scenes between Page and fellow-traveler Rebecca DeMornay, and Page's conversation with sheriff Richard Bradford as he drives her the final few miles to Bountiful. It's a journey destined to enrich the lives of all three principals, and many of us in the audience, as well. Page is inspired, and DeMornay proves once again to be one of the more under-appreciated actresses of her generation.

1985. 102m. DIR: Peter Masterson. WRIT: Horton Foote. CAST: Geraldine Page, John Heard, Rebecca DeMornay, Carlin Glynn, Richard Bradford.

AN UNMARRIED WOMAN...

stars Jill Clayburgh as a woman living all too complacently within her seventeen-year marriage, when hubby informs her he has fallen in love with a salesgirl from Bloomingdale's. The free fall begins as our beleaguered heroine attempts coping

with the tribulations facing any woman who has depended on one man for love and happiness her entire adult life. Among many crises, there's her initial hatred of all men—aided and abetted by the harrowing singles scene—a teenaged daughter who blames the divorce on Mom, and an ex-husband who actually plans on marrying the new love in his life. But through all the pain and self-doubt, and with the help of those near and dear, this 'unmarried woman' gains a more assured sense of where her strengths lie and what she wants out of her life. The movie put Clayburgh on the Hollywood map, and deservedly so. (As a case in point, her reaction to her husband's confession of new love is a visceral highlight.) Special mention is due a screenplay which allows Clayburgh's psychiatrist to give her frequent and needed advice.
1978. 124m. DIR&WRIT: Paul Mazursky. CAST: Jill Clayburgh, Michael Murphy, Lisa Lucas, Pat Quinn, Kelly Bishop, Linda Miller, Alan Bates, Cliff Gorman.

WAITING TO EXHALE...

based on Terry McMillan's best-selling novel and co-written by McMillan, is your paramount female-bonding flick, with a script that throws no punches; male-bashing abounds. Whitney Houston, Angela Basset, Loretta Devine, and Lela Rochon co-star as the upwardly mobile working girls seeking that most elusive of entities: a compassionate, faithful, unmarried man. That these four women also happen to be African-American gives our story a perspective sorely lacking in contemporary cinema. The story opens on New Year's Eve, when Angela's husband has just announced he's leaving her and their two children to marry his white secretary. Our other three heroines aren't faring much better. Whitney, hoping to extricate herself from a long-term affair with a married man, is in the process of moving from Denver to Houston. Divorcée Loretta long ago gave up any personal life to bring up her only son. And Lela's love life, which includes drug-dealers and fat, oily bosses, is as vapid as they come. But over the next twelve months, through all their romantic and professional turmoils, their mutually supportive sisterhood flourishes.

Special mention is due Gregory Hines and Wesley Snipes as Loretta and Angela's charming love interests, and Dennis Haysbent as a smooth-talking, suave devil of a married man, who manages to convince Houston again and again that he's going to leave his wife. Uh-huh.

1995. 121m. DIR: Forest Whitaker. WRIT: Terry McMillan, Ronald Bass. CAST: Angela Bassett, Whitney Houston, Loretta Devine, Lela Rochon, Gregory Hines, Dennis Haysbert, Michael Beach, Wesley Snipes, Toyomichi Kurita.

WALKING AND TALKING...

directed and scripted by a woman, stars Anne Heche and Catherine Keener as lifelong friends who are going through a crisis of confidence after Heche—'grotesquely in love'— moves in with boyfriend Todd Field, leaving Keener and cat to manage the single life on their own. Episodic in structure, we follow each woman's personal struggles, together and separately, as they attempt to make sense out of a life which has reached that baffling turn in the road called adulthood. The opening segment is slow-going, but stick with this one and you will be awarded with an endearing cinematic offering, one with its female perspective firmly in place. Special mention is due a script which fleshes out its characters and to the engaging leading performances by Heche and Keener. Liev Schreiber, as Keener's ex-boyfriend-turned-confidant, is destined to grow on you.

1996. 83m. DIR&WRIT: Nicole Holofcener. CAST: Catherine Keener, Anne Heche, Liev Schreiber, Todd Field, Kevin Corrigan.

THE WASH...

is a marvelous, unassuming film about starting over, quietly reminding us that it's never too late. Nobu McCarthy stars as the sixty-ish Japanese-American wife of dour and silent retiree Mako, who decides she can't take this twilight existence any longer and moves out, leaving hubby dazed and confused. After forty years of marriage, the couple's two daughters are scandalized as well, but none of this stops our heroine from initiating a lovely romance with local fisherman

Sab Shimono. The movie's title refers to the only event which keeps the now separated couple in contact; once a week she still does her ex-hubby's wash. An insider's intimate look at California's Japanese-American culture is the added attraction to this shamefully overlooked gem.

1988. 94m. DIR: Michael Toshiyuki Uno. WRIT: Philip Kan Kotanda. CAST: Nobu McCarthy, L.V. Mako, Sab Shimono.

WHAT'S LOVE GOT TO DO WITH IT?...

scripted by a woman and based on Tina Turner's own story, chronicles the charismatic rock star's turbulent life: her move as a teenager from Tennessee to St. Louis to live with her Mom and sister; her first encounter with the already famous Ike Turner, who sees a unique and powerful talent in this young singer; and their early success together before Ike's escalating drug addiction, flagrant infidelities, and physical abusiveness finish off their marriage. Our bloodied heroine is so desperate to finalize the split that she surrenders royalty rights to every song or album the two ever recorded together, only asking the court for the right to keep her show-business name. The film goes on to portray Tina's gradual rebirth, with the considerable help of the Buddhist faith, leading up to her amazing 1980 musical comeback. Neither writer nor director gloss over Ike's cruelty to his wife, nor Tina's tortured attempts to put up with it, which ultimately is what makes this such a strong and uncompromising cinematic experience. Special mention is due Angela Bassett and Laurence Fishburne's powerful leading performances and that sensational finale.

1993. 118m. DIR: Brian Gibson. WRIT: Kate Lanier. CAST: Angela Bassett, Laurence Fishburne, Cora Lee Day, Vanessa Bell Calloway, Jenifer Lewis, Phyllis Yvonne Stickney.

THE WIZARD OF OZ...

is a must-see for those listless days when we feel our life is stuck in the sepia plains of Kansas; it's time to take a flight over the proverbial rainbow with one of the most memorable leading ladies of all time. Sixteen-year-old Judy Garland, as the restless young farm girl who yearns for something more in her life, brings Dorothy to the screen as no other actress could ever hope to. The story-within-our-story begins when a tornado whirls Dorothy and her beloved dog Toto out of Kansas and into the wondrous land of Oz, where she meets up with three helpmates, The Scarecrow, The Tin Man, and The Cowardly Lion. Like Dorothy, her three new friends are yearning for something which, unbeknownst to them, they already have. ('If Only I Had a Brain/a Heart/the Nerve.') So it's 'Off To See The Wizard,' who insists they must kill off the Wicked Witch of the West before he can help them out. Enter Margaret Hamilton as our dastardly villainess, and the dark side of Oz begins to deliciously emerge. It's the most engaging of musical fantasies, which doubles as an archetypal heroine journey, Dorothy facing a series of trials and challenges which ultimately transform her into a young woman ready 'to go home again.' The supporting cast, including Jack Haley, Ray Bolger, Burt Lahr, and Frank Morgan doesn't get any better than this. Additional kudos is due Harold Arlen and E.Y. Harburg's outstanding musical score.

1939. 101m. B&W/C. DIR: King Vidor, Victor Fleming. WRIT: Noel Langley. CAST: Judy Garland, Ray Bolger, Burt Lahr, Margaret Hamilton, Jack Haley, Frank Morgan, Billie Burke.

A WOMAN'S TALE...

is a finely-wrought story of one indomitable elderly woman, living with her cat in a small apartment which she long ago made into her home and castle. At 78, she is also a serious chain-smoker and paying the price with terminal lung cancer. If this sounds depressing, well yes, there are those moments. But in general, it's an uplifting tale of resilience and love. Numerous scenes stay in one's memory: the soothing ritual of her evening bath; going to sleep listening to a radio talk show; visiting a magnificent waterfall with the young day nurse who becomes so tightly bonded to her; a dance she shares with a next-door neighbor; a death-bed reconciliation with her middle-aged son. In spite of everything, even the cruelties this frail old lady must endure from loutish downstairs neighbors who wish to evict her, our heroine maintains an unassailable conviction that life 'is a very beautiful thing.' Of note: the actress Sheila Florence herself died of cancer shortly after starring in this film.

1992. 94m. DIR&WRIT: Paul Cox. CAST: Sheila Florence, Gosia Dobrowolska, Norman Kaye, Chris Haywood, Myrtle Woods.

YENTL...

is Barbra Streisand's tour-de-force directorial debut. Twelve years in the making, the movie relates the travails of a Jewish girl striving for the impossible—an education—in the conservative early 1900s of Eastern Europe. Our heroine shears her locks, dons pants, and masquerades as a boy named Ansel in order to gain acceptance at a nearby rabbi-run academy. Enter Mandy Patinkin as the older classmate who takes this greenhorn under his wing, at which point the sexual miscues begin flying in earnest. A sublime subplot emerges when circumstances stop Patinkin from marrying true love Amy Irving. In order to prevent another man from getting his hands on his girl, and to ensure himself an occasional visit, Patinkin convinces 'Ansel' to marry Irving in his stead. It is a marriage of convenience which initiates some of the movie's tenderest scenes, as Irving's character finds herself falling in love with this most unusual of men. A husband who actually listens? And respects her as his equal? Bliss everywhere but in the bedroom is the new bride's bewildering lament. Lush cinematography, a rich musical score song by one of the best in the business, and a high-spirited feminist slant all combine to make Streisand's first film an unqualified success.

1983. 134m. DIR: Barbra Streisand. WRIT: Barbra Streisand, Jack Rosenthal. MUS: Michel Legrand. LYR: Marilyn & Alan Bergman. CAST: Barbra Streisand, Mandy Patinkin, Amy Irving, Nehemiah Persoff, Steven Hill.

COMEDY WITH A HEART

"Well, it's not the men in your life that count. It's the life in your men."
May West rephrasing a reporter's question,
I'M NO ANGEL

"I'm keeping my expectations very low. Basically, I'm just searching for a mammal. I'm even flexible on that."
Janeane Garofalo to blind date Randy Quaid,
on her prospects for a future relationship,
BYE BYE, LOVE

ABSOLUTELY FABULOUS...

is scripted by comedy genius Jennifer Saunders, who also co-stars in this landmark British TV series. Each 90-minute cassette revolves around best friends and confidantes Saunders and Joanne Lumley, who smoke, drink, and bed their way down the rocky road of middle-aged paranoia, while running a fashion PR business on the side. The two are equally self-centered, exploitive, disparaging, and shameless; in sum, without a single redeeming characteristic aside from being uproariously funny. The fact that Saunders' daughter 'Saffron' is as straight as they come, forces Mom into the awkward situation of forever attempting to make amends for her own outrageous behavior. Among their various escapades is Saunders' bout with liposuction, Lumley getting a disastrous chemical peel, Saunders' time in the hospital with a broken toe ("I want total sensory deprivation and back-up drugs."), Lumley becoming the center of a Parliament sex scandal and relishing every moment of it, and the two gals staging an orgy in order to get back in touch with their inner selves. Need we say more? Now pour out a glass of your favorite libation and indulge in the kind of devilish entertainment which would never have come out of American network programming. *1991-96. 90m/per cassette. DIR: Bob Spiers. WRIT: Jennifer Saunders. CAST: Jennifer Saunders, Joanna Lumley, Julia Sawalha, Jane Horrocks, June Whitfield.*

ADAM'S RIB...

another comic gem from the pens of Ruth Gordon and Garson Kanin, makes the most out of the chemistry between co-stars Katharine Hepburn and Spencer Tracy as married attorneys on opposing sides of an attempted murder case. The supporting contributions are just as noteworthy, Tom Ewell a sleazy delight as the unfaithful spouse, and Judy Holliday perfect at playing the ditzy, jealous wife now on trial for taking aim at Ewell's mistress. Hepburn chooses to represent Holliday, determined to prove that the prosecution's case, as argued by assistant D.A. Tracy, is a clear reflection of sexist double standards. (Hepburn: "All I'm trying to say is that there's lots of things that a man can do and in society's eyes it's all hunky-dory. A woman does the same thing—the *same* thing mind you—and she's an outcast.") As the trial goes forward, courtroom resentments between our battling spouses begin percolating to the surface on the home front, as well. The scenario is light years ahead of its time—a deft mix of slapstick, sophisticated wit, and saucy romance—making it a battle-of-the-sexes not to be missed.

1949. 101m. B&W. DIR: George Cukor. WRIT: Ruth Gordon, Garson Kanin. CAST: Katharine Hepburn, Spencer Tracy, Judy Holliday, Tom Ewell, David Wayne, Jean Hagen.

ALADDIN...

is a movie for the kiddies, no doubt about it, but comes endorsed all the same, due to Robin Williams' unique contribution, his kinetic performance as the voice of the Genie transforming this Disney production into one surprisingly hip outing. (Disney illustrators wisely did not complete their animation work on the Genie until after Williams had recorded his dialogue, thereby allowing them to take full advantage of his trademark free-association riffs.) The storyline is a familiar one. Lowly boy falls in love with young maiden he believes to be equally lowly. But she's actually the princess of the land, whom her weak-kneed father is marrying off to the villain of our piece, whereupon Aladdin saves the day with the aid of the capricious, motor-mouthed Genie. Among highlights, there are those magnificent magic carpet rides and the savvy supporting cast. Ultimately, however, praise must come back around to Williams' achievement and the undeniable fact that animation is a perfect medium for this comic genius.

1992. 90m. DIR: John Musker, Ron Clements. WRIT: Ron Clements, John Musker, Ted Elliot, Terry Rossio. VOICES: Robin Williams, Scott Weinger, Linda Larkin, Jonathan Freeman, Frank Welker, Gilbert Gottfried.

ANNIE HALL...

Woody Allen's breakthrough achievement, with his gifts as a director/writer coming into full flower, is a comic rendition of the rise and fall of one particular modern-day romance. It is also Allen's consummate valentine to ex-love Diane Keaton, as his clever, wistful script hands the movie over to his leading lady on a silver platter. (Who among us did not fall instantaneously in love with this most unique of heroines, quirky wardrobe and all?) Woody co-stars as Alvy Singer, a stand-up comic and Manhattan paranoid ("I was having lunch with some guys from NBC. So I said, 'Did you eat yet or what?' And Tom Christie said, 'No, jew?'"), semi-depressive ("Life is divided up into the horrible and the miserable."), neurotic ("I'm one of the few males who suffers from penis envy."). He takes a wry look at his past—his childhood and the failure of his first two marriages—while falling hard for aspiring nightclub singer Keaton. Among countless highlights, there's Keaton arranging a ride home with Allen after a tennis match, the subtitles underlining their first drink together, parallel sessions at their psychiatrists' offices, the two being driven to the airport by Keaton's demented younger brother Christopher Walken, Keaton's rendition of 'You'd Be So Nice,' Jeff Goldblum's cocktail party walk-on, and Allen's decidedly un-Hollywood finale.
1977. 94m. DIR: Woody Allen. WRIT: Woody Allen, Marshall Brickman. CAST: Diane Keaton, Woody Allen, Tony Roberts, Paul Simon, Shelley Duvall, Carol Kane, Colleen Dewhurst, Christopher Walken.

ARSENIC AND OLD LACE...

part screwball, part black comedy, is a showcase for Cary Grant's super-kinetic performance as a drama critic who makes a most disconcerting discovery upon visiting his maiden aunts' Brooklyn boarding house. There's a corpse in their window box, and another thirteen buried in the basement below. It seems these two sweet spinsters, played to wide-eyed perfection by Josephine Hull and Jean Adair, have taken to poisoning lonely gentlemen with arsenic-laced elderberry wine, thereby sending them on to ostensibly happier resting grounds. (Adair, apprising nephew Grant of her secret recipe: "For a gallon of elderberry wine, I take one teaspoon of arsenic. Then I add a half teaspoon of strychnine and just a pinch of cyanide.") While Grant makes increasingly frantic attempts at concealing both the corpses and his aunts' insanity from the police, his predicament is further complicated by the arrival of murderous brother Raymond Massey, 'plastic surgeon' Peter Lorre, and looney uncle John Alexander, who fancies himself as Teddy Roosevelt and has adopted his sisters' basement as his own personal Panama Canal. (And you thought *your* family was dysfunctional?)

1944. 158m. B&W. DIR: Frank Capra. WRIT: Julius & Philip Epstein. CAST: Cary Grant, Josephine Hull, Jean Adair, Raymond Massey, Peter Lorre, Edward Everett Horton, Jack Carson, James Gleason.

THE AWFUL TRUTH...

scripted by a woman, is classic screwball featuring high-energy performances from two of the best in the genre. Irene Dunne and Cary Grant co-star as a married couple who suspect each other of having affairs. After they rashly opt for divorce, Dunne meets aw-shucks Oklahoma cattleman Ralph Bellamy, while Grant begins seeing high society girl Molly Lamont. It's all for naught, of course, since our two principals are still crazy for one another and spend the remainder of the film sabotaging each other's fledgling relationships. Among highlights, there's Bellamy's straight-faced, gullible reactions to a series of barbs Grant tosses his way, Alexander D'Arcy's gleefully fey contribution as Dunne's singing teacher, and a sexy reconciliation in a secluded cabin at film's finale.

1937. 92m. B&W. DIR: Leo McCarey. WRIT: Vina Delmar. CAST: Cary Grant, Irene Dunne, Ralph Bellamy, Alexander D'Arcy, Cecil Cunningham, Molly Lamont.

BABE...

is one talking-animal film that can be enjoyed as much, or more so, by adults. This wondrous tale focuses on the misadventures of an adorable piglet who is raised for slaughter in an Orwellian assembly-line breeding pen. Fortunately for Babe, he is saved from the cruel fate of his brethren when a kindly sheep farmer wins him in a raffle at the county fair. At his new home on the Hoggett farm, our lonely orphan is quickly taken underwing by Border Collie 'Fly' and her many pups. Another new pal is Ferdinand the duck, who has long been trying to turn himself into a rooster in the hope of being more indispensable alive and crowing than as somebody's Christmas dinner. In point of fact, however, the carnivorous Mrs. Hoggett has her eyes on Babe for that particular holiday celebration. But providence is once again on Babe's side when farmer Hoggett begins suspecting the implausible: that this intelligent little piggy just might make one great herder of sheep. ("Farmer Hoggett knew that little ideas which tickled and nagged and refused to go away should never be ignored. For in them lie the seeds of destiny.") Subsequent adventures lead up to the National Grand Sheepherding Championship, where Babe's performance will decide his final fate. Spectacular indeed are the training and special effects which make us believe these animals really are talking. Also notable is Christine Cavanaugh's poignant rendition of Babe's voice, James Cromwell's contribution as Farmer Hoggett, and last, but certainly not least, the performance of our astute leading player. After viewing this little gem, pork chops and bacon might never look or taste the same.

1995. 94m. DIR: Chris Noonan. WRIT: George Miller, Chris Noonan. CAST: Christine Cavanaugh (Voice of Babe), James Cromwell, Miriam Margolyes (Voice of Fly), Hugo Weaving (Voice of Rex), Danny Mann (Voice of Ferdinand), Miriam Flynn (Voice of Ma).

BACK TO THE FUTURE...

stars Michael J. Fox as a high school student whose sorry home life features a wimp of a father and an alcoholic mother. When his grown-up mentor, 'mad' and savvy scientist Christopher Lloyd, assembles a time machine from a recon- stituted DeLorean, Michael is accidentally hurtled back thirty years to 1955. It's the same small town but definitely *not* the same era. To make matters worse, Michael's presence inadvertently prevents his teenaged parents from meeting and falling in love. To the contrary, it's now Michael who becomes the romantic interest of his sweet, 17-year-old 'Mom' Lea Thompson. Thus begins the convolutions of a plot that spins toward a two-pronged denouement which takes place in the past *and* the future. Much of the entertainment value of this film, aside from Lloyd and Fox's dead-on performances, springs from the considerable cultural gap between the fifties and the eighties. (Having had a brief look at Fox's underwear, Lea assumes his name is Calvin Klein.) Fox's skateboarding expertise and his Chuck Berry-inspired duck-walking guitar solo deserve special mention, as does a scenario which is fast-paced and imaginative throughout.

1985. 114m. DIR: Robert Zemeckis. WRIT: Robert Zemeckis, Bob Gale. CAST: Michael J. Fox, Christopher Lloyd, Crispin Glover, Lea Thompson, Thomas F. Wilson, Claudia Wells.

THE BAKER'S WIFE...

is a black-and-white French classic, a humorous and knowing tale of a village's new baker and the young wife who deserts him for the local shepherd. The all-trusting baker refuses to believe his wife could have left him—she must be visiting her mother—but out of grief and confusion shuts down his bakery, nonetheless. The townspeople, deprived of their daily bread, jump into action, organizing a hunting party to track down the wanderlust spouse. The peerless Raimu imbues our baker with such kindness and empathy, we have no trouble understanding how his young wife rediscovers her love for him. And the final scene, where our couple are ostensibly discussing the bakery's two cats, but in reality are talking about one another, is as tender as they come.

1938. 124m. B&W. In French w/English Subtitles. DIR&WRIT: Marcel Pagnol. CAST: Raimu, Ginette Leclerc, Charles Moulin, Charpin, Robert Vattier, Robert Bassac.

BEAUTIFUL GIRLS...

is one of those 'guy-bonding' films which surprises you by turning into thoughtful, entertaining cinema. The ensemble effort is spearheaded by Timothy Hutton's bemused performance as the going nowhere piano man who returns to wintry small-town Massachusetts for his tenth year high school reunion, only to find that his former high school buddies are faring no better than he is. If anything, these sorry losers are doing far worse. Snow-plow entrepreneur Matt Dillon, in spite of being inside a warm relationship with girlfriend Mira Sorvino, is carrying on a none-too-furtive affair with ex-flame and married Lauren Holly, apparently because she represents the long-ago high school glory for which he still pines. Business partner Michael Rapaport spends his free moments wreaking churlish revenge on ex-girlfriend Martha Plimpton, when he isn't obsessing on the supermodels whose scantily clad portraits cover every inch of his bedroom walls. And the 'happily married' foursome to this group, Noah Emmerich, is obviously harboring his own unresolved frustrations, which come into play at a key moment in our scenario. Uma Thurman is understatedly splendid as the visitor who sets off each of these misguided souls' hopeless fantasies, and Natalie Portman is surprisingly adept as the precocious thirteen-year-old who the increasingly befuddled Hutton finds himself falling for. Among highlights, there is Rosie O'Donnell's rap on 'real' women, and Rapaport's equally humorous rant on letting us gals 'behind the curtain.' At heart, what this story suggests is that men are so fixated on finding the 'perfect ten,' they overlook—to their own considerable emotional detriment—all the lovely ladies right in their midst.

1996. 110m. DIR: Ted Demme. WRIT: Scott Rosenberg. CAST: Timothy Hutton, Matt Dillon, Michael Rapaport, Noah Emmerich, Max Perlich, Uma Thurman, Natalie Portman, Mira Sorvina, Martha Plimpton, Rosie O'Donnell.

BETSY'S WEDDING...

quintessential Alan Alda, is a gentle, non-sexist comedy starring Mr. Alda and Madeleine Kahn as a forty-something, happily married couple who get way over their heads when trying to throw the kind of extravagant wedding for their
daughter which they assume their wealthy future in-laws
expect. The increasingly desperate father-of-the-bride, a self-
employed building contractor not having one of his better
years, is eventually obliged to go to questionable extremes to
raise funds, a scheme which involves smarmy mob-connected
brother-in-law Joe Pesci. Molly Ringwald, the Betsy of our
title, and Ally Sheedy as her insular older sister, are both
delineated in sympathetic, intelligent lights.

*1980. 94m. DIR&WRIT: Alan Alda. CAST: Alan Alda, Madeleine
Kahn, Molly Ringwald, Ally Sheedy, Joe Pesci, Joey Bishop, Anthony
LaPaglia.*

BIG...

co-scripted and directed by women, is the best of the
child/adult transference flicks that abounded in the late
eighties. When 13-year-old Joshua is refused a shot at a
souped-up amusement park ride because he's too young, he
approaches a mysterious fortune-telling machine and makes a
fervent wish to 'become big.' By next morning, our kid's
dream has come true. Enter Tom Hanks as the young Joshua
now trapped inside a thirty-five-year old body and about to
embark upon a bizarre and giddy adventure. Josh's mom
doesn't recognize him. To the contrary, she assumes he has
kidnaped her 'real' son, and frantically notifies the police,
thereby obliging our boy-man to leave home and survive in
the adult world without money or work, not to mention such
amenities as a social security number or a driver's license.
When he finally secures a job, not surprisingly as a consultant
at a toy company, this thirteen-year-old is further compelled

to deal with board meetings, office rivalries, and an incipient romance with co-worker Elizabeth Perkins. Hanks is delightfully gawky and guileless as the innocent who revitalizes the cynical adult world around him. Among highlights, there is Hanks and boss Robert Loggia dancing on an electric piano, Hanks cashing his first check, and his 'one night stand' with Perkins at his apartment. ("Okay, but I get to sleep on top.") *1988. 98m. DIR: Penny Marshall. WRIT: Anne Spielberg, Gary Ross. CAST: Tom Hanks, Elizabeth Perkins, John Heard, Robert Loggia, Jared Rushton, David Moscow, Jon Lovitz, Mercedes Ruehl.*

THE BIG CHILL...

co-scripted by a woman, is ensemble acting at its finest, no doubt due to the extended time director Lawrence Kasdan gave his talented cast to rehearse and settle into their roles before filming began. It's the story of seven former sixties activists—each one adroitly introduced to us in the opening 'Grapevine' sequence—who reunite fifteen years later at their common friend Alex's funeral. They decide to make a weekend of it by holing up at married couple Kevin Kline and Glenn Close's South Carolina antebellum home, and throughout the next two days share reminiscences, regrets, and revelations over meals and drinks. It's a reflective, piquant script, underscored by one pervasive question mark: how did a group of committed activists in the '60s become such material yuppies in the '80s? Or as the minister at the funeral so plaintively asks us: "Where did Alex's hope go?" Among many highlights is the sequence which has everyone unpacking his or her suitcase, William Hurt interviewing himself on video, Jeff Goldblum 'the morning after,' and Don Galloway's touching midnight soliloquy on life and marriage. Save for Galloway, who makes an early exit from the scenario, the entire cast became instantaneous household names after the release of this landmark film. Special mention is due the fabulous sixties soundtrack.

1983. 108m. DIR: Lawrence Kasdan. WRIT: Lawrence Kasdan, Barbara Benedek. CAST: Kevin Kline, Glenn Close, Jeff Goldblum, Tom Berenger,

William Hurt, Meg Tilly, Mary Kay Place, JoBeth Williams, Don Galloway, James Gillis.

THE BIG PICTURE...

takes broad swipes at the Hollywood movie industry while relating the misadventures of a promising young filmmaker in Los Angeles. Kevin Bacon stars as the up-and-comer signed by a large studio, only to see his 'serious' screenplay mutated by a formula-minded producer into moronic, sexist trash. It's a world of amoral opportunists, and no one is more opportunistic than our young hero, as he sacrifices any artistic vision, not to mention loyalties to a girlfriend and best buddy, at the altar of Fame, Fun, and Fortune. It all backfires, of course, forcing this would-be director to take a long, hard look at his life. Bacon gives another in a string of dexterous performances, while Martin Short is sublimely fatuous as his wacked-out agent.

1989. 100m. DIR: Christopher Guest. WRIT: Christopher Guest, Michael McKean, Michael Varhol. CAST: Kevin Bacon, Emily Longstreth, Jennifer Jason Leigh, Teri Hatcher, Martin Short, Michael McKean, J.T. Walsh.

THE BIRDCAGE...

scripted by Elaine May, is oft-hilarious cinema starring Robin Williams and Nathan Lane as long-term lovers who own and run a popular drag revue nightclub in Miami's South Beach. As our story opens, the two are suddenly called upon to create a facade of 'normalcy,' due to Williams' son's upcoming visit, accompanied by his fiancée and her arch-conservative parents. For the occasion, ultra-swishy Lane is going to attempt appearing 'straight,' which sets up some of the movie's funnier moments, as Williams gives Lane a crash course in Being Male. It's to no avail, of course, and Williams decides it would be wiser if the in-laws never meet Lane; Williams' ex-wife Christine Baranski will take on the temporary role as William's mate. But Lane has no intentions of being excluded from this family reunion and shows up unexpectedly, *also* masquerading as Williams' wife. High-spirited hijinks ensue. Special mention is due Gene Hackman in drag, and May's politically savvy script.

1996. 118m. DIR: Mike Nichols. WRIT: Elaine May. CAST: Robin Williams, Nathan Lane, Gene Hackman, Diane Wiest, Dan Futterman, Calista Flockhart, Hank Azaria, Christine Baranski.

BORN YESTERDAY...

features Judy Holliday's greatest—and funniest—screen performance as Billie Dawn, the blond, not-so-dumb chorus girl moll of gangster Broderick Crawford. When Crawford's ambitions seem to outstrip his mistress' intelligence, he engages handsome newspaperman William Holden to tutor Billie in the finer points of life. (Typical repartee between tutor and student: "Nobody's *born* smart, Billie. You know what the stupidest thing on earth is? An infant." "What do you've got against babies, all of a sudden?" "Nothing. I've got nothing against a brain that's three weeks old and empty. But after it hangs around for 30 years and hasn't absorbed anything, I begin to wonder about it." "What makes you think I'm 30?") As the lessons proceed, the inevitable amorous entanglements transpire. Moreover, as Billie smartens up, she rebels against her boyfriend's disrespectful treatment, as well as his dubious business practices. Revenge will be sweet in this fifties Hollywood classic.

1950. 103m. B&W. DIR: George Cukor. WRIT: Albert Mannheiner. CAST: Judy Holliday, Broderick Crawford, William Holden, Howard St. John, Frank Otto, Larry Oliver.

BREAKING AWAY...

follows the misadventures of four high school buddies as they putter away the summer after graduation, trying to fathom what to do with the rest of their lives. It doesn't help any that their hometown of Bloomington, Indiana quarters a Big Ten university, obliging our declassé 'cutters'—so named after the local quarrying, or stone-cutting industry—to play constant witness to thousands of collegiate success stories. All four co-stars are excellent, but Dennis Christopher is the stand-out as the innocent, Italian-obsessed young cyclist who is training for the bike race of a lifetime. Paul Dooley and Barbara Barrie lend able comic support as the loving if bewildered parents attempting to guide their son through the troubled waters of early adulthood. Love, disillusionment, heartbreak, and new beginnings; it's all here, with the bonus of genuinely exciting two-wheeled competition, and a picture-perfect final scene. *1970. 100m. DIR: Peter Yates. WRIT: Steve Tesich. CAST: Dennis Christopher, Daniel Stern, Jackie Earle Haley, Dennis Quaid, Paul Dooley, Barbara Barrie, Robin Douglas.*

BROADWAY DANNY ROSE...

opens in Manhattan's Carnegie Deli, where a group of old-time borscht-belt comics, all playing themselves, are swapping their favorite Danny Rose stories. Danny, one of Woody Allen's more lovable creations, is a theatrical agent with a heart of gold—a man who takes on any and all clients, no matter how hopeless their talent, and then proceeds to give them his unconditional support. The 'most famous Danny Rose story of all' centers around boozing nightclub singer Nick Apollo Forte, whom our agent has nurtured to the brink of stardom. As the story-within-the-story opens, tonight is the big night; Milton Berle is looking for guests for his upcoming TV special and has agreed to catch this lounge crooner's act. But the trouble begins when the very married Apollo convinces agent Danny to be his 'Beard' on this all-important occasion, thereby escorting his gum-snapping mistress Mia Farrow to the performance for emotional support. In the meantime, Mia and Apollo have a huge fight over the phone, and she refuses to attend the event. Danny attempts to drag her there, nonetheless, and they run into a series of frantic complications, most of them involving Mia's mafioso ex-boyfriend. Among highlights, there's Danny's yearly Thanksgiving dinner for his motley crew of losers, and a redux of his run through the streets of Manhattan to correct a hasty miscall. To quote from his Uncle Harry's philosophy of life: "Acceptance, forgiveness, and love." Amen! *1984. 85m. B&W. DIR&WRIT: Woody Allen. CAST: Woody Allen, Mia Farrow, Nick Apollo Forte, Sandy Baron, Milton Berle, Corbett Monica, Jackie Gayle, Morty Gunty, Will Jordan, Howard Storm, Jack Rollins.*

BROTHER FROM ANOTHER PLANET...

one of director John Sayles' many low-budget miracles, is a creatively comic send-up of the sci-fi genre, offering us a black extra-terrestrial mute who crash-lands in a Manhattan harbor, then wends his way to a Harlem bar where all the fun begins. The underlying premise, milked to such good effect, is that nobody who meets this friendly outlander—immigrant shopkeepers, hookers, tourists from Indiana—find anything peculiar about the chap. Even his muteness is taken on faith, which means that everybody *but* our protagonist does the talking. Joe Morton stars as the erstwhile alien, managing to establish a distinctive, sympathetic presence without uttering a single word. Of note: that's director Sayles as one of the bad guys trying to trap our E.T. *1984. 100m. DIR&WRIT: John Sayles. CAST: Joe Morton, Darryl Edwards, Dee Dee Bridgewater, Ren Woods, Steve James, Maggie Renzi, David Strathairn, John Sayles.*

THE BROTHERS MCMULLEN...

writer/director Edward Burns' brilliant screen debut, co-stars Burns himself, along with Jack Mulahy and Mike McGlone, as three Irish-Catholic brothers temporarily living under the same roof while attempting, together and separately, to get a grip on their relationships and their lives. (And en route, hopefully not becoming clones of their ne'er-do-well Dad: "Our favorite wife-beating, child-abusing, alcoholic.") Mulahy is the 'stable' married one who slips much too easily into an adulterous affair; McGlone is the Church-obsessed, highly principled one, coping with the novel responsibility of being out of college; and Burns is a hoot as "Mr. Hot-Shot non-committal." Considering the movie's excellent production values, not to mention the hip and witty dialogue, it's truly remarkable to learn that the film was made on a budget of under $100,000.

1995. 97m. DIR&WRIT: Edward Burns. CAST: Jack Mulahy, Mike McGlone, Edward Burns, Connie Button, Maxine Bahns, Elizabeth McKay, Shari Albert, Jennifer Jostyn, Elizabeth McKay, Catherine Bolz.

BYE BYE, LOVE...

is a comically sweet meditation on divorce from a man's point of view; the struggle to get a life, find romance, and maintain solid relationships with one's children when no longer living under the same roof with them. In so doing, we follow dads Paul Reiser, Matthew Modine, and Randy Quaid through one weekend with and without their offspring. Modine is the jerk who wants to bed every woman he meets; Reiser is still pining for his Ex; and Quaid is prepping for his third official date since The Divorce. (The latter scenario features a riotous contribution from Janeane Garofalo, who comes close to stealing the entire flick.) In an opening cameo, sanctimonious talk radio host Rob Reiner sets the stage, admonishing his listeners that "we're creating a whole generation of kids who have *Nick At Night* for a father." The bittersweet irony underlining our story—poignantly expressed by Quaid at film's finale—is that it often takes the wrenching process of being physically separated from one's children before a man learns to appreciate what being a father truly means.

1994. 106m. DIR: Sam Weisman. WRIT: Gary David Goldberg, Brad Hall. CAST: Paul Reiser, Matthew Modine, Randy Quaid, Janeane Garofalo, Lindsay Crouse. Amy Brennan, Eliza Dusk, Ed Flanders, Rob Reiner, James Whitworth, Maria Pitillo.

CALIFORNIA SUITE...

is Neil Simon's West Coast riposte to his Manhattan-based *Plaza Suite*, filmed seven years earlier. The swank Beverly Hills Hotel serves as the setting for four overlapping stories, with predictable 'Simon-ized' results. Maggie Smith and Michael Caine take top honors—she as an aging actress nominated for her first Oscar, and he as her roving-eyed, gay husband—the two of them flying into Los Angeles for the Academy Awards. Sharp-tongued New Yorker Jane Fonda ("L.A. is Paradise with a lobotomy."), has headed west to confront ex-hubby Alan Alda about the future custody of their teen-age daughter. And married couple Walter Matthau and Elaine May are hilarious in an episode which defies description. Bill Cosby and Richard Pryor's installment starts off promisingly enough, but deteriorates into puerile slapstick before their time runs out. With the exception of this final entry, expect snappy dialogue and pacing throughout.

1978. 103m. DIR: Herbert Ross. WRIT: Neil Simon. CAST: Maggie Smith, Michael Caine, Jane Fonda, Alan Alda, Elaine May, Walter Matthau, Richard Pryor, Bill Cosby.

CLUELESS...

written and directed by Amy Heckerling, is a sharply observed and funny spoof of upper-middle-class high school U.S.A. Alicia Silverstone stars as this, like, super hip Beverly High senior who hangs out with best pal Stacey Dash, while meditating on the crucial matters of life, including fitness, fashion, music, boys, and everyone's social standing. (Typical repartee between Alicia and Stacey: "What did you do in school today?" "Broke in my new clogs.") But matters get serious for Alicia when she goes altruistic by transforming klutzy new girl in town Brittany Murphy into 'Miss Popularity,' first by upgrading her wardrobe, and secondly by engineering a romance between Brittany and the high school's 'Mr. Cool.' But like Jane Austen's Emma, this is one obtuse and hapless matchmaker, a failing which extends to her own love life when she falls hard for the handsome, sloe-eyed new boy in town who—natch—turns out to be gay. ("I guess it was meant to happen. I mean, he does dress better than me.") Unbeknownst to our myopic heroine, true love is right at her finger tips. But it's going to take her most of the film to open those pretty blue eyes and see the light. Special mention is due Heckerling's amazing script—an endless string of hilarious one-liners and antic vignettes—and Silverstone's impeccable comic turn in the leading role.

1995. 97m. DIR&WRIT: Amy Heckerling. CAST: Alicia Silverstone, Stacey Dash, Brittany Murphy, Paul Rudd, Dan Hedaya, Donald Adeosun Faison, Elisa Donovan, Brekin Meyer.

DADDY'S DYING AND WHO'S GOT THE WILL?...

brings a large group of talented, underused actors under one roof, including Judge Reinhold, Beverly D'Angelo, Tess Harper, Keith Carradine, and Beau Bridges, as extended members of a family reuniting around their father's deathbed, only to learn that the comatose old man has misplaced the all-important will. Nostalgia, greed, affection, and long-simmering hostilities commingle and play themselves out as this crew of eccentrics lock horns at their Texas homestead. In spite of a few uneven patches, this bittersweet comedy will win over most of its viewers. Patrika Darbo, as the lovable wife of boorish hubby Bridges, is the surprise here. And that makes it all the more satisfying when she takes a hike from her sorry marriage with one of our assembled guests.

1990. 95m. DIR: Jack Fisk. WRIT: Del Shores. CAST: Judge Reinhold, Amy Wright, Beverly D'Angelo, Patrika Darbo, Tess Harper, Keith Carradine, Molly McClure.

DAVE...

stars Kevin Kline as regular guy Dave Klovic, who also happens to be a dead ringer for the president of the United States. He is retained by White House chief-of-staff Frank Langella as a temporary stand-in for the president, thereby giving the boss time to dally with his mistress of the hour. But things go terribly awry when the Prez has a critical heart attack at a most inopportune moment. The Machiavellian Langella now persuades Dave to continue his masquerade awhile longer, thereby giving Langella time to plot a power-grab end-run around vice president Ben Kingsley. But much to the chief-of-staff's displeasure, Dave begins taking his job seriously, making a series of thoughtful decisions which—unlike those of his look-alike predecessor—start to turn the country around. Highlights of this far-ranging, seamlessly edited political satire include the growing love interest between Dave and First Lady Sigourney Weaver, accountant Charles Grodin's balancing act with our government's budget, and above all, Langella's deliciously wicked contribution as the oh-so-dastardly villain of our piece.

1983. 105m. DIR: Ivan Reitman. WRIT: Gary Ross. CAST: Kevin Kline, Frank Langella, Sigourney Weaver, Kevin Dunn, Ben Kingsley, Charles Grodin.

DAY FOR NIGHT...

co-scripted by a woman, is François Truffaut's loving homage to the profession of filmmaking. It's a highly entertaining insider's view of how a movie actually gets made, including the inevitable crises, cost overruns, clashes of egos, and fly-by-night affairs. Jacqueline Bisset heads this ensemble effort as an American actress just recovering from a nervous break-down when she flies to France to star in the film-within-the-film, *Pamela*. Then there's Jean-Pierre Léaud as the patheti-cally insecure, self-centered actor who will be playing her husband, Jean-Pierre Aumont as the middle-aged but still dashing leading man, and Valentina Cortese as the tipsy 'over-the-hill' actress relegated to playing the part of the abandoned wife. Truffaut more or less plays himself as the increasingly frantic director who is attempting the seemingly impossible: to get this feature completed, on budget and on time. Georges Delerue's effervescent musical score ensures our story's breezy pace.

1973. 116m. In French w/English Subtitles. DIR: François Truffaut. WRIT: Suzanne Schiffman, Jean-Louis Richard, François Truffaut. CAST: Jacqueline Bisset, Jean-Pierre Léaud, Valentina Cortese, Jean-Pierre Aumont, François Truffaut, Nathalie Bay, Dani.

THE DAYTRIPPERS...

stars Hope Davis as a happily married Long Island housewife who wakes up one morning to discover an Elizabethan love poem in her husband's jacket. ("Our love is truly parallel. Though infinite, we can never meet.") Naturally suspicious that this bespeaks of a secret love affair, Hope stops off at her mother Anne Meara's house for some impromptu advice. Mom thinks that the sooner they get to the bottom of this amorous sonnet, the better off her daughter will be. And so it is that Hope, Mom, Dad and sister Parker Posey, with boyfriend Liev Schrieber in tow, all pile into the family station wagon and head into Manhattan to confront hubby Stanley Tucci with the incriminating evidence. It's going to be a long day's journey into night, replete with misadventures, family squabbles, and revelations, before they manage to track Tucci down, at which point the movie treats us to a rather surprising denouement.
1996. 87m. DIR&WRIT: Greg Mottola. CAST: Hope Davis, Anne Meara, Parker Posey, Pat McNamara, Liev Shreiber, Stanley Tucci, Campbell Scott.

THE DREAM TEAM...

opens with an encounter session in a mental ward which is worth the rental fee alone. But the real story commences when inmate-friendly psychiatrist Dennis Boutsikaris persuades clinic administrators that his four patients are stable enough to enjoy a field trip to Yankee Stadium. En route to the ballpark, the good doctor gets knocked out by vicious thugs, and our four misfits are stranded without pilotage in the mean streets of the Big Apple. Misadventures ensue. This is Michael Keaton at his jazzy, manic best. Ditto for Christopher Lloyd, who is side-splitting one moment, surprisingly touching the next. Special mention is due our inmates' shared rendition of 'Hit The Road, Jack,' and a great twist near film's finale which wryly addresses the ongoing 'drug treatment debate.'

1989. 133m. DIR: Howard Zieff. WRIT: Jon Connelly, David Loucka. CAST: Michael Keaton, Christopher Lloyd, Peter Boyle, Stephen Furst, Lorraine Bracco, Dennis Boutsikaris.

THE ELECTRIC HORSEMAN...

stars Robert Redford in one of his most amiable screen performances as an over-the-hill rodeo celebrity who now makes a living as a touring spokesman for a breakfast cereal company. But all that is about to change when this cowboy outrages his corporate bosses by skipping town with the firm's mascot, a multimillion-dollar racehorse who's been pumped full of steroids to insure his docility when on parade. Redford's plan is to set the beautiful creature free at an as yet unknown destination, where the stallion can join up with wild horses in the area. But TV journalist Jane Fonda is hot on his trail, and after some cagey investigative work catches up with Redford and thoroughbred, proceeding to befriend them both before making the tough decision between good copy and a great horse. Among highlights, there is Redford making his case for the stallion's freedom, before and after he thinks Fonda's camera is running, the growing attraction between our two principals, and a stirring pictorial rendition of 'America the Beautiful.'

1979. 120m. DIR: Sydney Pollack. WRIT: Robert Garland. CAST: Robert Redford, Jane Fonda, Valerie Perrine, Willie Nelson, John Saxon, Nicolas Caster.

THE ENGLISHMAN WHO WENT UP A HILL BUT CAME DOWN A MOUNTAIN...

is a whimsical tale of two British mapmakers who come to a small Welsh community, circa 1917, to ascertain the status of the large knoll behind their village. According to the 'Queen's standards,' a mountain must stand one thousand feet above the ground, but the cartographers assess the rise at only 984 feet, thereby officially down-sizing it to a hill. Their deduction is heresy for the citizens of this rural communiy who have considered the landmark to be Wales' first mountain from time immemorial. Barkeep and roustabout Colm Meaney comes to the rescue by ensuring that the surveyors are kept in town long enough for the villagers to build up their mountain the required sixteen feet. And such is the slim plot around which this charming comedy evolves. Hugh Grant is at his best as the young English officer who develops a lasting affinity for this Welsh community. Ditto for publican Meaney and local cleric Ian Hart, two lifelong adversaries who, in the course of their shared crisis, come to understand and love one another. Special mention is also due Ian McNeice's hilarious contribution as Grant's chronically inebriated superior.

1995. 99m. DIR&WRIT: Christopher Monger. CAST: Hugh Grant, Colm Meaney, Ian McNeice, Ian Hart, Tara Fitzgerald, Kenneth Griffith.

EVERYONE SAYS I LOVE YOU...

won't be for everyone; a Woody Allen film where the cast is repeatedly breaking into song? But this sweet, old-fashioned entertainment is refreshingly free of the neurotic ramblings of more typical Allen offerings. Edward Norton of Primal Fear fame is terrific in the leading role as a guy wearing his heart on his sleeve for true love Drew Barrymore. Among highlights is Norton's opening 'Just You, Just Me,' a nifty song-and-dance number in a jewelry story, succeeded by a somewhat crazed dance number in the hospital, and a divine sequence between an airborne Goldie Hawn and Allen on the banks of the Seine. Although other sequences are not quite as inspired, Carlo Di Palma's on-location cinematography in New York, Paris, and Venice shimmers throughout.

1996. 97m. DIR&WRIT: Woody Allen. CAST: Edward Norton, Goldie Hawn, Alan Alda, Drew Barrymore, Tim Roth, Lukas Haas, Julia Roberts.

FATHER OF THE BRIDE...

both the original 1950 version and the 1991 remake are co-scripted by women and come recommended. The earlier rendition has its dated aspects, including Papa Spencer Tracy never out of a suit and tie, the obligatory black maid, and the inexplicable fact that Dad hasn't met his daughter's fiancé even though the chap lives in the neighborhood. But Tracy's sardonic contribution more than compensates for such caveats. Among highlights is his and his wife Joan Bennett's visit to the future in-laws, and Tracy's attempt to get to know his prospective son-in-law. (Guess who does all the talking?) This version is more pensive than the remake, which has Steve Martin's requisite wild-and-zany touch. He stars as the doting father who can't get it through his head that daughter Kimberley Williams—a delight in her film debut—is old enough to be getting married. What follows are the preparations for an insanely extravagant wedding, with Martin Short over the top as their wedding consultant. Like the original, Pop begins wrestling with spiraling costs and a diminishing sense of self, with his beloved daughter about to fly the nest. It's predictable yet charming entertainment, which occasionally doubles as a surprising heart-tugger.

1950. 93m. DIR: Vincent Fleming. WRIT: Frances Goodrich, Albert Hackett. CAST: Spencer Tracy, Elizabeth Taylor, Joan Bennett, Billie Burke, Leo G. Carroll, Don Taylor, Russ Tamblyn.

1991. 105m. DIR: Charles Shyer. WRIT: Nancy Myers, Charles Shyer. CAST: Steve Martin, Diane Keaton, Kimberly Williams, Kieran Culkin, George Newbern, Martin Short.

THE FAVOR...

scripted by women, is a romantic comedy built around a shaky premise which translates surprisingly well to the screen. Harley Jane Kozak stars as a mother of two who is slightly bored with her perfectly happy marriage to husband Bill Pullman, when an impending 15th-year high school reunion triggers fantasies about long-ago teenaged steady

Ken Wahl. Upon learning that best friend Elizabeth McGovern plans a trip to Wahl's hometown of Denver, Kozak convinces her to look up the hunk and see how he's weathered the years. Since Kozak and Wahl never actually went 'all the way' back in high school, she even suggests that McGovern go to bed with the guy, enabling Kozak to live vicariously through the experience. McGovern does her one better by spending an entire night with Wahl—who apparently has weathered very well indeed—and returns to give Kozak all the juicy details. Jealous, angry, and confused, our horny housewife takes a secret trip to Denver herself. Suspicious hubby follows in quick pursuit, as does girlfriend McGovern, hoping to stave off disaster, *as does* McGovern's suspicious boyfriend Brad Pitt. It's a great change of pace to find the men playing second fiddle in this particular sexual farce, with both female leads, particularly Kozak, giving strong comic contributions. Special mention is due Pullman on that harmonica!

1994. 97m. DIR: *Donald Petrie.* WRIT: *Josann McGibbon.* CAST: *Harley Jane Kozak, Elizabeth McGovern, Bill Pullman, Brad Pitt, Ken Wahl, Larry Miller, Holland Taylor.*

FLIRTING WITH DISASTER...

is a '90s update of the classic 'screwball' genre. Ben Stiller and Patricia Arquette co-star as a young married couple with a 4-month-old child they haven't christened yet, because Stiller—an adoptee—feels incapable of giving his son a namesake until he can locate his own birth mother and father. Stiller's obsessive need to find his 'roots' infuriates his adoptive parents Mary Tyler Moore and George Segal. Stiller persists, nonetheless, enlisting adoption agency rep Tea Leoni in his crusade. The young couple, with long-legged Leoni in tow, commence a cross-country quest which begets a series of uproarious misadventures before they finally hit pay dirt in California in the persons of ex-hippies Lily Tomlin and Alan Alda. At which point Moore and Segal come blustering back onto the scene. It's a great ensemble effort, enhanced by surprisingly touching contributions from relative unknowns Josh Brolin and Richard Jenkins.

1996. 92m. DIR&WRIT: David O. Russell. CAST: Ben Stiller, Patricia Arquette, Tea Leoni, Mary Tyler Moore, George Segal, Lily Tomlin, Alan Alda, Josh Brolin, Richard Jenkins.

THE FRONT...

a comedy about a tragedy, stars Woody Allen as a book-maker/delicatessen cashier who 'fronts' for several blacklisted TV writers during the communist witch hunt of the 1950s. Our no-talent bookie puts his name on the outcasts' scripts, thereby serving as their go-between with the producers. In turn, he receives ten percent of their take. Along the way, Allen falls in love with comely network administrator Andrea Marcovicci, who's under the false impression he is the genius churning out all these brilliant teleplays. Allen himself comes close to forgetting he's not the real author, until a congressional investigating committee subpoenas him, and a battle of conscience ensues. The fact that many of the participants in this film, including comic Zero Mostel, screenwriter Walter Bernstein, and director Martin Ritt actually *were* blacklisted in the fifties, adds both poignancy and authority to our story.

1976. 95m. DIR: Martin Ritt. WRIT: Walter Bernstein. CAST: Woody Allen, Zero Mostel, Herschel Bernardi, Michael Murphy, Andrea Marcovicci, Remak Ramsey.

THE FULL MONTY...

opens with a newsreel showing us the town of Sheffield a quarter century ago, as "the beating heart of England's industrial north." But the ensuing years have seen the town's steel mills closed down, leaving the once-prosperous citizenry of this Yorkshire community to cope in a jobless Brave New World. When ex-mill worker Robert Carlyle takes note of the huge popularity of touring Chippendale strippers among the local female population, he convinces a few of his equally desperate mates to form a striptease act of their own. These fellows are far from representing 'Playgirl' photo-op material, being variously overweight, skinny, middle-aged, depressed, and uniformly skittish about appearing on stage baring it all. But stripping down to the 'full monty' is exactly what they are promising to do, in the hopes of drumming up a suitable audience. Among highlight of this quirky, entertaining film, there is our chaps practicing their routine while standing in line at an unemployment office, and that memorable finale. *1996. 90m. DIR: Peter Cattaneo. WRIT: Simon Beaufoy. CAST: Robert Carlyle, Tom Wilkinson, Mark Addy, Steve Hulson, William Snaps.*

THE GENERAL...

a 1927 silent masterpiece from Buster Keaton, stars the comic genius as a would-be fighting man at the onset of the Civil War. But the Confederate Army turns him down, believing he's more important to the cause as a locomotive engineer, a job for which he is eminently suited. ("There were two great loves in Johnny Gray's life—his engine and his girl.") Unfortunately, the aforementioned girlfriend, Marion Mack, assumes that Keaton is simply too cowardly to enlist in the war effort and jilts him. But en route to visiting her father, the train she is traveling on—Keaton's beloved 'General'—is commandeered by a group of Union spies, who promptly barrel northward with Mack still on board. Keaton speeds singlehandedly to the rescue, in a string of dazzlingly choreographed sight gags which reveal him to be an acrobat and stunt man of the first order. Not only does Keaton rescue his girl and steal back the General, he also learns of a major offensive being planned by the Union Army. And now the chase is reversed, Keaton racing the General back south to warn the Confederate forces, with Union soldiers in hot pursuit. Mack's wonderfully ditzy performance is the perfect foil for 'Stone-face' Keaton's trademark deadpan delivery. And incredibly enough, the scenario is based on a true story! *1927. 78m. B&W. DIR&WRIT: Buster Keaton. CAST: Buster Keaton, Marion Mack, Glen Cavender, Jim Farley, Joe Keaton.*

GET SHORTY...

a comedic hodgepodge of *The Player* meeting *The Godfather*, features a consummate leading performance from John Travolta. He plays a Miami-based loan collector who heads for Los Angeles to exact an outstanding debt from shlock movie producer Gene Hackman. But soon enough mafia business takes second fiddle to movie-making, as Travolta, a self-described film buff, begins pitching deals to Hackman, while fending off a two-pronged assault from sleazy drug-dealer Delroy Lindo and Miami gangland boss Dennis Farina. Travolta exploits his underworld skills with a measured and knowing touch, foiling all comers, in the process recouping the mob money and going on to produce his first Hollywood film. Catchy dialogue, Farina's hysterical take as a vengeful goon, and John Lurie's jazzy soundtrack all combine with Barry Sonnenfeld's deft direction to make this one of the best Elmore Lenord novels to be translated to the silver screen. *1995. 105m. DIR: Barry Sonnenfeld. WRIT: Scott Frank. CAST: John Travolta, Gene Hackman, Rene Russo, Danny DeVito, Dennis Farina, Delroy Lindo, James Gandolfini, Jon Gries, David Paymer.*

GETTING EVEN WITH DAD...

co-stars Ted Danson, Saul Rubinek, and Gailard Sartain as bumbling crooks planning one last heist. (How bumbling? This trio just finished a lengthy prison stint for stealing *Betamax* video machines.) The plan is to pilfer an allotment of precious coins being shipped to the San Francisco mint. But when Danson's eleven-year-old son suddenly shows up on his doorstep—the boy our wayward father hasn't seen or written to in four years—it's payback time. This kid, ably played by Macaulay Culkin, is far more clever than our would-be con artists. Not only does the resourceful Culkin secretly video-tape the men hiding the stolen coins, he then shifts the loot to an unknown location and proceeds to blackmail his dad; Danson and his partners-in-crime won't be seeing those coins again unless Pop agrees to spend a week entertaining his son.

Most reluctantly, Danson submits to his kid's form of extortion, and so it's seven days of baseball games, miniature golf, amusement parks, and aquariums, with dumb and dumber tagging along for the ride. Among highlights is the sweet rapport which develops between father and son, a dash of romance between Danson and undercover FBI agent Glenne Headly, and any number of delightfully silly moments between Rubinek and Sartain, all adding up to a charming little film.

1994. 110m. DIR: Howard Deutch. WRIT: Tom S. Parker, Jim Jennewein. CAST: Ted Danson, Macaulay Culkin, Saul Rubinek, Gailard Sartain, Glenne Headly, Hector Elizondo.

THE GOLD RUSH...

features Charlie Chaplin's 'Little Tramp' looking for gold and romance in nineteenth-century Alaska. When we first meet Charlie ("Three days from anywhere, a Lone Prospector"), he's down on his luck, freezing and broke. Bad goes to worse when he stumbles into a cabin inhabited by the villainous Mack Swain, who promptly kicks Charlie back into the cold. But the same ill wind that keeps blowing Charlie into that cabin, sweeps prospector Tom Murray their way, whereupon a deliciously choreographed waltz sets in, Mack and Tom fighting over a gun which, no matter *where* Charlie runs, keeps pointing right in his direction. As matters develop, Charlie and Tom form an alliance of sorts, and our Tramp, in possibly his most famous scene, cooks up their Thanksgiving dinner: his right shoe. Charlie eventually moves into town, where he falls hard for beautiful dance hall girl Georgia Hale. Soon enough he's inviting Georgia and her snobbish friends over to his new residence for dinner, and the fantasy he entertains about the prospective meal, with Charlie's face cavorting over two dinner rolls speared with forks, is one of the more inspired moments in cinema. All said and done, this is possibly Chaplin's finest silent film.

1925. 85m. B&W. DIR&WRIT: Charlie Chaplin. CAST: Charlie Chaplin, Mack Swain, Tom Murray, Georgia Hale.

GROUNDHOG DAY...

stars Bill Murray as a self-important and cynical TV weatherman sent to Punxatawney, Pennsylvania for his annual coverage of the only-in-America festivities of Groundhog Day. But something goes terribly askew when Murray gets trapped in a time warp which obliges him to live through the same miserable day, over and *over* again. Out of desperation, Murray finally opts for suicide. But when even that doesn't work, our obnoxious weatherman is left with no choice but to gradually, day after the very same day, clean up his act, until he gets it absolutely and totally right, living through one selfless, creative, life-affirming 24-hour span. Along with the laughs, in this cleverly premised comedy, comes a charming romance, as TV producer Andie MacDowell finds herself falling in love with this Neanderthal-turned-jazz-playing-poetry-loving-Good-Samaritan. Who wouldn't?
1993. 103m. DIR: Harold Ramis. WRIT: Danny Rubin, Harold Ramis. CAST: Bill Murray, Andie MacDowell, Chris Elliott, Stephen Tobolowsky, Brian Doyle Murray, Marita Geraghty.

GRUMPY OLD MEN...

unites Walter Matthau and Jack Lemmon for their seventh film together. This time around they are former boyhood friends, now retired widowers and neighbors in small-town Minnesota, who have been feuding for so many years, the root cause of their dispute has long since been forgotten. Their ongoing verbal jousts and exchanges of moronic practical jokes have quite simply become their reason for getting out of bed every morning. When sexy new gal Ann-Margaret arrives in town, their rivalry shifts into high gear. The scenario is a perfect springboard for two old pros, letting one of the most enduring and endearing comedy teams in cinematic history do exactly what they do best. You may wish to stay put through the closing credits for a final choice outtake.
1993. 104m. DIR: Donald Petrie. WRIT: Mark Steven Johnson. CAST: Jack Lemmon, Walter Matthau, Ann-Margaret, Burgess Meredith, Daryl Hannah, Kevin Pollack, Ossie Davis.

GUARDING TESS...

stars Nicolas Cage as a play-it-by-the-book Secret Service agent, presently wrapping up a three-year stint protecting Tess Carlisle (Shirley MacLaine), the ex-President's widow. Restless to move on to a meatier assignment, Cage is stunned to learn that Tess has requested that he stay on in her rural hometown for another three years. (Cage to his supervisor: "I can't stay with that woman another three years! I can't stay for another three minutes!") But since the current president has seconded the widow's request, Cage has no option but to return to Ohio, where over time our uptight, insular agent loosens up to the point of developing true affection and respect for the tough old broad he had originally despised. It's an unusual and tender buddy flick concerning two lonely souls who learn to care deeply for one another, with some nice comic touches from the supporting cast.

1994. 98m. DIR: Hugh Wilson. WRIT: Peter Torokvei, Hugh Wilson. CAST: Nicolas Cage, Shirley MacLaine, Austin Pendleton, Edward Albert, James Rebhois, Richard Griffiths.

HARVEY...

co-scripted by Mary Chase and adapted from her Pulitzer Prize-winning play, stars an endearing Jimmy Stewart as small-town tippler Elwood P. Dodd. Elwood's best pal and soul mate happens to be an invisible, six foot tall white rabbit named Harvey, otherwise explained as a 'pooka' or mischievous imp from Irish folklore. Elwood's abiding affection for this invisible rabbit is complimented by an unfettered love for all of mankind, including the loners he meets in bars and habitually invites home for dinner. After a disastrous tea party, at which Elwood insists on introducing Harvey to all of his sister's high society guests, addled Josephine Hull reluctantly decides she must have her brother committed. All does not go as planned, however, and when by mistaken assumptions Hull finds herself in the mental institution, the ordeal is so ghastly, she has serious reservations about committing her beloved brother. By film's finale, Josephine even admits to having seen that darn rabbit herself. ("And what's more, he's every bit as big as Elwood says he is!") It's an original charmer, which is bound to leave a lingering glow long after the final credits.

1950. 104m. B&W. DIR: Henry Kosher. WRIT: Mary Chase, Oscar Brodney. CAST: James Stewart, Josephine Hull, Victoria Horn, Peggy Dow, Cecil Kellaway, Charles Drake, Jesse White.

HEART & SOULS...

opens in 1959 San Francisco, when and where a bus accident kills its four passengers—Kyra Sedgwick, Charles Grodin, Tom Sizemore, and Alfre Woodard—and places them in limbo as around-the-clock playmates of the baby boy born at the moment of their death. Cut to 1965, where our seven-year-old kid, ably portrayed by Eric Lloyd, is relating to his four buddies in his usual natural and chatty fashion. The kink in the program is that while he can see, talk, and play with his ghostly companions, they are invisible to everyone else, and that includes his parents, who are considering committing their son to an institution. To save the child from such a fate, our four ghosts reluctantly become invisible to him as well. But their sudden, if well-intentioned leave-taking has long-lasting emotional effects on the boy, a fact that we learn when the film jumps forward another twenty three years to find him, now in the person of Robert Downey Jr., as a high-powered businessman with serious commitment problems to girlfriend Elizabeth Shue. Circumstances bring his four long-lost sidekicks back into his life, whereupon we learn why they've been forced to stay attached to this young man all these years. By temporarily borrowing Downey's physical body, each of them is finally going to have the opportunity to accomplish the one thing they didn't have time to complete before that fatal traffic accident thirty years before. Now let the fun begin!

1993. 104m. DIR: Ron Underwood. WRIT: Brent Moddock, S.S. Wilson, Gregory & Erik Hansen. CAST: Robert Downey Jr., Kyra Sedgwick, Alfre Woodard, Charles Grodin, Tom Sizemore, Eric Lloyd.

HEAVEN CAN WAIT...

co-scripted by Elaine May, and based on the 1941 chestnut *Here Comes Mr. Jordan*, stars Warren Beatty as an L.A. Rams quarterback who is a victim of a car crash and whisked off to heaven before his time. When celestial dispatcher James Mason realizes the error, Beatty is sent back to earth in the body of the man who had been scheduled to die at that moment, a corrupt businessman whose unnatural exit has been engineered by greedy wife Dyan Cannon and lover Charles Grodin. Imagine their surprise when the 'neatly executed' hubby turns up alive, rejuvenated, and ethically transformed. Julie Christie plays the environmentalist and love interest who opens Beatty's eyes to the pollution crisis his predecessor's firm is aggravating. Although the two principals are fine indeed, the film's success is clinched by the contributions from a supporting cast which includes Cannon and Grodin as the haplessly conniving murderers, and Jack Warden as the football coach who senses correctly that he's met this aging executive before.

1978. 101m. DIR: Buck Henry, Warren Beatty. WRIT: Elaine May, Warren Beatty. CAST: Warren Beatty, Julie Christie, Dyan Cannon, Charles Grodin, Jack Warden, James Mason.

HIGH SEASON...

directed and co-written by a woman, stars Jacqueline Bisset as a celebrated British photographer who has been living with her daughter on the beautiful Greek isle of Rhodes for the last several years. But financial difficulties will force her to give up her magnificently placed, white-washed house unless she can sell a rare Roman vase given to her by best friend and art expert Sebastian Shaw. The elderly Shaw pays a visit in order to help Bisset arrange a profitable sale, but he has ulterior motives for coming to this island, which brings pompous British spy Kenneth Branagh into the picture, along with his put-upon young wife Lesley Manville. Last but certainly not least, there is Bisset's estranged hubby James Fox, a faddish sculptor who has just been commissioned by local shopkeeper 'Yanni' to create a statue to the Unknown Tourist, much to the disgust of Yanni's tourist-hating mother, Irene Pappas. Director/screenwriter Clare Peploe juggles this array of characters with admirable savoir-faire, intertwining the various stories into a tangled romantic web which ignites on the night of Bisset's celebratory bash. Among highlights, there is Bisset's sympathetic leading performance, Shaw's touching portrayal of a man ruing his past and all that might have been, and truly magnificent on-location scenery.

1988. 104m. DIR: Clare Peploe. WRIT: Clare & Mark Peploe. CAST: Jacqueline Bisset, James Fox, Sebastian Shaw, Kenneth Branagh, Leslie Manville, Irene Pappas, Paris Tselios.

HIS GIRL FRIDAY...

co-stars comedy virtuosos Rosalind Russell and Cary Grant, she as a soon-to-be-remarried ace reporter, he as her ex-husband and editor of the big-city newspaper where she formerly worked. When Russell comes to Grant's office announcing her upcoming nuptials to insurance salesman Ralph Bellamy, Grant resolves to stop at nothing to get her back on the paper and out of Bellamy's arms. Grant is superb as the cajoling, intimidating editor, and Russell every bit his equal; which is to say that these two were ideally suited to the relentlessly staccato-like, overlapping dialogue that became director Howard Hawks' unique contribution to the screwball formula. Also terrific is Bellamy's supporting contribution as the bumpkin of a Mama's boy who is never quite sure what fast-talking Grant is getting at. (Bellamy, concerning his profession: "Of course, we don't help you much when you're alive. But afterwards—that's what counts.") The plot device of an impending execution of a possibly innocent man takes a back seat to banter and waggery in this '40s comedy classic.

1940. 92m. B&W. DIR: Howard Hawks. WRIT: Ben Hecht, Charles Lederer. CAST: Rosalind Russell, Cary Grant, Ralph Bellamy, Gene Lockhart, John Qualen, Porter Hall.

HONEYMOON IN VEGAS...

opens in a New York City hospital in 1987, where dying mom Anne Bancroft cons son Nicolas Cage into promising he will never marry. Four years later, we find Cage very much in love with the comely Sarah Jessica Parker, but still struggling with the 'mother thing,' leading to difficulty with the 'commitment thing.' Under pressure from Parker, Cage finally agrees to tie the knot, and they opt for a quick wedding in Las Vegas. Enter gangster James Caan, who sees Parker as a dead ringer for his deceased wife and decides he wants her for his own. Towards that end, he tricks Cage into an all-night poker game which generates far-reaching and zany complications. In early scenes with Parker, Caan is surprisingly touching as the aging racketeer who is desperately seeking a new lease on life. But this film belongs to Cage as the ambivalent fiancé who finally sees the light when threatened with losing his woman. Toss an international Elvis impersonation contest into the festivities and you have the makings for a felicitously flipped-out romantic comedy. (But Gawd, some of the dresses they pour Parker into!)

1992. 95m. DIR&WRIT: Andrew Bergman. CAST: Nicolas Cage, Sarah Jessica Parker, James Caan, Noriyuki Morita, John Capodice, John Boyle.

HOUSE CALLS...

stars Walter Matthau as a recently widowed surgeon who finds his suddenly single status has its unexpected benefits. In particular, nurses in his hospital appear more than willing to be wined, dined, and bedded by their celebrated older colleague. Enter Glenda Jackson as a sassy, wise-cracking divorcée, and the unexpected happens to our swinging bachelor—he finds himself falling in love with a woman who is vaguely his own age. To complicate matters for our would-be playboy, Jackson insists on all or nothing. Matthau reluctantly agrees to a month-long experiment with monogamy and the film takes wing. Matthau and Jackson work wonderfully together, both verbally and physically, and Art Carney gives great comic support as the increasingly senile chief-of-staff. (When the hospital CEO suggests to Carney that they install closed circuit television in their newborn baby nursery, Carney objects: "Television? But that's insane! What the hell would they watch? They can't even focus yet!")

1978. 98m. DIR: Howard Zieff. WRIT: Charles Shyer, Max Shulman, Julius J. Epstein. CAST: Walter Matthau, Glenda Jackson, Art Carney, Richard Benjamin.

HOW TO MARRY A MILLIONAIRE...

boasts a delectable ensemble effort from Lauren Bacall, Marilyn Monroe, and Betty Grable as a trio of comely dames determined to snare themselves wealthy mates. Their modus operandi is to pool all their resources and rent temporary penthouse digs, thereby lending themselves an aura of elegance which they hope will attract monied suitors in kind. Nothing quite works out as planned, of course, Grable falling for a forest ranger, Monroe for an on-the-lam tax evader, and Bacall for another in a long line of 'gas attendant jockies.' There is a bit more here than meets the eye, however, which makes for a happily serendipitous finale. Of note: you may wish to fast-forward through the opening orchestra sequence, apparently tacked on by the studio to show off the formerly new technique of stereophonic sound.

1953. 96m. DIR: Jean Negulesco. WRIT: Nunnally Johnson. CAST: Lauren Bacall, Marilyn Monroe, Betty Grable, David Wayne, William Powell, Cameron Mitchell.

I LOVE YOU TO DEATH...

a black comedy of macabre dimensions, serves up many side-splitting moments as it relates the travails of hard-working Italian-American wife and mother Tracy Ullman, who is saddled with philandering pizza-man hubby Kevin Kline. When Ullman discovers just how extensive are his infidelities, she and mom Joan Plowright start plotting what they consider to be his well-deserved demise. The major hitch in the scheme is their appointed hit men, two stoned-out cousins played with riotous abandon by William Hurt and Keenu Reeves. Although the would-be victim is in a dead sleep—Ullman and Plowright prepped Kline for slaughter by feeding him spaghetti spiked with three bottles of sleeping pills—they still can't manage to get the job done. Kline is poisoned, shot, stabbed, and ultimately prevails, only to refuse pressing charges against his 'passionate' wife. Of note: this crazy scenario is allegedly based on a true story!

1990. 110m. DIR: Lawrence Kasdan. WRIT: John Kostmayer. CAST: Tracy Ullman, Kevin Kline, Joan Plowright, William Hurt, Keenu Reeves, River Phoenix.

I'LL DO ANYTHING...

has such a strong female perspective, it's surprising to discover the script was penned by a man. (Then again, James L. Brooks is the same writer/director whose creative efforts brought us *Terms of Endearment* and *Broadcast News*, two earlier films featuring strong, sympathetic women.) Nick Nolte stars as the out-of-work actor who is obliged to take custody of the six-year-old daughter he hasn't seen in three years. In need of immediate funds, he will 'do anything' for a few bucks, which includes becoming chauffeur for insufferable Hollywood producer Albert Brooks. Subplots abound, including Nolte's interlude with his boss' winsome assistant Joely Richardson, and Julie Kavner's struggling relationship with the crass producer. But the heart of the story concerns an estranged father and daughter who come to love and understand one another. The genuine performance elicited from young co-star Whittni Wright is a delightful bonus.

1993. 115m. DIR&WRIT: James Brooks. CAST: Nick Nolte, Whittni Wright, Julie Kavner, Albert Brooks, Joely Richardson, Tracey Ullman.

IMPROMPTU...

scripted by a woman, is a satirical imagining of the social and sexual interactions among a group of celebrated 18th century artists, including author George Sand, composers Frederic Chopin and Franz Liszt, and painter Eugene Delacroix. Judy

Davis stars as the decidedly lusty Sand. ("I used to think I'd die of suffocation when I was married. Now it's my freedom that's killing me.") The acclaimed writer has bedded her way through an impressive list of lovers, a fact which drives ex-hubby Mandy Patinkin to mad distraction. But as our film opens, it is the retiring and consumptive Chopin who she perceives as her soul mate. Upon making her intentions clear, she both intimidates the timorous Chopin and infuriates her most recent conquest, the young tutor who has the annoying habit of challenging all his prospective rivals to a duel at dawn. One of the film's many felicitous touches is Emma Thompson's comic cameo as the batty duchess who hosts this band of wags and parasites at her country estate. A perfect impromptu, as Chopin explains to Sand, should seem to be spontaneous and free, with no evidence of the painstaking origins of its construction. Ditto for this original cinematic gem.

1990. 108m. DIR: James Lapine. WRIT: Sarah Kernochan. CAST: Judy Davis, Hugh Grant, Mandy Patinkin, Julian Sands, Bernadette Peters, Ralph Brown.

IN & OUT...

stars Kevin Kline as a popular high school English teacher, who is about to marry long time fiancée Joan Cusak. But big problems set in for this bike-riding, poetry-loving professor when ex-student Matt Dillon wins an Academy Award and unintentionally 'outs' Kline on national television: "He's a great teacher, and he's gay!" Soon enough camera crews from around the country have pitched camp at Kline's high school, while he continues to insist to Cusak, parents Debby Reynolds and Wilford Brimley, and his increasingly confused students that he's as straight as they come. Openly gay TV newscaster Tom Selleck believes otherwise, however, and comes to town both to do a documentary on Kline and to persuade him to emerge from the closet. Aside from a silly detour into Dillon's film-within-the-film, it's an entertaining, life-affirming scenario, whose highlights include the entire community giving Kline their support at high school graduation, and a hilarious macho 'instructional' video. ("Truly manly men drink beer and have bad backs. But under any circumstances, they do *not* dance!") That said, watch our leading man strut his stuff!

1997. 110m. DIR: Frank Oz. WRIT: Paul Rudnick. CAST: Kevin Klein, Joan Cusak, Tom Selleck, Debbie Reynolds, Wilford Brimley, Shalom Karlow, Zak Orth, Bob Newhart.

IRRECONCILABLE DIFFERENCES...

co-scripted by a woman, stars Shelley Long and Ryan O'Neal as a hopelessly backbiting couple whose daughter Drew Barrymore has decided to 'divorce' in order to be placed in the custody of the family's loving Mexican maid. As hokey as that pretext may sound, it sets up a most effective satire. Through a series of flashbacks, we first see how Long and O'Neal meet and fall in love while making their way across country to Los Angeles. She's an aspiring author of children's books, while he's dreaming of hitting the big time as a Hollywood director. They marry, co-write a screenplay, and produce a highly successful film. But in true Hollywood fashion, he's the one who gets all the credit, leaving Long feeling increasingly dissatisfied. A creaky marriage gets far worse when O'Neal discovers a sizzling starlet for their next movie—you guessed it, Sharon Stone. From this point forward, the movie focuses on the mercurial professional fortunes of this combative, now separated pair. After a successful second film, O'Neal loses his shirt directing a musical version of *Gone With the Wind*, while Long puts her writing talents back to work penning a bestselling novel. Through all of their travails, neither of our preoccupied winner/losers manages to give daughter Barrymore the attention she so obviously craves. It's an entertaining comedy about an all-too-familiar tragedy: how parents' busy careers often leave their children whistling in the dark.

1984. 112m. DIR: Charles Shyer. WRIT: Nancy Myers, Charles Shyer. CAST: Shelley Long, Ryan O'Neal, Drew Barrymore, Sam Wanamaker, Allen Garfield, Hortensia Colorado.

JUNIOR...

plays with the timeworn supposition—'what if men could give birth?'—with comic and gratifying results. Arnold Schwarzenegger is perfectly cast as the cold fish of a bio-scientist who has developed an anti-miscarriage fertility drug. But when the FDA denies approval for a test run of the medication on pregnant women, business partner Danny DeVito persuades our scientist to be the guinea pig himself. Thus Arnold will be impregnated via the wonders of test-tube insemination and retain the fetus throughout the first trimester, whereupon a miscarriage will be induced. But after three months of pregnancy, Schwarzenegger turns the tables on DeVito, deciding he wants to keep the baby ("My body, my choice."), at which point the loopy complications set in. This flick took a dive at the box office, apparently because men were discomfited by the paradox of seeing their favorite action hero 'heavy with child.' But for the rest of us it's a real hoot watching Hollywood's foremost macho-man portraying a preggo, and a most sympathetic one, at that. Schwarzenegger plays it sweet and straight, making the preposterous appear remarkably feasible as he experiences the customary phases of pregnancy, including morning sickness, the wonders of the first ultra-sound, and natural childbirth classes. In the process, he picks up the best aspects of the female psyche, becoming a better man for having carried and bore a child. Special mention is due Emma Thompson as Arnie's ultra-klutzy love interest.

1994. 100m. DIR: Ivan Reitman. WRIT: Kevin Wade, Chris Conrad. CAST: Arnold Schwarzenegger, Danny DeVito, Emma Thompson, Frank Langella, Pamela Reed, Judy Collins.

THE LADY EVE...

is quintessential screwball, pairing Barbara Stanwyck with Charles Coburn as father-and-daughter con artists who travel the luxurious ocean-liner-circuit in search of wealthy prey. Enter Henry Fonda as the scientist millionaire, just back from a year in the Amazon and poised for the kill. (Coburn's assessment of Fonda: "There's as fine a specimen of the species Sucker Sapiens as I've ever seen. Bet he even performs card tricks.") But it doesn't take long for our confidence dame to fall in love with her would-be victim, and the flimflam begins in earnest. Stanwyck is expectedly savvy, sexy, and fast-talking, but Fonda is the revelation here, giving a jubilantly straight-faced performance as the babe-in-the-woods beer tycoon just waiting to be hooked, again and again. It's one of director Preston Sturges' finer efforts.

1941. 94m. B&W. DIR&WRIT: Preston Sturges. CAST: Barbara Stanwyck, Henry Fonda, Charles Coburn, William Demarest, Eric Blore, Eugene Pallette.

LES COMPERES...

is a French farce which exploits the superb comic chemistry between odd-couple Pierre Richard and Gerard Depardieu. At the opening of the film, 16-year-old Parisian runaway Tristan is hitch-hiking down to Nice with his ruffian girlfriend in tow. When the police refuse immediate assistance to desperate Mom Anne Duperey, she takes matters into her own hands by phoning old flame Depardieu and claiming that he is Tristan's real father, in the hope that paternal responsibility will persuade him to go looking for her son. But he claims to be too busy to offer her any help, and so she tries the same scheme on former boyfriend Richard. The suicidal, manic-depressive Richard is thrilled to learn he has an offspring and quickly agrees to try tracking him down. Meanwhile, a guilt-ridden Depardieu has reconsidered, and the two men meet down in Nice—in typically riotous fashion—and join forces in finding Tristan, each remaining convinced that he is the real papa of the young runaway. Among highlights is the eternally weepy Richard suddenly finding himself unable to cry when it suits their purposes.

1983. 92m. In French w/English Subtitles. DIR&WRIT: Francis Verber. CAST: Pierre Richard, Gerard Depardieu, Anne Duperey, Michel Aumont, Stephane Bierry.

LILY IN LOVE...

makes fine use of a couple of old pros, with Christopher Plummer and Maggie Smith playing divinely off each other as a couple whose marriage has seen better days. He plays a boozing, self-absorbed actor, and she is a lonely, albeit successful screenwriter who offends hubby Plummer with the notion he is too old to undertake the romantic lead in her next film. Against his protestations, she seeks a younger, unknown actor to play the role, whereupon Plummer returns, masquerading by virtue of an Italian accent and theater cosmetics as the very man Lily seems to be looking for. Not only is he a more than adequate performer, but the epitome of graciousness and romance—everything her husband decidedly is not. Roberto/Plummer lands the role, crew and cast fly off to Budapest to shoot the film-within-the-film, and a uniquely comic offering unfurls. Lily falls in love! (An exchange between the increasingly fuming Plummer and his increasingly frantic producer: "My wife is actually falling for that slimy piece of mozzarella!" "But might I point out that *you* are that slimy piece of mozzarella!") The comic tempo suffers whenever Elke Sommer takes center stage.

1985. 105m. DIR: Karoly Makk. WRIT: Frank Cucci. CAST: Maggie Smith, Christopher Plummer, Adolph Green, Elke Sommer.

LIVING IN OBLIVION...

gives us two uproarious days in the life of the cast and crew of one of those proverbial 'independent' low-budget films, as everyone attempts the seemingly impossible—to wrap up production. Steve Buscemi is perfectly cast as the frenzied director, having a nervous breakdown while anything that can go wrong on the set *does* go wrong, including sound mikes in the frame, exploding smoke props, misplaced libidos, the outrageous ego of our leading man, and the general chaos of anyone's worst nightmare. The opening sequence sets the tone as leading lady Catherine Keener plays a particularly emotional scene and, due to pervasive disturbances in the field, must re-enact the all-important moment over and over again. Give Keener credit for bringing a different nuance to every take. Special mention is due Dermot Mulroney's contribution as the oh-so-hip cinematographer, and Rica Martens' touching offering as our director's slightly demented Mom. *1994. 92m. DIR&WRIT: Tom Dicillo. CAST: Steve Buscemi, Catherine Keener, Dermot Mulroney, Danielle von Zemeck, James LeGros, Rica Martens, Robert Wightman, Hillary Gilford, Kevin Corrigan, Peter Dinklage, Matthew Grace.*

LOST IN AMERICA...

co-written by a woman, stars Albert Brooks as a full-fledged, high-flying yuppie who gets overlooked for an expected promotion at his ad agency. ("I've seen the future and it's a bald-headed man from New York.") In rebellion and disgust, he quits his job, buys a Winnebago, and with wife Julie Hagerty sets out to find out what makes America tick. Think of it as *Easy Rider* meeting *Honeymoon in Vegas*, which is where our would-be adventurers' pilgrimage begins. Among the movie's highlights is Brooks' harangue on the 'Nest Egg Principle' and his stint as an elementary school crossing guard. Although this tale ultimately takes a cautionary view of the 'drop-out' syndrome, its collage of cross-country vistas makes a persuasive argument for taking the plunge all the same. *1985. 91m. DIR: Albert Brooks. WRIT: Albert Brooks, Monica Johnson. CAST: Albert Brooks, Julie Hagerty, Michael Greene, Tom Tarpey.*

LOVER COME BACK...

is the second romantic comedy pairing Doris Day and Rock Hudson, with Tony Randall again portraying the ever-suffering third wheel. In this outing, Day and Hudson are competing advertising execs who have never met. When the unscrupulous Hudson pirates away one of Day's clients, she is determined to get revenge by wooing the research chemist working on Hudson's firm's mysterious new product, 'VIP.' Dropping into VIP's Greenwich Village laboratory, she finds Hudson himself in lab coat, wrongly assumes that he's the aforementioned chemist, and all the fun begins. Hudson is a kick as the notorious playboy courting Day with his aw-shucks, virginal-scientist routine—a wolf in sheep's clothing if ever there was one—and Day is a superb foil as his wide-eyed prey. Watch for a lot of inside jokes in this early sixties flick, with marijuana and Hudson's gayness among them. The magnetism between Hudson and Day, comic and otherwise, is a joy to behold.

1961. 107m. DIR: Delbert Mann. WRIT: Stanley Shapiro, Paul Henning. CAST: Rock Hudson, Doris Day, Tony Randall, Edie Adams.

MARRIED TO THE MOB...

was Michelle Pfeiffer's breakthrough role, in a film which pits her against mobsters in one corner and government agents in the other, their black and white hats increasingly indistinguishable as the scenario spins merrily along. The opening gambit has Pfeiffer married to philandering hit man Alec Baldwin, a chap not long for this world when he is discovered messing around with mafioso boss Dean Stockwell's main squeeze. Widowhood has unexpected compensations for Pfeiffer, enabling her to flee her Long Island home for the Lower East Side of Manhattan, where she struggles to make a more honorable if decidedly humbler life for herself as a hairdresser. But complications arise when Stockwell takes an obsessively romantic interest in her, at the same time that the FBI is trying to prove that Pfeiffer engineered her husband's untimely demise. In the process, FBI operative Matthew Modine falls for our comely hairdresser, realizes she is indeed innocent, and starts laying down tracks to trap the real culprit. But his methods are so inept that his cover is quickly blown, at which point he and Pfeiffer become seriously endangered species. Good-humored vitality, old-fashioned romance, and a musical score that keeps the whole proceedings zipping along, are a few of the movie's virtues. Still another is Mercedes Ruehl's scene-chewing performance as Stockwell's jealous, vengeful wife.

1988. 102m. DIR: Jonathan Demme. WRIT: Mark Burns. CAST: Michelle Pfeiffer, Dean Stockwell, Matthew Modine, Mercedes Ruehl, Anthony Nici.

THE MATCHMAKER...

far superior to the overly long musical remake *Hello, Dolly!*, stars Shirley Booth as a professional cupid in turn-of-the-century Yonkers, New York. Paul Ford is the middle-aged, tight-fisted shop owner who has decided it's time to remarry, and the younger the bride the better. Booth feigns to further Ford's ambitions, setting him up for a trip to Manhattan to meet bonny milliner Shirley MacLaine. But Ford's young sales clerks Tony Perkins and Robert Morse take advantage of their boss' rare absence by traveling to the City as well, whereupon they meet MacLaine first and Perkins falls head-over-heels in love. Which is no reason for concern, since our wily matchmaker has other plans for merchant Ford's future. Aside from an excusably corny scene in the milliner's shop, the film is a nostalgic delight, spearheaded by Booth and Ford's comic contributions.

1958. 101m. DIR: Joseph Anthony. WRIT: Thorton Wilder. CAST: Shirley Booth, Paul Ford, Anthony Perkins, Robert Morse, Shirley MacLaine.

MAX DUGAN RETURNS...

is an heartfelt comedy starring Marsha Mason as a widowed school teacher, struggling to raise teenage son Matthew Broderick on spunk and humor while living from paycheck to paycheck. To add to Mason's already plentiful economic woes, her dilapidated Ford Bronco gets stolen, which ushers in romantic interest Donald Sutherland as the police lieutenant who is assigned to her case. Matters now take an unexpected turn, when Mason's long-lost father Max Dugan (Jason Robards) shows up on her doorstep after a thirty-year hiatus, bearing a mysterious suitcase of cash. Papa Max claims its money he swindled from heavies in Las Vegas to even an old score, but the more presents he showers on daughter and grandson, the more suspicious becomes Mason's new police-man beau concerning the source of his bounty. It's an excellent cast, highlighted by Broderick's amazing film debut—his low-key comic timing can't be faulted—and

Robards' touching contribution as a man determined to make the most of what little time he has left.

1983. 98m. DIR: Herbert Ross. WRIT: Neil Simon. CAST: Marsha Mason, Matthew Broderick, Jason Robards, Donald Sutherland.

MICKI & MAUDE...

stars Dudley Moore as a TV journalist happily married to district attorney Ann Reinking, the 'Micki' of our title, when *his* biological clock starts ticking. The guy wants kids in the worst way, while Micki, whose career is just taking off, is determined to postpone childbearing a few more years. Enter Amy Irving as the sweet-faced cello player 'Maude,' whom Dudley interviews one afternoon and joins at a concert the same evening. After some serious canoodling, Maude becomes pregnant, and Dudley decides the only decent thing to do is to divorce Micki and marry Maude. But then *Micki* turns up pregnant, as well. Dudley—in love with both women and still struggling for the 'high moral ground'— decides there is only one viable option: bigamy. It's a slightly uneven farce blessed by Moore's considerable comic talents and the likability of our two budding Moms. Does our bigamist eventually get his just desserts? Yes. And no. Special mention is due Richard Mulligan's contribution as Dudley's addled best friend and confidant.

1984. 115m. DIR: Blake Edwards. WRIT: Jonathan Reynolds. CAST: Dudley Moore, Ann Reinking, Amy Irving, Richard Mulligan, Wallace Shawn, George Gaynes.

MIDNIGHT RUN...

stars Robert De Niro as an ex-cop-turned-bounty-hunter who is enlisted by bondsman Joe Pantoliano to haul embezzler Charles Grodin back to Los Angeles. It seems that accountant Grodin stole $15 million from the Chicago mob, gave it away to charity, got arrested, then skipped town after being released on bail. The frantic bondsman stands to lose the entire $450,000 of Grodin's bail unless De Niro can bring our embezzler back within five days time. Due to Grodin's non-violent temperament, the assignment appears to be a piece of cake, what is known in the business as a 'midnight run.' But complications abound, including the FBI's determination to place Grodin in their witness protection program, and Chicago mob boss Dennis Farina's equally determined effort to have Grodin eliminated ASAP. De Niro quickly traces Grodin to New York City, and their perilous cross-country odyssey begins. It's destined to be a four-day high-wire act, wherein an atypical fellowship evolves between this decidedly odd couple. Grodin is a proven comedic entity; it's De Niro who is the surprise here, giving a deft portrayal of a man who's funny without meaning to be, without even realizing he's funny. Special mention is due the supporting contributions from Farina as our vengeful mobster and Yaphet Kotto as the enraged FBI agent whom De Niro trips up time and again. Considering all the thrills and chills, not to mention the laughs, this is a surprisingly warm-hearted gem, one not to be missed.

1988. 123m. DIR: Martin Brest. WRIT: George Gallo. CAST: Robert De Niro, Charles Grodin, Yaphet Kotto, John Ashton, Dennis Farina, Joe Pantoliano.

MODERN ROMANCE...

opens with leading man Albert Brooks asking girlfriend Kathryn Harrold if she understands the essence of a 'lose-lose' situation: "You know—like Vietnam. Or us." Having her relationship compared to that quagmire of a war is all too emblematic of this woman's problems. She is romantically involved with a chap who believes they have nothing in common and is forever breaking up with her, only to instantly panic and insist on getting back together again. Brooks is alternately very funny—catch his scene on quaaludes—and downright exasperating, as a man who hasn't a clue what he really wants or needs from a woman. All he *does* know is that he can't stomach the idea of any other fellow wooing his sexy lady after he's split the scene, and therein lies the rub.

1981. 102m. DIR&WRIT: Albert Brooks. CAST: Albert Brooks, Kathryn Harrold, Bruno Kirby, George Kennedy.

MOTHER...

co-written by a woman, gives Debbie Reynolds the opportunity to remind us, after a 25-year hiatus from the movies, of just how accomplished a comedienne she really is. Director Albert Brooks co-stars as a twice-divorced forty-something sci-fi writer who concludes that his ongoing trouble with women must stem from an unresolved relationship with his mother. His solution to the problem is to move back in with Mom for as long as it takes for him to figure out what went wrong. An exasperated Reynolds does not initially take kindly to the idea of her son as roommate, suspicious that she is being unfairly blamed for his emotional shortcomings. But over time their relationship prospers, Brooks realizing that he made a serious mistake in assuming that—for all practical purposes—his mother 'first came to life when he was born.' By delving into his mother's past and learning of the aspirations she cherished before having her two sons, Brooks unlocks the key to their sometimes troubled relationship and feels happily ready to move on. This kind of scenario could easily have descended into bathos if not for Brooks' wry and steady hand, making for a most entertaining night at the movies. Special mention is due Rob Morrow's mincing contribution as the younger brother who is increasingly jealous of all the attention Mom is giving his older sibling, and once again to Debbie Reynolds for her pitch-perfect performance.
1996. 104m. DIR: Albert Brooks. WRIT: Albert Brooks, Monica Johnson. CAST: Debbie Reynolds, Albert Brooks, Rob Morrow, Lisa Kudrow, John C. McKinley, Isabel Glasser, Peter White.

MR. DESTINY...

is an amusing, if slightly lightweight update of the classic *It's a Wonderful Life*, focusing on the 'only ifs' which haunt us as the years go by. James Belushi stars as our everyman, still tormented by the missed opportunity to be the big hero back in high school, when he blew an all-important baseball game by striking out at bat. Now happily married to Linda Hamilton, but experiencing your standard mid-life crisis, Belushi drops into a corner pub and meets cryptic barkeep Michael Caine. Caine, alias Mr. Destiny, serves him a bewitching cocktail and suggests that if there is anything Belushi wants altered in his past, the time to ask is now. Belushi makes his wish—a whopping home run at that critical moment twenty years before—downs the cocktail and presto! his dream has come true. But with the domino theory firmly in place, his life is now as it would have been, should he have become the town's champion those many years ago, one modified exploit transforming his entire adult life. Will it be for better or worse? You make the call.

1990. 100m. DIR: James Orr. WRIT: James Orr, Jim Cruckshank. CAST: James Belushi, Linda Hamilton, Michael Caine, Jon Lovitz, Rene Russo, Hart Bochner.

MY FAVORITE YEAR...

is a humorous and poignant portrait of early television, back when there was still some innocent exuberance to the proceedings. As the story opens, Mark Linn-Baker, the youngest television writer for the top-rated *King Kaiser's Comedy Hour*, is given the assignment to keep close watch over the week's guest star, a former-matinee-idol-turned-womanizing-alcoholic played to delightful abandon by Peter O'Toole. O'Toole arrives in New York already tipsy and unmanageable, and turns the tables on the young Linn-Baker by leading him on a series of wild and crazy escapades around Manhattan. As misfortune would have it, this little romp leaves O'Toole dead-drunk on the day he is to participate in a live TV skit. Amongst all the hilarity, there are notable small and moving moments, including a loving husband asking O'Toole if he would be so kind as to take his awestruck wife for a turn on the dance floor, and O'Toole getting a glimpse of his estranged daughter and all that might have been. Special mention is due Joseph Bologna's exceptional contribution as the acerbic and brawling King Kaiser. Of note: the scenario is based on a real-life incident, when a young Mel Brooks was delegated to attempt reining in Errol Flynn before he was to perform live on Sid Caesar's *Show of Shows*.

1982. 92m. DIR: Richard Benjamin. WRIT: Norman Steinberg, Dennis Palumbo. CAST: Peter O'Toole, Mark Linn-Baker, Joseph Bologna, Jessica Harper, Bill Macy, Lainie Kazan, Anne DeSalvo, Basil Hoffman, Lou Jacobi, Adolph Green.

THE ODD COUPLE...

features comedy team Walter Matthau and Jack Lemmon in their most memorable screen pairing, as Yin and Yang trying to live under the same roof together. Lemmon is the neat freak whose wife has just asked for a separation. Matthau is the divorced, quintessential slob who reluctantly agrees to share his apartment with Lemmon, in the hopes of staving off his suicidal frame of mind. Predictably disastrous results ensue. (Matthau, in the middle of still another rage: "I can't take it anymore, Felix! I'm cracking up. Everything you do irritates me. And when you're not here, the things I know you're gonna do when you come back irritate me. You leave me little notes on my pillow. I told you 158 times I cannot stand little notes on my pillow! 'We are all out of cornflakes. F.U.' It took me three hours to figure out F.U. was Felix Ungar!") Among highlights, there's Carole Shelley and Monica Evans' choice act as the 'Pigeon Sisters' from upstairs whom our odd couple make the big mistake of meeting on a double-date.

1968. 106m. DIR: Gene Saks. WRIT: Neil Simon. CAST: Walter Matthau, Jack Lemmon, Carole Shelley, Monica Evans, John Fiedler, Herbert Edelman, David Sheiner, Larry Haines.

PAPER MOON...

is remarkable for the performance given by nine-year-old Tatum O'Neal in the co-starring role. She plays an orphan who might or might not be the 'illegitimate' daughter of phony Bible salesman Ryan O'Neal, her real-life father. By scrutinizing her mentor as he swindles poor widows into buying Bibles at the height of the Depression, our kid adopts the tricks of the trade as if they were her own, becoming a better fast-talking con artist than Ryan himself. In addition to a smart and funny screenplay, the film boasts beautiful black-and-white cinematography modeled on the work of director Bogdonovich's own mentor, John Ford. Madeleine Kahn's predictably comic contribution is another bonus.

1973. 102m. DIR: Peter Bogdonovich. WRIT: Alvin Sargent. CAST: Tatum O'Neal, Ryan O'Neal, Madeleine Kahn, John Hillerman, Randy Quaid.

PETER'S FRIENDS...

co-scripted by a woman, is a British take on the same college-reunion theme pioneered by *The Return of the Secaucus 7*, and cashed in by *The Big Chill*. Seven members of a former collegiate musical troupe are invited by the eighth member of the troop—the Peter of our title—to spend the New Year's weekend at the elegant manor house which he recently inherited from his late beloved father. There's going to be the usual reminiscences, revelations, and general partying going on through this gala forty-eight hours, and more than a few touching denouements. The luxury of the setting, the likability of our cast, including the talents of Emma Thompson and Kenneth Branagh, and the over-all sympathy of the direction and script ("Adults are just kids who owe money."), make for a satisfying night at the movies. If there be a caveat, it is the unnecessarily strident characterization of Branagh's Hollywood wife, Rita Rudner. Of note: there are deeper reasons than nostalgia for Peter having planned this reunion, motivations which may be surmised before the film's finale.

1992. 102m. DIR: Kenneth Branagh. WRIT: Rita Rudner, Martin Bergman. CAST: Emma Thompson, Stephen Fry, Kenneth Branagh, Rita Rudner, Hugh Laurie, Imelda Staunton, Alphonsia Emmanuel, Tony Slattery, Alex Lowe, Alex Scott, Phyllida Law.

PILLOW TALK...

co-stars Doris Day as an interior decorator, and Rock Hudson as the songwriter-cum-playboy who drives her batty monopolizing their joint party line, wooing one or another of his very long string of girlfriends. Their phone relationship—they've never actually met face-to-face—becomes increasingly antagonistic. ("Mr. Allen, this may come as a shock to you, but there are some men who don't end every sentence with a proposition!") Upon inadvertently overhearing a restaurant conversation, Hudson learns Day's identity and sets about seducing his gorgeous nemesis. He's not going to court her as himself, of course, but as a rich, innocent Texan, in town for a convention. ("I get a nice warm feeling being near you, Ma'am. It's like being 'round a pot-bellied stove on a frosty morning.") Among highlights is Day's housekeeper Thelma Ritter drinking Hudson under the table, Day's sexy delivery of 'Possess Me,' and the tongue-in-check comic rapport between our two leads.

1959. 102m. DIR: Michael Gordon. WRIT: Stanley Shapiro, Maurice Richlin. CAST: Doris Day, Rock Hudson, Tony Randall, Thelma Ritter, Nick Adams, Lee Patrick.

PLANES, TRAINS & AUTOMOBILES...

not to mention the tackiest of motel rooms, figure prominently in this buddy flick about two erstwhile travelers who are attempting the deceptively simple task of getting from New York to Chicago to celebrate Thanksgiving with their respective families. This is a one-trick pony which rides due to the comic talents of our two leads, Steve Martin playing the uptight advertising exec, and John Candy the motor-mouth-from-hell curtain ring salesman. When their flight gets re-routed to Wichita, Kansas, Candy uses his 'connections' to get them the last available motel room in town. But there's a catch: the room in question has only one bed. Bigger catch: Candy leaves a six pack on the vibrating mattress. Bad goes to worse, and worse on to catastrophic. What can possibly go wrong next, is the question you find yourself asking. Rest assured, something always does, with our antagonists becoming comrades-in-arms in the process. The pleasant surprise here is the warm-hearted finale.

1987. 93m. DIR&WRIT: John Hughes. CAST: Steve Martin, John Candy, Edie McClurg, Michael McKean, William Windom, Laila Robbins.

THE PLAYER...

is an uncannily authentic satire of Hollywood filmmaking, courtesy of someone who knows from whence he speaks, director Robert Altman. Tim Robbins stars as the writer executive at his movie studio, responsible for deciding which of the innumerable scripts and pitches he reads and/or hears each day will see the light of day. (Robbins responding to yet another pitch from yet another aspiring screenwriter: "I see. So it's kind of a psychic, political-comedy-thriller, with a heart?" Writer: "With a heart, and um, not unlike *Ghost* meets *The Manchurian Candidate.*") Amid our power broker's daily rituals—the speaker phone conferences, the power lunches, the private screenings—trouble brews in the form of up-and-comer exec Peter Gallagher, who's eyeing Robbins' job. There is also the matter of the anonymous threatening postcards Robbins is receiving from a writer whose script he recently rejected. When the warnings become increasingly more alarming, he feels he has no choice but to confront his would-be assassin and attempt negotiation. And now the predicaments really set in. The scenario is biting if good-natured fun, enhanced by cameos from innumerable Hollywood luminaries. Special mention is due Robbins' jaunty starring performance and that capper of a finale.
1992. 123m. DIR: Robert Altman. WRIT: Michael Tolkin. CAST: Tim Robbins, Cynthia Stevenson, Greta Scacchi, Fred Ward, Whoopi Goldberg, Peter Gallagher, Vincent D'Onofrio, Dean Stockwell.

PLAZA SUITE...

gives comedy genius Walter Matthau the opportunity to do his schtick, portraying three different men in very divergent situations, all three acts taking place in Manhattan's landmark Plaza Hotel. Due credit must be given each of Walter's talented leading ladies: Maureen Stapleton as the lonely wife attempting to celebrate her 24th wedding anniversary with a less than enthusiastic spouse, Barbara Harris as the New Jersey housewife agreeing to an afternoon tryst with an old flame-turned-famous-Hollywood-producer, and Lee Grant as the anxious mother-of-the-bride who watches the entire wedding go up in smoke while her husband vainly coaxes their stage-frightened daughter out of the bathroom. The last skit is the funniest, with Grant in top form. ("All right, so we yell and scream a little. So we fight and curse and aggravate each other. So you blame me for being a lousy mother, and I accuse you of being a rotten husband. That doesn't mean we're not happy, does it?") The first skit, as pulled off by Matthau and Stapleton, rings pathetic and true.

1971. 115m. DIR: Arthur Hiller. WRIT: Neil Simon. CAST: Walter Matthau, Maureen Stapleton, Barbara Harris, Lee Grant.

THE PURPLE ROSE OF CAIRO...

is Woody Allen's whimsical ode to the joy and sanctuary of the movies. Mia Farrow stars as a Depression-era waitress who seeks escape from her dismal marriage to abusive hubby Danny Aiello by attending the local cinema night after night. One evening the unexpected occurs, when one of the characters starring in the present feature—"Tom Baxter, Explorer and Adventurer, on the verge of a madcap Manhattan weekend"—walks off the screen and into Mia's life, wherein a bittersweet love story unfolds. Among highlights, there's the ultra-naive Baxter (Jeff Daniels) stumbling into a cathouse, a sequence where he takes Mia back into the movie-within-the-movie for a night on the town, and a poignant finale. Farrow and Daniels both contribute shimmering, letter-perfect leading performances.

1985. 82m. DIR&WRIT: Woody Allen. CAST: Mia Farrow, Jeff Daniels, Danny Aiello, Dianne Wiest, Van Johnson, Zoe Caldwell, John Wood, Michael Tucker, Edward Herrmann.

QUICK CHANGE...

features one of the more ingenious bank heists in cinema, and for that alone is worth a look-see. But after the original success, the real trouble sets in, as our unlikely trio of bank robbers—Bill Murray, Geena Davis, and Randy Quaid—are incapable of finding an escape route out of New York City to

COMEDY WITH A HEART

JFK airport. Manhattan and its boroughs now become the leading players, making for an oft-hilarious 'anti-city' scenario, one which can be appreciated by anyone who has ever even thought about spending time in the Big Apple. Among highlights is Tony Shahoub's comic contribution as a non-English speaking cab driver who becomes intertwined in their troubles—just *what* language he is speaking is a matter of pure conjecture—and a spirited turn by Jason Robards as the police chief who is trying to crack the case. This quirky, entertaining comedy was Murray and screenwriter Howard Franklin's directorial debut, and should have presaged many more to follow. What about it, fellas?

1990. 89m. DIR: Bill Murray, Howard Franklin. WRIT: Howard Franklin. CAST: Bill Murray, Geena Davis, Randy Quaid, Jason Robards, Bob Elliot, Victor Argo, Kathryn Grody, Philip Bosco.

THE REF...

co-scripted by a woman, gives stand-up comedian Denis Leary the role of a lifetime. When a Christmas Eve robbery goes haywire, and police roadblocks prevent burglar Leary from making his getaway, he takes a married couple hostage in order to obtain temporary shelter. The pair whom Leary randomly chooses, Judy Davis and Kevin Spacey, are the dysfunctional couple from hell; these two people *never* stop bickering, to the considerable chagrin of their abductor. ("I went and hijacked my fucking parents.") When an obnoxious mother-in-law and company descend on the household, Leary plots his escape while masquerading as our scrapping couple's marriage counselor, thereby becoming their unofficial 'ref.' Superb comic turns from all four principals—including Richard Bright as Leary's dipsomaniacal partner-in-crime—and a surprisingly affective contribution from Robert Steinmiller as the lonely and neglected son, easily overcome a slightly haphazard storyline.

1994. 92m. DIR: Ned Demme. WRIT: Marie Weiss, Richard LaGravenese. CAST: Denis Leary, Judy Davis, Kevin Spacey, Richard Bright, Robert Steinmiller.

RUTHLESS PEOPLE...

stars Bette Midler as the brassy wife of Danny DeVito, a philandering, sleazeball of a garment tycoon. DeVito is busy planning his wife's demise with the help of mistress Anita Morris, when Judge Reinhold and Helen Slater save him the trouble by abducting Midler for ransom. But these hapless kidnappers—who are attempting to make DeVito pay for ripping off one of Slater's designs—are in real trouble if they expect him to hand over any money to get back his obnoxious wife. No matter how far they lower their ransom demand ("I've been kidnaped by K-Mart!" Midler bemoans), DeVito stands firm, leaving this most insufferable of hostages in Reinhold and Slater's wretched custody. Given no other choice, our three unhappy campers eventually join forces to plot retribution against DeVito. Revenge will be both ingenious and sweet.

1986. 93m. DIR: Jerry & David Zucker, Jim Abrahams. WRIT: Dale Lanner. CAST: Bette Midler, Danny DeVito, Judge Reinhold, Helen Slater, Anita Morris, Bill Pullman.

THE SEVEN YEAR ITCH...

plays with the axiom that after seven years of marriage, one or the other member of the partnership is bound to develop a wandering eye. When Tom Ewell's wife and son head to the lake during a blistering Manhattan summer, happily married hubby begins fantasizing about the oh-so-fetching newcomer upstairs, Marilyn Monroe. The resulting escapades take place largely inside our would-be philanderer's overheated imagination. (Ewell, conjuring up another 'frank' conversation with wife Evelyn Keyes: "What you don't realize, Helen, is this thing about women and me. I walk into a room and they sense it instantly. I arouse something in them. It's kind of an animal thing I've got. It's really quite extraordinary.") The under-used Ewell is in top form. Ditto for Monroe as the innocent who ultimately helps Ewell make sense of his marriage and his life. Rachmaninoff's Second Piano Concerto and the most famous subway grate in cinematic history are among the notable props in this classic farce from master director Billy Wilder.

1955. 105m. DIR: Billy Wilder. WRIT: George Axelrod, Billy Wilder. CAST: Tom Ewell, Marilyn Monroe, Evelyn Keyes, Sonny Tufts, Victor Moore, Robert Strauss, Oscar Holmolka.

SINGIN' IN THE RAIN...

co-scripted by a woman, is a musical satire of the era when Hollywood studios were making the awkward transition from silent films to sound. Gene Kelly stars as a cinematic heart-throb of the late twenties who has the misfortune of co-starring—in-the-film-within-our-film—with silent movie queen Jean Hagen, whose heretofore unheard screechy delivery is not going to cut it in the age of talkies. Donald O'Connor plays Kelly's former Burlesque partner, and Debbie Reynolds is the mellow warbler who will be dubbing Hagen's songs. The fact that the movie's titular centerpiece is the most famous song-and-dance number in cinema, shouldn't obscure the other great routines, in particular O'Connor's deliciously kinetic rendition of 'Make 'Em Laugh.' Special mention is due Reynolds for her amazing screen debut, holding her own along side her two seasoned co-stars every step of the way.

1952. 103m. DIR: Stanley Donen, Gene Kelly. WRIT: Betty Comden, Adolph Green. CAST: Gene Kelly, Donald O'Connor, Debbie Reynolds, Jean Hagen, Millard Mitchell, Cyd Charise.

SOAPDISH...

stars Sally Field in a wonderfully zany performance as an 'aging' soap opera diva struggling against falling ratings and a backstage plot to get her off the show. In an effort to jump-start the show's popularity, management decides to resurrect a character written out of the series via decapitation twenty years earlier. Enter Kevin Kline as Field's former co-star, as well as former lover, and all the fun begins. This is an example of comic ensemble acting at its finest, with everyone from Kline as the hammy has-been, to Whoopi Goldberg as the increasingly unhinged scriptwriter, to Cathy Moriarty as the conniving wanna-be, to Robert Downey Jr. as the sleazy producer, separately and in concert keeping this farce bubbling merrily along.

1991. 97m. DIR: Michael Hoffman. WRIT: Andrew Bergman, Robert Harling. CAST: Sally Field, Kevin Kline, Robert Downey, Jr., Cathy Moriarty, Whoopi Goldberg, Elizabeth Shue, Carrie Fisher, Garry Marshall, Teri Hatcher.

SOME LIKE IT HOT...

ace director Billy Wilder's greatest comedy, puts jazz musicians Jack Lemmon and Tony Curtis on the run from the mob after accidentally witnessing Chicago's 1929 St. Valentine's Day Massacre. With necessity being the mother of invention, our two desperados bluff their way out of a tight spot by masquerading as women, thereby getting work with an all-girl jazz band headed for a gig down in Miami. En route, they both fall hard for the ukulele-playing, booze-swilling lead singer, Marilyn Monroe. The train ride south is worth the rental fee alone. But there are countless other highlights, including Curtis playing a caricature of Cary Grant, George Raft and Pat O'Brian lampooning themselves, and last, but certainly not least, Joe E. Brown's contribution as the millionaire who is thoroughly smitten with Lemmon-in-drag. Which brings us to the movie's peerless closing line...

1959. 120m. B&W. DIR: Billy Wilder. WRIT: I.A.L. Diamond, Billy Wilder. CAST: Jack Lemmon, Tony Curtis, Marilyn Monroe, Joe E. Brown, George Raft, Pat O'Brien.

STARTING OVER...

stars Burt Reynolds in his best comic performance as a lonely and befuddled divorced fellow, still madly in love with ex-wife and aspiring singer-songwriter Candice Bergen. With support from older brother Charles Durning and sister-in-law Frances Sternhagen, he is making a game effort to begin anew. But it's a torturous affair until blind date Jill Clayburgh comes onto the scene. In spite of matters getting off to a hilariously disastrous start, the two are soon falling earnestly in love. Nothing is going to be easy, of course, especially when the gorgeous Bergen returns, wanting back into her marriage. (The song Candice warbles for ex-hubby is worth the rental fee alone.) Heartbreak, reconciliations, new and old loves ensue, leading up to a most satisfying finale.

1979. 106m. DIR: Alan J. Pakula. WRIT: James L. Brooks. CAST: Burt Reynolds, Jill Clayburgh, Candice Bergen, Charles Durning, Frances Sternhagen, Austin Pendleton, Mary Kay Place.

THE STING...

opens in Joliet, Illinois, where Robert Redford and fellow con man Robert Earl Jones are running a scam to defraud a local racketeer of a $5,000 delivery. They succeed all too well, unintentionally crossing paths with their victim's mob lord, Robert Shaw. In the process, Jones is killed, and Redford—who narrowly escapes—becomes obsessed with revenging his good buddy's death. Towards that end, he heads into Chicago to enlist the help of a man he has yet to meet, a character described by Jones as "the greatest con artist of them all." That would be Paul Newman, of course, who after a little friendly persuasion agrees to assist Redford in conceiving the ultimate sting, one which will fleece the nefarious Shaw of a literal fortune. This is one elaborate swindle, with the ultimate con job being played on us dupes in the audience. Special mention is due the magical pairing of Redford and Newman, nostalgia-steeped cinematography which convincingly evokes another time and place, and Marvin Hamlisch's buoyant adaptation of Scott Joplin's ragtime jazz.

1973. 129m. DIR: George Roy Hill. WRIT: David Ward. CAST: Robert Redford, Paul Newman, Robert Shaw, Eileen Brennan, Charles Durning, Ray Walston, Harold Gould.

STRANGER THAN PARADISE...

is an off-beat, slice-of-life classic starring John Lurie as an Americanized Hungarian who claims to hate his native country as much as he loves his new one. Yet, with no apparent irony, this fellow has embraced the worst features of American life, frittering away his days in a Brooklyn slum, sleeping, watching TV, and 'socializing' with equally clueless buddy Richard Edson. Enter Willie's sixteen-year-old cousin Eszter Balint, just off the plane from Hungary and needing to camp out for a few days. It's an awkward visit—she can't fathom what her older cousin is doing with his life—but a friendship of sorts evolves before the teenager heads west. Months later John and Richard drive to Cleveland for a visit with Eszter and aunt Cecilla Stark (the latter treating us to a show-stealing performance), at which point our three young gad-abouts opt for the traditional all-American road trip to Miami. But this isn't going to be a Florida you've ever seen before. To say that the dialogue is minimalist and their adventures stillborn would be an understatement. But once you adapt to the movie's spare, almost real-time rhythm, an ongoing inner chuckle is your reward. The inside joke for director Jarmusch, one suspects, is that his black-and-white cinematography and relentlessly drab locations look suspiciously like the barren Soviet bloc landscapes of the American imagination. *1984. 90m. DIR&WRIT: Jim Jarmusch. CAST: John Lurie, Richard Edson, Eszter Balint, Cecilla Stark.*

SWEET LIBERTY...

stars director/writer Alan Alda as a history professor who gets much too involved with the film crew shooting a movie based on his Pulitzer Prize-winning book. Alda's smug delight soon turns to dismay, when he realizes that screenwriter Bob Hoskins and director Saul Rubinek are intent on turning his high-brow entertainment into moronic trash. Enter Michelle Pfeiffer as the starring actress in the film-within-the-film who threatens to steal Alda's heart away, and a delightfully smarmy Michael Caine as her leading man. It's an occasionally aimless, but ultimately charming outing due to an ingratiating cast which includes Lise Hilboldt as the woman in Alda's life not so willing to stand waiting in the wings, and Lillian Gish as Alda's paranoid, invalid Mom.

1986. 107m. DIR&WRIT: Alan Alda. CAST: Alan Alda, Lise Hilboldt, Michelle Pfeiffer, Michael Caine, Bob Hoskins, Lillian Gish, Saul Rubinek.

THAT THING YOU DO!...

written and directed by Tom Hanks, is an entertainingly convincing movie about the world of '60s rock and roll. Tom Everett Scott stars as the jazz-loving, talented drummer who turns a struggling band around by pepping up their beat. When Playtone Records discovers the group, they are catapulted from playing pizza joints to the national touring route, while their titular hit song rides to the top of the charts. It's the straightforward story of four young men and a girl having the time of their lives with instant fame and fortune, until self-absorbed songwriter Jonathan Schaech rocks the boat by insisting on recording more of his own material. Among highlights, there is the magic moment when the group first hears their song on the radio, Scott meeting his jazz idol Del Paxton, and the group's rendition of the film's best song, 'Come On and Dance With Me Tonight.' Director Hanks elicits fine performances from the entire cast, with special mention due Scott's appealing leading contribution, and Steve Zahn's breezily comic take as the band's lead guitarist. Of note: the gorgeous cocktail waitress teasing Scott in a bar is Hank's real-life wife Rita Wilson.

1996. DIR&WRIT: Tom Hanks. CAST: Tom Everett Scott, Liv Tyler, Steve Zahn, Jonathan Schaech, Ethan Embry, Tom Hanks, Alex Rocco, Bill Cobbs, Rita Wilson, Chris Isaac, Kevin Pollack.

TO BE OR NOT TO BE...

the black-and-white original, is an amazing sleight-of-hand, managing to be an exuberant farce wrought from a most tragic subject. The year is 1939, and the place is Warsaw, where an idiosyncratic troupe of Polish actors, masquerading as Nazis, outwit Hitler and his storm troopers at the outbreak of WWII. Jack Benny, as 'that great, great actor Josef Tura,' gives his funniest screen performance. (A Nazi officer's assessment of Benny's acting ability: "What he did to Shakespeare, we are now doing to Poland.") Carole Lombard's comedic flair is also in full flower, in a film which was to be her last. Later in 1942, her plane crashed in the Sierra Nevada mountains en route from a War Bonds tour. In her memory, treat yourself to a genuine Lubitsch classic.

1942. 102m. B&W. DIR: Ernst Lubitsch. WRIT: Edwin Justus Mayer. CAST: Jack Benny, Carole Lombard, Robert Stack, Lionel Atwill, Felix Bressart, Sig Ruman.

TOOTSIE...

is a romantic comedy about a man who becomes a better man, for having been a woman. Dustin Hoffman stars as the unemployed actor who's so desperate for work, he auditions for a soap opera role disguised as the lady administrator they have in mind. When he actually lands the part, he is obliged to continue the charade for weeks on end, and the ongoing cross-dressing and gender-bending opens him up to an entirely new world of emotions and feelings. One problem, however, is 'Dorothy's' growing attraction to soap opera co-star Jessica Lange. Lange returns the affection in kind, but what's to become of their blossoming relationship when Lange learns that she is actually a *he*? Among highlights of this delightful scenario, there's 'Dorothy' flirting with talent agent Sydney Pollack at the Russian Tea Room, 'Dorothy' and Lange sharing girl talk before going to sleep, Bill Murray's wry comic contribution as Hoffman's roommate and in-house playwright, and Lange at her most luminous.

1982. 100m. DIR: Sydney Pollack. WRIT: Larry Gelbart, Murray Schisgal. CAST: Dustin Hoffman, Jessica Lange, Bill Murray, Dabney Coleman, Sydney Pollack, Estelle Getty, Geena Davis, Charles Durning, George Gaynes.

TOP HAT...

spotlights fabulous art deco sets, a plethora of exuberant musical numbers, and a nostalgically joyful scenario, making it easily Fred Astaire and Ginger Rodgers most memorable cinematic pairing. The story line of mistaken identities, predictably contrived and occasionally silly, opens with song-and-dance man Astaire falling hard for Rodgers, and vice versa. But Rodgers wrongly deduces that Astaire is her best friend Helen Broderick's husband and rebuffs his advances. When she flees to Venice with Helen, Astaire and Helen's 'real' husband Edward Everett Horton follow in hot pursuit. And now Ginger compounds the confusion by marrying her dress designer Erik Rhodes. But not to worry, since Horton's valet Eric Blore will save the day for all and sundry. Among highlights is Blore's comic contribution, Ginger and Fred gliding to 'Isn't It A Lovely Day?' and 'Cheek to Cheek,' and Fred's brilliant solo—which he himself choreographed—'Top Hat, White Tie and Tails.'

1935. 101m. B&W. DIR: Mark Sandrich. WRIT: Dwight Taylor, Allan Scott. COMP: Irving Berlin, Max Steiner. CAST: Ginger Rodgers, Fred Astaire, Edward Everett Horton, Helen Broderick, Eric Blore, Erik Rhodes.

A TOUCH OF CLASS...

stars Glenda Jackson as a reasonably content divorcée who meets married executive George Segal in a London park, bumps into him again when flagging down a cab, and without further ado agrees to a weekend rendezvous in Spain. The tryst threatens to become an unmitigated disaster when their escalating war-of-words explodes into a free-for-all wrestling match. But enmity quickly turns to amity, the weekend is saved, and what was to have been a brief, convenient affair evolves into something far more serious. The remainder of our story, however predictable, is carried off with convincing chemistry and panache by two of the wittiest in the business. One quibble: whatever happens to Jackson's two kids once she and Segal rent their pied-a-terre?

1973. 105m. DIR: Melvin Frank. WRIT: Jack Ross. CAST: Glenda Jackson, George Segal, Paul Sorvino, Hildegarde Neil.

TRUE LOVE...

co-written and directed by Nancy Savoca, explores the gender gulch with wry comic flair. You will detect more than a little irony in our film's title while following a Bronx couple and their respective families through the weeks between the couple's engagement and their impending marriage. It becomes increasingly apparent to everyone involved that these two should not be getting hitched, principally because the future groom is far too foot-loose and fancy free to settle down. (As a case in point, he wants to spend his honeymoon night hanging out at his favorite bar with the boys.) But the inexorable march toward premature matrimony seems oddly unstoppable. Savoca has succeeded remarkably well in bringing the real-life nuances of this Italian-American neighborhood to the screen, imbuing the film with an authentic, slice-of-life feel from start to finish. And Annabella Sciorra and Ron Eldard give solid leading performances as the young love birds headed for troubled waters through no fault of their own. It's all been written in the stars, as they say. Or in the differing orbits of their two planets.

1989. 104m. DIR: Nancy Savoca. WRIT: Nancy Savoca, Richard Guay. CAST: Annabella Sciorra, Ron Eldard, Aida Turturro, Roger Rignack, Star Jasper, Keely Cinnante.

WAY OUT WEST...

is a classic Laurel and Hardy comedy, featuring the duo journeying out to Brushwood Gulch to deliver the deed of a gold mine to the daughter of their deceased prospector pal. Getting there is half the fun, of course, but once they arrive in Brushwood, the villain of our piece, barkeep Finlayson, purposely directs them to the wrong girl. Quintessential Stan and Oliver predicaments ensue, with sight gags, slapstick, and witty repartee culminating in a bar duet and soft-shoe sequence that are bound to steal your heart away. Other highlights include Ollie forcing a weepy Stan to eat his own hat, and Ollie almost drowning in a shallow pond, time and again.

As Stan proudly reminds Ollie at one of their many problematic junctures: "Any bird can build a nest, but it isn't everyone who can lay an egg." This is the film to convert the uninitiated or unconvinced to L&H fanhood.

1937. 86m. B&W. DIR: James W. Horne. WRIT: Charles R. Roger, Felix Adler, James Parrott. CAST: Stan Laurel, Oliver Hardy, Rosina Lawrence, James Finlayson, Sharon Lynne, ZaSu Pitts.

WHAT ABOUT BOB?...

starts Richard Dreyfuss as a pompous psychiatrist and author of the best-selling self-help manual *Babysteps*, who is about to meet his Waterloo in the form of needy paranoid-neurotic patient, Bill Murray. ("Roses are Red, Violets are Blue, I'm a schizophrenic, And so am I.") Murray sees Dreyfuss as his savior—the one person who can cure him of his array of phobias. But it's August, and Dreyfuss and family have headed for the lake. Murray follows in quick pursuit and proceeds to endear himself to the wife and kids, while unintentionally driving Dreyfuss right over the edge. The ongoing joke milked to such perfection is that no matter how desperate and mean-spirited become Dreyfuss' attempts to get rid of Murray, our lovable neurotic assumes it's just another ingenious strategy in Doc's 'babysteps' approach.

1991. 99m. DIR: Frank Oz. WRIT: Tom Schulman, Alvin Sargent. CAST: Bill Murray, Richard Dreyfuss, Julie Hagerty, Charlie Korsmo, Fran Brill.

WINDOW TO PARIS...

is a charming, modern-day Russian fairy tale concerning a scuffling music teacher who moves into communal lodgings and discovers that the window in his small room opens directly onto the streets of the City of Light. The contrast between the sumptuousness of Paris and the desperation of post-Soviet Russia serves as the initial fascination—in particular the dizzying, euphoric reaction of our impoverished Muscovites to such opulence at every turn. But the story is far more poetic and profound than this opening gambit might suggest. Our protagonist quickly perceives that neither communism nor capitalism speaks to what is best in the human heart, and by staying true to himself, reminds us of the generous soul buried in us all. Among highlights are the magical dance segments, and Serguei Dontsov's whimsical leading performance.

1995. 92m. In Russian w/English Subtitles. DIR: Yuri Mamin. WRIT: Arkadi Tigai, Yuri Mamin. CAST: Serguei Dontsov, Agnes Soral, Victor Mekhailov, Nina Oussatova

A YEAR IN PROVENCE...

based on Peter Mayle's best-selling book, relates in comic fashion the true travails of an English couple who opt for early retirement, leaving behind the rat race of London to restore a 200-year-old 'fixer-upper' in southern France. What we are privy to on four 90 minute cassettes—each depicting one season of the year—are the droll, nigh-absurd adventures of forging a new life in a new country. There's a farmhouse which refuses to get renovated, as well as decidedly quirky neighbors, and an ongoing procession of English friends who use the place as their own private hotel. Permeating the entire scenario is the good food, drink, and sunshine of gorgeous Provence. At first glance, John Thaw seems too old for the part of Peter, and Lindsay Duncan too young. But they work so well together, the disparity in ages quickly becomes moot. You may decide to disregard the fourth cassette, really just a re-working of *The Baker's Wife*, and opt to see the sublime 1938 French original.

1989. 4 cassettes/90m. DIR: David Tucker. WRIT: Michael Sadler. CAST: John Thaw, Lindsay Duncan, Bernard Spiegel, Jean-Pierre Delage, Maryse Kuster, Louis Lyonnet.

HEARTBREAK HOTEL

*"I was born when you kissed me. I died when
you left me. I lived a few days while you loved me."*
Gloria Grahame to Humphrey Bogart,
IN A LONELY PLACE

*"I'll be everywhere—everywhere you look. Wherever
there's a fight so hungry people can eat, I'll be there.
Wherever there's a cop beatin' up a guy, I'll be there.
I'll be in the way guys yell when they're mad.
I'll be in the way kids laugh when they're hungry
and know their supper's ready. And when people
are eatin' the stuff that they raise, and livin' in the
homes they build, I'll be there, too."*
Henry Fonda in a final farewell
to his beloved mother Jane Darwell,
THE GRAPES OF WRATH

AFTERGLOW...

is quintessential Alan Rudolph—original, quirky, and poignant. Julie Christie and Nick Nolte co-star as a deeply estranged married couple, and although the root cause of their long-standing alienation is not revealed until midway through the film, their problems are surely exacerbated by Nolte's philandering disposition. Younger couple Jonny Lee Miller and Lara Flynn Boyle are having trouble as well, principally because Miller is a workaholic with no interest in committing to rearing a family, while Boyle desires a baby in the worst way. Re-enter Nolte as the builder whom Boyle engages, purportedly to construct a nursery in her home, but in reality to sire that much wanted child. Then Christie and Miller, who are both spying on their wayward spouses at Montreal's Ritz-Carlton hotel, meet and fancy one another enough to spend the weekend together. Sound contrived? Under Rudolph's crafty direction it all works quite naturally, and that includes the moment when our four principals simultaneously learn about their two intertwining liaisons. It's a foreseeably explosive, yet unexpectedly comic scene. The ultimate consequence of all this bed-hopping might well be redemption for all concerned. Or is it that easy? Our four leads give uniformly convincing performances, with Christie's wrenching contribution the undeniable highlight.

1997. 114m. DIR&WRIT: Alan Rudolph. CAST: Julie Christie, Nick Nolte, Jonny Lee Miller, Lara Flynn Boyle.

ALL THE WAY HOME...

a black-and-white American classic, is based on *A Death in The Family*, James Agee's moving account of how his mother and himself as a young boy struggled to cope with his father's accidental death. Amazingly enough, the film matches the power of the book, as it tackles the tragedy of premature death with visceral and heartfelt results. When the story opens, father Robert Preston is taking his eight-year-old son Rufus for an afternoon on the town, before returning to loving wife and mother Jean Simmons. The following day they are joined by Preston's parents and his brother's family for a momentous auto trip to Preston's grandmother, a shriveled old soul who feels re-born upon setting eyes on her great-grandson for the first time. That evening, Preston and Simmons make love, in a scene whose verbal foreplay is as tender as it comes, followed by a late-night phone call from Preston's inebriated brother, claiming that their father is dying. Preston has no choice but to drive over to his brother's funeral parlor and confirm his father's condition, at which point our tragedy unfolds. Preston and Simmons give equally commanding performances, he as the doting, strong-minded patriarch, and she as the young wife who has to cope with the sudden and irretrievable loss of her dearly beloved soul mate. Special mention is due Aline MacMahon's sympathetic contribution as Aunt Hannah, who sits out the long night with Simmons while they await news of Preston's fate.

1963. 97m. B&W. DIR: Alex Segal. WRIT: Philip Reisman. CAST: Jean Simmons, Robert Preston, Pat Hingle, Aline MacMahon, Thomas Chalmers, Michael Kearney.

AND THE BAND PLAYED ON...

is docu-drama at its finest, a gripping behind-the-scenes look at the race against time within both the French and American medical communities as they attempt to isolate the virus causing AIDS. It was a pursuit hampered by ignorance, one-upmanship, lack of funding, and frightful government neglect. (Among other salient details, we are reminded that President Reagan never uttered the 'A' word until 1987.) The scenario introduces us to several prominent scientists in both countries, as well as to key members of the gay community who lead the fight against and/or succumb to this relentless disease. Matthew Modine, as a dedicated investigator at CDC, heads a remarkably talented all-star cast which includes Alan Alda, Richard Gere, and Ian McKellan, among others. But this film doesn't rely on its star power. Screenwriter Arnold Schulman has fashioned a tragic spellbinder whose central

mystery remains unresolved to the present day. Among highlights is a particularly stirring finale.

*1993. 140m. DIR: Roger Spottiswoode. WRIT: Arnold Schulman. CAST:
Matthew Modine, Alan Alda, Ian McKellan, Saul Rubinek, Glenne
Headly, Richard Gere, Lily Tomlin, Richard Masur, Anjelica Houston,
Swoozie Kurtz.*

ANNA KARENINA...

Tolstoy's epic of forbidden love, has spawned many cinematic
interpretations over the years. We are recommending a made-
for-television production from the '80s starring Jacqueline
Bisset and Christopher Reeve. Bisset co-stars as the rebellious
Anna of our title, a married woman who defies the mores of
19th century Russian society by leaving her elderly husband
and child for the dashing calvary officer Count Vronsky.
Because her husband refuses to give her a divorce, remarriage
to Vronsky is impossible, leaving Anna in a perilous and
increasingly isolated situation. Due to the genuine vibes
between our two leads, it is no stretch to believe in the intensity of this couple's mutual passion, the 'original sin' whence
the remainder of the tragedy must unfold. Special mention is
due Paul Scofield's deeply nuanced performance as Anna's
abandoned spouse. Of note: considering the movie's length, a
champagne-caviar intermission might well be in order.

*1985. 150m. DIR: Simon Langton. CAST: Jacqueline Bisset, Christopher
Reeve, Paul Scofield, Ian Ogilvy, Anne Massey.*

AWAKENINGS...

broadly directed by Penny Marshall as is her wont, is the true
story of neurologist Dr. Oliver Sacks' 1969 experimental use
of the drug L-dopa at a Bronx mental hospital. He works his
magic in a ward commonly referred to as 'The Garden' due to
the autistic nature of the patients who reside there. The other
practitioners at the hospital are convinced these inmates are
nothing more than walking ghosts. Sacks believes otherwise
and, while researching his patients' medical histories, discov-

ers an intriguing shared ailment in their pasts which leads to the good doctor's 'cure.' There is a real poignancy to this film as we encounter a cast of characters who wake up middle-aged, only to realize that they have completely missed their youth. Accolades are due Robin Williams for his subdued performance, going completely against type as the shy and retiring neurologist. Ditto for Robert De Niro, as the patient aroused from an incredible thirty-year withdrawal to joyfully experience the grace and wonder of the world around him.

1990. 120m. DIR: Penny Marshall. WRIT: Steve Zaillian. CAST: Robin Williams, Robert De Niro, John Heard, Julie Kavner, Penelope Ann Miller, Max von Sydow, Steve Vinovich.

BIRD...

is the biography of saxophone genius Charlie Parker, the man who almost single-handedly revolutionized jazz in the 1940s with the creation of bebop. Due to director/writer Eastwood's decision to concentrate on Parker's lifelong battle with heroin, the audience plays witness to a messy, complicated life on screen. But from that first wrenching sequence in Parker's kitchen, we sense that Forest Whitaker *is* Bird, and Diana Verona matches him scene for scene as his beleaguered, ever-loyal common-law wife. The action moves in flashbacks through his hard-fought rise to fame, to his brief but brilliant reign as the leader of the most influential group in jazz, and onto his heartbreaking decline. The story is punctuated by Parker's frequent, ultimately futile attempts to kick the drug habit destined to kill him at age thirty-four. (The coroner on the scene at his death thought he was over sixty.) This is no doubt the best jazz-orientated film to date, with Charlie Parker's own improvised solos—his soaring, searing, distinctive sound—serving as its heart and soul. Because of the film's length and generally somber tone, an intermission comes recommended.

1988. 160m. DIR: Clint Eastwood. WRIT: Clint Eastwood, Joel Oliansky. CAST: Forest Whitaker, Diane Verona, Michael Zelniker, Samuel E. Wright, Keith David.

BREAKFAST AT TIFFANY'S...

showcases a most affecting finale—that cat, that rain, those two lost souls who finally break through the layers of pride, illusion, and miscues to fall into each other's lives. Audrey Hepburn is the very embodiment of Holly Golightly, the rural hick-turned-mod-Manhattanite who is out to bag herself the richest husband those gorgeous brown eyes can buy. She is, of course, far more vulnerable than her chic exterior might suggest. (Or to paraphrase agent Martin Balsam summing up her personality: "She's a phony, alright. But a *real* phony.") Which might explain why, in spite of all intentions to the contrary, Holly finds herself falling for her handsome new neighbor, impoverished and 'kept' aspiring novelist George Peppard, at his most congenial. Aside from being a memorable love story, the scenario features excellent contributions from the supporting cast, including a sizzling Patricia Neal as Peppard's patroness, a poignant Buddy Ebsen as Holly's bewildered hillbilly ex-husband, and, in a perverse bit of casting, Mickey Rooney as Holly's 'Japanese' upstairs neighbor. George Axelrod's adaptation of Truman Capote's novella is faithfully and sturdily wrought, and Henry Mancini's world famous 'Moon River' serves as its beguilingly bittersweet leitmotif.

1961. 115m. DIR: Blake Edwards. WRIT: George Axelrod. CAST: Audrey Hepburn, George Peppard, Patricia Neal, Buddy Ebsen, Martin Balsam, John McGiver.

BREAKER MORANT...

takes place during the turn-of-the-century Boer War and is all the more tragic for being based on true events. Three Australian soldiers, stationed in South Africa to assist the British fight against the rebelling Dutch colonialists, are court-martialed for following orders which dictated that they execute all enemy prisoners. Unfortunately, one of these murdered prisoners was a German fighting for the Boer cause, and the powers-that-be back in England, anxious to maintain good relations with Germany, opt to make scapegoats out of the Australians. The scenario is shown in flashback as this riveting courtroom drama unfolds, with us in the audience turned into the unwitting jury. Expect fine acting throughout, highlighted by Edward Woodward and Bryan Brown's penetrating leading performances.

1980. 107m. DIR: Bruce Beresford. WRIT: Bruce Beresford, Jonathan Hardy, David Stevens. CAST: Edward Woodward, Bryan Brown, Jack Thompson, John Waters, Rod Mullinar, Lewis Fitz-Gerald, Charles Tingwell.

THE BRIDGES OF MADISON COUNTY...

a tale of middle-aged passion based on the famous best-seller, vastly improves on the original by telling the story from the perspective of forty-five-year-old Italian-American housewife Francesca, and by enlarging on the roles of the two grown children who return to Iowa for a reading of their mother's will. To their initial chagrin, the sister and brother learn via diaries that Mom had a profoundly erotic four-day love affair some thirty years back, when the kids and their father were off at a county fair. Extended flashbacks reveal how Francesca and globe-trotting National Geographic photographer Robert Kincaid first meet and over the course of the next few days fall deeply in love. This is a highly charged romantic tale, driven by the exquisitely genuine performances of our two leads, Meryl Streep and Clint Eastwood. Streep becomes a veritable schoolgirl before our eyes as she experiences the breathless wonder of falling in love for the first time in her life, while Eastwood has never displayed such raw vulnerability on screen. (The scene where he stands in the pouring rain, telepathing to Streep all the love in his heart and soul, is priceless.) Honorable mention is due Richard LaGravenese's script for allowing Francesca's character the moxie to encourage each phase of the affair, an evocative musical score highlighted by Lennie Neihaus & Eastwood's haunting 'Bridges' theme song, and Ella Fitzgerald and Johnny Hartman's smoky renditions of many romantic blues classics. That sprawling farm kitchen is apt to linger in your mind's eye long after the final credits.

1996. 135m. DIR: Clint Eastwood. WRIT: Richard LaGravenese. CAST: Meryl Streep, Clint Eastwood, Ann Corley, Victor Slezak, Jim Haynie.

BRIEF ENCOUNTER...

is a gracefully crafted scenario concerning two people who, against all intentions, find themselves falling in love. Trevor Howard and Celia Johnson co-star as the doctor and house-wife, both relatively happy in marriages to others, who meet at a train station one fateful afternoon. As coincidence would have it, Celia comes into London every Thursday to do her weekly shopping, while Thursday is the one day of the week Trevor works in a city hospital. Theretofore, one chance encounter evolves into a series of weekly rendezvous, and a casual friendship ripens into a bittersweet, compassionate romance. Special mention is due the excellent performances from our leading players, as well as Cyril Raymond's contri-bution as Celia's stodgy yet somehow lovable mate. The film's Rachmaninoff musical score is used to great advantage.

1945. 86m. B&W. DIR: David Lean. WRIT: Noel Coward, David Lean, Anthony Havelock-Allan. CAST: Celia Johnson, Trevor Howard, Cyril Raymond, Stanley Holloway, Joyce Carey, Everley Gregg.

CAMELOT...

is a rare Hollywood musical for boasting a genuine dramatic conflict, one which pulsates with human pathos and compas-sion. It's a proverbial love triangle set to Lerner & Loewe's musical score and steeped in the mythical history of King Arthur's court. Richard Harris stars as the 12th century English monarch ('I Wonder What The King Is Doing Tonight?'), whose restless young wife Guinevere, played by a radiant Vanessa Redgrave ('The Lusty Month Of May'), falls hard for the dashing Sir Lancelot ('If Ever I Would Leave You.'). It doesn't hurt this flick any that Redgrave and Franco Nero as Lancelot had a love affair during and after produc-tion, their mutual vibes translating palpably to the silver screen. But the last word is certainly due Harris' affecting contribution as the sovereign who strives to bring peace to war-torn Europe, while remaining fathomless on how to control the wiles of his own wandering spouse. ('How To Handle A Woman?')

1967. 150m. DIR: Joshua Logan. WRIT: Alan Jay Lerner. COMP: Frederick Loewe. CAST: Richard Harris, Vanessa Redgrave, Franco Nero, David Hemmings, Lionel Jeffries.

CAMILA...

written and directed by a woman (who made her directorial debut four years earlier at age 58!), is based on a tragically true story. Camila, a young woman from a 19th century family of Buenos Aires aristocrats, makes the mistake of falling in love with, and seducing, the handsome local Jesuit priest. He's an initially reluctant, then passionate conquest, and the two young lovers run off to attempt the impossible: making an independent life for themselves in the Argentinian outback. Conservative government authorities afford one obstacle to lasting connubial bliss, and the ex-priest's deep and abiding love for his Church—and guilt for having abandoned it—affords the other. The film depicts its love story in a quietly beautiful yet powerfully erotic manner that is heightened by the stirring performances of the two leads.

1984. 121m. In Spanish w/English Subtitles. DIR&WRIT: Maria-Luisa Bemberg. CAST: Susu Pecoraro, Imanol Arias, Hector Alterio, Elena Tasisto.

CARMEN...

based upon Bizet's opera of passion and jealousy and set among a modern-day troupe of flamenco dancers, is a unique and exhilarating collaboration between director Carlos Saura and choreographer Antonio Gades. Gades himself stars as the dashing dance instructor in search of his ideal Carmen, whom he finds in the person of twenty-one-year-old dancer Laura Del Sol. In the process of tutoring the young woman for the part, life imitates art and our Latin Pygmalion falls passionately in love with his firebrand Galatea—a situation which is further complicated when her ex-lover appears on the scene. The film interweaves performance with 'reality' as dress rehearsals dissolve into 'real life,' and 'actual' fights become choreographed rumbles, until the thin line between fact and fiction goes up in fire and smoke. The supercharged duets danced by Gades and Del Sol are the movie's erotic highlights. *1983. 102m. In Spanish w/English Subtitles. DIR: Carlos Saura. CHOR: Antonio Gades. CAST: Antonio Gades, Laura Del Sol, Paco DeLucia, Christina Hoyes.*

CHARLY...

an arresting amalgam of sentimentalized documentary, romance, science fiction, and social drama, is the story of a severely retarded man who becomes the object of a series of scientific experiments. It's all done in the best of intentions, of course. Via a brain operation, our medical researchers hope to duplicate the miracle they wrought on the lab mouse they've turned into a veritable prodigy, capable of running intricate mazes at the drop of a hat. When the surgery appears to be a success, caseworker Claire Bloom is brought in as Charly's tutor, giving all that manifest intelligence discipline and form. As she progresses, there seems to be no limit to how high Charly's brilliance will soar. And that is the fascination to this scenario—watching a mentally impaired young man credibly evolve into genius. Ultimately, however, everyone is flying a little too close to the sun. Cliff Robertson gives one of his more intriguing performances in the title role. *1968. 103m. DIR: Ralph Nelson. WRIT: Sterling Silliphant. CAST: Cliff Robertson, Claire Bloom, Lilla Skala, Leon Janney, Dick Van Patten, William Dwyer.*

THE CHRISTMAS WIFE...

scripted by a woman, stars Jason Robards as a recently widowed gentleman who can't tolerate the idea of spending his first holiday season alone. To remedy the situation, he goes to an escort agency and rents himself a temporary wife. Twenty-four hours of good company is all he is requesting; no connubial bliss, simply conversation and companionship to stave off the holiday blues. Julie Harris is the hired hand who reluctantly accommodates Robard's wishes, under one ironclad condition: no questions may be asked about her personal life. The action takes place over the course of Christmas Eve and Christmas Day, which underscores both the poignancy of our story and the sense of mystery surrounding Harris' situation. It's an eloquently quiet scenario, well acted by two old pros. *1988. 73m. DIR: David Jones. WRIT: Katherine Ann Jones. CAST: Jason Robards, Julie Harris, Don Francks.*

CITY LIGHTS...

stars Charlie Chaplin as the 'Little Tramp,' who, despite the abuse of rich and poor alike, manages to maintain his dignity and abiding infatuation for the world around him. Like all of Chaplin's silent masterworks, the scenario is essentially a love story, this time around Charlie falling hard for the blind flower girl in his neighborhood, Virginia Cherrill. He proceeds to do everything possible, from shoveling manure to entering boxing matches, to help Cherrill and her grandmother pay their rent. Enter Hank Mann as the alcoholic millionaire whom Chaplin befriends, hoping to exploit the man's wealth for funds toward an eye operation for his beloved flower girl. (A running gag used to great effect is that our wealthy dipsomaniac can only recognize Chaplin when he's drunk, never when he's sober.) Charlie's triumphs and failures in his amorous and altruistic quests make for a grand tragicomedy, perfectly encapsulated by the film's final image. *1931. 86m. B&W. DIR&WRIT: Charlie Chaplin. CAST: Charlie Chaplin, Virginia Cherrill, Florence Lee, Hank Mann, Harry Myers.*

CYRANO DE BERGERAC...

Edmond Rostand's celebrated play turned into film, is loosely based on the heroics of an authentic 17th century poet and swordsman, a champion of the poor and censor of the corrupt on high who had the misfortune of possessing an oversized

nose. In this 1990 French production, Gerard Depardieu is utterly convincing as our rabble-rousing gallant. There are many subplots, but the central story revolves around Cyrano's hopeless passion for his beautiful cousin Roxanne, who in turn pines for the handsomer, if decidedly less brilliant Christian. As an exercise in vicarious courtship, Cyrano agrees to become Christian's romantic counselor, ghost-writing eloquent love letters to Roxanne which his rival signs in his stead. Roxanne falls in love with Christian, believing him to be the author of these passionate missives, with bittersweet consequences. Special mention is due novelist Anthony Burgess' lyrical English subtitles.
1990. 138m. In French w/English Subtitles. DIR: Jean-Paul Rappeneau. WRIT: Jean-Paul Rappeneau, Jean-Claude Carriere. CAST: Gerard Depardieu, Anne Brochet, Vincent Perez, Jacques Weber, Roland Bertin.

DANCES WITH WOLVES...

Kevin Costner's amazing directorial debut, shames the countless narrow-minded, racist westerns which came before it. Costner himself stars as a disillusioned Union officer who—as our story opens—is brought to a makeshift army hospital to have his mutilated foot amputated. But he escapes before the operation takes place, makes a suicidal ride into Confederate lines, miraculously survives the charge, and becomes an instant war hero with his choice of future assignments. He opts for an isolated post on the frontier of the Dakotas, hoping to see a bit of the 'Wild West' before it entirely disappears. And now the heart of the scenario unfolds, as the lieutenant sets up shop on a remote stretch of prairie and gradually befriends his only neighbors, a tribe of Lakota Sioux Indians. In the process, Costner goes native with a vengeance and experiences a spiritual and psychological conversion which transforms him into the title character. Among highlights of this carefully observed and visually stunning epic, is the delicate love story which develops between Costner and Mary McDonnell, the white woman who has lived with the

Sioux tribe ever since her family was killed many years before. There is also Graham Greene's typically knowing and wry contribution as the Sioux chief, as well as magnificent cinematography from Dean Semler and a lovely musical score from ace composer John Barry. The film's final sequence, reminding us of the natural beauty and humanity sacrificed to 'white man's destiny,' is as wrenching as they come. Of note: the longer, 237-minute 'director's cut' is not the selection herein reviewed.

1990. 183m. In English and Lakota Sioux w/English Subtitles. DIR: Kevin Costner. WRIT: Michael Blake. CAST: Kevin Costner, Graham Greene, Mary McDonnell, Rodney A. Grant, Floyd Red Crow Westerman, Tantoo Cardinal, Robert Pastorelli.

DEAD MAN WALKING...

based on the autobiographical memoirs of Louisiana nun Helen Prejan, is the story of one woman's introduction to the hellish world of Death Row. At the request of condemned inmate Matthew Poncelet, Prejean helps the young man file a last minute appeal. But in so doing, she stirs up the wrath of the parents of the two teenagers he brutally raped and murdered. And now Prejean attempts the seemingly impossible: to understand and empathize with both the sick and tortured person who committed the crime, and the shattered families who must forever live with the horror of their loved ones' deaths. It is an anguishing journey she undertakes, full of contradictions, complexities, and deep sorrow. But Prejean never stops struggling to reach that part of Poncelet—long buried in the anger and hate of his own impoverished upbringing—where the human heart resides. In the process, she helps him to find a grace in death he never found in life. While Susan Sarandon is outstanding as our heroine, it is Sean Penn who delivers the performance of a lifetime as the cynical, embittered soul who ultimately attains redemption.

1995. 122m. DIR&WRIT: Tim Robbins. CAST: Susan Sarandon, Sean Penn, Robert Prosky, Raymond Berry, Celia Weston, R. Lee Erney, Mary Beth Percy, Scott Wilson.

E.T.—THE EXTRA-TERRESTRIAL...

scripted by a woman, tells the story of an endearing, limpid-eyed alien who is accidentally abandoned by his spaceship crew on Planet Earth. Trapped in the bewildering world of suburban America, with threatening two-legged hunters chasing him down, the diminutive E.T. is given shelter by ten-year-old Henry Thomas. While hiding out in Thomas' home, our lovable alien struggles with the inscrutable oddities of modern-day Earth—telephones, TVs, beer cans—while establishing a profound telepathic bond with his resourceful guardian. But despite his new-found friendship, E.T. is so homesick he will surely perish unless he is returned to his own planet ASAP. The race against time and big-wig military types is fraught with chills, thrills, and a most touching finale.

1982. 115m. DIR: Steven Spielberg. WRIT: Melissa Mathison. CAST: Henry Thomas, Dee Wallace, Peter Coyote, Robert MacNaughton, Drew Barrymore.

AN EARLY FROST...

was the first TV drama to deal with the AIDS crisis and has held up extremely well with the passage of time. As our story opens, part-time piano teacher Gena Rowlands and lumber-yard proprietor Ben Gazzara are enjoying a loving, long-term marriage, made all the more satisfying by the success of their two grown-up children. But their middle-class, provincial existence is about to meet the ultimate challenge, when beloved son Aidan Quinn discloses to his family that he has AIDS, when they don't even know that he is gay. Quinn is excellent in the difficult leading role, with veterans Rowlands and Gazzara giving able support as his distraught and perplexed parents. Special mention is due John Glover's performance as the lonely but persevering fellow-AIDS patient whom Quinn belatedly befriends. As might be expected, the film is emotion-packed, aided and abetted by a solid, unsentimental script.

1985. 97m. DIR: John Erman. WRIT: Ron Cowan, Daniel Lipman. CAST: Aidan Quinn, Gena Rowlands, Ben Gazzara, John Glover, D.W. Moffett, Sylvia Sydney.

THE ELEPHANT MAN...

is based on the heartbreakingly true story of one John Merrick, the victim of a childhood disease which left him so hideously deformed that he spent the greater part of his life as a sideshow freak. He eventually is 'saved' by a Dr. Frederick Treves, who wishes to study him and towards that end hides him away in a ward of his hospital. While under Treves' care, an intelligent, sweet, and introspective soul is allowed to emerge from its crusty shell, wherein our 'elephant man' becomes a darling/oddity of Victorian society. The film is occasionally tough viewing, particularly the opening sequences with Merrick under the control of his brutish carny, Freddie Jones. But John Hurt is nothing short of magnificent in the leading role, capable of conveying deep-felt emotions merely through his lisp of a voice and the subtle carriage of his encased body. Special mention is due Anthony Hopkins' typically shaded performance as the doctor who gives Merrick his first taste of human dignity, as well as the arresting black-and-white cinematography which so aptly reflects the shadowy underside of turn-of-the-century London.

1980. 125m. B&W. DIR: David Lynch. WRIT: Christopher DeVore, Eric Bergren, David Lynch. CAST: John Hurt, Anthony Hopkins, Anne Bancroft, John Gielgud, Wendy Hiller, Freddie Jones

GHOST...

stars Patrick Swayze as a murdered investment consultant whose spirit struggles to reconnect with lover Demi Moore, so as to warn her of impending danger from unlikely sources. But try as he might, Moore remains out of his psychic reach. Not so for 'medium' Whoopi Goldberg, whom Swayze enlists as his go-between. Whoopi is a hoot as a fake clairvoyant completely baffled by her sudden ability to connect with 'the other side.' And her kinetic performance is a necessary bless-

ing for a romantic thriller which seeks to entertain on one too many levels. (i.e. The true climax of this film does not come with the resolution of the crime, but at the cathartic moment when Swayze is given one last chance to hold true love Moore in his arms.) Don't miss those sensual potter's wheel sequences early on. Demi knows how to handle that clay!
1990. 127m. DIR: Jerry Zucker. WRIT: Bruce Joel Rubin. CAST: Patrick Swayze, Demi Moore, Whoopi Goldberg, Tony Goldwyn, Rick Aviles.

GOODBYE AGAIN...

based on Françoise Sagan's high-class soaper *Aimez-Vous Brahms?*, comes recommended for the Ingrid Bergman fans among us. Bergman stars as a forty-something interior decorator in love with the very wrong man, a handsome and debonair Yves Montand who is as unfaithful as they come. The couple has an understanding of sorts; he enjoys the occasional fling with a pretty young thing, and she is given no choice but to 'understand.' Anthony Perkins enters as the callow, if lovable puppy dog of a suitor, smitten with Bergman in spite of—or perhaps because of—the fact that she is fifteen years his senior. Flattered and touched by his attentions, as well as being emotionally drained from Montand's habitual philandering, Bergman slips into the foreseeable affair with decidedly mixed results. An added plus to this scenario is its Parisian backdrop.
1961. 120m. B&W. DIR: Anatole Litvak. WRIT: Samuel Taylor. CAST: Ingrid Bergman, Yves Montand, Anthony Perkins, Jesse Royce Landis, Diahann Carroll.

GRAPES OF WRATH...

based on John Steinbeck's classic novel, is melodrama at its most anguishing, while recounting the odyssey of the thousands of 'Okies' who fell victim to the 1930s Dust Bowl. This national tragedy is told up-close-and-personal by concentrating on the travails of the extended Joad family, who are leaving their foreclosed family farm for the promise of a better future further west. Unfortunately, the flyer which falls into Pa Joad's hands, advertising ample employment in the California vineyards, is the same deceptive hand bill which has enticed countless other refugees to travel to the Golden State. Instead of work, the Joads find over-crowded migrant camps, managed by harsh 'law' officers. But although physically displaced and economically bereft, the Joad family—in the person of Henry Fonda as older brother Tom, and Jane Darwell as his stalwart mother—come to embody an abiding faith in our country's future. This story of poor, decent people struggling for dignity against overwhelming odds brims over with unforgettable moments of drama and compassion, highlighted by Fonda's soul-searching leading performance. Special mention is due Gregg Toland's black-and-white cinematography, his use of available light and documentary techniques making for a stark and moving vision of Depression-era America.

1940. 129m. B&W. DIR: John Ford. WRIT: Nunnally Johnson. CAST: Henry Fonda, Jane Darwell, John Carradine, Charley Grapewin, Dorris Bowdon, Russell Simpson.

HEARTSOUNDS...

scripted by a woman and based on Martha Lear's non-fiction bestseller, is an unflinching account of a loving marriage torn asunder by the husband's heart attack, his follow-up double-bypass surgery, and its four-year aftermath. Mary Tyler Moore and James Garner co-star as the couple who must deal together and separately with a patriarchal medical system which arrogantly insists on talking down to its patients. (As the wife points out in mounting frustration: "It's always *your* fault, never theirs!") In explicit detail, the film portrays the harrowing wake of heart failure: the fever, the chills, the coughing spells and memory loss, up to one particularly horrific night when Garner almost drowns in his own lung fluids because nurses are afraid to wake up a sleeping intern.

Although occasionally grueling, the scenario is ultimately a most affective love story, featuring memorable performances from two actors at the top of their craft.
1984. 135m. DIR: Glenn Jordan. WRIT: Fay Kanin. CAST: Mary Tyler Moore, James Garner, Sam Wanaker, Wendy Crewson, David Garner, Carl Marotte.

HOWARDS END...

is another illustrious Merchant-Ivory production based on an E.M. Forster novel. The story takes place in the dying days of Edwardian England, a time when the homes people owned still served as essential reflections of who they were. And so it is with the sumptuous country manor which has been in Ruth Wilcox's upper-class family for generations, an estate which both defines the dying matriarch and gives her refuge from her husband's crowded London life. After her death, her husband and daughter are dismayed to find that she has bequeathed the ancestral home to a woman friend they barely know, and an emancipated middle-class 'spinster,' at that. And so they selfishly decide to keep Howards End for themselves. But time has a way of rectifying past grievances, and in its own ingenious way justice will be served. Class struggles, rapacity, deceit, love, and honor all play equal parts in what is ultimately the tragic confluence of three families from London's various social strata. Special mention is due the luminous performances from Vanessa Redgrave as Mrs. Wilcox and Emma Thompson as her younger beneficiary.
1992. 140m. DIR: James Ivory. WRIT: Ruth Prawer Jhabvala. CAST: Vanessa Redgrave, Emma Thompson, Helena Bonham Carter, Anthony Hopkins, Sam West, Prunella Scales, Joseph Bennett.

IN A LONELY PLACE...

is a brooding film noir which features one of Humphrey Bogart's finest dramatic performances, both chilling and complex, as a hard-drinking, belligerent Hollywood screenwriter. One evening he brings hat-check girl Martha Stewart back to his bungalow—purportedly so she can summarize the potboiler which he has been assigned to turn into film—and new neighbor Gloria Grahame observes them from across the courtyard. The next morning, Stewart's disfigured dead body is found by Los Angeles police, and our screenwriter, thought to have been the last person to see her alive, is brought in for questioning. When the detectives come calling at his apartment complex, the comely Grahame gives Bogie the much needed alibi. His curiosity and appreciation for her inexplicable assistance spark a passionate, if difficult love affair. In spite of an uncharacteristically corny opening vignette, it's both a moody and moving scenario, made all the more effective by Grahame's genuinely sensual performance and the startling chemistry between our two leads. Honors also go to Burnett Guffey's ravishing black-and-white cinematography. *1950. 94m. B&W. DIR: Nicholas Ray. WRIT: Andrew Solt. CAST: Humphrey Bogart, Gloria Grahame, Frank Lovejoy, Carl Benton Reid, Art Smith, Jeff Donnell.*

INTERMEZZO...

soars on the heartrending contributions from its two co-stars, Ingrid Bergman as the talented young piano teacher, and Leslie Howard as the married concert violinist whose child she is tutoring. Against their better judgment, the two slip into an adulterous affair, with bittersweet, and, by today's standards, slightly dated results. Although this was Bergman's first English-speaking film, her warmly infectious performance eclipses that of the seasoned Howard, undoubtedly because this is a remake of the original Swedish version which catapulted her to stardom in her native land. The emotional impact of the film is aided and abetted by the passionate and pervasive Robert Henning-Heinz Provost love theme, and by the great violinist Jascha Heifetz' behind-the-scenes dubbing of Howard's performance sequences. *1939. 70m. B&W. DIR: Gregory Ratoff. WRIT: George O'Neill. CAST: Ingrid Bergman, Leslie Howard, Cecil Kellaway, Edna Best, Ann Todd.*

IT'S MY PARTY...

is a love story which deals trenchantly with the AIDS crisis. Eric Roberts and Greg Harrison co-star as two people who care deeply for one another until Roberts tests HIV positive. Harrison proves incapable of dealing with the situation and within a few months has asked his stricken lover to move out. One year later Roberts is diagnosed with AIDS-related PML, a fast-moving cerebral lesion which will almost certainly leave him brain-dead within a matter of days. Roberts has witnessed the grisly, incontinent fate of others dying of PML and opts for a more dignified exit, deciding on an overdose as his modus operandi, with a 24-hour farewell party to precede his suicide. The stellar cast of family and friends who gather around Roberts to help him celebrate his final hours includes Marlee Maitlin and Olivia Newton-John as his two sisters, Lee Grant as his loving Greek-American mom, George Segal as his estranged alcoholic father, and Margaret Cho as the only friend who understands how important it is for Roberts and Harrison to reconcile before Roberts take his leave. Considering the subject matter, it's an amazingly entertaining film, with special mention due Roberts' powerhouse leading performance.

1996. 109m. DIR&WRIT: Randal Kleiser. CAST: Eric Roberts, Greg Harrison, Margaret Cho, Lee Grant, Bronson Pichot, Marlee Maitlin, Roddy McDowell, Olivia Newton-John, Bruce Davidson, George Segal, Paul Regina, Ron Glass.

KRAMER VS. KRAMER...

opens with wife and mother Meryl Streep desperate for a respite from a marriage which is so unsatisfying, it is emotionally drowning her. The main source of her discontent is hubby Dustin Hoffman, a self-absorbed workaholic who spends little if any quality time with his wife and their six-year-old son Justin Henry. All that's about to change when Streep takes a hike from this sorry situation in the hopes of 'finding herself,' leaving our ambitious Ad exec to care for the boy he hardly even knows. (The first morning Dustin takes his son to school, he has to ask him what grade he is in.) Over the weeks and months to follow, Hoffman learns to care deeply for his son, with his high-rolling business career suffering accordingly. Then Streep returns to Manhattan, wanting young Justin back in her life, and an excruciating custody battle ensues. There is no doubt that the film is a set-up, as evidenced in the bias of a trial which conveniently passes over how truly absent Hoffman was as a parent before his wife's sabbatical. But the acting is uniformly superb, including a surprisingly moving performance from young Henry, turning what could have been standard fare into a compassionate study of the familial ties which forever bind us. The increasingly tender scenes between Hoffman and his son are indelible highlights.

1979. 105m. DIR&WRIT: Robert Benton. CAST: Dustin Hoffman, Meryl Streep, Justin Henry, Jane Alexander, Howard Duff, George Coe, JoBeth Williams.

LE GRAND CHEMIN...

based on director Hubert's own childhood experience, is the story of a seriously estranged married couple who are blessed with the miracle of redemption and reconciliation during the summer that the wife's nephew comes to stay at their farm. The young boy's presence at first heightens the bitterness between our two principals, then via crisis brings them back together in a manner not soon to be forgotten. The scenario stands as a powerful reminder that where love once walked the earth, it may well walk again. Of note: that is the director's own son playing the young interloper who unwittingly transforms this couple's lives.

1987. 107m. In French w/English Subtitles. DIR&WRIT: Jean-Loup Hubert. CAST: Christine Pascal, Richard Bohringer, Antoine Hubert, Vanessa Guiedj.

A LONG DAY'S JOURNEY INTO NIGHT...

presents 24 hours in the life of a tragically dysfunctional family; four people who are hopelessly entangled in a web of jealousy, resentment, and guilt, with an indomitable glimmer of love shining through every wrenching scene. Based on the autobiographical play by Eugene O'Neill, who insisted that it not be premiered until after his death, the film offers four performers the dramatic roles of a lifetime. Katharine Hepburn is the lonely, morphine-addicted matriarch ("One day, long ago, I could no longer call my soul my own."), Ralph Richardson is her philandering miser of a husband, Jason Robards is the drunkard roustabout older son, and Dean Stockwell rounds out this quartet as the incipient poet who has just been diagnosed with consumption. Hepburn, in her finest dramatic performance, is nothing short of devastating. It's an extended cinematic outing, as the film is close to three hours long, but once settled in, you can expect a great night at a small theater.

1962. 174m. DIR: Sidney Lumet. WRIT: Eugene O'Neill. CAST: Katharine Hepburn, Ralph Richardson, Jason Robards, Dean Stockwell.

LONGTIME COMPANION...

is the euphemism commonly employed by newspaper obits when referring to the surviving half of a gay relationship. Credit this Hollywood production for giving the AIDS epidemic a human face, as we follow a close-knit group of Manhattan gays and a common woman friend throughout the travails of the eighties, the decade in which the magnitude of the AIDS crisis became painfully evident to America and the world at large. Early mystifying reports of a 'gay cancer' give way to puzzling medical evaluations, leading up to the realization that a new and devastating plague is in our midst. Craig Lucas' script is both insightful and heart wrenching, as well as being slightly cornball upon occasion. Among highlights is everyone's excitement at witnessing the first openly gay kiss on daytime TV, and uniformly convincing performances from our ensemble cast.

1990. 100m. DIR: Norman Rene. WRIT: Craig Lucas. CAST: Campbell Scott, Bruce Davison, Stephen Caffrey, Patrick Cassidy, Brian Cousins, Mary-Louise Parker, John Dosset, Mark Lamos, Dermot Mulroney, Michael Schoeffling.

LOVE LETTERS...

scripted and directed by a woman, stars Jamie Lee Curtis as a public radio disc jockey whose beloved mother dies of cancer, leaving the twenty-two-year-old to cope alone with a self-pitying alcoholic father whom she appears to loathe. When sifting through her deceased mother's belongings, she stumbles across a box of old love letters which, to her astonishment, document her mother's longstanding passionate affair with a man she obviously cherished. Curtis doesn't condemn her mother's secret liaison; on the contrary, she romanticizes it to the extent of falling into an adulterous relationship of her own with married photographer James Keach. The longer her affair with Keach proceeds, and the more often she re-reads her mother's letters, the more she identifies with the man who wrote them. Ultimately, she decides to take action in ways her mother's ex-lover did not. Fireworks, revelations, and a lot of growing up ensues.

1984. 98m. DIR&WRIT: Amy Jones. CAST: Jamie Lee Curtis, James Keach, Amy Madigan, Matt Clark.

LOVE MATTERS...

tells the story of two very troubled marriages as they chaotically converge one fateful weekend. The story opens with an extended glimpse into the lives of Griffin Dunne and Annette O'Toole as their relationship approaches that awkward crossroads where love may still be in the offing, but the passionate spark has all but disappeared. At this point our couple receives an inopportune late night visit from hubby's best friend Tony Goldwyn, squiring sexy new mistress Gina Gershon and announcing his plans to divorce wife Kate Burton. The havoc these X-rated lovebirds wreak on O'Toole and Dunne's faltering rapport is predictably devastating. But more is happening in this movie than first meets the eye, and as the weekend progresses, surprises await all and sundry. Special mention is due Burton's performance as the anguished, abandoned wife.

1993. 97m. DIR&WRIT: Ed Lottimer. CAST: Griffin Dunne, Annette O'Toole, Tony Goldwyn, Gina Gershon, Kate Burton.

THE MAN IN THE MOON...

scripted by a woman, is an incisive coming-of-age tale set in rural Louisiana of the 1950s. Fourteen-year-old tomboy Reese Witherspoon is beginning to wonder if she will ever grow up, and in particular, if she will ever blossom into the beautiful, sought-after young woman her older sister Emily Warfield has become. Our adolescent heroine is at the dawn of her sexual awakenings, awhirl with unfamiliar sensations and nowhere to focus them until the new boy moves in next door. But handsome newcomer Jason London is three years her senior and more interested in Older Sis. There are several love stories at work in this film, not the least of them being the deep and abiding affections between the two sisters—a mutual devotion which must survive unexpected tragedy. The beautifully understated scenario is given added appeal by the talents of the supporting adult cast.

1991. 100m. DIR: Robert Mulligan. WRIT: Jenny Wingfield. CAST: Reese Witherspoon, Emily Warfield, Jason London, Tess Harper, Sam Waterston, Gail Strickland.

MY LIFE...

might easily have slipped into melodrama without Michael Keaton's deft starring performance, managing to parry the thin line between poignancy and soap opera throughout. He plays a successful public relations exec and confirmed workaholic who learns he is dying of cancer at the very moment wife Nicole Kidman becomes pregnant with their first child. Not assured that he is even going to be alive for the birth, Keaton spends much of his final months videotaping himself, elaborating on his background and family, while offering his unborn son a lot of tongue-and-cheek parental advice. The ultimate goal, of course, is to introduce his child to the father he might never meet. But the very act of videotaping, as well as his numerous visits to acupuncturist Haing S. Ngor, together and separately serve as catalysts for Keaton to work through many unresolved conflicts in his life. All plot devices to the contrary, this is essentially a film about the art of living, with the art of dying getting the last word. Or as Ngor advises Keaton: "The final second of your life is the most important of all. It is everything you are, everything you ever said or ever thought, all rolled into one. There is the secret of your life. Until that last moment, you still have time, you can change everything."

1993. 114m. DIR&WRIT: Bruce Joel Rubin. CAST: Michael Keaton, Nicole Kidman, Haing S. Ngor, Bradley Whitford, Queen Laftifah.

ON THE BEACH...

anticipated later apocalyptic films such as *Testament* and *The Day After* by almost thirty years, and in our opinion remains the best of the lot. Based on the novel by Nevil Shute, the film opens after a devastating nuclear war has rendered the planet inhabitable save for the continent of Australia, where a group of survivors have amassed. But it's a tortuous waiting game they are playing, since it is only a matter of months before Australia too will be buried under the clouds of deadly radiation. Gregory Peck and Ava Gardner head the stellar cast as two very lonely people who start up an affair out of desperation, only to fall desperately in love. Despite the dire circumstances, there is a warm, uplifting edge to their story. Not so, alas, for Anthony Perkins' compelling portrayal of a man attempting to cope with the impending enforced suicide of his wife, his baby daughter, and himself, when every nerve in his body tells him their lives have only just begun. Fred Astaire, in his first non-dancing role as a scientist and erstwhile speedway driver, is strong indeed. The variations on the Australian ballad 'Waltzing Matilda' serve as an effective emotional counterpoint throughout.

1959. 135m. B&W. DIR: Stanley Kramer. WRIT: John Paxton. CAST: Gregory Peck, Ava Gardner, Anthony Perkins, Fred Astaire, Donna Anderson.

PASCALI'S ISLAND...

is set on the exotic Greek isle of Simi in the year 1908, when the Turkish empire is on the brink of collapse. Ben Kingsley is the low-level Turkish bureaucrat and occasional spy who is forever scribbling off missives to his superiors in Istanbul concerning suspicious activities on the island. He is convinced of an incipient rebellion, but his communications go unheeded, perhaps even unread. Charles Dance is the dashing mystery man who has come to the island to attempt an archeological dig—or so he claims—and convinces Kingsley to act as his mediator with the island's Turkish regent. In the process, the two slip into a wary alliance where danger looms, as does romance between Dance and Australian expatriate Helen Mirren, a painter who is involved in her own furtive activities on this isle. This is a beautifully crafted story of three people whose lives become tragically intertwined.

1988. 106m. DIR&WRIT: James Deardon. CAST: Ben Kingsley, Charles Dance, Helen Mirren, Sheila Allen, Vernon Dobtcheff.

PHILADELPHIA...

based on a true story, works on two dovetailing levels, both as a tense courtroom drama and as a chronicle of a dying man. Tom Hanks stars as the rising young attorney of a high-powered law firm, about to be fired when superiors discover he has AIDS. The irony of his situation, predictable but effective, is that Hanks can't find another lawyer willing to take on his case of unjust dismissal until homophobic ambulance-chaser Denzel Washington agrees to litigate, purely for the money and exposure it will afford him. Among highlights, there's the subtle treatment of Washington's change of heart vis-a-vis his client, the scenes between Hanks and Mom Joanne Woodward, and a theme song by Bruce Springsteen, 'Streets of Philadelphia,' which brings home the extent of the AIDS tragedy with understated eloquence. Hanks' affecting leading performance vouches for his amazing versatility on the silver screen.

1994. 119m. DIR: Jonathan Demme. WRIT: Ron Nyswaner. CAST: Tom Hanks, Denzel Washington, Mary Steenburgen, Jason Robards, Charles Glenn, Antonio Banderas, Joanne Woodward.

THE PIANO...

directed and written by Jane Campion, gives us a distinctly woman's point of view on the question of eroticism and desire. The scenario also boasts leading characters, a setting, and a storyline which are all as singular as they come. Holly Hunter stars as a 19th century Scottish woman of imposing intelligence who also happens to be mute. ("I have not spoken since I was six years old. Nobody knows why, least of all myself. This is not the sound of my voice; it is the sound of my mind.") As the story opens, our heroine is sailing with daughter Anna Paquin to New Zealand for an arranged marriage with taciturn farmer Sam Neill. Against all odds, she has also managed to ship her piano to these bleak foreign shores. It is an act of necessity, not of luxury, since playing the instrument is both her spiritual salvation and a means of communicating her emotional landscapes to the outside world. But the indifferent Neill refuses to have the piano hauled to his inland farm, preferring to leave it stranded on the beach. Enter Harvey Keitel as a former whaler turned Maori convert, who trades a piece of land for the piano and then arranges for Hunter to give him piano lessons in his hut. In the process, a most unusual and increasingly mutual seduction takes wing, Keitel offering to sell the piano back to Hunter key by ivory key, in exchange for sensual/sexual 'favors.' It's an intense and original scenario portraying both the triumphs and tragedies a grand passion can beget. Special mention is due Paquin's supporting performance as her mother's young interpreter, carrying the majority of the film's lines with audacious panache, and for Hunter's remarkable executions at that piano. (She was a concert-pianist-in-training in her youth.)
1993. 120m. DIR&WRIT: Jane Campion. CAST: Holly Hunter, Harvey Keitel, Anna Paquin, Sam Neill, Kerry Walker, Genevieve Lemon.

THE PRINCE OF TIDES...

co-scripted by a woman, stands as Barbra Streisand's second successful directorial outing. It's the lovingly fashioned, if oft-harrowing story of a dysfunctional South Carolinian family, whose dark secrets are gradually revealed as grown-up twins Nick Nolte and Melinda Dillon—both undergoing consultation with Manhattan psychiatrist Streisand—come to terms with their tragic upbringing. Technically Nolte isn't one of Streisand's patients; he has come to New York to help the good doctor reconstruct the fragmented mirror of his suicidal sister's past. And that is how the script deals with the question of doctor-patient ethics when Nolte and Streisand fall passionately in love. Nolte gives one of his finest screen performance as an aimless, unhappily married man, on the verge of leaving his family when he gets the SOS call to fly north. Appearances to the contrary, psychiatrist Streisand isn't faring any better, suffering through a bitter marriage with philandering virtuoso-violinist Jeroen Krabbé and contending with a rebellious teenaged son. There will be a lot of healing going on, both in and out of that psychiatrist office, this particular love affair offering our two principals new leases on lives destined to be lived with other people than each other.

1991. 132m. DIR: Barbra Streisand. WRIT: Pat Conroy, Becky Johnston. CAST: Nick Nolte, Barbra Streisand, Blythe Danner, Kate Nelligan, Jeroen Krabbé, Melinda Dillon, George Carlin, Jason Gould.

RED SHOE DIARIES...

stars a pre-*X-files* David Duchovny as a man trying to make sense out of his beloved fiancée's suicide. When he unearths her secret journal, we go backward in time to be introduced to girlfriend Bridgette Bako, a comely young lady who is suffering from an embarrassment of riches. In spite of being inside a sexy and satisfying relationship with Duchovny, when she encounters handsome stranger Billy Wirth—a working-class hunk who appears to be everything her boyfriend is not—she steps over the edge, red shoes and all, taking us into a sexual netherworld perhaps best experienced vicariously from our living room sofas. The film's conflict arises when our so-called hunk turns into a genuine person with genuine needs; what Bako had intended as a casual fling, he wants to turn into the real thing. The scenario is raw and erotic, but unlike the many mediocre 'Red Shoe' sequels, this selection sports a credible story and very decent performances. *1992. 105m. DIR&WRIT: Zalman King. CAST: Bridgette Bako, David Duchovny, Billy Wirth, Brenda Vacarro.*

THE REMAINS OF THE DAY...

scripted by Ruth Prawer Jhabvala, is a variation on the 'Upstairs/Downstairs' theme graced by the elegant Merchant-Ivory touch. Anthony Hopkins stars as the repressed, fiercely loyal butler of Nazi sympathizer Lord Darrington (James Fox), who in the years prior to WWII hosts a series of 'diplomatic' conferences with the idea of establishing a separate peace between England and Germany. It's amateurish meddling which will soon have Darrington labeled a dangerous traitor, yet our butler appears to have no idea what his employer is up to. Hopkins' hermetic veneer cracks ever so slightly under the influence of Darrington Hall's new housekeeper Emma Thompson, whereby a subtle, wordless romance begins germinating. But Hopkins' stubborn refusal—his seeming inability—to reach out with any intimacy toward Thompson gives her little choice but to leave Darrington for a marriage proposal elsewhere. This is all told in flashback, the film opening when an older Hopkins is beginning a car trip across England, in the hopes of convincing Thompson to return to Darrington Hall to serve under its new owner, retired American congressman Christopher Reeve. Highlights include an exquisitely opulent setting, a literate, well-wrought screenplay, and excellent contributions from our two leads. *1993. 135m. DIR: James Ivory. WRIT: Ruth Prawer Jhabvala. CAST: Anthony Hopkins, Emma Thompson, James Fox, Christopher Reeve, Peter Vaugh, Hugh Grant, Tim Piggot-Smith.*

ROOM AT THE TOP...

offers a grim picture of class differences in England's industrial north, circa 1950. Laurence Harvey stars as the slumbred opportunist determined to leave his working-class origins far behind him. When he takes work as a government accountant in a town dominated by self-made millionaire Donald Wolfit, our anti-hero quickly sets his cap for the powerful man's teen-age daughter Heather Sears. But Pop knows exactly what Harvey is up to and sends his daughter off to the Continent until her passions can cool. In the meantime, Harvey falls genuinely in love with unhappily married Simone Signoret, and their scenes together become the film's highlight. All too soon, Harvey will be obliged to make the classic choice between love and money. Will it be Signoret's knowing sensuality or Sears' virginal, if gilded callowness? This particular 'room at the top' might give a man everything he could ever wish for, while obliging him to sacrifice the one thing he truly desires. Harvey and Signoret's performances are equally sublime.

1959. 115m. B&W. DIR: Jack Clayton. WRIT: Neil Paterson. CAST: Laurence Harvey, Simone Signoret, Heather Sears, Hermione Baddeley, Anthony Eigar, Donald Wolfit, Allen Culbertson.

SHADOWLANDS...

is based on the true life story of American poet Joy Gresham, who traveled to England in the 1950s to pay homage to celebrated author, theologian, and Oxford don C.S. Lewis. Her presence is a pleasant if disturbing distraction for Lewis and his brother, who have been living the comfortable, clubby bachelor life for decades. Neither of them, nor any of their male colleagues, know quite what to do with this 'brassy' female in their midst. In time, however, if with some trepidation, Lewis offers Joy a marriage of convenience so that she and her son may remain legally in England. And it is only now, slowly and subtly, that a lasting passion is born between them, the two falling deeply in love just as Joy is diagnosed with bone cancer. Stirring shadowlands ensue. Although

Debra Winger's New York accent is irregular at best, both she and Anthony Hopkins give excellent leading performances in this complex and poignant film.

1993. 130m. DIR: Richard Attenborough. WRIT: William Nicholson. CAST: Debra Winger, Anthony Hopkins, Edward Hardwicke, Joseph Mazzello, John Wood.

SOPHIE'S CHOICE...

co-stars two of our finest actors—Meryl Streep and Kevin Kline—in a love story for the ages, exuberant and devastating by turn. Based on William Styron's autobiographical novel, it is the tale of an Auschwitz concentration camp survivor who is still deeply haunted by her past when she settles in postwar Brooklyn and falls in love with a high-spirited charmer whose soul turns out to be as tortured as her own. Events unfold through the eyes of young narrator Peter MacNicol, an aspiring novelist who has moved into the rooming house where the troubled lovers reside. They adopt him as a comrade-in-arms, unintentionally introducing him to an emotional kaleidoscope of highs and lows heretofore imagined only in his wildest dreams and nightmares. Be forewarned that the flashbacks to the camp, wherein we learn the significance of 'Sophie's choice,' are bone-chilling.

1982. 157m. DIR&WRIT: Alan Pakula. CAST: Meryl Streep, Kevin Kline, Peter MacNicol, Rita Karin, Stephen Neuman, Josh Mostel.

A STREETCAR NAMED DESIRE...

can be tough, claustrophobic theater, as we watch the brutally savage Stanley Kowalski deliberately strip his sister-in-law of whatever flimsy hold she still has on her sanity, making her mental meltdown complete. But the 1951 adaptation of playwright Tennessee William's classic, starring Vivien Leigh and Marlon Brando, is not to be missed. As the story opens, thirty-something widow Blanche Dubois has just been fired from her present teaching position and arrives on her sister Stella's doorstep looking for temporary refuge. But this New Orleans tenement is going to be no port-in-the-storm for our embattled heroine. Her brother-in-law, who is every bit her opposite, distrusts her from the onset, fearing the effect which her genteel airs might have on his friendship with poker-playing buddy Mitch, and more importantly, on his marriage to the much desired, if abused Stella. And so he digs into Blanche's past, eventually exposing her as a promiscuous waif. Ironically, but oh-so-rightfully, it is not Blanche's, but rather Stanley's own sadistic actions which will lead to the destruction of everything he holds near and dear. In the starring roles, Leigh as Blanche is the very embodiment of unraveling magnificence, while Brando's Stanley is such a convincing mix of physical threat and sexual potency, that we have no doubt where this story is leading from the first moment he appears with Leigh on screen.

1951. 125m. B&W. DIR: Elia Kazan. WRIT: Tennessee Williams, Oscar Saul. CAST: Vivien Leigh, Marlon Brando, Kim Stanley, Karl Malden, Rudy Bond, Nick Dennis.

TABLE FOR FIVE...

features a wrenching performance from leading man Jon Voight as a divorced, former golf pro who still carries a serious torch for ex-wife Millie Perkins. She left him five years earlier for all the right reasons, and is now happily married to Richard Crenna, who is both a loving husband and a devoted stepfather to Perkins and Voight's three children. As our story opens, Voight has just put himself deeply in debt in order to take his kids on a lavish Mediterranean cruise. It's all part of a ruse to prove to his ex-wife he has become a changed man. But she knows better and begs him not to give their children false hopes. ("You can take them to the Pyramids. Let Richard take them to the dentist.") The trip starts off on a predictably sour note; in truth, Voight has never spent more than a few days with his kids in the past four years and barely knows how to communicate with them anymore. Then tragedy strikes on the home front, and Voight and Crenna are obliged to work through very painful decisions concerning the future of the children. The acting is uniformly excellent, with special mention due Marie-Christine Barrault's sympathetic contribution as Voight's helpmate through an emotional shipwreck, and Crenna for his steady, understated portrayal of a man who stands to lose everything he loves through no fault of his own. The on-location settings on the luxury liner, with brief lay-overs in Italy, Greece, and Egypt, are predictably resplendent. Of note: the title of the film will take on varying nuances as the scenario unfolds.

1983. 120m. DIR: Robert Liebman. WRIT: David Seltzer. CAST: Jon Voight, Richard Crenna, Marie-Christine Barrault, Millie Perkins, Robbie Kiger, Roxanna Zal, Son Hoang Bui.

TERMS OF ENDEARMENT...

is a film about two equally remarkable women who also happen to be mother and daughter, and the ebb and flow of their relationship over ten years' time. Shirley MacLaine is the mother, a widow who hasn't slept with a man since her husband's death many years before. Debra Winger is the daughter who marries feckless English professor Jeff Daniels as a means of putting distance between herself and her overbearing mom. After a brief and revealing prologue, this high-quality soap opera moves from Winger's wedding—an event that in protest MacLaine doesn't even attend—to the newlyweds' move to Iowa, through the birth of Winger's three children, and the predictable deterioration of her marriage when hubby finds the grass greener elsewhere. Back in Texas, MacLaine is dealing with the trauma of turning fifty and becoming a grandmother, while taking a vain stab at romance with playboy ex-astronaut Jack Nicholson. The two stories intermittently converge via countless long-distance phone calls and Winger's occasional visits to Texas, before an agonizing medical crisis ushers in the five-hankie finale. MacLaine received the Oscar for her contribution, but this is Winger's movie, as she brings a remarkable authenticity to her role, inhabiting the character from start to finish. A caveat to the script is its vaguely denigrating approach to the single-working-girl.

1983. 132m. DIR&WRIT: James L. Brooks. CAST: Debra Winger, Shirley MacLaine, Jeff Daniels, Jack Nicholson, Danny DeVito.

TRULY, MADLY, DEEPLY...

is a poignant examination of grief and mourning, and how it can leave us emotionally adrift. Leading lady Juliet Stevenson has prematurely lost lover Alan Rickman to the Grim Reaper and is finding it impossible to get on with the task of living. When he suddenly reenters her life—phantom-wise—her joy is without measure. The kink in the program is that he can never again be a part of her 'real' world, the one lived outside the four walls of her apartment. Another wrinkle comes in the form of his ghostly comrades, who lust after her video player and hang out night after night watching their favorite flicks. Our heroine must eventually come around to the painful yet inevitable denouement, which the film conveys via an eloquent passage from Pablo Neruda:

Forgive me, if you are not living,
You my beloved who have died.
All the leaving will fall on my breast,
It will rain on my soul all night, all day.
My feet will want to march the way you are sleeping,
But I will go on living
For I must...

Co-stars Stevenson and Rickman are superbly convincing in the leading roles.

1991. 107m. DIR&WRIT: Anthony Minghella. CAST: Juliet Stevenson, Alan Rickman, Bill Paterson, Michael Maloney, Christopher Rozychi, Keith Bartlett, David Ryall, Stella Maris.

VALMONT...

manages to be far more erotic and involving than the earlier *Dangerous Liaisons*. And chief credit for this distinction must go to co-stars Annette Bening and Colin Firth, both of whom possess a rare blend of thespian expertise and sizzling sensuality which makes for powerful cinema. The story itself is a devilish one. In the year 1782, two members of the French aristocracy entertain themselves by way of a heartless game of sexual one-upmanship, in which they seduce and undo the lives of selected innocent bystanders. Meg Tilly is one of their victims, as is the distressingly young Fairuza Balk. No winner will emerge from their cruel, if tantalizing diversions. The ultimate loser may be too easy to divine. Special mention is due Bening's oh-so-sweetly devious persona.

1989. 137m. DIR: Milos Forman. WRIT: Jean-Claude Carriere. CAST: Colin Firth, Annette Bening, Meg Tilly, Sian Phillips, Fairuza Balk.

THE WAY WE WERE...

charts a romance buffeted by class and political differences over the span of twenty years. Robert Redford plays the quintessential all-American ("In a way, he was like the country he lived in. Everything came too easy for him."), who against all indications falls in love with Jewish working-class radical Barbra Streisand, a woman for whom things never come easy at all. After a brief prologue, the movie flashes back to the college days of 1937, then on to 1944 Manhattan, when and where the two meet again to fall in love and marry. The next chapter joins our couple's loving albeit tumultuous life together in Hollywood, where Redford is writing for the movies. And the film's finale treats us to a most poignant 1950s postscript. Our co-stars work tenderly and genuinely together, which is why the love scenes are the finest in the film. Special mention is due the splendid theme song, music by the ubiquitous Marvin Hamlisch, lyrics by Marilyn and Alan Bergman, as sung by the remarkable Ms. Streisand.

1973. 118m. DIR: Sydney Pollack. WRIT: Arthur Laurents, Alvin Sargent. CAST: Barbra Streisand, Robert Redford, Bradford Dittman, Lois Chiles, James Woods, Patrick O'Neal.

WEST SIDE STORY...

opens with aerial panning shots portraying Manhattan as a series of geometric patterns. Then the camera zooms into one particular neighborhood, suggesting that of all the fascinating stories New York could provide, you're about to see *this* one. Thus begins this groundbreaking musical update of

Romeo and Juliet, a tragic tale of the mounting rivalry between two New York City street gangs—a rivalry brought into sharp relief by the impossible romance between Tony, a member of the Anglo Jets, and the beautiful Maria, whose brother is the kingpin of the Puerto Rican Sharks. Among musical highlights, there's the Jets' hot 'Cool,' Tony's tender riff on 'Maria,' and Rita Moreno's sassy 'America.' The supporting cast, in particular the fiery Moreno and the positively pantherine George Chakiris, are terrific. On the other hand, leads Natalie Wood and Richard Beymer, dubbed by Marni Nixon and Jim Bryant, are blatantly miscast. The fact that this significant deficit doesn't sabotage the film speaks for the magnificent Leonard Bernstein and Stephen Sondhein musical score, and the jazzy choreography of Jerome Robbins.

1961. 151m. DIR: Robert Wise, Jerome Robbins. WRIT: Ernest Lehman. COMP: Leonard Bernstein, Stephen Sondheim. CAST: Natalie Wood, Richard Beymer, Rita Moreno, George Chakiris, Russ Tamblyn, Tucker Smith, Tony Mordente.

WHAT HAPPENED WAS...

an independent bare-bones feature, is one of the more searing chronicles of a first date on celluloid. Co-stars Karen Sillas and Tom Noonan are relative unknowns, which is one of the pleasures of this film—we've never met these people before. The scenario all takes place in Sillas' apartment, as she returns from work and heads directly to her answering machine, then on to the refrigerator for some white wine. There are no messages on her machine, but there *is* that bottle of Chardonnay, which she sips to ease jangled nerves while trying on numerous wardrobe options for the big date. Sillas is perfectly cast as everywoman wanting that something more in her life; ideally a partner to share it with. ("At one point, guys just stopped asking me out. I don't know if it was my age, or I gave off this serious vibe. But just when I started to have something interesting to say, nobody wanted to hear it.") Noonan is equally suited as a thirty-something, self-doubting man. ("It seems like something broke in me a long time ago.") The dinner rendezvous has an utterly credible rhythm,

as our pair circle hesitantly around each other's expectations and needs, leading up to the confessional finale.
1993. 91m. DIR&WRIT: Tom Noonan. CAST: Karen Sillas, Tom Noonan.

WHOSE LIFE IS IT, ANYWAY?...

based on Brian Clark's right-to-die play brought successfully to both the London and New York stage, is brought just as successfully to the silver screen due to Richard Dreyfuss' verbally energetic performance. Dreyfuss stars as a talented young sculptor who is paralyzed from the neck down by a horrific car accident. Kept alive by injections, drugs, machines, and often humiliating around-the-clock care from the hospital staff, the quadriplegic chooses to battle institutional authorities for his legal right to die with dignity. (Or, as Dreyfuss points out to his doctor, Christine Lahti: "As far as I'm concerned, I'm already dead.") All indications to the contrary, this is not as downbeat a scenario as one might expect. Black humor abounds, as does sterling supporting contributions from Lahti, and John Cassevetes as the hospital's chief-of-staff.
1981. 118m. DIR: John Badham. WRIT: Brian Clark, Reginald Rose. CAST: Richard Dreyfuss, Christine Lahti, John Cassevetes, Bob Balaban, Kenneth McMillan, Khaki Hunter, Janet Eilber.

WUTHERING HEIGHTS...

recounts the ill-fated love between the daughter of an early 19th century Yorkshire family and the urchin of a young boy whom the father takes into their home and raises as his own. Cathy and the orphaned Heathcliff form an immediate and profound bond, becoming inseparable soul mates while playing at their whimsical, imaginary games. Cathy's brother Hindley, on the other hand, harbors a guttural and obsessive jealousy for the newcomer. Years pass, and their father dies, whereupon Hindley becomes master of the domain and promptly orders Heathcliff to move into their stables. A further wedge is placed between Heathcliff and Cathy when she begins to be courted by upper crust neighbor Edgar Linton. Feeling increasingly betrayed by the woman who had pledged him her undying love, Heathcliff flees Wuthering Heights for destinations unknown. The despondent Cathy marries Edgar, only to have her beloved return, having amassed a large enough fortune to wreak his own brand of vengeance on all and sundry. William Wyler's deliberate direction force-fully captures both the madness and ferocity inherent to Emily Bronte's gothic romance classic. Highlights include one of Laurence Olivier's more memorable performances as the tortured Heathcliff, and appropriately brooding cine-matography from cameraman Gregg Toland.

1939. 103m. B&W. DIR: William Wyler. WRIT: Ben Hecht, Charles MacArthur. CAST: Laurence Olivier, Merle Oberon, David Niven, Donald Crisp, Flora Robson, Hugh Williams, Geraldine Fitzgerald, Leo G. Carroll, Cecil Humphreys, Miles Mander.

YANKS...

focuses on the chaotic effect legions of American soldiers had on British communities during WWII, when thousands of young and restless men were billeted throughout the coun-tryside awaiting action on the continent. Within this context, the film examines two parallel love stories. The first involves G.I. Richard Gere and the lovely Lisa Eichhorn, whose boyfriend happens to be off fighting on the European front. And as much as her parents come to appreciate the ingratiat-ing young American, their loyalties understandably lie with their daughter's fiancé. Eichborn, on the other hand, is con-siderably less certain where her loyalties belong. The film's second romance, more knowing and less equivocal, is between Gere's superior William Devane and married war-effort vol-unteer Vanessa Redgrave. All four leads contribute genuine, empathetic performances which convincingly reflect the pro-found uncertainties of those times.

1979. 139m. DIR: John Schlesinger. WRIT: Colin Welland, Walter Bernstein. CAST: Richard Gere, Lisa Eichhorn, William Devane, Vanessa Redgrave, Rachel Roberts, Chick Vennera.

TIMELESS TALES
WELL TOLD

*"My idea has always been if we could bring
the mothers of the various nations together, then there
would be no more war."*
Vanessa Redgrave to Emma Thompson,
HOWARDS END

"Fasten your seat belts, it's going to be a bumpy night."
Bette Davis to assembled guests,
before a predictably turbulent soiree,
ALL ABOUT EVE

ALL ABOUT EVE...

is writer/director Mankiewicz's masterwork, a tour-de-force of wit and sophistication that by Hollywood standards has never been bettered. In the voice-over technique used throughout, unctuous drama critic George Sanders sets the stage: "To those of you who do not read, attend the theater, listen to unsponsored radio programs, or know anything of the world in which you live, it is perhaps necessary to introduce myself. My name is Addison DeWitt." His urbanely barbed observations acquaint us with the principal players, in particular with Eve Harrington, whose meteoric rise to the top of the theater world leaves plenty of bloody tracks in her wake. Anne Baxter plays our up-and-comer to Machiavellian perfection, as she inveigles her way into an entourage of Broadway veterans in order to launch her career. But as good as Baxter is, this is unquestionably Bette Davis' movie, her portrayal of first lady of the stage Margo Channing running the gamut from impeccable comic timing one moment to heartrending vulnerability the next. The supporting roles are carried off with equal panache, including a sprightly cameo by newcomer Marilyn Monroe.
1950. 138m. B&W. DIR&WRIT: Joseph Mankiewicz. CAST: Bette Davis, Anne Baxter, George Sanders, Gary Merrill, Celeste Holm, Hugh Marlowe, Thelma Ritter, Marilyn Monroe.

ALWAYS...

opens on the Friday evening that our melancholy couple is about to sign their divorce papers, after five years of marriage and two years of separation. But the notary brought in to legalize the proceedings comprehends just how much these two still care for one another and refuses to countersign until Monday morning, insisting that they use this Fourth-of-July weekend to reconsider. What follows is director Henry Jaglom's affectionate rendition of the break-up of his marriage to former wife Patrice Townsend, as their relationship is critiqued, dissected, and evaluated amongst the family and friends who join the couple to celebrate the holiday weekend. Jaglom and Townsend play themselves in the movie, which makes for some stilted moments in the opening scenes. But the directing and acting wax steadily more accomplished, affording us a probing look into the mysterious forces which can bring two people together, and just as effectively work in tearing them apart.

1985. 105m. DIR&WRIT: Henry Jaglom. CAST: Henry Jaglom, Patrice Townsend, Bob Rafelson, Melissa Leo, Andre Gregory, Michael Emil.

AMADEUS...

director Forman's triumphant adaptation of scenarist Shaffer's Broadway hit, focuses on the all-consuming jealousy which 18th century composer Antonio Salieri felt for his divinely gifted contemporary, Wolfgang Amadeus Mozart. The movie opens in a mental institution where Salieri is recounting his life story to a priest. Forthwith, we are swept back thirty years to the late 1700s and the palaces of Hapsburg Emperor Joseph II, when and where the exuberant twenty-six-year-old Mozart is about to perform. Salieri himself—as the Emperor's court composer—plays witness to the musical brilliance of this boorish young man, and his envy is visceral and immediate. 'Why should this buffoon be blessed with such dazzling talent and not *I*?' is the question that bedevils Salieri over the next three years, as he plots his nemesis' demise. It's an unusually sumptuous period piece which uses its location setting of Prague to great advantage. But far more than mere spectacle, this film is a thoughtful and entertaining meditation on genius and madness, greatness and mediocrity, ingenuousness and guilt. The vivid performances from co-stars Tom Hulce and F. Murray Abraham are further enhanced by Mozart himself, who posthumously has given us one of the greatest movie soundtracks of all time.

1984. 158m. DIR: Milos Forman. WRIT: Peter Shaffer. CAST: F. Murray Abraham, Tom Hulce, Jeffrey Jones, Elizabeth Berridge, Roy Dotrice.

AND BABY MAKES SIX...

scripted by a woman, co-stars Colleen Dewhurst as a middle-aged mother of five who unexpectedly gets pregnant and to the shock of the entire family chooses to keep the baby. Dismay gradually gives way to acceptance for all but hubby Warren Oates, who is frankly outraged by his wife's unilateral decision. After twenty five years of raising and supporting a family, he's anticipating life without the kids around, reveling in the proverbial sailing-around-the-world fantasies which are decidedly out-of-synch with the responsibilities of raising still another child. It is a rawly honest dilemma which this once happily married couple now face, with no easy solution in sight. Strong performances by leading players Dewhurst and Oates give the film its depth. Watch for Timothy Hutton in his film debut.

1979. 104m. DIR: Waris Hussein. WRIT: Shelley List. CAST: Colleen Dewhurst, Warren Oates, Mildred Dunnock, Maggie Cooper, Timothy Hutton.

ANNE OF THE THOUSAND DAYS...

co-scripted by a woman, features a grand leading performance from Genevieve Bujold as Anne Boleyn, the woman who resisted King Henry VIII's advances for six long years, until he would marry her, thus making any of their offspring legitimate heirs to the throne of England. When Henry (Richard Burton at his most blustery) discards first wife Katherine of Aragon—circa 1926—to wed the younger and prettier Boleyn, it precipitates a final break with the Vatican and the creation of the Church of England. Boleyn quickly becomes pregnant, but to the King's chagrin, gives birth to a baby girl. When her second child arrives stillborn, Henry sees reason enough to begin wooing the still younger and prettier Jane Seymour. Although the defiant Boleyn's fate is now sealed, a posthumous sequence reminds us who really triumphed in this royal battle of wills; the abandoned little girl who has just lost her mother to her father's rapacious ways is none other than the future Queen Elizabeth. It's a consummately-acted costume drama, with special mention due Irene Pappas' fierce contribution as the King's spurned first wife. *1969. 145m. DIR: Charles Jarrott. WRIT: Bridget Boland, John Hale. CAST: Genevieve Bujold, Richard Burton, Irene Pappas, Anthony Quayle, John Colicos, Michael Hordern.*

BAD BEHAVIOR...

offers us a good-natured seriocomedy of domestic relations co-starring the equally marvelous Sinead Cusak and Stephen Rea. They play a long-married Irish couple whose North London row house is suddenly in need of repairs. What follows is a month-in-the-life of two people whose complacent, slightly bored relationship may well be masking impending turmoil. Rea tramps off to work every day as a city planner, where he half-heartedly evades the flirtations of a younger officemate. Cusak works part-time in a bookstore, when she isn't writing her first novel or overseeing a somewhat turbulent extended household, which includes identical twin repairmen and lonely girlfriends who envy Cusak her 'perfect' husband. The film successfully paints a portrait of two people still deeply in love, in spite of—and because of—all the years they have spent together. Of note: director Les Blair wrote a bare-bones outline for a script and over a long rehearsal period allowed the actors to improvise and fine-tune their dialogue, resulting in an unusually realistic production. *1993. 100m. DIR&WRIT: Les Blair. CAST: Sinead Cusak, Stephen Rea, Philip Jackson, Clare Higgins, Phil Daniels, Mary Jo Randle, Saira Todd.*

BARCELONA...

focuses on a kinship between two twenty-something cousins who, for better or worse, have always depended on each other for the rudiments of a sibling relationship. Taylor Nichols is the overly earnest, self-questioning half of this pair, posted in Spain near the end of the Cold War as a sales representative for a Chicago firm. And he is most decidedly *not* in the mood for an impromptu visit from imperious cousin Christopher

Eigeman, presently a Navy attaché assigned as 'advance man' for the sixth fleet's upcoming shore leave. Our first impressions of the acerbically witty and self-absorbed Eigeman support Nichol's apprehensions. But the two young men are destined to grow on each other—and us—over the weeks of the naval officer's extended visit. Director/writer Whit Stillman's script has its sophomoric moments, but also its share of moving ones, and he has elicited impressively natural performances from the two leads.

1994. 100m. DIR&WRIT: Whit Stillman. CAST: Taylor Nichols, Christopher Eigeman, Tushka Bergen, Mira Sorvina.

BEFORE AND AFTER...

tells the story of a young teenager who did or did not murder his girlfriend in a fit of rage, and the traumatic effects his escape, capture, and trial have on his family—parents Meryl Streep and Liam Neeson, and little sister Julie Weldon. It's the younger child who sums up their predicament: "Your whole life can change in a second. And you never know when it's coming. Before, you think you know what kind of world this is. But after, everything is different. Not bad maybe. Not always. But different. Forever." Neeson plays the father who is willing to do anything, even destroy possible evidence, in order to save teenager Edward Furlong from going to prison. Streep is the mother who has enough faith in her son to simply care desperately for the truth. This conflict between devotion and honor lies at the movie's core, and is delineated with riveting clarity by our two leads.

1996. 110m. DIR: Barbet Schroeder. WRIT: Ted Tally. CAST: Meryl Streep, Liam Neeson, Edward Furlong, Julia Weldon, Alfred Molina, John Heard, Daniel Van Burgen.

THE BEST INTENTIONS...

scripted by Ingmar Bergman, is a bleak yet fascinating chronicle of Bergman's parents' courtship and the early years of their stormy marriage. Set in Sweden at the turn of the century, we first meet the distinctly upper-middle-class Pernilla August, a young woman who, through the matchmaking machinations of her older brother, meets and falls in love with an impoverished theology student played by Samuel Froler. Pernilla's mother is adamantly opposed to the relationship and 'misplaces' an all-important love letter in the hopes of thwarting the fledgling liaison. The lovelorn pair manage to reunite and marry, of course, only for our young heroine to discover she has wedded her life to a very proud and puritanical man. There are superb performances from the entire cast, but since the movie is a weighty three hours, an intermission comes well-advised.

1992. 182m. In Swedish w/English Subtitles. DIR: Bille August. WRIT: Ingmar Bergman. CAST: Pernilla August, Samuel Froler, Ghita Norby, Max von Sydow, Lennart Hjultrom, Mona Malm, Lena Edre, Anita Bjork.

THE BEST MAN...

is a taut dramatization of a behind-the-scenes political power struggle which pits idealistic Henry Fonda against ruthless Cliff Robertson, as the two men vie for their party's presidential nomination. Between these two adversaries stands the imposing figure of Lee Tracy as the dying ex-president who, by the eve of their political convention, has yet to put his support behind one man or the other. The brass knuckles emerge when Robertson digs up dirt concerning Fonda's emotional/psychological past and doesn't hesitate to use it to his own advantage. Fonda now appears to be out of the running, until he comes across proof of a sex scandal in Robertson's past. Is he going to resort to his opponent's smear tactics in order to get back in the race, or will the high road prevail? Accolades are due the still and potent performance from Margaret Leighton as Fonda's estranged wife, and Haskell Wexler's stunning black-and-white cinematography.

1964. 102m. B&W. DIR: Franklin J. Schaffner. WRIT: Gore Vidal. CAST: Henry Fonda, Cliff Robertson, Lee Tracy, Edie Adams, Margaret Leighton, Shelley Berman, Ann Southern, Richard Arlen, Mahalia Jackson.

BETRAYAL...

takes an innovative approach to the classic love triangle by playing it backwards, opening with the end of a seven-year adulterous affair and wending its way back to that magic/tragic moment when it all began. This novel approach to our story is both absorbing and unsettling, as we play witness to the passionate euphoria which ushers in this illicit romance long after having been shown the emotional heartbreak which comes in its wake. Jeremy Irons as a clever, charming literary agent, and Ben Kingsley as an older, wiser publisher who is truly in love with beautiful wife Patricia Hodge, bring Pinter's elliptical mood piece magnificently to life. But Hodge is the revelation here, those soulful eyes speaking a thousand words in scene after scene. Of note: don't fuss with the volume control at the opening sequence, which is seen through livingroom windows and, frustratingly enough, not intended to be heard.
1983. 95m. DIR: David Jones. WRIT: Harold Pinter. CAST: Patricia Hodge, Ben Kingsley, Jeremy Irons.

BORN ON THE FOURTH OF JULY...

based on the true experiences of veteran Ron Kovic, concentrates on the Vietnam War's lasting effects on one individual soldier and his family. Tom Cruise plays the gung-ho eighteen-year-old volunteer whose war wounds render him paralyzed from the chest down. We follow this young man's spiritual and emotional evolution from naive high school student, to terrified combatant, to embittered paraplegic, and finally to active anti-war protester. It is compelling and gritty cinema. When our soldier finds it impossible to adjust to life on the home front, he takes a sabbatical south of the border, where—in the company of other traumatized war-vets—he drowns his pain and self-pity in tequila and truncated prostitute-aided sex. (A ferocious confrontation between Cruise and fellow paraplegic Willem Dafoe is a definitive highlight.) Director Oliver Stone and co-screenwriter Kovic have fashioned what is ultimately an uplifting tale of one man's political and emotional awakening, made wrenchingly believable by Cruise's committed performance.

1989. 145m. DIR: Oliver Stone. WRIT: Ron Kovic, Oliver Stone. CAST: Tom Cruise, Kyra Sedgwick, Raymond J. Barry, Jerry Levine, Tom Berenger, Willem Dafoe.

BROADCAST NEWS...

is an entertaining, if ultimately lightweight analysis of network news shows, starring Holly Hunter as the talented, high-powered TV producer who grooms sportscaster William Hurt as the anchor for her station's evening news. Albert Brooks co-stars as the 'reporter's reporter' and admirable linguist who deserves the anchor spot, but in the flashy vacuity of current television programming is destined to be kept safely behind the camera. (Then again, his priceless one-time shot in front of the camera might prove the TV execs were right, after all. Or, as one crewman observes: "This is more than even *Nixon* sweated.") A love triangle emerges, with Brooks desperately in love with Hunter, Hunter hopelessly in love with Hurt, and Hurt incorrigibly in love with himself. Among highlights, there's Joan Cusak's race to get an edited tape to the station on time, Hunter coaching Hurt via earphones while he's covering a live event on TV, and a soundtrack which includes François Cabrel's 'L'Edition Speciale' and Gladys and the Pips' 'Midnight Train to Georgia.'

1987. 132m. DIR&WRIT: James L. Brooks. CAST: Holly Hunter, William Hurt, Albert Brooks, Joan Cusak, Jack Nicholson, Robert Prosky.

THE BUDDY HOLLY STORY...

features Gary Busey's galvanizing leading performance as the legendary 50s pop star who died in a plane crash at the age of twenty-one. It is no stretch to believe that Busey *is* Holly. The actor disappears into the role, playing a hot guitar and singing the arrangements himself rather than resorting to the conventional method of lip-synching. And incredibly enough, he manages to improve on a few of Holly's originals, with 'True Love Ways' as a case in point. The film correctly portrays the composer-singer as a true original. Like Glenn Miller before him, Holly, in the dawning era of Rock, knew that his own arrangements were essential to the sound he wished to put across. He therefore insisted on producing his recordings, a most unusual demand for any singer/songwriter to make back in the fifties, and even more so for a neophyte who had yet to prove his mettle. But it might explain why, after all these years, Holly's music still so clearly reflects his unique genius. 'That'll Be The Day.' 'Peggy Sue.' 'It's So Easy.' 'True Love Ways.' Holly lives!

1978. 113m. DIR: Steve Rash. WRIT: Robert Gittler. CAST: Gary Busey, Don Stroud, Charles Martin Smith, Conrad Janis, William Jordan, Maria Richwine.

CABARET...

a groundbreaking musical which doubles as serious drama, stars Liza Minnelli—flying on all cylinders—as a young American singer struggling to launch a successful career in early 1930s Berlin. Minnelli befriends the new boarder in her rooming house, attractive English tutor Michael York, and the two slip into a casual affair. A second romance would appear in the offing between lovely Jewess Marisa Berenson and fellow English student Fritz Webber. But do not come to this film looking for illusory walks into the sunset. The signs of approaching apocalypse are everywhere to be seen, Nazism sinking its talons ever deeper into the German psyche while our amiable cast of characters remains tragically unaware. Minnelli's show-stopping performance is effectively counter-balanced by Joel Grey's devilish contribution as our androgynous Master of Ceremonies. Musical highlights which Grey and Minnelli bring to that cabaret stage include 'Money, Money,' 'Cabaret,' 'Wilkommen,' and 'Maybe This Time.'

1972. 119m. DIR: Bob Fosse. WRIT: Jay Presson Allen. CAST: Liza Minnelli, Joel Grey, Michael York, Marisa Berenson, Fritz Webber, Helmut Griem.

CAT ON A HOT TIN ROOF...

features Burl Ives' most memorable screen performance as Big Daddy, the tyrannical millionaire who is about to learn a lesson in love at the end of a materially successful, emotionally bereft existence. Tennessee Williams' play, as adapted for the screen by director Richard Brooks and James Poe, offers our principal characters more epiphanies in the course of a single evening—Big Daddy's sixty-fifth birthday party—than most of us experience in a lifetime. But it works most satisfactorily, due in no small part to the volatile chemistry which Paul Newman and Elizabeth Taylor bring to their roles of Brick and Maggie, the deeply estranged married couple who painfully mend on this dramatic night. The reason for Brick's longstanding refusal to make love to, or even to touch his young wife (making Maggie feel "like a cat on a hot tin roof"), is gradually revealed, allowing for a denouement which neatly ties together all the disparate threads of the plot. Greed, an ongoing theme of this story, is ultimately eclipsed by passion and redemption.

1959. 108m. DIR: Richard Brooks. WRIT: Richard Brooks, James Poe. CAST: Burl Ives, Paul Newman, Elizabeth Taylor, Judith Anderson, Jack Carson.

A CHRISTMAS CAROL...

the landmark 1951 adaptation stars an inimitable Alistair Sim as Ebenezer Scrooge, the meanest, most miserly, holiday-hating skinflint in all of London. This fellow is so closefisted and misanthropic, he even begrudges his loyal clerk the day off to celebrate Christmas with his loving family. That is all about to change, of course, as Ebenezer lives through one harrowing, soul-transforming night. His first visitor on this fateful Christmas Eve is his late business partner, who is enduring enchained and eternal purgatory due to sins of avarice in his past life. He warns the quaking Ebenezer that he will be receiving three more visits in the night ahead, from the ghosts of Christmas Past, Present, and Future, each of whom will be taking our money-grubber on a pilgrimage through his own life, showing him how his petty ways have hurt so many around him, most particularly himself. After the third and most harrowing journey, Ebenezar wakes up Christmas morning deliriously happy to be alive, with his inner self radically recast. The ebullient sequence to follow is bound to steal your heart away.

1951. 86m. B&W. DIR: Brian Desmond Hurst. WRIT: Noel Langley. CAST: Alistair Sim, Kathleen Harrison, Jack Warner, Michael Horem, Patrick Macnee, Mervyn Johns, Hermione Baddeley, Clifford Mollison, George Cole, Carol Marsh.

CITIZEN COHN...

might be one of those films you overlook, simply because the topic seems so innately unappealing. Why spend two hours reviewing the life of Roy Cohn, the sleazy, opportunistic lawyer who stood guard over Joe McCarthy's 1950s communist witch-hunt? James Woods is the reason, as his hypnotic performance brings this gay-bashing, Jew-hating, right-wing sociopath strikingly to life. It's an oddly entertaining look at a human monster, told via hallucinatory flashbacks as Cohn lies dying in a hospital ward. The profound irony which is revealed as his past literally comes back to haunt him is that Cohn was both gay *and* Jewish, and that the disease laying waste to him is AIDS.

1992. 112m. DIR: Frank Pierson. WRIT: David Franzoni. CAST: James Woods, Joe Don Baker, Joseph Bologna, Ed Flanders, Fredric Forrest, Lee Grant.

CITIZEN KANE...

director Orson Welles and cinematographer Gregg Toland's masterpiece, boasts dramatic camera angles and deep focus photography, as well as groundbreaking frame compositions and a soundtrack as vivid as they come, all underpinning a jig-saw plot device. But what often gets buried under the flurry of technical praise is the tragic story of a man who succeeds beyond his wildest dreams, only to lose his very soul in the process. Based on the life of newspaper tycoon William

Hearst, the scenario is set up as a mystery, opening at the end of Kane's life, when this most powerful of men lies dying alone at his palatial Florida manor. The last word he utters on his deathbed is the cryptic 'Rosebud.' Newsreel editor Philip Van Zandt is convinced the word holds the key to this man's mysterious past and dispatches reporter William Allard to interview Kane's family and ex-friends, hoping to get at the truths behind the myth. Via a series of flashbacks, we follow Kane from his humble beginnings—all fire and optimism— on to his ruthless peak, and down to that cold and lonely finale, wherein the riddle behind Kane's dying murmur provides the most heartbreaking moment of all.

1941. 119m. B&W. DIR: Orson Welles. WRIT: Herman J. Mankiewicz, Orson Welles. CAST: Orson Welles, Joseph Cotton, Everett Sloane, Dorothy Comingore, Ruth Warrick, Ray Collins, Erskine Sanford.

CLEAN AND SOBER...

features one of Michael Keaton's finest dramatic performances as a drug and alcohol addicted real estate hotshot whose situation is so desperate he's prepared to borrow his parents' last dime to fuel his habit. Oblivious to the severity of his problem, our anti-hero wakes up one morning to find that last night's pick-up has overdosed herself into a coma, while embezzlement charges are brewing against him at his real estate firm. In a user's panic, he hides from the police by taking refuge in a rehab clinic, where against his will he is obliged to undergo treatment. It will take an uncompromising attitude from counselor Morgan Freeman, the trauma of enforced abstinence, and considerable emotional sustenance from AA support buddy M. Emmet Walsh, before our addict starts making a turn-around. This is a somber look at the detox process, as well as the challenges which follow an addict when he or she heads back into the real world. Freeman's convincing supporting contribution is an added bonus.

1988. 124m. DIR: Glenn Gordon Caron. WRIT: Tod Carroll. CAST: Michael Keaton, Morgan Freeman, Kathy Baker, M. Emmet Walsh, Tate Donovan, Henry Judd Baker, Claudia Christian.

COAL MINER'S DAUGHTER...

is an only-in-America success story detailing country singer Loretta Lynn's phenomenal journey from a tumbledown shack in the coal fields of Kentucky to the stage of the Grand Ole Opry. Lynn hand-picked Sissy Spacek to play the lead in this film and wisely so, for the actress creates an amazingly credible character at all points over a thirty-year span. Lynn's life is not an easy one. For starters, she is a mere thirteen years of age when she weds Doolittle 'Mooney' Lynn, and he is far from being a perfect man. To his credit however, it is Mooney—played with predictable panache by Tommy Lee Jones—who gets them out of that dead-end Kentucky mining town, and Mooney who buys his wife her first guitar, and Mooney whose determination to get his wife's songs on the radio jump-starts her career. But with Loretta's growing success, the inevitable troubles set in, as she endures her husband's chronic alcoholism and infidelities, as well as her own increasing health problems. Thomas Rickman's screenplay doesn't pull any punches. In spite of the thriving love affair between Lynn and her adoring fans, it is the story of a very lonely woman whose family life, not to mention the simple joys of every day living, are sacrificed at the altar of fame and fortune. Spacek deserves extra kudos for singing Lynn's songs and making them her own.

1980. 125m. DIR: Michael Apted. WRIT: Tom Rickman. CAST: Sissy Spacek, Tommy Lee Jones, Levon Helm, Beverly D'Angelo, Phyllis Boyen, Bill Anderson.

CONRACK...

co-scripted by a woman, tells the true story of a white teacher attempting to educate underprivileged black children in a decrepit two-room schoolhouse on an island off the South Carolina coast. The film transcends the educator-produces-miracles-in-the-classroom genre, in large part due to Jon Voight's free-wheeling performance. It is a daunting task this instructor takes on. Most of his kids literally can't add up 2+2 and are further handicapped by a principal who refers to her charges as babies and treats them as such. But Conrack's ped-agogical approach, one which becomes central to the film's entertainment value, is his absolute refusal to talk down to his students. He expects them to meet him at his own level, and for the most part they succeed.

1974. 111m. DIR: Martin Ritt. WRIT: Harriet Frank Jr., Irving Ravitch. CAST: Jon Voight, Madge Sinclair, Hume Cronyn, Paul Winfield, Martin Ritt.

CRIMES AND MISDEMEANORS...

Woody Allen's Dostoevskian take on the morals of our times, posits the question—is murder irredeemable?—and comes up with a most unsettling answer, in the process offering us a brutally honest meditation on adultery. Martin Landau stars as a successful ophthalmologist, esteemed by family and col-leagues alike, who lapses into an affair with airline stewardess Anjelica Huston. But it's now two years down the road, and Landau wants out of the increasingly stressful situation at the very moment when Huston is pressing him to leave wife Claire Bloom, as he had originally promised. 'Marriage or *else*' is her ominous demand, with plenty of ammunition to back up her threat. A secondary plot line involves unhappily mar-ried documentary-maker Allen, falling in love with public television producer Mia Farrow while filming a portrait of smug television director Alan Alda. It is pure genius how seamlessly Allen pulls these two disparate stories together by film's finale. Special mention is due Huston's searing contri-bution as the spurned mistress, a performance bound to stay with you long after the final credits.

1989. 104m. DIR&WRIT: Woody Allen. CAST: Martin Landau, Anjelica Huston, Woody Allen, Alan Alda, Mia Farrow, Jerry Orbach, Sam Waterston, Joanna Gleason, Claire Bloom.

A CRY IN THE DARK...

asks what greater tragedy could befall a couple on a family camping trip than to have their thirteen-week-old little girl killed by a wild dog. Something more tragic could and did befall such a couple in 1980 Australia when public opinion refused to believe that a dingo—an Australian wild dog—was capable of dragging a twelve pound baby from her tent and into the wilderness. Fueled by irresponsible press coverage and public innuendo, an aberrant government turned on the grieving mother, who happened to be a Seventh-Day Adventist, accusing her of murdering her own child. This inexorable rush to judgment makes for a chilling scenario, showcasing Meryl Streep in yet another of her astonishing, accent-perfect performances. Can there be any doubt that she is the finest actress of her generation?

1988. 120m. DIR: Fred Schepisi. WRIT: Fred Schepisi, Robert Caswell. CAST: Meryl Streep, Sam Neill, Bruce Myles, Charles Tingwell, Nick Tate, Neil Fitzpatrick.

DRIVING MISS DAISY...

set against the backdrop of the evolving American South, follows the twenty-five-year friendship between an eccentric and wealthy Jewish widow and the wily African-American chauffeur her son insists she employ. As Miss Daisy and Hoke, Jessica Tandy and Morgan Freeman are equally superb, the magical chemistry between them making their many leisurely scenes together eminently satisfying. Part of the charm, of course, is how their relationship evolves over the years, from caution, to camaraderie, to a deep and abiding affection, with Daisy ultimately realizing that Hoke is her best friend. It's a straightforward, eloquent scenario, giving us a telling look at how the changes wrought by the civil rights movement affected this country on a most personal level. Special mention is due Dan Aykroyd's wry contribution as Tandy's doting son.

1989. 99m. DIR: Bruce Beresford. WRIT: Alfred Uhry. CAST: Jessica Tandy, Morgan Freeman, Dan Aykroyd, Esther Rolle, Patti LuPone.

THE ENTERTAINER...

a bleak yet fascinating film, offers one of Laurence Olivier's finest screen performances. Only an actor of his obvious genius could so authentically bring to life the mediocrity and self-conceit at the core of this particular entertainer. Vaudeville is in its death throes, a reality which cut-rate song-and-dance man Archie Rice refuses to accept. Bankrupt in every sense of the word, Archie paves his road to rack and ruin on the stubborn if heartfelt credo: 'I perform, therefore I *am*.' Olivier is ably assisted by Brenda de Banzie as his long-suffering, alcoholic wife, and Joan Plowright as the daughter who struggles to keep this wildly dysfunctional family afloat. Look for early performances by Albert Finney and Alan Bates as Archie's two sons.

1960. 97m. DIR: Tony Richardson. WRIT: John Osborne, Nigel Kneale.
CAST: Laurence Olivier, Brenda de Banzie, Joan Plowright, Roger Livesey, Alan Bates, Albert Finney.

EVE'S BAYOU...

is Kasi Lemmons' striking writing-directing debut, and speaks mightily for her future. The film's opening lines set the tone for everything to follow, as our grown-up narrator reflects back on her youth: "Memory is a selection of images, some elusive, others printed indelibly in the brain. The summer I killed my father, I was ten years old." And so unfolds a stirring drama of guilt, consequence, and the paranormal, which doubles as a Roshomon-like psychological thriller, all set within the menace and magnolias of 1950s rural Louisiana. Jurnee Smollett stars as the second daughter of prosperous Creole parents Samuel L. Jackson and Lynn Whitfield. Jackson is the respected local physician, bedeviled by a philandering bedside manner which deeply hurts his elegant wife. But matters get far more complex when our unsuspecting young protagonist begins to discover what is going on beneath the surface of her apparently happy family. Bad goes to worse when she decides to 'fix' the situation by making a pact with the mysterious local voodoo woman. Ultimately, we are reminded that the secrets which can hold a family together can work just as powerfully in tearing it apart, with—in this case—the deep-rooted bonds of sisterhood prevailing, nonetheless. Special mention is due the young Smollet's stirring leading performance, Debbi Morgan's fiery contribution as her thrice-widowed aunt, Amy Vincent's shimmering cinematography, and Terence Blanchard's languorous musical score.

1997. 100m. DIR&WRIT: Kasi Lemmons. CAST: Samuel L. Jackson, Jurnee Smollett, Lynn Whitfield, Meegan Good, Debbi Morgan, Diahann Carroll.

THE FALCON AND THE SNOWMAN...

based on Christopher Boyce and Dalton Lee's true story, is surely one of the more peculiar cases of treason on record. Timothy Hutton co-stars as the seminary school drop-out with a lot of time on his hands, when his father lands him a job at a telex-routing center deep inside the CIA's 'black operation' beat. Initially, it's a kick for Hutton working this Pentagon vault, a department privy only to the highest of security-cleared personnel. Margaritas and Bloody Marys whipped up in shredding machines are the order of the day for him and his two co-workers, as they perform repetitive, elementary tasks. Then our 'Falcon' takes a closer look at one of these top-secret telexes and discovers just how intrusive CIA policy can be—in this case, the Agency attempting to influence an Australian election. In self-righteous outrage, Hutton opts to expose our government's darker side by unwisely passing photocopies of the incriminating documents to the Russian Embassy in Mexico City. Even more unwisely, he chooses 'Snowman' Sean Penn, a former buddy now heavy into cocaine-trafficking south of the border, as his envoy. Penn plays a guy out of control, a paranoid drug dealer looking for a quick buck, and his pathetic attempts to wheel and deal the KGB provide some of the film's more farcical moments. Strong, textured performances by both leads highlight what amounts to a real-life tragicomedy.

1985. 131m. DIR: John Schlesinger. WRIT: Steven Zaillian. CAST: Timothy Hutton, Sean Penn, Pat Hingle, Joyce Van Patten, David Suchet.

FIDDLER ON THE ROOF...

stars the masterly Chaim Topol as Tevye, the irrepressible milkman and father of five dowry-less daughters in a turn-of-the-century Russian village. Tradition! is his mantra and battle cry. ("Without traditions, our lives would be as shaky as a fiddler on the roof.") Change is what his three strong-willed older daughters demand, desperate to be free of the age-old strictures of matchmaking in order to have the right to choose their own husbands. When the third daughter goes so far as to fall in love with a gentile, our milkman is stretched to the breaking point. Among highlights, there's the fiddler's rooftop serenade, Topol's rendition of 'If I Were a Rich Man' and 'Do You Love Me?' Nonna Crane's 'Sunrise, Sunset,' and the three daughters 'Matchmaker.' Much credit is due Sheldon Hamick and Jerry Bock's rousing, oft-poignant musical score, adopted for the screen by John Williams.

1971. 184m. DIR: Norman Jewison. WRIT: Joseph Stein. CAST: Chaim Topol, Nonna Crane, Leonard Frey, Molly Picon, Rosalind Harris, Paul Mann, Michelle Marsh, Neva Small.

FIRST DO NO HARM...

scripted by a woman and inspired by real events, hits hard at our medical profession while telling the story of a family's anguishing attempts to deal with a young son's epilepsy. Painful spinal taps and an inordinate amount of prescriptive drugs are the only answers the various medical 'experts' can offer our despairing parents—superbly played by Meryl Streep and Fred Ward—as they watch their beloved child deteriorate under the influence of increasingly heavy medication. (As Streep laments: 'What are *side* effects? As if a 102 degree temperature and a rash all over his body is off to the side somewhere.') Their situation is made all the more burdensome due to a bureaucratic glitch which deprives them of any medical insurance, ultimately forcing them to foreclose on their home in order to continue giving their son any medical care. With no solutions in sight, Streep begins doing her own research into her son's condition, poring over medical texts at the library day after day. Ultimately, she comes across promising information concerning a high protein 'ketogenic' diet and its positive effect on child epilepsy. But when the good doctors brush off the regime's recuperative powers as useless anecdotal evidence and insist on a perilous operation in its stead, Streep takes matters into her own hands.

1996. 110m. DIR: Jim Abrahams. WRIT: Ann Beckett. CAST: Meryl Streep, Fred Ward, Seth Atkins, Mayo Martindale, Allison Janney, Oni Lamphrey.

FRIENDLY PERSUASION...

is a slightly dated, bucolic adaptation of Jessamyn West's novel about a southern Indiana Quaker family's struggle to maintain the ideals of peace amidst the outbreak of the Civil War. Gary Cooper and Dorothy McGuire co-star as the loving husband and wife, one of them less convinced than the other that their pacifist Quaker principles must prevail. And Anthony Perkins gives one of his best screen performances as the son who fears he is using his religion to mask a deeper cowardice, and thus resolves to 'prove himself' by taking up arms against the Confederates. A sensitive story is peppered with humorous touches, among them Samantha the Goose's non-stop tormenting of our eight-year-old narrator, Little Jess. There are countless evocative moments, as well, including daughter Phyllis Love running out barefoot to say a last farewell to her battle-bound beau, and the night Cooper and McGuire pass in the family barn. Dmitri Tiomkin's moving theme song, 'Thee I Love,' resonates throughout.

1956. 140m. DIR: William Wyler. WRIT: Michael Wilson. CAST: Gary Cooper, Dorothy McGuire, Anthony Perkins, Marjorie Main, Charles Halton, Phyllis Love, Richard Eyer, Robert Middleton.

GIANT...

based on Edna Ferber's novel and just as sprawling, chronicles the life and times of Texas cattle baron Rock Hudson and the woman he loves, Maryland society princess Elizabeth Taylor. After her elegant and pampered upbringing, it isn't going to be easy for this strong-willed blueblood to adapt to the harsh realities of ranch life out west. But Liz prevails on all fronts, in the process hammering away at her husband's conservative beliefs. With Hudson and Taylor's stormy albeit loving marriage taking center stage, our story follows the rise of Big Oil interests in Texas, epitomized by upstart oil baron James Dean. In his cinematic swan song—Dean died in a car accident before the film was released—he gives us a poignant, compellingly bizarre performance as a man who gets everything he has ever desired, while forbidden the one thing he truly wants. Which brings us to his early scenes with Taylor, which are genuine heart-tuggers. The film also provides us with Hudson's finest dramatic performance.

1956. 201m. DIR: George Stevens. WRIT: Fred Guiol, Ivan Moffat.
CAST: Rock Hudson, Elizabeth Taylor, James Dean, Mercedes
McCambridge, Carroll Baker, Jane Withers.

THE GIG...

is an independently made gem about a band of white, middle-aged amateur Dixieland jazz musicians who have been jamming once a week for years on end, when they are unexpectedly offered a paying two-week engagement at a Catskills resort. But the group's bass player has to undergo emergency surgery for cancer, which ushers in Cleavon Little as the black professional they hire as his replacement. Further complications set in, including deplorable housing conditions at the resort, the new member's temperament and bona fide musical artistry, and the resort proprietor's musical predilections—he hates Dixieland and had been expecting soft-shoe dance entertainment. Everything resolves itself in unexpected fashion by film's finale, with each of our principals leaving this gig a little wiser, a little sadder, a little more reverential. There are uniformly fleshed out performances, highlighted by Little's graceful contribution.

1985. 95m. DIR&WRIT: Frank D. Gilroy. CAST: Wayne Rodgers,
Cleavon Little, Warren Vache, Joe Silver, Daniel Nelbach, Andrew Duncan,
Jay Thomas, Jerry Malz.

THE GLENN MILLER STORY...

stars James Stewart in a typically convincing performance as the illustrious trombone-playing bandleader whom we follow from the late twenties up to his untimely death in a WWII plane crash. Considering the film's genre, Hollywood showbiz biography, one might expect a dated, even corny storyline. Not so! Among many pluses, the script wisely acknowledges the considerable influence Miller's wife had on his development as a musician, and June Allyson plays this important role with intelligence and sympathy. At the heart of the film, however, is Miller's unique and lasting contribution to the era of Swing—his conviction that every band should develop its own sound by using its own arrangements of the music they played. The great soundtrack is evidence enough of Miller's genius, delivering such swing classics as 'In The Mood,' 'String of Pearls,' 'Moonlight Serenade,' 'Tuxedo Junction,' 'Pennsylvania 6-5000,' and 'Chattanooga Choo-Choo.' A parade of musical greats, including Louis Armstrong and Gene Krupa, play themselves in snappy cameos.

1954. 113m. DIR: Anthony Mann. WRIT: Valentine Davies, Oscar Brodney. CAST: James Stewart, June Allyson, Charles Drake, George Tobias, Harry Morgan, Frances Langford, Louis Armstrong, Gene Krupa.

THE GREAT SANTINI...

is another Pat Conroy autobiographical novel brought successfully to the silver screen. The film tells the story of Conroy's father, a frustrated, stateside career Marine officer who long ago turned family life into boot camp and his wife and four children into his permanent recruits. Robert Duvall is superb in the starring role, a breakthrough performance which made him a Hollywood leading man. There are some difficult scenes to be sure, particularly Dad browbeating sensitive teenaged son Michael O'Keefe. But the movie provides many moments of warmth, humor, and tenderness, as well. Ultimately, via Lewis John Carlino's inspired screenplay, it's a tale of love transcending familial dysfunction. Honors go to

O'Keefe's sympathetic contribution, as well as Blythe Danner's characterization of the doting mother and long-suffering wife.

1980. 118m. DIR&WRIT: Lewis John Carlino. CAST: Robert Duvall, Blythe Danner, Michael O'Keefe, Lisa Jane Persky, Stan Shaw, David Keith, Anne Haddock, Brian Andrews.

A GREAT WALL...

co-scripted by a woman, stars director Peter Wang as a San Francisco computer programmer overlooked for a well-deserved promotion, very possibly because of his Chinese-American background. In disgust, Wang quits his job and takes his wife and son back to mainland China to visit the sister and brother-in-law he hasn't seen in over twenty years. It's both an entertaining and intriguing story, as our principals experience the inevitable culture shock before gradually adapting to the traditions and culture of present-day China. Special mention is due a largely non-professional yet most amiable cast in this first ever Chinese/American co-production. Of note: the film's title is derived from an interview with President Nixon on his groundbreaking trip to China. When asked his opinion of China's most popular tourist attraction, Nixon answered, "The Great Wall is...a great wall."

1986. 103m. In English and Chinese w/English Subtitles. DIR: Peter Wang. WRIT: Shirley Sun, Peter Wang. CAST: Peter Wang, Sharon Iwai, Kelvin Han Yee, Lin Oingin, Hy Xiaoguang.

HANNAH AND HER SISTERS...

depicts one year in the life of three thirty-something siblings—Mia Farrow, Barbara Hershey, and Dianne Wiest—as they struggle to find emotional and professional fulfillment in modern-day Manhattan. Mia appears to be the stable one as a happily married stage actress who is constantly striving to keep everyone in her family happy, including bickering, boozing Mom and Dad, Maureen O'Sullivan and Lloyd Nolan. Hershey is the lost soul who is tiring of a live-in relationship with reclusive painter Max von Sydow and slipping ever so precariously into an adulterous liaison with brother-in-law Michael Caine. Wiest isn't any better off, presently competing with her own catering partner Carrie Fisher for the affections of architect Sam Waterston, while working on her first novel on the side. And finally there is Woody Allen himself as the hypochondriac of a TV producer who is about to fall in love with one of our sisters. Special mention is due Wiest's most endearing contribution to date, and a surprisingly poignant finale.

1986. 103m. DIR&WRIT: Woody Allen. CAST: Mia Farrow, Diane Wiest, Barbara Hershey, Woody Allen, Sam Waterston, Carrie Fisher, Maureen O'Sullivan, Max von Sydow, Lloyd Nolan.

HARRY AND TONTO...

is a sweet, sentimental road flick starring Art Carney as Harry, a 72-year-old widower and retired college professor who moves in with his oldest son after being forcefully evicted from his apartment building. His original plan is to look for new lodgings, but motivated by his grandson's interest in Zen philosophy, Harry decides to gratify his own life-long ambition of traveling to California. With his beloved cat Tonto as faithful companion, Harry begins his cross-country odyssey, making family stopovers in New Jersey, Chicago, and Los Angeles, while meeting new friends and visiting old lovers en route, and becoming rejuvenated in the process. This warm, humorous, and occasionally heartbreaking scenario is highlighted by Carney's sympathetic performance, and a fine supporting cast which includes Ellen Burstyn, Larry Hagman, Geraldine Fitzgerald, and that beautiful kitty. (Cats *can* travel, after all!)

1974. 115m. DIR: Paul Mazursky. WRIT: Paul Mazursky, Josh Greenfeld. CAST: Art Carney, Ellen Burstyn, Chief Dan George, Geraldine Fitzgerald, Larry Hagman, Arthur Hunnicutt, Philip Bruns, Josh Mostel.

HESTER STREET...

scripted and directed on a shoestring by Joan Micklin Silver, is a disarming period piece which takes us back to turn-of-the-century Lower East Side Manhattan to witness the cultural adjustments of Jewish immigrants embarking on a new life. Carol Kane co-stars as the young wife who leaves her homeland with her son in tow, to join the husband she hasn't seen in almost three years. To her and hubby Steven Keats' mutual chagrin, the two barely recognize one another anymore. Keats—whose circumstances in New York open the first ten minutes of the film—has Americanized with a vengeance and can't hide the shame and condescension he feels towards his wife's Orthodox look and old-fashioned ways. The situation goes from bad to worse, when he all but deserts his wife for the wiles of sexy milliner Doris Roberts, who boasts a sizeable dowry to boot. But not to worry. With the help of a kindly, tough-minded neighbor, Kane's future is destined to brighten by leaps and bounds. This may well be Kane's best screen performance, her silences worth a thousand words. Keats deserves special mention, as well, for his droll portrayal of a man who can't shed the Old World traditions fast enough, blithely unaware of the price he might be paying down the road. Be forewarned that a low budget makes for fuzzy production values early on.

1975. 89m. B&W. DIR&WRIT: Joan Micklin Silver. CAST: Carol Kane, Steven Keats, Doris Roberts, Mel Howard, Dorrie Kavanaugh, Stephen Strimpell.

HONEYSUCKLE ROSE...

co-scripted by a woman, is a country-western twist on the *Intermezzo* theme, except that this time around we're rooting for the abandoned wife. Willie Nelson co-stars as the Texas singer Buck Bonham, with Dyan Cannon playing his gutsy spouse and singing partner in the Bonham Band's road show. When Cannon decides she can't take the traveling any longer,

Nelson's good buddy Slim Pickens suggests his daughter Amy Irving as Cannon's replacement. On the road again, the expected dalliance takes place between Nelson and adoring young thing. But when Cannon finds out about it, there's hell to pay for all and sundry. It's a predictable story, entertainingly told, with the sound track the icing on the cake. *1980. 120m. DIR: Jerry Schatzberg. WRIT: Carol Sobieski, William Wittliff, John Binder. CAST: Willie Nelson, Dyan Cannon, Amy Irving, Slim Pickens, Joey Floyd, Charles Levin.*

HOSTAGES...

a very fine HBO production, tells a composite story of the fifty Western citizens who were abducted off the streets of Beirut between 1984 and 1992. In so doing, we follow the misfortunes of five real-life hostages—British journalist John McCarthy, Irishman Brian Keenan, and Americans Terry Anderson, Frank Reid, and Thomas Sutherland—as one by one they fall prey to capture by radical Muslim groups who hope to parley these kidnappings into the collection of much-needed funds. But the British, Irish, and American governments all insist they can do nothing toward the release of their countrymen, claiming that by dealing with terrorists they will only be encouraging further abductions. If it had not been for the tireless efforts of female relatives, in particular Terry Anderson's sister, Brian Keenan's two sisters, and John McCarthy's wife, these men might well have died in captivity. It's a compelling and convincing docu-drama, made all the more realistic for being based on actual conversations and interviews with relevant persons involved. The acting is first-rate throughout, with particular praise due Colin Firth and Ciaran Hinds' performances as cell mates who develop a deep and mutual affinity for one another. The squalid, isolating conditions of these men's predicament is made viscerally clear, as is the humor and humanity which allows them to survive their impossible plight. Or, as Hinds reminds us in a most memorable scene: "It's better to light a candle, than to sit and curse the dark."

1996. 95m. DIR: David Wheatley. WRIT: Bernard MacLaverty. CAST: Colin Firth, Ciaran Hinds, Kathy Bates, Natasha Richardson, Jay O. Sanders, Josef Sommer, Harry Dean Stanton.

I REMEMBER MAMA...

a heartwarming, unsentimental reworking of Kathryn Forbes' memoirs, *Mama's Bank Account*, stars Irene Dunne as the loving, strong-willed matriarch of a Norwegian immigrant family, scraping by in turn-of-the-century San Francisco. Barbara Bel Geddes is our narrator and future writer, affectionately sketching out the portrait of a woman who provided her family with wisdom, inspiration, a joy for living, and a generous spirit which gave without question to the more needy whenever the occasion arose. Among highlights, there is their elderly boarder's nightly story hour, as the gentleman reads from a procession of classics to the most rapt of audiences, and Mama sneaking into a hospital ward to serenade her ailing younger daughter with a Norwegian lullaby. When we learn the truth about Mama's bank account at film's finale, it's the loveliest moment of all.

1948. 95m. DIR: George Stevens. WRIT: DeWitt Bodeen. CAST: Irene Dunne, Barbara Bel Geddes, Barbara O'Neil, Florence Bates, Peggy McIntyre, June Hedin, Oscar Homolka, Philip Dorn, Cedric Hardwicke, Edgar Bergen.

IN THE NAME OF THE FATHER...

stars Daniel Day-Lewis in a riveting performance as the real-life Gerry Conlon, a ne'er-do-well Irish lad who is in the wrong place at the very wrong time, and winds up being ruthlessly scapegoated by British police. Under pressure to find a culprit for a recent 1974 IRA bombing, the police randomly accuse Conlon and his father of having committed the terrorist acts, then go to convoluted and outrageous extremes to prove to the public that they have found the right men. (What they put Conlon's entire family through in the interest of 'justice,' has to be seen to be believed.) With the help of a dogged lawyer played by Emma Thompson, Conlon is finally proven innocent. But not before countless lost years in prison, and the death of his father just months before their release. Special mention is due Peter Postlethwaite's affecting, understated performance as Conlon's father, and Day-Lewis for his uncanny ability to get inside Conlon's skin and stay there from the opening gambit right through to the film's thrilling finale.

1993. 133m. DIR&WRIT: Jim Sheridan. CAST: Daniel Day-Lewis, Peter Postlethwaite, Emma Thompson, John Lynch, Corin Redgrave, Beatie Edney, John Benfield.

IT'S A WONDERFUL LIFE...

the venerable Frank Capra classic co-scripted by women, gives eloquent testimony to the fact that each of us can and does make a difference. James Stewart, in one of his finest per- formances, plays George Bailey, a man whose problems have so defeated him, he's about to commit suicide. In a series of flashbacks, we witness the many good deeds that George did as a boy, then move on to find him a restless young adult, impatient to set off for college, but thwarted by fate to remain in his hometown, take on his father's business, and raise a family. Years pass and he becomes so overwhelmed by finan- cial problems, he can't see any way out of his predicament but to jump off the nearest bridge. Enter elderly gentleman Henry Travers, who beats him to the punch by hurtling him- self into the water and crying out for help. When George comes to his rescue, Travers reveals himself to be our strug- gling banker's guardian angel, intent on taking him on a spe- cial voyage which will allow him to see the sorry state of Bedford Falls—and his family and friends—in a world that would exist if he had never been born. By journey's end, George's urgent desire to resume his 'ordinary' existence is so infectious ("*Please*, God. Let me live again!"), that we find ourselves, regardless of our situations, feeling likewise. And therein lies the reason for this film's ever-growing popularity, as it continues to remind us that mundane, run-of-the-mill life is undoubtedly the greatest gift of all.

1946. 125m. B&W. DIR: Frank Capra. WRIT: Frank Capra, Frances Goodrich, Albert Hackett, Jo Swerling. CAST: James Stewart, Donna Reed, Lionel Barrymore, Henry Travers, Thomas Mitchell, Samuel S. Hinds, Frank Faylon, Gloria Grahame.

THE JEWEL IN THE CROWN...

an epic *Masterpiece Theater* production, revolves around members of the British community living in India during its turbulent transition to home rule, circa 1942-1947. The axis of the extended cast is Hari Kumar—magnificently rendered by actor Art Malik—as the Indian journalist who is wrongly arrested by the bigoted villain of our story for the rape of Daphne Manners. Although starred-crossed lovers Daphne and Kumar all but disappear early on in the story, they remain the provocative echo affecting everything which follows. Special mention is due Geraldine James' performance as the self-contained army nurse committed to keeping her dysfunctional family intact, and Charles Dance as the dashing officer who walks into her life.

1984. 750m. DIR: Christopher Morahan, Jim O'Brien. WRIT: Charles Rennie MacIntosh. CAST: Art Malik, Susan Wooldredge, Geraldine James, Charles Dance, Tim Piggott-Smith, Peggy Ashcroft.

JUDGMENT...

is a well-executed, if disturbing film based on the true story of a devout Catholic Louisiana couple, played by Blythe Danner and Keith Carradine, who begin to suspect that their young boy has been the victim of sexual abuse. Worse still, the unlikely perpetrator is apparently the popular parish priest. When our distressed couple and several other parish parents try to confront their bishop with the gravity of the problem, they are consistently stonewalled. A cash settlement is eventually offered, but no admission of guilt, either on the part of the priest or the church itself. When the parents are not even given assurance that the offending cleric will not be returning to parish work, Danner and Carradine refuse the hush money and take the case to court. There are adept performances from all concerned, including David Strathairn's spooky portrayal of an ostensibly gentle, well-meaning individual who rationalizes sodomizing these young boys as a means of bringing God's love into their lives.

1990. 89m. DIR&WRIT: Tom Topor. CAST: Blythe Danner, Keith Carradine, David Strathairn, Jack Warden, Bob Gunton, Mitchell Ryan, Michael Faustino.

THE LION IN WINTER...

is an intensely personal drama envisioning the going-ons of the 1183 court of Henry II and his family at Christmastime, as the king and queen battle over whom is to be Henry's successor to the English throne. Wife Eleanor of Aquitaine and their three royal sons have all been released from exile for the occasion, and intrigues, shifting alliances, and revelations ensue. ("I know. You know I know. I know you know I know. We know Henry knows, and Henry knows we know. We're a very knowledgeable family.") Peter O'Toole and Katharine Hepburn are equally brilliant in the leading roles, their ongoing clash of wits making the most of James Goldman's incisive screenplay. It is a scenario which intimates that the great moments in history, and those playing party to them, are driven by the same human needs which influence the rest of us less historical but equally hysterical embattled souls.

1968. 134m. DIR: Anthony Harvey. WRIT: James Goldman. CAST: Peter O'Toole, Katharine Hepburn, Jane Merrow, Nigel Terry, Timothy Dalton, Anthony Hopkins, John Castle.

LOCAL HERO...

the embodiment of Scottish director Bill Forsyth's cinematic style, is a gentle, offbeat comedy, somewhat fuzzy around the edges. Peter Riegert stars as the emissary for a giant Texas oil corporation, sent by firm president Burt Lancaster to buy off a sleepy fishing hamlet on the coast of Scotland and turn it into a giant refinery. The citizens of this little village are all too willing to trade in their cozy lives for the millions in the offing. It is Riegert himself who begins to doubt his mission, as he slowly falls in love with the area, finding something in this ravishing coastline and its quirky, congenial inhabitants which is sorely lacking from his yuppie existence back in Houston. Progress, and all we stand to lose by its fated advance, is the meditation at the heart of this enchanting tale. *1983. 112m. DIR&WRIT: Bill Forsyth. CAST: Peter Riegert, Denis Lawson, Burt Lancaster, Fulton Mackay, Jenny Seagrove.*

THE LONG HOT SUMMER...

both the 1958 original and the 1986 remake are based on a William Faulkner short story about a hotshot young drifter with a dubious past who meanders into a small southern town and is adopted by the local patriarch. What the tyrannical Varner sees in the cocky Ben Quick is not only husband material for his obstinate and unmarried daughter, but future overseer material for his extensive properties—a responsibility he does not believe his own weakling son is up to carrying out. Then an outbreak of arson makes everyone suspicious of the new boy in town, and big trouble is in the offing. The earlier, more celebrated version of this steamy Freudianesque tale boasts a talented, star-studded cast which cannot be faulted. But it's the longer, more fleshed out made-for-television update which is the one not to be missed, if for no other reason than to see Don Johnson in top form as our man Quick. Then too, this latter production boasts such sizzling chemistry between Johnson and Judith Ivy, that the scenario becomes a love story of the first order. Check it out! *1958. 117m. DIR: Martin Ritt. WRIT: Harriet Frank Jr., Irving Ravetch. CAST: Paul Newman, Joanne Woodward, Orson Welles, Lee Remick, Anthony Franciosa, Angela Lansbury.*
1986. 172m. DIR: Stuart Cooper. WRIT: Rita Mae Brown, Dennis Turner. CAST: Don Johnson, Judith Ivy, Jason Robards, Cybill Shepherd, William Russ, Ava Gardner, Wings Hauser.

THE MAMBO KINGS...

scripted by a woman, showcases Armand Assante and Antonio Banderas at their sexiest, the latter in his first English-speaking role. The two actors co-star as Cuban brothers who flee the sinister forces of pre-revolutionary Cuba with the hope of hitting the big time in the mambo clubs of New

York. The remainder of our story highlights hot Latin-beat musical numbers interwoven with romance and heartbreak. But the most tangible love affair in this flick is between the two Castillo brothers themselves—the blood ties that bind them to one another and to the music they were raised on. Among highlights is Desi Arnez Jr. playing his own father in a sequence out of the *I Love Lucy* show. (Back in the fifties, Desi Arnez Sr. became a champion of the Cuban community for legitimizing that country's musical tradition in the United States.)

1992. 100m. DIR: Ame Glimcher. WRIT: Cynthia Cidre. CAST: Armand Assante, Antonio Banderas, Cathy Moriarty, Maruschka Detmers, Desi Arnez Jr., Celia Cruz, Tito Puente.

THE MAN IN THE GRAY FLANNEL SUIT...

offers us a finely etched depiction of married life in 1950s suburbia, as the wife and children deal with one reality on the home front, while the husband faces quite different circumstances in the dog-eat-dog world of Madison Avenue downtown. With the help of a few martinis each evening, husband and wife attempt bridging the gap, reconnecting and redefining the meaning of their hectic lives. Gregory Peck and Jennifer Jones—she, in surely her finest screen performance—are equally convincing in the starring roles. Ditto for the ever reliable Fredric March as the powerful advertising mogul who long ago made the choice between family and career and is now paying the price. Due to the story-within-our-story, WWII experiences still haunting Peck, this is an unusually long film, but absorbing throughout.

1956. 153m. DIR&WRIT: Nunnally Johnson. CAST: Gregory Peck, Jennifer Jones, Fredric March, Lee J. Cobb, Keenan Wynne, Anne Harding, Marisa Paven, Arthur O'Connell.

MANHATTAN...

Woody Allen's valentine to the city he loves, showcases a glorious opening sequence, with fireworks exploding over the skyline of New York to the rhythm of a Gershwin score. Allen himself stars as a successful, middle-aged TV writer who is presently involved with high school senior Mariel Hemingway. (Sound uncomfortably familiar?) But when he meets married best friend Michael Murphy's secret girlfriend Diane Keaton, he finds himself falling in love with a woman who is vaguely his own age. Then complications set in, among them Keaton's romantic whims, and Allan's ex-wife-turned-lesbian Meryl Streep, who is writing a book about their failed marriage. Special mention is due Gordon Willis' magnificent black-and-white cinematography and one of Allen's typically heartfelt finales.

1979. 96m. B&W. DIR&WRIT: Woody Allen. CAST: Woody Allen, Mariel Hemingway, Diane Keaton, Michael Murphy, Meryl Streep, Anne Byrne, Karen Ludwig.

A MONTH IN THE COUNTRY...

takes us back to the early 1900s, when British policy for shell shocked veterans was to give them temporary assignments in rural areas, in the hope that a tranquil setting would allow the psychic healing to begin. Two fine English actors, Kenneth Branagh and Colin Firth, both at the beginning of their distinguished careers, co-star as the battle-scarred soldiers who have been given a month-long furlough in the Yorkshire countryside. The former is assigned to work on a modest archaeological dig, the latter to exhume an original 14th century mural from a medieval church wall. A cautious friendship blooms between our two walking wounded, as does a love interest between unhappily married Natasha Richardson and Firth. (The scene where she stumbles across him having a leisurely smoke in the noonday sun packs enough sensual wallop to be worth the rental fee alone.) But don't come to this reverently quiet film expecting lust and fireworks. The story remains true to its characters and era throughout.

1987. 92m. DIR: Pat O'Connor. WRIT: Simon Gray. CAST: Colin Firth, Kenneth Branagh, Natasha Richardson, Patrick Malahide, Richard Vernon, Elizabeth Hanson.

NEVER CRY WOLF...

based on Canadian nature writer Farley Mowat's firsthand experiences, stars Charles Martin Smith as the young biologist who is dropped into the Arctic tundra for the purpose of making a long-term study of the breeding, hunting, and migration patterns of the Yukon wolf. In particular, he is there to prove whether or not wolves are responsible for the declining herds of Caribou, at a time when Canadian conservation policy is considering lifting its long-term ban on wolf-poaching. The movie works on three different levels: firstly, as a coming-of-age story, as our green-horned biologist learns to adjust and ultimately to thrive in the stark conditions of the far North; secondly, as a gorgeously photographed documentary-like study of one of our more beautiful and misunderstood creatures; and lastly, as a love story between one scientist and the animals he seeks to understand and ultimately to rescue from man's rapacious ways.
1983. 105m. DIR: Carroll Ballard. WRIT: Curtis Hanson, Sam Hamm. CAST: Charles Martin Smith, Brian Dennehy, Samson Jonah.

NOTHING IN COMMON...

stars Tom Hanks as a thirty-something creative director of an ad agency, an ultra-yuppie gad-about-town who is forced to ask himself some serious questions when his mother walks out on Dad after thirty-six years of marriage. Jackie Gleason, in his final film role, gives an unflinching performance, with no hint of the curmudgeon Ralph Kramden in his portrayal of a relentlessly unfaithful husband who never took the time to love, relate, or even talk to his wife and son. By film's final curtain, we suspect that this learning process might possibly, if belatedly, be launched. Comic touches include Hanks' boss Hector Elizondo and his toupees, and the many scenes at Hanks' ad agency. Screenwriter Podell must have penned from firsthand experience to have captured such an on-target satire of the business. In the leading role, Hanks is predictably on target, and Eva Marie Saint is fine indeed as a woman attempting to salvage the last precious years of her life. But ultimately this is Gleason's show, making us ponder why his considerable talents weren't allowed to surface in many more films.

1986. 119m. DIR: Gary Marshall. WRIT: Rick Podell. CAST: Tom Hanks, Jackie Gleason, Eva Marie Saint, Bess Armstrong, Hector Elizondo, Barry Corbin, Sela Ward.

ORDINARY PEOPLE...

based on Judith Guest's best-selling novel, is a cinematic rarity, in that the movie improves on the written original. It was also Robert Redford's directorial debut, which is an amazing fact, considering the letter-perfect integrity of what is essentially a modern-day classic. The story revolves around one family's disintegration in the wake of the beloved eldest son's accidental death, and all four leads—Timothy Hutton, Mary Tyler Moore, Donald Sutherland, and Judd Hirsch—give first rate, high-definition performances. How did Redford elicit such a frosty, austere characterization from lovable comedienne Moore? And at seventeen years of age, Hutton may well have delivered the finest performance of his career, taking center stage as the guilt-ridden young man who is struggling to rebuild his life after a failed suicide attempt. It's a personal battle which is made all the more complicated due to the unarticulated resentment his mother relentlessly channels his way. Hutton's sessions with psychiatrist Hirsch—scenes which are uncommon gems—and his growing affection for classmate Elizabeth McGovern, together and separately help move our young man toward rebirth.

1980. 124m. DIR: Robert Redford. WRIT: Alvin Sargent. CAST: Timothy Hutton, Mary Tyler Moore, Donald Sutherland, Judd Hirsch, Elizabeth McGovern, M. Emmet Walsh, Dinah Monoff.

A PAPER WEDDING...

a Canadian film made in Montreal, induces one to suspect that whoever was responsible for *Green Card* saw this flick first, and then 'Americanized' it with predictable results. This production presents the more serious side to illegal immigration: the plight of thousands of political refugees who literally can never go home again. Genevieve Bujold stars as a just-turned-forty literature professor, mired in a dead-end love affair with a married man when her immigration attorney sister entreats her to enter into a marriage of convenience with Chilean refugee Mañuel Aranguiz. Because the man faces imprisonment or worse should he return to his homeland, Bujold reluctantly agrees. And now two complete strangers are obliged to spend three days together becoming intimately acquainted with one another, in hopes of convincing Canadian officials that they are entering into genuine connubial bliss. The ending is vaguely unsatisfactory, but it remains an intriguing night at the movies, with Bujold, as always, a joy to behold.

1989. 90m. In French & Spanish w/English Subtitles. DIR: Michel Brault. CAST: Genevieve Bujold, Manuel Aranguiz, Dorothee Berryman.

PREFONTAINE...

is a naturalistic dramatization—character development over hero worship—of the brief and celebrated life of controversial track star Steve Prefontaine. After a telltale prologue, the story opens in Coos Bay, Oregon circa 1968, with top one-miler 'Pre' being courted by collegiate track coaches from near and far. But he has his heart set on the University of Oregon and the opportunity to work with celebrated track coach Bill Bowerman. Once in Eugene, Bowerman persuades the cocky young runner to forgo the one-miler in the interest of training for the three-miler, convinced that Pre can *own* that event. And over the next four years that is exactly what Prefontaine accomplishes, breaking all NCAA records for the 5000 meter, while becoming the James Dean of the track world. After a heartbreaking performance in the 1972 Munich Olympics, Pre returns to Oregon to train for another shot at the gold in Montreal, in the process becoming an outspoken activist for amateur athletes' rights. The story is told in flashback via a series of on-camera interviews with Pre's parents, former teammates, coaches, and friends, some twenty years after the magnetic sport star's untimely death. And the technique is amazingly effective due to the likability of the supporting cast, and to the astonishing make-up feat which has these actors age two decades in an entirely credible manner. Among highlights of a scenario which gets better as it unfolds, there is R. Lee Ermey's contribution as Pre's crusty coach and the man who put jogging on the map, and Jared Leto's mesmerizing leading performance, those steely blue eyes artfully conveying the unquenchable ambition which was to become Prefontaine's lasting legacy.

1996. 107m. DIR: Steve James. WRIT: Steve James, Eugene Corr. CAST: Jared Leto, R. Lee Ermey, Ed O'Neill, Lindsay Crouse, Amy Locane, Breckin Meyer, Laurel Holloman, Brian McGovern, Kurtwood Smith, Peter Anthony Jacobs.

A PRIVATE MATTER...

directed by Joan Micklin Silver, is based on the true story of Sherry Finkbine, mother of four and hostess of the kids' show 'Romper Room,' who begins using tranquilizers during her fifth pregnancy. The sleeping pills in question happen to be medication which her husband brought back from Europe the previous summer, and unbeknownst to either of them, the capsules contain an obscure compound called thalidomide, a chemical which causes severe birth defects in pregnant women. Upon discovering their plight, Sherry's doctor recommends a private, officially illegal abortion—the year is 1964—and in the interest of their other children, the parents sadly concur. Although the procedure will be performed under strict secrecy, Sherry puts out an anonymous alert about her situation, in the interest of alerting other women to the inherent dangers of thalidomide. As is the media's wont, reporters track her down as the source of the story, whereupon the Finkbines' lives turn into a living nightmare. Co-stars Sissy Spacek and Aidan Quinn give strong, measured performances in a film which serves as a vital reminder of how traumatic life can be for women when the question of choice remains unlawful and out of bounds.

1992. 89m. DIR: Joan Micklin Silver. WRIT: William Nicholson. CAST: Sissy Spacek, Aidan Quinn, Estelle Parsons, Sheila McCarthy, Leon Russom, William Macy.

PROVIDENCE...

presents one long, intimate night in the life of elderly dying novelist John Gielgud, as he attempts to transcend the knife-stabbing pain of advanced cancer with a little help from his friends: morphine, white wine, and a fertile imagination. As the hours pass, he mentally composes and decomposes what appears to be his last novel, basing his characters on his own children. In his malefic fiction, son Dirk Bogarde and daughter-in-law Ellen Burstyn are a dueling, unhappily married couple, whereas illegitimate son David Warner is falling in love with Burstyn while being prosecuted for murder by district attorney Bogarde. When morning finally dawns, we actually meet Gielgud's three grown-up children, who turn out to be a far cry from the characters who peopled the man's midnight hallucinations. What follows is an idyllic outdoor feast celebrating Gielgud's 78th birthday, and considering the circumstances, it serves as an astonishingly uplifting finale. Fair warning: Gielgud's narcotic-fueled fantasies include an ongoing autopsy which occasionally hits the screen.

1977. 104m. DIR: Alain Resnais. WRIT: David Mercer. CAST: John Gielgud, Ellen Burstyn, Dirk Bogarde, David Warner, Elaine Stritch.

A QUESTION OF FAITH...

is the true story of one woman's fight against a form of cancer known as nodular lymphoma. What makes this story so singular is that nodular lymphoma is one of the few malignancies the medical community openly admits does not respond to orthodox treatment—neither surgery, radiation, nor chemotherapy—thereby leaving our protagonist with no choice but to pursue unorthodox therapies. Many alternative healing methodologies are explored in this film, including visualization, psycho-therapeutic counseling, and a middle-of-the night outdoor exercise program. (Cancer cells become most active after 3 a.m. due to the growing scarcity of oxygen in our body at this time.) Since this scenario is based on real events, it makes for a most educational and encouraging film experience. One year later, our protagonist is not only free of cancer, but has become pregnant in the bargain, making one question if the medical establishment isn't seriously missing the boat on this one.

1993. 90m. DIR: Stephen Gyllenhaal. WRIT: Bruce Hart. CAST: Anne Archer, Sam Neill, Frances Lee McCain, James Tolkan, James Hong.

QUIZ SHOW...

as directed by Robert Redford, transforms a TV scandal of the 1950s into a modern Greek tragedy. Ralph Fiennes stars as the real-life Charles Van Doren, an innocent who is all-too-easily corrupted by the unscrupulous, rating-obsessed bosses running the quiz show *Twenty One*. John Turturro is Fiennes' over-the-top counterpart, the Jewish, self-proclaimed loser who is instructed by the powers-that-be to take a dive on the show in order that our urbane, gentile literature professor may become the new reigning champ. Enter Rob Morrow as a member of Congress' Subcommittee of Legislative Oversight, an investigative dynamo who feels "like a race horse whose gate won't open." When a New York judge seals a Congressional inquiry into quiz show ethics, a step which had not been taken since 1869, Morrow smells a rat, shoots out that gate, and our story takes wing. Among many quiet gems in this scenario, there is Fiennes—his world about to crash in around him—sitting up late with patrician father Paul Scofield, waxing nostalgic about coming home from school as a kid and going into the refrigerator to find a cold bottle of milk and a piece of chocolate cake. "The simplicity of it. I don't think I'll ever be that happy again." Relish masterly performances from all three leads, as well as the typically distinguished contribution from Scofield as the one person whose love and respect our fallen hero so dearly craved.

1995. 110m. DIR: Robert Redford. WRIT: Paul Athens. CAST: Ralph Fiennes, John Turturro, Rob Morrow, Paul Scofield, David Paymer, Hank Azario, Christopher McDonald, Johann Carlo, Elizabeth Wilson, Mira Sorvino.

RAIN MAN...

serves as an intriguing look at an autistic 'idiot savant,' a person capable of memorizing entire telephone books at the drop of a hat, while lacking the mental or emotional ability to lead an independent life. Dustin Hoffman purportedly did an entire year of research before taking on the central role, and it shows, as he acts from inside the very heart and soul of his character. Tom Cruise co-stars as the self-centered yuppie hustler who gets the shock of his life upon learning his father bequeathed his entire $3 million estate to an institutionalized older brother whom Cruise didn't even know existed. Outraged that he has been left out of the will, Cruise decides to take matters into his own hands by kidnaping his brother from the institution and flying him to Los Angeles, where Cruise imagines he can force the trustee to hand over half of the inheritance. Unfortunately for Cruise, Hoffman has a phobia about flying. ("Flying is very dangerous. In 1987, there were 30 airline accidents, 211 fatalities.") And so begins a most unconventional and tender road trip, giving our brothers the opportunity to get to know, understand, and ultimately to love one another. It's a journey destined to profoundly transform them both.

1988. 118m. DIR: Barry Levinson. WRIT: Ronald Bass, Barry Morrow. CAST: Dustin Hoffman, Tom Cruise, Valerie Galen, Jerry Molen, Jack Murdoch.

REUNION...

stars Jason Robards as a Jewish businessman, now a resident of the United States, who is taking a trip to his native Germany, both literally and figuratively, as he flashes back fifty years to a boyhood friendship aborted by the rise of Hitler. Enter Christian Inhaled and Sam West as the young men whose considerable social differences—one is a middle-class Jew, the other a gentile from an Aryan aristocratic family—are easily surmounted by their natural affinities for one another. They are intelligent, sensitive, and curious young men, and surely would have enjoyed a lifelong fellowship if fascism had not played its bitter hand. The increasingly belligerent Nazi Party influences our young aristocrat's sensibilities, while simultaneously persuading the Jewish boy's parents to send their son to safer climates abroad. The movie now returns to the present, with Robards arriving in his hometown of Stuttgart to learn the fate of the long-ago friend who remained behind. Special mention is due the performances elicited from young Inhaled and West, and for Harold Pinter's thought-provoking script.

1988. 120m. DIR: Jerry Schatzberg. WRIT: Harold Pinter. CAST: Jason Robards, Christian Inhaled, Sam West, Françoise Fabian, Maureen Kerwin, Barbara Jefford, Alexander Trauner.

RUNNING ON EMPTY...

scripted by a woman, tells the moving story of two former sixties radicals, Christine Lahti and Judd Hirsch, who—due to an anti-Vietnam war protest which fatally misfired—are still on the lam from the FBI after seventeen long years. It is an eternally transitory existence this fortyish couple and their two teenaged kids have been obliged to live, foregoing roots, steady neighbors, and constant friends in order to keep one step ahead of the Feds on their trail. Their peripatetic lifestyle is wearing thin on all concerned, and particularly on older son River Phoenix. He is falling in love for the first time in his life and is soon to be accepted into the Julliard School of Music, two happy developments which give him good reason to want out of his family's never-ending decampments. The crisis of heart and conscience for this young man is that once he leaves his parents, he may never be able to contact them again. Among highlights, there is an excruciatingly poignant scene when Lahti reunites with the father she hasn't seen in twenty years, and excellent performances from the entire cast.

1988. 116m. DIR: Sidney Lumet. WRIT: Naomi Foner. CAST: River Phoenix, Christine Lahti, Judd Hirsch, Martha Plimpton, Jonus Arby, Ed Crowley.

SCHINDLER'S LIST...

is based on the life of one Oskar Schindler, a gentile German entrepreneur and aspiring war profiteer, who moves to Nazi-occupied Poland and opens an enamelware plant so he can employ ghetto Jews at starvation wages. The situation begins to shift—along with Schindler's moral conscience—when Jewish bookkeeper Itzhak Stern persuades his boss to look the other way while Stern starts classifying their factory employees as essential workers, thereby exempting them from 'resettlement' in the concentration camps. But within the year the Krakow ghetto is destroyed and all surviving Jews are shipped to a forced labor camp, at which point Schindler convinces Nazi Commander Amon Goeth to move his factory inside the labor camp as well. Within camp walls it is business as usual, except that Schindler is now taking an active and increasingly dangerous role in saving the lives of his workers, ultimately spending all of his profits to save over 1,000 Polish Jews from certain death. This is a morally somber, artistically staggering historical epic, with special mention going to the leading performances from Liam Neeson as Schindler and Ben Kingsley as his worthy and wily accountant. If there be a caveat to the production, it is Ralph Fiennes' over the top characterization of the heinous Goeth. *1993. 195m. C/B&W. DIR: Steven Spielberg. WRIT: Steven Zaillian. CAST: Liam Neeson, Ben Kinglsey, Ralph Fiennes, Embeth Davidtz, Caroline Goodall, Jonathan Sagalle.*

SCHOOL TIES...

a story about bigotry at a posh east coast prep school, comes recommended for the modulated talents which Brendan Fraser brings to the leading role. He plays an outstanding high school quarterback, who also happens to be Jewish. When the film opens, he has just been offered a scholarship to play his senior year at ultra-waspy St. Matthews, chiefly because the school's alumni are determined to have a winning season. Fraser's loving and supportive father sends his son off to the new school with some bad advice, unwisely counseling him to keep his Jewish background under wraps. At St. Matthews, the 'closeted' Fraser quickly becomes Big Man on Campus, not only because of his skills on the football field, but due to his unswerving sense of self—a deeply entrenched dignity which his more privileged but less confident brethren find admirably tantalizing. Then one of his classmates discovers Fraser's ethnic credentials and 'outs' him, at which point the lines are drawn and the battle of wills and conscience is launched.

1992. 110m. DIR: Robert Mandel. WRIT: Dick Wolf, Darryl Ponicsan. CAST: Brendan Fraser, Matt Damon, Chris O'Donnell, Randall Batinkoff, Andrew Lowrey.

SEARCHING FOR BOBBY FISCHER...

only tangentially concerned with ex-World Chess Champion Fischer, is the true-life story of one Josh Waitzkin, an otherwise normal seven-year-old-kid who suddenly reveals a genius aptitude for the game of chess. (He picks up the complexities of the game by observing a few matches in Manhattan's Washington Square Park.) How should parents encourage such a prodigal son is one of the central questions asked in this film. What does it take to win? And is it worth the price? Ben Kingsley is touchingly pathetic as the victory-at-all-costs chess pro whom father Joe Mantegna initially retains to tutor his son. And Laurence Fishburne is predictably authentic as Kingsley's foil, a chess hustler who becomes Josh's most empathetic teacher. But to single out two performances is not to slight the excellence of the entire cast, in particular the young Max Pomeranc, a ranked player in his own right, who brings an impressive legitimacy to the leading role.

1993. 111m. DIR&WRIT: Steve Zaillian. CAST: Max Pomeranc, Joe Mantegna, Joan Allen, Ben Kingsley, Laurence Fishburne .

SECRET HONOR...

is a tour-de-force solo performance from Phillip Baker Hall as the tortured, post-presidential Richard Nixon, drinking his way through a bottle of Scotch as he tries to set the record straight one last time—on tape of course—by giving us a

look at the 'face behind the mask that is behind the mask.'
Intriguing insights are mixed with comic pathos, as we play
witness to a man who seems oddly driven, even inspired, by
two essentials: a profound hatred of the Kennedys and an
ever-present self-pity. ("I'm just like my old man. He sold his
grapefruit grove, and *then* they found oil.") The screenwriters
obviously did their homework, including reading transcripts
of the Nixon tapes, for the former president's verbal idiosyn-
crasies are brought uncannily to life. One is left hoping that
many of the frightening theories this film proposes—including the idea that California's so-called Committee of 100 has
been covertly running this country for years—are the invention of a brilliant script. (This particular 'Nixon' summing up
how our government works: "What the rich, Ivy League
princes never realized is that what these people really wanted
was a dogcatcher. Okay, so I was their dogcatcher. Dogcatcher
as King! And these cheats and shysters, and these mobsters,
and these lobsters—I mean lobbyists—all the well-fed bums
and tramps in this country, that is your palace guard.")
1985. 90m. DIR: *Robert Altman.* WRIT: *Donald Freed, Arnold Stone.*
CAST: *Phillip Baker Hall.*

SEX, LIES, AND VIDEOTAPES...

co-stars Andie McDowell and Peter Gallagher as a couple
whose marriage has seen better days. He's off making
whoopie with sexy sister-in-law Laura San Giacomo, while
Andie idles in her psychiatrist's office ruminating on the
garbage crisis and her present vapid emotional state. ("Being
happy isn't all that great. Last time I was happy, I put on 25
pounds. I thought John was going to have a stroke.") Enter
James Spader as a former college buddy of Gallagher's, who is
staying at their home a few days while looking for more permanent digs. Andie has been dreading his arrival, but appre-
hension turns to curiosity when she realizes he's not at all like
her self-indulgent, yuppie husband. (At their first dinner
together, Spader probably asks Andie more questions about
herself than her husband has lobbed in her direction through-

out their entire relationship.) Spader *does* have an eccentric quirk however—an obsession with videotaping women's confessions as they talk about their real or imagined sex lives. In fact, his own sexual life is pretty much circumscribed to jerking-off while re-viewing his subjects' intimate revelations. Not to worry. Through a series of innocent trysts with Spader and that camera, our heroine is able to work through her fears and walk out of a bad situation. The truism grounding this unusual film is that conversation can often be sexier than sex. *1989. 101m. DIR&WRIT: Steven Soderberg. CAST: Andie MacDowell, James Spader, Peter Gallagher, Laura San Giacomo.*

SIX DEGREES OF SEPARATION...

loosely based on a true story, takes its title from the notion that each of us can be linked to any other person on the planet via six intervening people. Although ostensibly about a robbery, the film borders on becoming a love story between wealthy New York matron Stockard Channing and the young black man who walks into her life as 'Sidney Poitier's son.' He has just been mugged in Central Park—or so he claims—and is invited to stay the night at Channing and husband Donald Sutherland's posh Manhattan digs. It's all told in a series of flashbacks as the wealthy couple divert a group of friends with the strange events of the night before. Expect a scenario heavy on dialogue, always clever, and often thought-provoking. Will Smith is dazzlingly charming as the midnight interloper, and Channing and Sutherland give superbly comic portrayals as two smug Manhattanites who have never questioned their privileged place in life until their intruder's visit. *1993. 111m. DIR: Fred Schepisi. WRIT: John Guare. CAST: Stockard Channing, Donald Sutherland, Will Smith, Mary Beth Hurt, Bruce Davison, Richard Masur, Ian McKellan.*

SOUL FOOD...

is a bittersweet melodrama which tells the story of an extended Chicago family held together by the strong spirit of its matriarch—'Big Mama Joe'—and her bountiful weekly

Sunday dinners. But serious troubles are in store when Mama falls into a surgery-induced coma, leaving her three daughters and their various spouses to cope on their own. Rich, successful lawyer Vanessa L. Williams is forever squabbling with happily married younger sister Vivica Fox, when she isn't turning bitchy on her aspiring musician of a husband Michael Beach, ultimately pushing him into a liaison with trouble-making cousin Gina Ravera. Sister number three Nia Long isn't faring much better. Her misguided attempts at getting ex-con hubby Mekhi Phifer a job results in the jealous Phifer playing stupid and landing himself right back in jail. Bad keeps going to worse for this contentious clan until our young narrator, ten-year-old Brandon Hammond, comes up with an unlikely solution to everyone's estrangements. Special mention goes to Kenneth 'Babyface' Edmonds' memorable soundtrack, and to those truly mouth-watering Sunday feasts. (Deep fried catfish, chicken and dumplings, cornbread, black-eyed peas, greens, peach cobbler, to name a few of the delectables set out on that table. Yum!)

1997. 115m. DIR&WRIT: George Tillman Jr. CAST: Brandon Hammond, Vanessa L. Willaims, Irma P. Hall, Vivica Fox, Nia Long, Michael Beach, Mekhi Phifer, Jeffrey D. Sams, Gina Ravera.

THE TALE OF TWO CITIES...

the 1936 black-and-white classic, is the version which comes recommended, in no small part due to Ronald Coleman's splendid leading performance. The story takes place during the turbulence of the French Revolution, with Coleman playing dual roles, both as Sydney Carton, a world-weary London barrister hopelessly in love with the comely Elizabeth Allan, and French nobleman Charles Darnay, who has just been sentenced to death for his connections with a hated and tyrannical Marquis. Elizabeth is married to the doomed Darnay, and in desperation turns to Carton for help, at which point Carton travels to Paris, frees Darnay, and takes his place in the stockade to await execution. Among visual highlights of our scenario is the fall of the Bastille, and the chilling, ferocious rabble-rousers at the guillotine. But spectacle never eclipses this essential character-study of a lawyer frittering his life away until called upon to make the ultimate sacrifice. The dark and shadowy cinematography suits one of novelist Charles Dickens' more brooding masterworks.

1935. 120m. B&W. DIR: Jack Conway. WRIT: W.P. Lipscomb, S.N. Behrman. CAST: Ronald Coleman, Elizabeth Allan, Edna May Oliver, Blanche Yurks, Reginald Owen, Basil Rathbone, Henry B. Walthall.

TALK RADIO...

stars real-life monologuist Eric Bogosian as an in-your-face, acerbic talk radio host, renowned for belittling and badgering callers and listeners alike. He is about to get a big break—his talk show possibly going nationwide—and persuades ex-wife Ellen Greene to fly into town for moral support. Although flashbacks reveal how he got where he is today, sabotaging his marriage while solidifying his career, the bulk of the film's action takes place right in the studio. Bogosian's character is a bona fide misogynist and bully, while remaining hypnotically watchable throughout. Credit is certainly due a script which gives him something to say, and to Oliver Stone's kinetic direction, making the most of that claustrophobic radio studio. Be advised that our anti-hero is not of the rabid, right-wing variety hosting so many present-day talk radio shows, but quite the opposite.

1988. 110m. DIR: Oliver Stone. WRIT: Eric Bogosian, Oliver Stone. CAST: Eric Bogosian, Ellen Greene, Alex Baldwin, John Pankow.

TO KILL A MOCKINGBIRD...

is a lyrical, hauntingly nostalgic scenario starring Gregory Peck as an Alabama lawyer defending a black man who has been accused of raping a white woman in the bigoted atmosphere of 1930s South. En route, our lawyer attempts making sense of the unfolding events to his two children and friends. The story is narrated from the viewpoint of young daughter Scout, and as such, winds up being as much about childhood's imagination, fears, and memories, as it is about social injustice. The end result is an arresting mix of sun-dappled front porches, tree-lined streets of yesteryear, and terrifying bogeymen waiting in dark places, including the ever-present bogeyman of racial prejudice. Peck's subtle performance is the reason for seeing this film, with special mention going to Elmer Bernstein's musical score.

1962. 129m. B&W. DIR: Robert Mulligan. WRIT: Horton Foote. CAST: Gregory Peck, Mary Badham, Philip Alford, Brock Peters, Robert Duvall.

THE TURNING POINT...

serves as an entertaining meditation on that dangerous tendency when hitting middle-age to second guess life choices made in our youth—the proverbial paths not taken and all that might have been. Shirley MacLaine and Anne Bancroft co-star as the two forty-something women whose renewed friendship, after a twenty year hiatus, acts as the catalyst for the mid-life crises to follow. They both want what the other now has. For MacLaine, it is the glamour and excitement of Bancroft's life as a star ballerina, a future she traded in for marriage and family those many years ago. For Bancroft, whose career is in its twilight, it is the love and security of MacLaine's family life which looks so attractive. Fireworks, revelations, and many ballet sequences ensue. Real-life ballerina Leslie Browne is admirably credible as the daughter MacLaine is chaperoning to New York City for a stint with the American Ballet Company, and Mikhail Baryshnikov is a kick at playing—well—Baryshnikov. A quibble: with MacLaine available, why was the obvious non-dancer Bancroft chosen to play our diva ballerina?

1977. 119m. DIR: Herbert Ross. WRIT: Arthur Larents. CAST: Shirley MacLaine, Anne Bancroft, Leslie Browne, Tom Skerritt, Mikhail Baryshnikov, Martha Scott, Marshall Thompson.

TURTLE DIARY...

reminds us in muted, delicate tones—as is screenwriter Harold Pinter's wont—of the tragedy our zoos and reservoirs perpetrate by trapping wild creatures in confined environs for years on end. In this particular case, it is the plight of three ocean turtles who have been imprisoned in a six-foot-square aquarium for an incredible thirty years. Ben Kingsley and Glenda Jackson co-star as two strangers brought together by their mutual compassion for these turtles' predicament. With the help of a sympathetic guard, they work out a scheme to return the turtles to their natural habitat. The process of plotting freedom for these unfortunate creatures serves as a catalyst, encouraging two private, passive individuals to break through their own self-made prisons and reach out to the world around them. Don't expect romance in the usual sense of the word; it is as co-conspirators in rightful action where our two principals will meet.

1986. 90m. DIR: John Irwin. WRIT: Harold Pinter. CAST: Ben Kingsley, Glenda Jackson, Richard Johnson, Michael Gambon, Rosemary Leach, Jeroen Krabbé, Eleanor Bron.

12 ANGRY MEN...

a '50s black-and-white classic, opens in a stifling Manhattan courtroom at the end of a murder trial, with the weary judge admonishing the equally exhausted jurors to heed the fundamental axiom that the defendant is 'innocent until proven guilty beyond a reasonable doubt.' Once back in the jury chamber, the foreman—believing they have an open and shut case—complies with the suggestion for an immediate vote. When the ballots are counted, eleven have elected to convict, with Henry Fonda as the lone holdout. It's not that he is convinced the boy is innocent of murdering his father. But he suggests, at the very least, that the defendant deserves to have his case briefly discussed. Deliberations ensue, tempers flare, personalities, motivations, and prejudices are delineated, as justice is slowly but grippingly served. Fonda and screenwriter Reginald Rose produced this gem and hand-picked the other eleven actors, all who make the well-wrought screenplay come vividly to life.

1957. 95m. DIR: Sidney Lumet. WRIT: Reginald Rose. CAST: Henry Fonda, Lee J. Cobb, Ed Begley, E.G. Marshall, Jack Warden, Martin Balsam, John Fiedler, Jack Klugman, Edward Binns, Joseph Sweeney.

VINCENT, FRANÇOIS, PAUL ET LES AUTRES...

is a profoundly moving tale of middle-age crisis told from the male point of view. Yves Montand heads the stellar French cast as a man who, in spite of his bravado exterior, is losing both his metallurgy business and his beloved estranged wife Stephane Audran, with no one but himself to blame. Then there's Michel Piccoli, who long ago traded in his caring, sensitive nature for material success, with his own marriage suffering accordingly. Serge Reggiani rounds out this trio, happily married but creatively blocked, incapable of finishing the novel he has been working on for the last twenty years. The scenario unfolds over communal feasts at Reggiani's country retreat—and over equally exuberant repasts in various Parisian cafes—with the three friends' assorted wives, friends, and mistresses sharing both the celebrations and the heartbreak. The performances are uniformly distinguished, but special mention must go to Audran's eloquent contribution. An extra bonus is Phillippe Sarde's delicate score, which manages to evoke life's evanescent beauty, as well as its everyday tragedies. Of note: the opening scene under the credits, blue on blue and thus only vaguely discerned, is a high point in Montand's life which becomes poignantly central to our story.

1974. 118m. In French w/English Subtitles. DIR&WRIT: Claude Sautet. CAST: Yves Montand, Michel Piccoli, Serge Reggiani, Stephane Audran, Marie Dubois, Gerard Depardieu.

THE WATERDANCE...

based on writer and co-director Neal Jimenez's personal experience, stars Eric Stolz as a promising young novelist who wakes up in a hospital to find himself locked into a 'halo' head brace, crippled for life due to injuries caused in a hiking accident. What follows is a unique comedy/drama, portraying Stolz' extensive and prolonged physical therapy, while he makes the painful emotional adjustment to life in a wheelchair. At the time of the tragedy, he had been having an affair with his married editor Helen Hunt, and although she continues to give him her total support, he cannot help but question the fairness of tethering her life to his own diminished existence. Other sub-plots involve the equally anguishing adjustments fellow paraplegics are undergoing in Stolz's ward. In particular, we meet and come to know redneck bigot William Forsythe—a member of a bike gang who was broadsided by an automobile while riding drunk—and former cadabout-town Wesley Snipes, whose wife is in the process of suing him for divorce. Unusual friendships supervene. It is a moving, but unsentimental scenario, made all the more effective by the obvious first-hand knowledge Jimenez has brought to the project. Special mention is due Stolz' typically genuine and unaffected leading performance.

1992. 106m. DIR: Neal Jimenez, Michael Sternberg. WRIT: Neal Jimenez. CAST: Eric Stolz, Wesley Snipes, William Forsythe, Helen Hunt, Elizabeth Peña.

WHO'S AFRAID OF VIRGINIA WOOLF?...

Richard Burton and Elizabeth Taylor's finest work together, serves up a devastatingly scathing night at the movies. Burton plays a defeated history professor, and Liz is his harridan of a wife, whose chief reason for getting out of bed every morning is to keep her hubby well aware of what a failure he has become. ("If you existed, I'd divorce you!") As the story opens, it is two a.m. in this small New England town, and our pair are slinging insults at each other while awaiting the arrival of the younger couple they invited back to the house for a drink. Enter Sandy Dennis and George Segal—she's a bit of a sniveling mouse and he a self-proclaimed ladies' man—add a goodly dose of wine and whiskey to the stew, and you have all the necessary ingredients for the emotional brawl to follow, one which is gut-wrenching, soul-baring, and unforgettable. Although dialogue doesn't get much more acidic than this, under Mike Nichols' skilled direction the comic touches as well as the pathos of the situation shine through.

1966. 131m. DIR: Mike Nichols. WRIT: Ernest Lehman. CAST: Elizabeth Taylor, Richard Burton, Sandy Dennis, George Segal.

WILD IS THE WIND...

made forty years ago, vaguely echoes the recent *Bridges of Madison County*, since both scenarios—the former directly and the latter indirectly—deal with the enormous adjustments a native-born Italian woman must make when dropped into rural America. Anna Magnani stars as the forty-ish Italian who comes to the States to marry brother-in-law Anthony Quinn after her sister dies in childbirth. But the bullheaded and overbearing Quinn is confounded by this lustier, more vibrant, and far more demanding version of his first wife. "Why aren't you more like Rosanna?" is the mantra which Magnani hears from her husband once too often before falling into an affair with Quinn's adopted son, Anthony Franciosa. There is genuine electricity between the magnificent Magnani and every other character on screen, including the stallion she saves from slaughter and attempts to tame.
1957. 114m. B&W. DIR: George Cukor. CAST: Anna Magnani, Anthony Quinn, Anthony Franciosa, Dolores Hart, Joseph Calleia.

WITH HONORS...

features Joe Pesci in an uncharacteristically poignant role as a homeless, self-proclaimed 'bum,' living in the furnace room of Harvard's campus library. Enter Brendan Fraser as a strictly-business-kind-of-guy, a Harvard senior who loses the only copy of his all-important thesis down the library air shaft and into Pesci's lap. A game of blackmail ensues, Pesci returning the thesis on a day-by-day, page-by-page basis for services rendered, including food, the occasional shower, and eventually a shot at a room in the house where Fraser lives. In the process, two very different people become close friends and Fraser's character undergoes a conversion of heart and soul. The fine performances from our two principals are further enhanced by the solid contributions from the supporting cast, particularly from roommate Patrick Dempsey and Fraser's incipient love interest Moira Kelly.
1994. 100m. DIR: Alek Keshishian. WRIT: William Mastrosimone. CAST: Joe Pesci, Brendan Fraser, Moira Kelly, Patrick Dempsey, Josh Hamilton, Gore Vidal.

WHODUNIT?

*"It was a hot afternoon, and I can still remember
the smell of honeysuckle all along that street. How
could I have known that murder sometimes smells
like honeysuckle?"*
Fred MacMurray in narration, upon leaving Barbara
Stanwyck's house for the first time,
DOUBLE INDEMNITY

"You're not too smart, are you? I like that in a man."
Kathleen Turner to William Hurt,
BODY HEAT

AMERICAN GIGOLO...

features Richard Gere in a sexy, textured performance as an upwardly mobile stud-about-town who not only services but appears to enjoy the company of the lonely matrons who make up his clientele. The opening sequence sets the tone, Gere tooling down a Southern California expressway to the driving beat of 'Call Me,' on top of a world which is on the verge of a serious meltdown. Unbeknownst to our morally ambiguous protagonist, he's about to be framed for a kinky sex murder committed by the spooky villain of the scenario. There are genuine vibes between Gere and Lauren Hutton, who plays the restless beauty falling in love with this paid-for-hire chaperon. And Hector Elizondo offers welcome comic relief as the detective hellbent on cutting his cocky antagonist down to size. The involving, poignant storyline suffers from a patchwork finale.

1980. 117m. DIR&WRIT: Paul Schrader. CAST: Richard Gere, Lauren Hutton, Hector Elizondo, Bill Duke, Nina Van Pallandt, Brian Davies.

APARTMENT ZERO...

is a bizarrely fascinating, multilayered psychological drama, fueled by an abundance of suggestion and innuendo. Set in the English-speaking quarter of Buenos Aires, the film stars Colin Firth as a repressed and fastidious Argentinian movie buff who runs a failing cinema revival house. In need of funds, he rents out half his flat to mysterious, freewheeling American Hart Bochner—an equal-opportunity seducer of old and young alike—and a parasite/host relationship takes flight. Then a series of gruesome political murders set this Argentine city on edge, and since the assassinations began with the arrival of Firth's new roommate, fellow tenants in the apartment building begin to question the effect of this odd couple on the public's safety. The film offers strong acting, a tantalizing script, and a finale which serves up leading man Firth transformed. And how!

1998. 124m. DIR: Martin Donovan. WRIT: Martin Donovan, David Koepp. CAST: Colin Firth, Hart Bochner, Fabrizio Bentivoglio, Liz Smith.

BODY HEAT...

a modern-day film noir, makes capital use of atmosphere, immersing us in the torrid paradoxes of the movie's small Florida town from the opening credits. William Hurt stars as a penny ante attorney just waiting to be hooked by the likes of married femme fatale Kathleen Turner. In her film debut, Turner delivers the most seductive performance of her career, as a temptress who is as smart and sexy as she is dangerous. Lawrence Kasdan, with a nod to *Double Indemnity*, has fashioned an ingenious, serpentine story, the plot twists handled with hair-raising aplomb. Rarely has lust—forget the hearts and flowers—come across so viscerally on screen. Expect steamy sex, decadent ambience, and crosses and double-crosses, with Ted Danson's supporting contribution and John Barry's insinuating musical score as bona fide bonuses.

1981. 113m. DIR&WRIT: Lawrence Kasdan. CAST: William Hurt, Kathleen Turner, Richard Crenna, Ted Danson, Mickey Rourke.

CAROLINE?...

is an exercise in quietly sustained suspense which eventually turns a most unexpected corner. Stephanie Zimbalist stars as the young woman presumed dead in a plane crash fifteen years earlier, who shows up on her father's doorstep claiming to be none other than the deceased Caroline, thereby making her privy to the substantial inheritance her father had bequeathed her. But is she who she claims to be, or are all her elaborate explanations an intricate deceit? Zimbalist is appropriately cryptic in the lead, as is Pamela Reed as the youngish second wife who is convinced that this Holly-come-lately is going to steal away her own well-deserved monetary legacy. Motives become central to our plot, as does the plight of the two young children who may or may not be Zimbalist's half-sister and brother. And yes, that is Dorothy McGuire as the beloved grandmother.

1980. 100m. DIR: Joseph Sargent. WRIT: Michael de Guzman. CAST: Stephanie Zimbalist, Pamela Reed, Dorothy McGuire, George Gizzard, Patricia Neal.

CHINATOWN...

set in Los Angeles of the late 1930s, stars Jack Nicholson as an honest cop turned 'bedroom dick' hired by Diane Ladd to prove that her husband—the city's Water Commissioner—is guilty of infidelity. But matters take a murky turn when Faye Dunaway arrives at his office, claiming *she* is the commissioner's wife and insisting her husband is not to be tailed. With more curiosity than forethought, Nicholson delves ever deeper into a mystery which gets more convoluted and dangerous by the minute, as he is hounded by villainous goons and resentful cops alike. But none of the above stops our wise-ass private eye from uncovering a scandal-in-progress of immense proportions. Among highlights of this classic detective flick is the convincing recreation of a particular time and place, Robert Towne's moody script, and John Huston's turn as the ruthless villain of the piece. Of note: that's director Roman Polanski playing Huston's creepy little henchman. *1974. 131m. DIR: Roman Polanski. WRIT: Robert Towne. CAST: John Nicholson, Faye Dunaway, John Huston, Perry Lopez, John Hillerman, Darrell Zwerling, Diane Ladd.*

COMPROMISING POSITIONS...

scripted by Susan Isaacs and based on her best-selling novel, stars Susan Sarandon as a bored Long Island housewife who, thanks to her status as a former journalist, cannot resist plugging into the murder investigation of a local philandering dentist. She is amazed to discover that several of her friends had been carrying on dalliances with our murdered dentist—trysts which included being photographed in those 'compromising positions'—and the women are now all paying the price by becoming prime suspects of the crime. It's a slightly bawdy plot, highlighted by Sarandon's provocative rapport with police detective Raul Julia, in one of his sexier performances. (To this investigator's chagrin, our housewife is solving the case faster than he is.) Co-stars include Judith Ivey as Sarandon's acid-tongued best friend, and Edward Herrmann as the loutish husband who finally wakes up and smells the coffee. It's Nancy Drew all grown-up and saucy, with tongue-placed-largely-in-cheek.

1985. 99m. DIR: Frank Perry. WRIT: Susan Isaacs. CAST: Susan Sarandon, Raul Julia, Judith Ivey, Edward Herrmann, Mary Beth Hurt, Joe Mantegna, Josh Mostel, Anne DeSalvo.

THE CONVERSATION...

stars Gene Hackman as a misanthropic wiretapper who accepts any and every assignment, as long as the price is right. All that is about to change, however, when our bugging expert and his assistant John Cazale are hired by a powerful business executive to record a young couple's conversation as they stroll in San Francisco's Union Square. After assembling a master tape in his editing studio and listening to the exchange over and over again, Hackman exposes a key phrase of the conversation which convinces him that murder is afoot. Still plagued by guilt concerning the assassinations triggered by his *previous* surveillance job, Hackman actively takes sides for the first time in his career, attempting to save the young couple's lives. Unfortunately for our cynic-turned-earnest-redeemer, all is not quite as it seems. Among memorable highlights of this harrowing condemnation of illegal espionage is the sequence where the increasingly paranoid Hackman turns his apartment into literal shreds.

1974. 113m. DIR&WRIT: Francis Ford Coppola. CAST: Gene Hackman, John Cazale, Allen Garfield, Harrison Ford, Cindy Williams, Fredric Forrest, Robert Duvall.

COURAGE UNDER FIRE...

gives *Rashomon* an update in this contemporary whodunit concerning a series of events which did or did not take place during the Persian Gulf War. The film opens with Lieutenant Colonel Denzel Washington leading a tank attack on enemy soldiers entrenched in the Iraqi desert. But night vision and air fusillade cause the commander to wrongly order the bombing of one of his own tanks. The colonel's mistaken order of 'friendly fire' is swept under the proverbial political carpet, but to Washington's emotional detriment, he is unable to do likewise. Now stateside, he is assigned to investigate the background of deceased Medevac pilot Meg Ryan—seen in a series of flashbacks as the scenario unfolds—in order to determine if she is worthy of a posthumous Medal of Honor. (If so, she would be the first woman to be this highly distinguished.) His legwork begins by interviewing a crew of soldiers whose lives were saved when Ryan's 'chopper' gave them essential cover from Iraqi attack. But in the process, her own helicopter crashed, and the real mystery to be probed is what happened over the next 12 hours, between sunset and sunrise, when rescue forces finally arrived. The central question which propels the inquiry is why everyone in Ryan's unit managed to survive except for Ryan herself. Wildly diverging stories abound; medic Matt Damon claims she died heroically in combat, while gunner Lou Diamond Philips, at his most scathingly misogynistic, describes her as a frightened, incompetent leader who died in shame. It's a complex inquiry, made all the more difficult by the guilt haunting Washington for his own actions in Desert Storm. But our investigator perseveres, gradually uncovering the gray area wherein lies the truth behind all the half-truths and lies. What follows is the scenario's stirring denouement. *1996. 120m. DIR: Edward Zwick. WRIT: Patrick Sheane Duncan.* *CAST: Denzel Washington, Meg Ryan, Lou Diamond Philips, Matt Damon, Michael Moriarty, Scott Glenn, Bronson Pinchot.*

DEAD AGAIN...

zigzags between 1940s Los Angeles, when an infamous Hollywood murder took place, and present-day L.A. where the participants of that decades-old tragedy—in contemporary incarnations—meet up once again. Revenge appears to be the motivation propelling this karmic rendezvous, but who will be avenging whom? And therein lies the rub. Two very different love stories approach, collide, and threaten to self-destruct, with Kenneth Branagh and Emma Thompson ideal as our time-cruising couple. In the present, Branagh is a private detective specializing in tracking down missing heirs, and Thompson is the gal who has wandered astray. In the black-and-white flashbacks, we cut to Branagh as a Hollywood composer who has recently escaped from Hitler's Germany and married a famous actress, once again played by Thompson. Andy Garcia is the intriguing third element of our story, as the reporter who has lived long enough to play witness to both love stories, and very possibly to both murders. (For tangential reasons, the film comes highly recommended for those attempting to give up the evil weed!)

1991. 107m. DIR: Kenneth Branagh. WRIT: Scott Frank. CAST: Kenneth Branagh, Emma Thompson, Andy Garcia, Derek Jacobi, Robin Williams.

DEATHTRAP...

is one roller-coaster of a thriller starring Michael Caine as a successful Broadway playwright whose latest efforts have been complete flops. Experiencing a crisis of confidence manifested in severe writer's block, he receives a timely manuscript from former drama student Christopher Reeve. To Caine's surprise, it's an out-and-out masterpiece. And now the plot thickens, as Caine sets out to dispose of this up-and-comer—with the reluctant help of ailing wife Dyan Cannon—thereby enabling him to call Reeve's work his own. Such is the deceptively modest foundation upon which this intricate murder mystery is launched. There are more twists, crosses, and double-crosses squeezed into two hours than most of us experience in a lifetime, which is all part of the fun, of course. Expect delightfully cagey contributions from all three leads.

1982. 116m. DIR: Sidney Lumet. WRIT: Jay Presson Allen. CAST: Michael Caine, Christopher Reeve, Dyan Cannon, Irene Worth.

DIAL M FOR MURDER/A PERFECT MURDER...

both the 1954 original and the 1997 re-make, focus on a money-grubbing husband intent on killing his very rich and unfaithful wife. The earlier production co-stars Ray Milland at his urbanely sleaziest as a has-been tennis player who goes to intricate extremes to plot wife Grace Kelly's demise. Since any detective worth his salt would first look to the husband as the culprit, Milland is going to need a rock solid alibi, thus someone else to commit the murder. He blackmails an old acquaintance into doing the dirty deed, and how he goes about this extortion is the first fascinating hook to our story. Nothing quite works out as planned, of course, and Milland's attempts to extricate himself from the mess he has created throws us a few more diabolical curves. Among highlights is the sterling contribution from John Williams as the crafty police inspector. Among caveats is Grace Kelly's inexplicably milk-toasty turn midway through the film. And that brings us to the 1997 re-make, featuring stock market wheeler-dealer Michael Douglas and heiress Gwyneth Paltrow in the leading roles. This time around, screenwriter Patrick Smith Kelly does not make the mistake of diminishing the wife's pluck and acumen after the first killing. To the contrary, she is the character who ultimately resolves the entire mystery. With the exception of one somewhat preposterous turn of events, this update makes for slick and engaging viewing throughout. Special mention is due the intriguing rapport which develops between Paltrow and Inspector David Suchet, as well as the sexy performance elicited from Viggo Mortensen as our heroine's shady love interest.

1954. 123m. DIR: Alfred Hitchcock. WRIT: Frederick Knott. CAST: Ray Milland, Grace Kelly, John Williams, Bob Cummings, Anthony Dawson. 1997. 108m. DIR: Andrew Davis. WRIT: Patrick Smith Kelly. CAST: Gwyneth Paltrow, Michael Douglas, Viggo Mortensen, David Suchet, Sarita Choudhury, Constance Towers.

DOLORES CLAIBORNE...

co-stars Kathy Bates as the small-town widow who did or did not push her wealthy invalid employer down the stairs to her death, and Jennifer Jason Leigh as the estranged journalist daughter who reluctantly returns home to give her mother needed emotional and legal support. Their common adversary is investigator Christopher Plummer, who is positive not only that Bates killed this time around, but that she murdered her husband twenty years earlier, a conviction Plummer was never able to prove in court. As he sees it, the opportunity for retributive justice is now at hand. The unraveling mystery behind the two deaths makes for fascinating cinema. But more than a clever plot, the movie hinges on the love/hate relationship between mother and daughter, a fiery kinship which Bates and Leigh bring home with brutal honesty. Special mention is due David Strathairn's chilling performance as Bates' abusive spouse.

1995. 131m. DIR: *Taylor Hackford.* WRIT: *Tony Gilroy.* CAST: *Kathy Bates, Jennifer Jason Leigh, Judy Parfitt, Christopher Plummer. David Strathairn, Eric Bogosian.*

DOUBLE INDEMNITY...

features a slinky Barbara Stanwyck conning cocky Los Angeles insurance salesman Fred MacMurray into murdering her husband. She gets so far under his skin that in spite of MacMurray's initial revulsion to the murder scheme, he winds up planning the entire homicide himself. Edward G. Robertson completes our cast of principals as the insurance company's suspicious fraud investigator who quickly becomes Stanwyck and MacMurray's wily nemesis. With the exception of a few dated moments, screenwriters Billy Wilder and Raymond Chandler have fashioned the consummate hard-boiled morality tale, with crisp, infectious dialogue to match. (MacMurray, confessing over the dictaphone to his boss: "You were pretty good in there for awhile, Keyes. You said it wasn't an accident. Check. You said it wasn't a suicide. Check. You thought you had it cold, didn't you? All wrapped up in tissue paper with pink ribbons around it. It was perfect except it wasn't, because you make one mistake. Just one little mistake. When it came to picking the killer, you picked the wrong guy. You want to know who killed Dietrichson? Hold tight to that cheap cigar of yours, Keyes...") Of note: the

film's title refers to a caveat in the doomed husband's insurance policy; if he dies in a train wreck the insurance remuneration will double.
1944. 106m. B&W. DIR: Billy Wilder. WRIT: Billy Wilder, Raymond Chandler. CAST: Fred MacMurray, Barbara Stanwyck, Edward G. Robinson, Jean Heather, Porter Hall.

FAMILY PLOT...
an entertaining exploration of coincidence and the criminal urge, showcases the other side of Alfred Hitchcock's genius— the mordant wit bubbling just under the surface of his more serious thrillers. Barbara Harris and Bruce Dern co-star respectively as the bogus clairvoyant and her seedy cab-driver boyfriend who team up to find a dead man who's not really dead, in the hopes of receiving the ten thousand dollar reward. Posthaste they find themselves way over the heads, pitted against two unscrupulous embezzlers played in high camp by William Devane and Karen Black. It's all in good fun, of course, even if there are some genuinely scary moments thrown in with a few genuinely silly ones. Harris and Dern contribute wonderful performances—they make a great comic pair—in what was to be Hitchcock's final film
1976. 120m. DIR: Alfred Hitchcock. WRIT: Ernest Lehman, Alfred Hitchcock. CAST: Barbara Harris, Bruce Dern, William Devane, Karen Black, Ed Lauter.

FATAL VISION...
was Gary Cole's starring debut as real-life Marine officer Jeffrey MacDonald, who did or did not murder his wife and two daughters. MacDonald blamed the bloody homicides on crazed hippies and had a serious stomach wound to lend credence to his story. The grieving father-in-law, here played by Karl Malden, initially believes his son-in-law's version of events, and as a witness for the defense helps deliver a verdict of 'not guilty' at MacDonald's military hearing. But as the months pass, MacDonald's behavior—in particular, the alacrity with which he begins dating other women, and his

obvious lack of remorse while plugging the talk-show circuit—gives Pop reason to begin harboring doubts about the doctor's innocence. He initiates his own inquiry into the triple-murders, becomes convinced that his son-in-law committed the crimes, and launches an exhaustive five-year one-man crusade, successfully petitioning the courts and Congress for MacDonald's trial. It's a gripping drama from start to finish, with Cole carrying off his problematic role with admirable distinction. Malden, as always, is superb. *1984. 192m. DIR: David Greene. WRIT: John Gray. CAST: Gary Cole, Karl Malden, Eva Marie Saint, Andy Griffith, Barry Neuman.*

IN THE HEAT OF THE NIGHT...

a 1967 black-and-white classic, hasn't dated one iota over the years due to the fine talents brought to the scenario by co-stars Sidney Poitier and Rod Steiger. When a wealthy businessman is found dead in small town Mississippi, prejudicial deputy Warren Oates arrests the most obvious suspect, the black stranger waiting at the local train station. But imagine Oates and police chief Steiger's surprise upon learning Poitier is far from being their assassin, that he is, in fact, a hotshot homicide detective on the Philadelphia police force. Poitier's big-city supervisor suggests that he remain in Mississippi long enough to assist his southern colleagues in solving the crime, but Poitier can't get out of this racist town fast enough. The defensive and blustering Steiger feels likewise, until various political pressures—namely the threat from wealthy widow Lee Grant to take her factory out of town unless her husband's murderer is found—force a most unlikely alliance between the white sheriff and his northern black counterpart. It is a working relationship which grows ever stronger, as Steiger is obliged to protect his collaborator from town bigots intent on running him out of town. But racism is a double-edged sword in this atmospheric mystery, brought to life by a complex and convincing script. Among highlights is the scene where our two principals confide over a couple of beers, discovering that they are more alike than they are different. Special mention goes to Oates' contribution as Steiger's horny and hapless deputy.

1967. 109m. B&W. DIR: Norman Jewison. WRIT: Sterling Silliphant. CAST: Sidney Poitier, Rod Steiger, Warren Oates, Lee Grant, James Patterson, Quentin Dean.

THE INCIDENT...

is a quiet political intrigue which succeeds by virtue of Walter Matthau's first-rate leading performance and the provocative storyline. Matthau plays a small-town Colorado lawyer, circa WWII, who becomes the community's pariah when a powerful judge railroads him into defending a German POW against a charge of murder. Complications abound. For starters, the town doctor whom our German is charged with killing, happens to have been Matthau's lifelong friend. And Matthau's own son stands to be killed by German soldiers while on the European front. The entire cast gives Matthau able support, particularly Peter Firth as the accused, and Susan Blakely as the daughter-in-law who has mixed feelings indeed about her father-in-law taking on this case.

1989. 95m. DIR: Joseph Sargent. WRIT: Michael & James Norell. CAST: Walter Matthau, Susan Blakely, Peter Firth, Harry Morgan, Robert Carradine, Bamard Hughes.

KEY LARGO...

stars Humphrey Bogart as an embittered WWII veteran who journeys to a dilapidated hotel in the Florida Keys to pay his respects to the family of a comrade killed in the war. He arrives to find widow Lauren Bacall and wheelchair-confined Pop Lionel Barrymore preparing for an approaching hurricane while being held hostage by previously-deported racketeer Edward G. Robinson and his gang of mobsters. They are demanding temporary refuge from the law, and for extra insurance are holding a town deputy prisoner in a guest room upstairs. There will be a lot of confrontations going on during this tropical storm, as well as death threats, boozing, and a blossoming love interest between Bogart and Bacall. It's a moody, atmospheric John Huston gem, aided and abetted by Max Steiner's musical score.

1948. 101m. B&W. DIR: John Huston. WRIT: Richard Brooks, John Huston. CAST: Humphrey Bogart, Lauren Bacall, Edward G. Robinson, Lionel Barrymore, Claire Trevor.

THE LAST OF SHEILA...

a murder mystery revved into high camp, is an ensemble effort which appears to have been as much fun to make as it is to watch. When the movie opens, Hollywood tycoon James Coburn is hosting a party at which, alas, his wife Shelia becomes the fatal victim of a hit-and-run car accident. Cut to the chase, one year later, when Coburn chooses to commemorate the anniversary of his wife's demise by inviting all the guests from that fatal evening—Richard Benjamin, Joan Hackett, Dyan Cannon, James Mason, Ian McShane, and Rachel Welch—to join him on a week-long yachting expedition. ("A study of six failures," Coburn snidely labels them upon snapping a photo of his assembled invitees.) Our master-of-ceremonies plans an elaborate round of 'whodunit' parlor games which he hopes will weed out his wife's murderer before the week is out. It's 'Murder He Wrote' meets the French Riviera, with a few unexpected twists.

1973. 119m. DIR: Herbert Ross. WRIT: Anthony Perkins, Steven Sondheim. CAST: James Coburn, Dyan Cannon, Richard Chamberlain, James Mason, Joan Hackett, Rachel Welch, Ian McShane.

THE LATE SHOW...

is a quirky, entertaining buddy flick of the first order. Art Carney stars as an over-the-hill private detective attempting to grind out a living in the underbelly of Los Angeles. (How far over-the-hill? He investigates his cases by city bus.) As the story opens, his ex-partner Howard Duff arrives at his doorstep with a fatal bullet lodged in his chest. Carney's fixation on solving the murder and exacting revenge on his longtime friend's death is turned on its ear by the appearance of kooky 'talent scout' Lily Tomlin, looking for professional help in locating her missing beloved kitty cat. Most reluctantly, Carney takes on her case, unaware that Tomlin's past connections—including that kitty—are going to help considerably toward solving his partner's murder. It's a familiar tale of blackmail and betrayal, given a unique twist by the unlikely pairing and knockout performances from our two leads. Tomlin is a heartrending wonder as the lonely, vulnerable urbanite who sees the aging Carney as her possible soul mate and future colleague. (She imagines them as a Nick-and-Nora for the 70s.) And Carney is equally affective as the crusty, ulcerous has-been who gradually senses that this screwy 'dolly' represents a new lease on life.

1977. 94m. DIR&WRIT: Robert Benton. CAST: Art Carney, Lily Tomlin, Bill Macy, Eugene Roche, Joanna Cassidy, John Considine, Howard Duff.

LAURA...

based on the novel by Vera Caspary, is a taut and stylish suspense yarn set within Manhattan's privileged upper crust. When Laura Hunt's body is discovered in her apartment by her maid, police detective Dana Andrews opens an investigation into her death, principally by interviewing the victim's friends and acquaintances. In particular, he seeks information from Laura's rich aunt Judith Anderson, and from her Svengali-like patron, prickly newspaper columnist Clifton Webb. Through flashbacks we learn of Laura's romantic and professional past, while our 'hard-boiled' detective proceeds to fall crazy in love with her painted portrait. The further his inquiry progresses, the more obsessed he becomes with a dead woman he can never have. To say anything more about the plot would risk the revelations to follow. Suffice it to say that the cast imparts uniformly stellar performances, backlit by David Raskins' haunting musical score.

1944. 85m. B&W. DIR: Rouben Mamoulian, Otto Preminger. WRIT: Jay Dratler, Samuel Hoffenstein, Elizabeth Reinhardt, Ring Lardner Jr. CAST: Dana Andrews, Clifton Webb, Gene Tierney, Lane Chandler, Vincent Price, Judith Anderson.

LONE STAR...

stands as independent filmmaker John Sayles' masterpiece, a complex and gripping mystery set amongst three cultures—Anglo, Mexican, and Black—which is so character-friendly that you leave the film feeling as if you have lived in the small Texas border town where the scenario unfolds. Nearly forty years after the mysterious disappearance of brutal, corrupt sheriff Kris Kristofferson, his skeletal remains are discovered in the neighboring desert terrain. The county's present sheriff Chris Cooper begins to suspect not only that Kristofferson was murdered, but that he was killed by Cooper's own father, the late, much-revered law officer whose memory is to be honored with a special unveiling in a few days time. The other locals advise Cooper to let those sleeping dogs lie, but he persists in his investigation, which turns into a layered quagmire with many unsuspected developments, one of the them involving Cooper's own birthright. Moving fluidly between past and present (so fluidly, you might not catch the transitions at times), it's an involving, contemporary whodunit which doubles as an American epic. The acting is uniformly excellent, as is Sayles' script, featuring one of the best last lines in cinema.

1996. 138m. DIR&WRIT: John Sayles. CAST: Chris Cooper, Elizabeth Peña, Kris Kristofferson, Matthew McConaughey, Joe Morton, Clifton James, Ron Canada, Frances McDormand.

MANHATTAN MURDER MYSTERY...

boasts another splendid opening ode to Woody Allen's favorite city, while celebrating his screen reunion with Diane Keaton after a fourteen year hiatus. Keaton, nearing that euphemism called 'middle-aged,' appears to be reveling in it. For rarely has she had so much fun with a role as in this characterization of an irrepressible amateur sleuth, out to prove the next-door neighbor murdered his own wife. Against his better judgment, hubby Allen gets dragged into her investigation, and Nick and Nora are reincarnated with a Jewish twist—no martinis but plenty of schtick. Alan Alda gives a predictably solid performance as the divorced family friend who hankers for Keaton until sexy author Anjelica Huston sashays into the picture, looking and acting better than ever. Together, these four Manhattanites hatch an ingenious scheme for trapping the villain, climaxing in a 'hall of mirrors' homage to *The Lady from Shanghai*.

1993. 105m. DIR: Woody Allen. WRIT: Woody Allen, Marshall Brickman. CAST: Diane Keaton, Woody Allen, Alan Alda, Anjelica Huston, Jerry Adler, Ron Rifkin, Joy Behar.

MASQUERADE...

pairs Meg Tilly, as the innocent, virginal heiress, with Rob Lowe as the all-too-handsome stranger who comes along to unleash all that pent-up passion. But from whence come his motives? And therein lies the rub. Just when we think we've solved that riddle, up pops another twist, keeping us guessing straight to the finish line of this romantic thriller. Among highlights to relish are the lush sequential paeans to the art of yacht racing, a clever script which avoids tripping over itself, an evocative theme song, and while we're at it—what the hell—Rob Lowe!

1988. 98m. DIR: Bob Swaim. WRIT: Dick Wolf. CAST: Rob Lowe, Meg Tilly, Kim Cattral, Doug Savant, John Glover, Dana Delany.

THE MIGHTY QUINN...

is an off-beat and exotic mystery starring Denzel Washington at his most alluring, as a play-it-by-the-book Jamiacan police chief. As the story opens, he is investigating the murder of a white mafioso who apparently had his hands in monied pies both on and off the island. The Jamaican powers-that-be seem intent on fingering a certain 'Maubee' as the culprit, a childhood buddy of Washington's who is in and out of trouble with the law. Our police chief tends to agree with their conclusion, having run into his old friend shortly after the murder, in the possession of a suitcase which came directly from the victim's room. But his estranged wife reminds him that Maubee is a lover, not a murderer. Then too, *why* are those same powers-that-be resisting the obvious need for an autopsy before the corpse is flown stateside? The deepening mystery is enhanced by fine supporting performances from the entire cast, with special mention due Robert Townsend's scene-stealing contribution as the trickster Maubee. Additional praise is due Anne Dudley's rocking original musical score. *1989. 98m. DIR: Carl Schenkel. WRIT: Hampton Fancher. CAST: Denzel Washington, James Fox, Robert Townsend, Mimi Rodgers, M. Emmet Walsh, Sheryl Lee Ralph.*

MURDER AT THE GALLOP...

stars the inimitable Margaret Rutherford as senior citizen/amateur detective par excellence, the feistiest, drollest Miss Marble to grace the silver screen. Our story opens with the death of a wealthy old codger whom the police are convinced died from natural causes. Miss Marble believes otherwise and cajoles her way into the investigation, learning of a mysterious horseback-riding lodge frequented by several possible suspects of the unsolved murder. Before you can say 'tally-ho,' Miss Marble has set herself up for a week at this lodge, where her determined inquiry begins. Many priceless scenes ensue, including Rutherford on horseback, and attending the club's annual dance. (Check out that dress!) Of note: the man who plays Miss Marble's faithful assistant, Mr. Stringer, was Rutherford's devoted real-life husband, Stringer Davis. *1963. 81m. B&W. DIR: George Pollock. CAST: Margaret Rutherford, Robert Morley, Flora Robson, Charles Tingwell, Duncan Lamont, Stringer Davis.*

MURDER IN TEXAS...

relates the eerie-but-true events surrounding the death of society woman and horse-lover Joan Robinson. She is the daughter of oil baron Ash Robinson and young first wife of renowned plastic surgeon Dr. John Hill, when she dies quite suddenly of an undiagnosed illness. It is Pop Robinson, here played brilliantly by Andy Griffith, who first suspects his son-in-law's culpability for his beloved daughter's quick demise. But such suspicions cannot be confirmed until similar sinister patterns develop around the second Mrs. Hill. Excellent performances from all four principals—Griffith, Farrah Fawcett as Hill's doomed first wife, Sam Elliot as the dangerous Dr. Hill, and Katherine Ross as the more fortunate second wife—make for a riveting cinematic outing. Interestingly enough, the script is based on *Prescription: Murder*, the memoir written by Hill's real-life second wife Ann Kurth.

1981. 200m. DIR: William Hale. CAST: Farrah Fawcett, Andy Griffith, Sam Elliot, Katharine Ross, Craig T. Nelson, Barbara Sammeth.

THE MUSIC BOX...

stars Jessica Lange as a Chicago criminal attorney who agrees to defend her immigrant father Armin Mueller-Stahl when—to her total bewilderment—he is charged with committing atrocious Nazi war crimes in WWII Hungary. As the case progresses, the nightmare deepens, facts turning up which leave Lange no choice but to begin suspecting her revered father might actually be guilty of such heinous acts. She eventually travels to Budapest to interview a vital witness and comes across the titular music box, which sets up one of the more understated yet chilling moments on screen. At heart, however, this is an intense legal drama, both in and out of the courtroom, as Lange and prosecutor Frederic Forrest play fast and loose with each other's reputations in a desperate attempt at gaining the upper hand. Special mention is due Mueller-Stahl's finely-tuned, enigmatic performance, in his first English-speaking film.

1989. 126m. DIR: Constantin Costa-Gavras. WRIT: Joe Eszterhas. CAST: Jessica Lange, Armin Mueller-Stahl, Frederic Forrest, Lukas Haas, Michael Rooker, Donald Moffatt.

NORTH BY NORTHWEST...

stars Cary Grant as New York advertising exec Roger Thornhill, who by a freak coincidence gets mistaken for American spy 'George Kaplan,' thus becoming the target of foreign agents who pursue him across the United States. En route, our ill-starred businessman is also framed for murder, whereby the interstate police take chase as well. When we finally learn George Kaplan's identity, it is only the first of several clever curve balls thrown our way. It's a thriller with a surprisingly amusing edge, due to Jessie Royce Landis' droll contribution as Grant's mother. (It would have been even a better film, if Landis' felicitous presence had not been entirely replaced midway through the film by Grant's love interest, Eva Marie Saint.) Hitchcock makes great use of locations throughout, including the United Nations building, the New York Plaza Hotel, Grand Central Station, boundless Illinois corn fields, and the climactic finale atop Mount Rushmore. Martin Landau deserves special mention as James Mason's creepy henchman. And as usual, whenever genius composer Bernard Herrmann pens the score, background music becomes foreground and part of the action itself. *1959. 136m. DIR: Alfred Hitchcock. WRIT: Ernest Lehman. CAST: Cary Grant, Eva Marie Saint, James Mason, Jessie Royce Landis, Leo G. Carroll.*

NOTORIOUS...

is possibly Hitchcock's finest effort, due to the unusual collaboration between the director and leading lady Ingrid Bergman throughout production. Together with screenwriter Ben Hecht, they have fashioned an intricately layered thriller which doubles as a convoluted love story. Desire, deception, contempt, and redemption are the film's running motifs, all which fuse brilliantly by the final curtain. Bergman plays the guilt-ridden daughter of a convicted Nazi spy who is persuaded by American agent Cary Grant to journey to post-WWII Brazil and romance repatriated German Claude Rains, thereby helping the State Department gain access to fascist activity in South America. Bergman must feign affection for Rains, even marry him if necessary, and the fact that she has fallen hopelessly in love with Grant does not change her assignment. Grant rightly credited this film for rejuvenating his flagging career. The supporting roles are solidly rendered, as well, particularly Rains as the oddly sympathetic villain— a man so smitten with his wife that he's blind to her increasing duplicity. Special mention is due Leopoldine Konstantin's contribution as Rains' overbearing, suspicious mother. At a key turning point, just watch that mind of hers spin its cunning wheels. Of note: the film's willingness to portray an amoral murkiness within America's intelligence community had to be a first in 1946 Hollywood.

1946. 101m. B&W. DIR: Alfred Hitchcock. WRIT: Ben Hecht. CAST: Ingrid Bergman, Cary Grant, Claude Rains, Leopoldine Konstantin, Louis Calhern

PRIMAL FEAR...

co-scripted by a woman, features a truly astounding performance from Edward Norton, in his screen debut, as the gentle alter boy who did or did not savagely murder Chicago's esteemed archbishop. As in any well-crafted mystery/thriller, unexpected twists and red herrings abound—including sexual perversion at the highest levels and a big monied real estate scandal—before the story confronts its central question. Among highlights is a uniformly excellent cast, including Richard Gere as the hotshot defense attorney who really *does* believe his clients are innocent until proven guilty, and Laura Linney as the fierce state prosecutor who also happens to be Gere's ex-lover. ("We had a one-night-stand, Marty. A six-month one-night-stand.") Their past history together predictably precipitates confrontations both in and outside the courtroom. Special mention is due cinematographer Michael Chapman's treatment of the city of Chicago, bringing out its shadowy underside as rarely before, and once again, Norton's spellbinding central conribution, one which is bound to stay with you long after the final credits.

1996. 130m. DIR: Gregory Hobitt. WRIT: Steve Shagan, Ann Biderman. CAST: Richard Gere, Laura Linney, Edward Norton, Margaret Colin, John Mahoney, Andre Braugher, Alfre Woodard, Frances McDormand, Terry O'Quinn, Steven Bauer.

PRIME SUSPECT...

a landmark BBC crime-drama scripted by Linda La Plante and starring the marvelous Helen Mirren, focuses on the homicide division of a London police department totally dominated by an ongoing male oligarchy. The opening sequence brings home the situation with casual perfection. (i.e. It is all-too-appropriate that Mirren does not appear on the scene for the first few minutes of film, and when she *does* first enter the picture, it is only to be summarily ignored by her male associates.) But the sexual politics turn far more vicious when the chief investigator of a murder inquiry dies of cardiac arrest and is replaced by Mirren, the only woman of senior police status on the force. In all its patronizing fury, the good-old-boys' network now kicks in with a vengeance. But not to worry, since Mirren proves more than up to the challenge, as she puts all her zeal, guts, and acumen into cracking the investigation, winning over several of her male colleagues in the process. As interesting as is the serial rape/murder case itself, the true fascination of this milestone in police procedure is its perspective on the glass ceiling which any and all women are obliged to confront when breaking into a field which men, since time immemorial, have considered theirs, and theirs alone. Of note: due to the unnecessary proliferation of blood, gore, and melodrama in the *Prime Suspect* sequels, you view the remainder of the Chief Inspector Jane Tennison series at your own risk.

1992. 240m. DIR: Christopher Menaul. WRIT: Linda La Plante. CAST: Helen Mirren, Tom Bell, Zoe Wanamaker, John Bowe, Tom Wilkinson, Ralph Fiennes.

THE PRIVATE LIFE OF SHERLOCK HOLMES...

alludes to the memoirs Dr. Watson requested to be kept under lock and key until fifty years after his death, due to their "delicate and sometimes scandalous nature." Now the time has come to open the strongbox, and we are transported back to 1887 London to relive one of Holmes and Watson's more intriguing misadventures. The film boasts top-notch performances from co-stars Robert Stephens and Colin Blakely, and a script which juggles wit, tragedy, and suspense with equal aplomb. Expect this Holmes to be a far more complex character than the one to which we have become accustomed—less super-sleuth, more mortal—as he tussles with cocaine addiction, feelings of inferiority toward his older brother, and a decided ambivalence vis-a-vis the fairer sex. Among highlights is Clive Revill's walk-on as director of the Russian National Ballet. And now, to quote from our dear Dr. Watson: "The game is afoot!"

1970. 125m. DIR: Billy Wilder. WRIT: I.A.L. Diamond, Billy Wilder. CAST: Robert Stephens, Colin Blakely, Genevieve Page, Irene Handl, Stanley Holloway, Christopher Lee, Clive Revill.

REAR WINDOW...

co-stars James Stewart as a magazine photographer who is temporarily wheelchair-bound due to a broken leg, and Grace Kelly as the gorgeous socialite girlfriend who keeps him company every night. Our bored invalid entertains himself by observing, through his binoculars, the activities of his courtyard neighbors night and day. It's an innocently lascivious diversion until he becomes convinced that one of these neighbors has just murdered his wife and is in the process of carting away her body in a series of suitcases. (Stewart to Kelly: "Just how would you start to cut up a human body?") In the intrigue to follow, it is Kelly, not Stewart, who will be risking all to solve the case. The two leading players—Stewart predictably, Kelly surprisingly—give three-dimensional, nuanced performances, and Thelma Ritter is her usual dry and droll self as Jimmy's sharp-tongued nurse. A few gratuitous and corny vignettes in the lives of the courtyard denizens don't mar this entertaining gem.

1954. 112m. DIR: Alfred Hitchcock. WRIT: John Michael Hayes. CAST: James Stewart, Grace Kelly, Thelma Ritter, Wendell Corey, Raymond Burr.

REBECCA...

co-scripted by a woman, is a gothic masterpiece which serves up an unlikely yet entirely successful pairing in the persons of Joan Fontaine and Laurence Olivier. She plays a rich lady's traveling companion, all awkwardness and humility, and he the world-weary, wealthy widower who is drawn to her shy and innocent ways. Fontaine can't believe her good fortune— either can we—when Olivier asks her hand in marriage, then takes her back to his magnificent estate of Manderley. But her elation is short-lived, when this tremulous, inexperienced heroine is thrust into a sophisticated world that absolutely terrifies her. Nasty housekeeper Judith Anderson exacerbates the situation ten-fold by harping non-stop on the superior qualities of Olivier's dead first wife, Rebecca. The woman drowned under mysterious circumstances over a year ago, and still more mysterious is Olivier's absolute refusal to talk about her death. Riddles abound, as does incipient danger from unexpected sources, all placed in eerie relief by Franz Waxman's haunting musical score.

1940. 130m. B&W. DIR: Alfred Hitchcock. WRIT: Joan Harrison, Robert E. Sherwood. CAST: Laurence Olivier, Joan Fontaine, Judith Anderson, George Sanders, Nigel Bruce, Florence Bates, Gladys Cooper.

SHADOW OF A DOUBT...

co-scripted by women, stars Joseph Cotton as an infamous serial murderer and object of a nationwide manhunt. Narrowly escaping the police, he hops a train west and takes advantage of his status as the long-absent, beloved Uncle Charley to hide out in his devoted sister's Santa Rosa home. His equally adoring niece Teresa Wright, named after her uncle and seeing him as her twin and soul mate, slowly begins to suspect the truth about her uncle, but hesitates to tell anyone, fearing how such a scandal would affect her mother's fragile health. So it comes down to a lethal game of cat-and-mouse between our two Charleys, with a curious sexual tension underlying the impending showdown. Wright shines as the dauntless heroine, as does the eerily soft-spoken Cotton as the woman-hating killer.

1943. 108m. B&W. DIR: Alfred Hitchcock. WRIT: Thorton Wilder, Alma Reville, Sally Benson. CAST: Joseph Cotton, Teresa Wright, MacDonald Carey, Patricia Collinge, Henry Travers, Wallace Ford, Hugh Cronyn.

SPELLBOUND...

an intriguing murder mystery set among a group of psycho-analysts, co-stars Ingrid Bergman as the young therapist who falls hard for Gregory Peck, the new director of their mental health foundation. But it quickly becomes apparent to Bergman that Peck is not who he is pretending to be, that in fact, he himself is ignorant of his own identity since he's suffering from acute amnesia. To compound his dilemma, he is an amnesia victim suddenly accused of murder. Bergman, convinced of his innocence, joins him on the lam, and in a race against time attempts to help Peck recover his past. In particular, they hope to piece together the traumatic events which triggered his original loss of memory. As in so many Hitchcock thrillers, we are treated to an artful blend of action, chills, and top-drawer romance. And for good measure, this one features a dream sequence art-directed by none other than Salvador Dali. Although the script sometimes tests the viewers credulity, the chemistry between Bergman and Peck is titillatingly authentic.

1945. 111m. B&W. DIR: Alfred Hitchcock. WRIT: Ben Hecht, Angus Macphail. CAST: Ingrid Bergman, Gregory Peck, Jean Acker, Leo G. Carroll, Michael Chekhov, John Emery.

SUDDEN FEAR...

co-scripted by a woman, was produced by leading lady Joan Crawford, who ponied up an incredible $800,000 to buy her way out of a studio contract so that she could participate in this independent feature. She plays a successful and wealthy playwright who decides that novice actor Jack Palance does not have the right 'look' as the leading man in her new production and has him replaced. Weeks later, she meets up with Palance again on a cross-country train ride, and after a whirlwind courtship the two get married. On the surface, the union appears to be idyllic. But all is not quite as it seems, and with the considerable help of a dictaphone machine, Crawford is called upon to use her own writing skills to elude her would-be murderers. This is Crawford at her finest, as she runs the emotional gamut from enraptured love, to fear, hate, and tremulous revenge, all the stronger, sadder, and wiser by film's finale.

1952. 110m. B&W. DIR: David Miller. WRIT: Lenore Coffee, Robert Smith. CAST: Joan Crawford, Jack Palance, Gloria Grahame, Bruce Bennett, Mike Connors.

THIEF OF HEARTS...

is the cinematic exploration of one woman's erotic fantasy/nightmare come true. Imagine yourself inside an uninspired marriage to a husband so absorbed in his career that you barely exist for the man. To offset the domestic tedium, you have fallen into the habit of keeping a confidential journal, wherein you inscribe all those erotic yearnings your mate has neither the time nor inclination to fulfill. All well and good until the evening you come home to find that the house has been burglarized, and the intimate diary is among the missing items. Meanwhile, the seductive interloper studies your journal, becoming wholly conversant with your secret 'other side' and exploiting this ill-begotten knowledge to his—and your?—advantage by taking you on a sensual roller coaster ride not soon to be forgotten. The complex chemistry between a very provocative Steven Bauer and Barbara Williams as his subconsciously willing victim, makes for both an erotic and spooky film.

1984. 100m. DIR&WRIT: Douglas Day Stewart. CAST: Barbara Williams, Steven Bauer, David Caruso, John Getz, George Wendt.

THE THIRD MAN...

a dark story further enhanced by appropriately menacing camera work, exemplifies classic film noir, all the more so for not depending on the proverbial manipulating female to further the plot line. Joseph Cotton stars as a self-described hack writer who journeys from the States to post-war, shell-shocked Vienna, in the hope of gaining work promised him by old buddy Orson Welles. But upon arrival, Cotton is promptly informed that Welles was killed in an accident, and that in fact, his funeral is presently taking place. Cotton attends the internment and meets British police inspector Trevor Howard, who claims that Welles was a black market racketeer whose shady dealings probably brought on his premature demise. Cotton doesn't believe his friend could have been capable of such nefarious activities and sets out to prove his innocence by carrying out his own investigation into Welles' life in Vienna. It's a convoluted inquiry which eventually comes down to locating the elusive 'third man' who allegedly helped carry Welles' body from the scene of the crime. Special mention is due Graham Greene's dramatic script, Anton Karas' haunting zither music, and top-notch performances from all three leads.

1949. 140m. B&W. DIR: Carol Reed. WRIT: Graham Greene. CAST: Joseph Cotton, Orson Welles, Trevor Howard, Alida Valli, Paul Hoerbiger, Ernst Deutsch.

THUNDERHEART...

loosely based on real events, stars Val Kilmer as a Native American FBI agent who reluctantly takes on the investigation of a murder on a North Dakota Sioux reservation. The only perk in this unwanted assignment is the opportunity to work and learn alongside the highly respected super agent Sam Shepard. Unfortunately, Shepard isn't quite who he appears to be, and before long Kilmer is depending upon reservation sheriff Graham Greene for any real assistance in solving the case. In the process of unraveling the crime, our leading man becomes immersed in the spiritual traditions of his ancestry and regains a legacy he had disowned in his youth. Powerhouse action and performances abound, with real Native Americans filling most of the supporting roles. Special mention is due Shepard's deceptively effortless performance, as well as Greene's contribution as the shrewd tribal police officer who serves as Kilmer's spiritual and professional guide. The dire poverty and injustice still dogging our country's first Americans serves as the film's sobering subtext.

1992. 118m. DIR: Michael Apted. WRIT: John Fusco. CAST: Val Kilmer, Sam Shepard, Graham Greene, Fred Ward, Fred Dalton Thompson, Sheila Toussey, Chief Ted Thin Elk, Dennis Banks, John Trudell, David Crosby.

TRUE BELIEVER...

based on a real-life court case, stars James Woods as a former champion of '60s radical causes now spending his days smoking pot and defending sleazeball drug dealers. Enter Robert Downey Jr. as the hero-worshiping law clerk who can't believe his idol has given up the good fight. When a poor Korean woman asks for help in freeing her son from a murder rap, the burnt-out Woods wants nothing to do with the case. Downey convinces him otherwise and a fascinating homicide investigation ensues. Among memorable moments, there's Downey's first meeting with his boss, the court scene where a key witness—a paranoid conspiracy freak—takes the stand for the defense, and the repeated re-enactments of the crime and its aftermath, as the truth behind the lies begins to slowly emerge. Special mention is due Yuji Okumoto's quietly charismatic performance as the defendant.

1989. 103m. DIR: Joseph Ruben. WRIT: Wesley Strick. CAST: James Woods, Robert Downey Jr., Margaret Colin, Yuji Okumoto, Kurtwood Smith, Tom Bower, Miguel Fernandez, Charles Hallahan.

2001: A SPACE ODYSSEY...

both brilliant and confounding, has to be taken on its own terms. But what better way to honor the late director Stanley Kubrick than by sitting down for a look at this visually stunning gem? Our story opens in prehistoric times, when the sudden appearance of an imposing black monolith works its magic on the apes in its midst, instantly evolving them into human-like beings. The scenario then shifts to the year 2001, when scientists have found a similar mysterious monolith dug into the moon's surface, which is flashing radio signals in the direction of Jupiter. This intriguing discovery sparks a follow-up space mission to that distant planet. But unfortunately for the astronauts aboard the space craft, the sophisticated computer under their supervision—Hal 9000—revolts and decides to take charge of the mission, at which point the battle for survival between Man and his out-of-control technology is launched. The fact that the special effects of this movie, made over thirty years ago, still stand up against the computer-generated hijinks of '90s filmmaking, is dazzling testimony to Kubrick's genius. Highlights include the opening 'Thus Spake Zarathustra' scene, the moment a bone-used-as-weapon morphs into a space craft to the tune of 'The Blue Danube,' and the spookiness of 'Hal' reading the lips of the two astronauts as they plot his imminent demise. One caveat of our scenario is the absolute, if intentional, blandness of the acting. Suffice it to say that a psychotic computer is the most lovable character on board.

1968. 139m. DIR: Stanley Kubrick. WRIT: Arthur C. Clarke, Stanley Kubrick. CAST: Keir Dullea, William Sylvester, Gary Lockwood, Daniel Richter.

VERTIGO...

is a slow-moving, but intriguing tale of romantic obsession which uses spectacular Northern California locations to great advantage. James Stewart stars as a police detective who takes a permanent mental health furlough from the force when his fear of heights indirectly causes the death of a fellow officer. An old college friend hires Stewart to start trailing his depressed, suicidal wife, a woman convinced that a long-dead relative has returned to possess her. In the process of following this mysterious lady around the streets of San Francisco, our hero falls hopelessly in love. Many unexpected complications ensue. Much of the story's tension is provided by its byzantine, paradoxical machinations which both prevent and allow the consummation of this obsessive love affair. Stewart is at his considerable best, and Kim Novak gives her finest screen performance, effectively playing two very different roles. It must be said, however, that due to the slow pacing, Bernard Herrmann's evocative musical score ultimately becomes the leading player.

1958. 126m. DIR: Alfred Hitchcock. WRIT: Alec Coppel, Samuel Taylor. CAST: James Stewart, Kim Novak, Barbara Bel Geddes, Tom Helmore, Henry Jones, Raymond Bailey.

WITHOUT A CLUE...

spoofs the Sherlock Holmes' mystique by suggesting it was actually Dr. Watson who solved the master's celebrated cases for Scotland Yard, with Holmes existing only as a creation of the good doctor's artistic imagination. But when the English press insist on meeting the celebrated detective, Watson is forced to hire a has-been actor to play the part. Enter Michael Caine as the bleary-eyed, skirt-chasing thespian Reginald Kincaid who does his inebriated best to impersonate Holmes, with Ben Kinglsey playing the part of the brilliant, ever-suffering Watson. (One of the many irate outbursts Watson directs at his blundering cohort: "Do you recall declaring with total conviction that the late Colonel Howard had been bludgeoned to death with a blunt *excrement?*") Caine and Kingsley are equally sublime in their respective roles, taking a hit-and-miss storyline and running away with it.

1988. 107m. DIR: Thom Eberhardt. WRIT: Garry Murphy, Larry Strawther. CAST: Ben Kingsley, Michael Caine, Peter Cook, Jeffrey Jones, Lysette Anthony, Paul Freeman.

YEAR OF THE COMET...

stars a winsome Penelope Ann Miller as the half-American daughter of an English wine merchant who finally gets the opportunity to demonstrate her multiple talents and outshine her insufferable half-brother, when her father sends her off to

Scotland to catalogue the wine cellars of a certain McPhearson castle. High wire adventure awaits, as does romance in the form of macho-blowhard turned knight-in-shining-armor Tim Daly. Louis Jourdan is the dastardly villain of our piece, an aging playboy who will stop at nothing to get his hands on the formula for eternal youth which unwittingly falls into Penelope's hands. Some farcical action sequences are too extended, but the lively chemistry between our two leads more than saves the day. Ditto for the gorgeous landscapes and talents of our supporting cast. (Catch the striking cameo by Art Malik of 'Hari Kumar' *Jewel in the Crown* fame. Now why isn't *he* playing more romantic leads?) Among other highlights, is a hilarious vignette that has Ian McNeice attempting to play a Scottish police investigator. Of note: the movie's title refers to the year 1811, the vintage of one particularly remarkable bottle of wine which Penelope discovers in that castle cellar.

1992. 135m. DIR: Peter Yates. WRIT: William Goldman. CAST: Penelope Ann Miller, Tim Daly, Louis Jourdan, Ian Richardson, Ian McNeice, Julia McCarthy, Art Malik.

NAIL-BITERS

"Mother—what's the phrase?—isn't quite herself today."
Anthony Perkins to hotel guest Janet Leigh,
PSYCHO

*"I like to put values on things, like the value of
eight years versus the value of a family. Interesting
calculations, wouldn't you say, Counselor?"*
Robert Mitchum making a-not-so-veiled threat
to Gregory Peck, the lawyer who put him behind bars
eight years earlier,
CAPE FEAR

ALIEN...

has to be one of the scariest movies ever made, with Sigourney Weaver's ferocious performance taking it right over the top. Cargo spaceship *Nostromo's* trip back to Earth is interrupted by orders from the Home Corporation to investigate a signal from a nearby planet. What the seven-member crew finds is a derelict vessel housing a mysterious hatchery, and when one of these embryos pops from its pod and attaches itself to scientist John Hurt, officer Ian Holm makes the big mistake of letting Hurt and his new friend back on board. In spite of everyone's trepidations, the creature drops off Hurt's face, inert and lifeless. And only now does the terror truly begin. If the first attack of this alien—actually more of an escape— is a graphically gory one, the remainder of the confrontations between crew and monster are virtually bloodless, Ridley Scott's great direction letting our imagination do the work. Weaver's no-nonsense rendering of co-Captain Ripley, in her amazing film debut, makes her one of the strongest heroines in the annals of cinema. Of note: if you enjoy this flick, its follow-up *Aliens* comes recommended as well.

1979. 116m. DIR: Ridley Scott. WRIT: Dan O'Bannon. CAST: Sigourney Weaver, Tom Skerritt, Veronica Cartwright, Yaphet Kotto, Harry Dean Stanton, Ian Holm, John Hurt.

ALL THE PRESIDENT'S MEN...

is director Alan Pakula's quasi-documentary adaptation of Carl Bernstein and Bob Woodward's best-selling book about the Watergate scandal. The movie shows us investigative journalism at its most tenacious: the heavy-duty phone work, the paperwork, the legwork, the bravado and intrusions, lies and manipulations, and whatever else it takes to get at the heart of a story. Robert Redford and Dustin Hoffman work most ably off each other as the two hard-pushing reporters, born competitors who are forced into a reluctant alliance. Redford put this excellent production together—buying up the rights to the book, hiring William Goldman to write the screenplay, and then persuading Hoffman to come on board due to the strength of Goldman's efforts. The end result is an edge-of-your-seat, yet bloodless political thriller.

1976. 138m. DIR: Alan Pakula. WRIT: William Goldman. CAST: Robert Redford, Dustin Hoffman, Jason Robards, Jack Warden, Martin Balsam, Jane Alexander, Stephen Collins, Meredith Baxter.

BAD DAY AT BLACK ROCK...

gives us just that—twenty four hours in one meanspirited western ghost town. Spencer Tracy stars, in perhaps his most commanding screen performance, as the wounded and dispirited WWII veteran who gets off the train at Black Rock one fateful morning in search of a Japanese-American farmer who allegedly lives in the area. Tracy is not saying why he's looking for the fellow, and the townspeople, who appear most unhappy at his arrival, aren't telling Tracy anything at all. Inauspicious beginnings get far worse when the demonic town boss Robert Ryan decides that this stranger is a menace who needs to be 'dealt with,' setting the stage for a grim battle of wits, stamina, and courage. This is a low-key thriller, as evocative and suspenseful as its title suggests, with special honors going to the incisive script, and to Walter Brennan's contribution as Tracy's reluctant ally.

1954. 81m. DIR: John Sturges. WRIT: Millard Kaufman, Don McGuire. CAST: Spencer Tracy, Robert Ryan, Ernest Borgnine, Lee Marvin, Walter Brennan, Anne Francis, Dean Jagger.

BEYOND RANGOON...

grounded on events taking place in Burma throughout the 1980s and '90s, is both a rousing political thriller and a tale of self-redemption imbued with a slightly mystical edge. Patricia Arquette stars as a young widow, devastated by the recent murder of her husband and son. Older sister Frances McDormand persuades Arquette that a trip to Asia might be just the prescription for her emotional recovery, and the two wind up in Burma ('a land of soldiers and monks'), with tour guide Spaulding Gray. When Arquette loses her passport, her companions have no choice but to leave the country without her, placing Arquette at the mercy of a vicious military dictatorship bent on smashing the student-led rebellion in its midst. Among highlights is U Aung Ko's contribution as Arquette's Burmese fellow-traveler, and the otherworldly courage of the young activist—embodying real-life Nobel Peace Prize winner Aung San Suu Kiji—who stands up to the throng of rifle-touting soldiers ordered to gun her down. *1996. 100m. DIR: John Boorman. WRIT: Alex Lasker, Bill Rubenstein. CAST: Patricia Arquette, U Aung Ko, Tiara Jacqueline, Ye Myent, Frances McDormand, Victor Slezak, Spaulding Gray.*

THE BIRDS...

features the film debut of Tippi Hedren as a flippant girl-about-town who initiates a flirtation with Rod Taylor in a San Francisco bird shop. The following day, she drives north to his weekend retreat in Bodega Bay with the intention of surreptitiously leaving a couple of lovebirds on his doorstep. But she is accidentally spotted by Taylor and attempts to save face by claiming to be visiting old school chum Suzanne Pleschette. As chance would have it, Pleschette is a former girlfriend of Taylor's, whose relationship was squelched by his jealous, widowed mother. Hedren and Taylor's mutual attraction seems headed for a similar fate. But then the birds arrive, first singly, then in clusters, then...Well, discover for yourself what Hitchcock has in store for his characters, both human and avian, in this most unique of nail-biters, not advised for the faint-hearted. Among highlights is a literal 'bird's-eye' view of Bodega Bay, the birds' ominous gathering on a playground's monkey bars, and that eerie finale. *1963. 120m. DIR: Alfred Hitchcock. WRIT: Evan Hunter. CAST: Tippi Hedren, Rod Taylor, Suzanne Pleschette, Jessica Tandy, Veronica Cartwright.*

BLACK ICE...

stars Michael Nouri as a struggling novelist/cab driver who picks up a fare from hell. Who *is* this mysterious beauty willing to shell out two thousand dollars for a cross-country commute? Through many detours and hair-raising escapes, it becomes obvious that among other things she is a consummate professional operative. But working for whom and running from what? When we finally learn the identity of Joanna Pacula's character and the reason for her involvement with a certain government official early in the film, the political implications are mind-boggling. It's an erotic, action-packed night at the movies, sporting great wintry landscapes and a surprisingly humorous edge.

1992. 90m. DIR: Neill Fearnley. WRIT: Arne Olson, John Alan Schwartz. CAST: Michael Nouri, Joanna Pacula, Michael Ironside.

BLACKMAIL...

a not-so-familiar story of greed and betrayal, stars Susan Blakely as a lonely, small-town widow who succumbs to the attentions of drifter Dale Midkiff. Unbeknownst to this vulnerable less-than-young lady, a con is in the works involving Midkiff and girlfriend Beth Toussaint. But when Midkiff starts caring for his would-be victim, complications arise, most of them involving sleazy newcomer Mac Davis, set on blackmailing the blackmailers. Matters get dangerously and elaborately crazed, with Miguel Tejado-Flores' dexterous script keeping you guessing up to the final curtain.

1991. 87m. DIR: Ruben Preuss. WRIT: Miguel Tejado-Flores. CAST: Susan Blakely, Dale Midkiff, Beth Toussaint, John Saxon, Mac Davis.

CAPE FEAR...

the 1962 original, is almost unbearably suspenseful due to Robert Mitchum's ultra-menacing performance. Set in the seemingly tranquil Louisiana Bayou, the story focuses on highly principled attorney Gregory Peck, whose family falls under the terror of the man whom Peck sent to jail for rape and assault eight years earlier. Through a series of chilling but credible scare tactics, ex-convict Mitchum begins exacting his single-minded revenge on Peck's family. Unfortunately for Peck, the police are helpless to jail this psychopath, since his sinister threats are too oblique to warrant arrest. Finally our lawyer—by now consumed by the basic instinct of survival for both himself and his family—takes matters into his own hands, which leads up to the heart-palpitating bayou climax. Among highlights, there are uniformly excellent performances, Sam Leavitt's brilliant black-and-white cinematography, and another remarkable musical score from Bernard Herrmann. (As a case in point, try watching that opening shot of Mitchum entering town with the sound turned down. Then review the scene with Herrmann's sound track firmly in place.) Of note: Polly Bergen's fine contribution makes one wonder why we never saw more of her on the silver screen. *1962. 105m. B&W. DIR: J. Lee Johnson. WRIT: James R. Webb. CAST: Gregory Peck, Robert Mitchum, Polly Bergen, Lori Martin, Martin Balsam, Jack Kruschen, Telly Savalas.*

CHARLEY VARRICK...

stars Walter Matthau as a penny ante bank robber who makes two major mistakes. The first error is his choice of partners in the person of proverbial loose cannon Andy Robinson. The second miscall is his choice of targets, a small-town New Mexico bank which just happens to be laundering money for the Mafia. Imagine Matthau's surprise when he opens the loot bag to find a load of cash, $750,00 to be exact, with 'organized crime' written all over it. This unexpected turn of events puts our two thieves smack in the cross-hairs of both the mob and—since a policeman was murdered during the robbery—the FBI. Matthau knows that the only way they are going to elude detection is by leaving the cache of money untouched for at least three years. But punk Robinson demands his share and begins to spend foolishly, which brings vicious hit-man Joe Don Baker hot on their trail. Special mention is due Matthau and Baker for their respectively droll and chilling performances, and that beaut of a finale. *1973. 111m. DIR: Don Siegel. WRIT: Howard Rodman, Dean Riesner. CAST: Walter Matthau, Joe Don Baker, Felicia Farr, Andy Robinson, Sheree North, Norman Fell.*

CHINA SYNDROME...

a tense tingler about the near meltdown of a nuclear plant, was originally dismissed by critics as apocalyptic nonsense. Weeks later, after the accident at Three Mile Island, the film gained instant credibility. Jane Fonda stars as a lightweight TV newscaster who yearns to be reporting on more serious material. While producing a promotional spot for a California nuclear plant, our newscaster gets more than she bargains for when she and cameraman Michael Douglas—his camera still running—play witness to impending disaster in the facility's control room below. It is obvious that catastrophe is only barely averted, and Fonda and Douglas race back to their network to get the footage of a lifetime on the six o'clock news. But the powers-that-be at the studio are persuaded it would be bad policy to air coverage of a nuclear accident just days before another nuclear plant is to get approval to go on line, and they confiscate the film. Douglas steals it right back, and our story takes wing. Jack Lemmon is very fine as the conscience-torn plant supervisor who agrees to help Fonda out, and Douglas, as the brash, hot-headed cameraman, gives one of the finest performances of his career.

1979. 123m. DIR: James Bridges. WRIT: Mike Gray, T.S. Cook, James Bridges. CAST: Jane Fonda, Michael Douglas, Jack Lemmon, Scott Brady, James Hampton, Peter Donat, Wilford Brimley, Daniel Valdez.

CRIMSON TIDE...

a variation on the *Caine Mutiny* theme, is a superbly paced submarine thriller co-starring Gene Hackman as the hard-nosed military lifer, and Denzel Washington as the idealistic college-trained officer. These two natural adversaries are forced into a reluctant alliance when Washington is appointed second-in-command of Hackman's ship. As the boat's executive officer, Washington's most important duty is to act as Captain Hackman's check point. In particular, the captain cannot order a missile launch without his E.O.'s green light. Enter a Russian fanatic who has taken control of a

Soviet silo site and is furiously trying to unlock the station's secret code. When the unthinkable has apparently been achieved, our sub receives a military wire ordering a preemptive strike on the Russian silos. Tense preparations for launch proceed, until a segment of a second message comes across a now damaged radio transmitter, either endorsing the previous command or nullifying it; the telex is too fragmentary to decipher. This precipitates the inevitable war of nerves between Hackman and Washington, culminating in a highly suspenseful, heart-palpitating finale. Special mention is due the crackling-hot script which amplifies the thrills and chills right up to the final scene.

1995. 115m. DIR: Tony Scott. WRIT: Michael Schiffer. CAST: Denzel Washington, Gene Hackman, Matt Craven, George Dzundza, Viggo Mortensen, James Gandolfini.

THE CRYING GAME...

features British actor Stephen Rea, in what will probably stand as his most memorable screen performance, as a conscience-stricken IRA man who gets in way over his head when he attempts to put a human face on his political activities. As the film opens, British soldier Forest Whitaker is kidnaped by the IRA and kept hostage at a rural 'safehouse.' Over the next few days, captor Rea comes to respect and understand his prisoner. Then a brutal British raid sabotages the entire operation, and Rea heads into London to inform Whitaker's former lover 'Dil' of the man's fate. Dil turns out to be an attractive, sympathetic hairdresser/chanteuse with whom Rea—to his befuddled amazement—finds himself falling in love. The film deals with some heady themes, including the nature of loyalty and desire, as well as the futility of violence. Rea, Jaye Davidson, and Whitaker's fine performances overshadow an occasionally clumsy storyline. On the other hand, Miranda Richardson's characterization is relentlessly overdrawn.

1992. 112m. DIR&WRIT: Neil Jordan. CAST: Stephen Rea, Jaye Richardson, Miranda Richardson, Forest Whitaker, Adrian Dunbar, Jim Broadbent, Ralph Brown.

THE DAY OF THE JACKAL...

a superior manhunt melodrama, stars Edward Fox as the 'Jackal,' the code-name for a fictional English hit-man hired by a cabal of conservative Frenchmen to assassinate President de Gaulle. The film's fascination comes from its parallel structure, the action alternating between the Jackal setting up the hit's complex groundwork, and the French and English intelligence services joining ranks to entrap him before disaster strikes. There are a few moments which stretch our credibility, among them Fox overhearing preciously important information by shear happenstance. But in large part this is a smoothly-paced thriller by veteran director Zinneman, boasting a first-rate performance from both Fox and Alan Badel, as the plodding but effective French intelligence officer.

1973. 142m. DIR: Fred Zinneman. WRIT: Kenneth Ross. CAST: Edward Fox, Alan Badel, Cyril Cusak, Olga Georges Picot, Delphine Seyrig.

DEAD CALM...

stars Sam Neill and Nicole Kidman as a bereaved young couple who embark on a yachting excursion off the coast of Australia in an effort to put distance between themselves and their son's untimely death. The unexpected latecomer into this solitary seascape is Billy Zane, who claims to be the lone survivor of a food poisoning attack which killed the other six people on a nearby sinking yacht. But when Neill—after letting Zane on board—rows over to the other vessel to investigate, things are not quite as they have been described. At this point our thriller diverges into two corollary stories, with Neill struggling to keep the boat he is trapped inside of from going under, while wife Kidman carries on a fierce psychological/physical battle with Zane in order to get her windjammer turned around in time to save Neill. The film's emotional center is the grieving wife's credible transformation into resourceful dynamo; as horrible as it was to lose her only child, current circumstances throw into dramatic relief the fact that life still matters, and her husband's life above all else. Haynes' screenplay keeps the violence, not the tension, largely off screen.

1989. 97m. DIR: Philip Noyce. WRIT: Terry Hayes. CAST: Sam Neill, Nicole Kidman, Billy Zane.

THE DEAD ZONE...

highlights Christopher Walken in one of his most sympathetic screen performances, as a man who comes out of a five-year coma with the sudden ability to predict the future of any person he touches. The seer retreats into self-pity and isolation, abdicating his frightening new powers until his one true love Brooke Adams—who married another while Walken was in his deep sleep—reminds him that life *is* still worth living. Partially reborn, Walken agrees to help local sheriff Tom Skerritt identify a serial murderer in their midst. They succeed all too well, with such devastating results that Walken withdraws into his solitary lifestyle once again. But when he impulsively saves the life of a young boy he has been tutoring, our psychic becomes aware of something known as the 'dead zone'—the part of the future which his visions can actually change. Ultimately, our hero is going to exploit his unusual talents to save the entire planet. Sound implausible? As mapped out in this flick, it is both a credible and provoking scenario, in large part due to screenwriter Jeffrey Boam's excellent adaptation of the Stephen King novel.

1983. 104m. DIR: David Cronenberg. WRIT: Jeffrey Boam. CAST: Christopher Walken, Brooke Adams, Tom Skerritt, Martin Sheen, Herbert Lom, Anthony Zerbe, Colleen Dewhurst.

DEATH AND THE MAIDEN...

stars Sigourney Weaver as a woman dealing with a mysterious reservoir of bitterness and rage. When the story opens, her husband's car has broken down, and he is returning home from work accompanied by his impromptu chauffeur, a mild-mannered and charming doctor played by Ben Kingsley. For inexplicable reasons, Weaver hides out in the bedroom upon their arrival, then while the two men are distracted over drinks, sneaks outside and drives off with the good doctor's car. Having little other choice, the two men bed down for the night, at which point Weaver returns, ties up the slightly tipsy Kingsley, and initiates a ferocious battle of wills. She is convinced she knows this man—that voice and particular way of speaking—as the person who repeatedly raped and tortured her when she was a political prisoner in some unnamed South American country. Kingsley insists it's a horrific case of mistaken-identity, and since she was blindfolded when the sessions took place, Weaver's shaken husband cannot unreservedly trust his wife's judgment. This long night's journey into day is riveting cinema up to the very last moment, with Weaver matching Kingsley's performance blow for blow.

1994. 103m. DIR: Roman Polanski. WRIT: Rafael Yglesias, Ariel Dorfman. CAST: Sigourney Weaver, Ben Kingsley, Stuart Wilson.

DIABOLIQUE...

the 1955 French classic, is a sinister, convoluted thriller of murder and intrigue. The story opens at a dreary boys' prep school run by a sadistic headmaster. This dime-store tyrant is so contemptible that his wife and mistress wind up not as foes but as allies, plotting their common nemesis' demise. Their plan is to drown him in a bathtub and then dump his body into the school's swimming pool, making it look like an accident or suicide. All appears to go as planned, until police investigators drain the pool and find no body. The pace of this classic thriller is slow getting out of the starting gate, partly due to the intentionally bleak black-and-white cinematography. But the scenario quickly picks up steam, building to what is surely one of the more spine-tingling climaxes in cinema history. It's a true original whose story line has been mimicked but never equalled in later films.

1955. 107m. B&W. In French w/English Subtitles. DIR: Henri-Georges Clouzot. WRIT: Henri-Georges Clouzot, Jerome Geronimi, Frederic Grendel, Rene' Masson. CAST: Simone Signoret, Vera Clouzot, Paul Meurisse, Charles Vanel.

DON'T LOOK NOW...

stars Julie Christie and Donald Sutherland as a young married couple in deep mourning over the recent accidental drowning of their little girl. For work-related reasons, they travel to winter-time Venice, where they have a chance encounter with a blind woman who claims to have 'seen' and spoken to their dead child. This sets in motion a bewildering chain of events, which builds in edgy spookiness right up to the final curtain. Among highlights of this arresting, occasionally confusing film is Sutherland's close call in the medieval church he is restoring, his final encounter with the red-cloaked figure—who may or may not be his daughter—and the reconciliation love scene between our two principals. Cinematic moments don't get much more erotic than this.

1973. 111m. DIR: Nicolas Roeg. WRIT: Allan Scott, Chris Bryant.
CAST: Donald Sutherland, Julie Christie, Hilary Mason, Clelia Matania, Massimo Serato, Renato Scarpa.

THE EXORCIST...

a horror flick not advised for the kiddies, stars twelve-year-old Linda Blair as an innocent who gradually falls prey to either a severe neurological disorder or possession by an exceedingly degenerate spirit. The story is set in the suburbs of Washington D.C. where divorced actress Ellen Burstyn is living with daughter Blair while starring in the on-location film-within-the-film. As Blair's condition continues to deteriorate, Burstyn seeks counsel from all manner of medical practitioners. But no one is able to pinpoint a physical or psychiatric ailment for her daughter's increasingly bizarre behavior. In desperation, Burstyn finally pursues religious guidance and a possible exorcism from local priest Jason Miller. Miller is reluctant to perform an exorcism himself and enlists the aid of seasoned colleague Max von Sydow, setting the stage for a visceral, savage, and prolonged battle between our exorcist and whatever is inside that little girl. Special mention is due Miller's multilayered performance as the tortured young priest who is experiencing a crisis of faith.

1973. 120m. DIR: William Friedkin. WRIT: William Peter Blatty.
CAST: Linda Blair, Ellen Burstyn, Max von Sydow, Jason Miller, Jack
MacGowran.

EYE OF THE NEEDLE...

is a taut, bloody, bizarrely sexy yarn, starring Donald
Sutherland as a Nazi agent who's been living in Britain disguised as an Englishman since 1938. He's kept a low profile
by residing in a string of dismal boarding houses, while
secretly keeping tabs on the English war effort. Known by his
compatriots as the 'Needle' for the ruthless manner in which
he dispatches those who get in his way, our spy successfully
penetrates British intelligence and learns the details of the
Allies' D-day invasion of mainland Europe. He immediately
heads for a rendezvous with a German submarine off the
British coast, but is waylaid via shipwreck on a Scottish isle
occupied by Kate Nelligan and her legless husband
Christopher Cazenove. Passion, betrayal, murder, and a fierce
battle for survival are the by-products of this chance
encounter. (Or, as Sutherland coolly observes to Nelligan near
film's finale: "The war has come down to the two of us.")
1981. 119m. DIR: Richard Marquand. WRIT: Stanley Mann. CAST:
Donald Sutherland, Kate Nelligan, Christopher Cazenove, Ian Bannen.

FAIL-SAFE...

is another in a long line of excellent films about the futility
of nuclear war. In this case, a computer malfunction in the
Strategic Air Command sends a detachment of aircraft to
drop nuclear bombs over Moscow. The military does everything in its power to stop the squadron, but when the planes
have flown beyond the point of no return, the only option left
is for our president to make an emergency call to the Russian
leadership. In a bomb shelter deep under the White House,
the President attempts the nigh-impossible: to persuade the
Russian Premier that this was all a horrible blunder and ask
him to work together with American officials in preventing
WWIII by finding a way to rectify the nightmarish situation.

The entire cast is top-flight in this gripping scenario, with special mention due Henry Fonda's low-keyed performance as the Commander-in-Chief, and Larry Hagman's contribution as his young interpreter. One caveat is a truly misguided early scene which suggests a young woman is sexually attracted to pro-nuke professor Walter Matthau because of the spectacle of mass-annihilation which he represents.
1964. 111m. B&W. DIR: Sidney Lumet. WRIT: Walter Bernstein. CAST: Henry Fonda, Walter Matthau, Frank Overton, Dan O'Herlihy, Fritz Weaver, Larry Hagman, Edward Binns.

FATAL EXPOSURE...

stars Mare Winningham as a single mother inadvertently trapped inside a terrifying mix-up. On summer vacation with her two sons, she enters a camera shop to collect last week's vacation photos and emerges with the very wrong set of snap shots—pictures which appear to document the surveillance of some middle-aged nobody. When a newspaper article reveals that this 'nobody' has just become the victim of an assassination, the bottom drops from under this family's vacation. In eluding the hit-man, who has learned that both she and her sons are aware of his identity, our heroine's resourcefulness and mettle are tested to their limit. The story, and the escalating risks which must be taken, remain credible due in large part to the talents Winningham brings to the starring role.
1991. 89m. DIR: Alan Metzger. CAST: Mare Winningham, Nick Mancuso, Christopher McDonald, Geoffrey Blake.

FIRE IN THE SKY...

based on a true story—and therefore all the more fascinating—concerns a group of loggers in a small southwestern town who report the disappearance of their co-worker. Bad goes to worse when they cough up the incredible details of their experience to family and friends; if the loggers' are to be taken seriously, their colleague was overpowered and then abducted by a UFO. Not surprisingly, very few citizens in this conservative mountain community can accept their incredible story. What *really* happened to the missing D.B. Sweeney is the question on everybody's lips, with murder being considered a far more plausible explanation. Who can say what the wheels of justice might have done to our five hapless loggers if the missing 'abductee' hadn't stumbled home dazed and petrified five days later. Sweeney's story, induced by hypnosis and shown in flashback, has to be seen to be believed. Special mention is due James Garner's contribution as the skeptical investigator, and Sweeney's performance as the tormented victim of this alien science project.

1993. 111m. DIR: Robert Lieberman. WRIT: Tracy Tormé. CAST: D.B. Sweeney, James Garner, Craig Sheffer, Robert Patrick, Henry Thomas, Peter Berg, Bradley Gregg.

FOUR DAYS IN SEPTEMBER...

opens with deceptively serene historical footage of Rio's celebrated beaches in the mid-sixties. Behind this lovely facade lays the brutal reality: in 1964, Brazil's democratic government was overturned by a military coup, and by 1968, all civil rights, including freedom of the press, had been abolished. It is in September of the following year that a small band of amateurish, if well-intended 'revolutionaries' decide to announce to the world their country's dire situation by kidnaping the American ambassador and threatening to kill him within 48 hours unless the government releases fifteen designated political prisoners. This tense and highly successful cinematic treatment of kidnapper Fernando Gabeira's autobiographical account affords us a surprisingly even-handed chronicle of the explosive escapade, in no small part due to director/writer Bruno Barreta's decision to show multiple viewpoints, thereby endowing the thriller with both objectivity and humanity. Special honors go to the inspired pairing of Alan Arkin as the kidnapped ambassador and Peter Cardosa as the impassioned young activist who finds himself befriending his hostage.

1997. 107m. In Portuguese and English w/Portuguese Subtitles. DIR&WRIT: Bruno Barreto. CAST: Alan Arkin, Peter Cardosa, Fernando Torres, Claudia Abren, Luis Fernando Guimaraes.

THE GODFATHER I & II...

launched Al Pacino's movie career, jump-started Marlon Brando's, established Robert De Niro as one of the premier actors of his generation, and ushered Francis Ford Coppola into the pantheon of great Hollywood directors. Along the way, an entire genre—that of the lowly 'gangster film'—was elevated to something approaching Greek tragedy. Part I opens with the lavish marriage of Don Vito Corleone's daughter to a small-time bookie, while the 'Capo' himself (Brando) is in a back room bartering favors for and from a variety of his faithful underlings. Also attending the wedding ceremony is second son Michael (Pacino), the much decorated marine who has just returned from WWII. College-educated, compassionate, astute, he is the family member everyone assumes is going to remain 'clean' and distant from the tribe's Syndicate affairs. The artistry of our story is how circumstances gradually transform Michael from lamb to lion to ruthless despot, a corruption fully realized in the devastating final scene between Michael and his wife (Diane Keaton).

Godfather II is a multi-generational saga which takes us back in time to play witness to Vito Corleone as a young husband and budding power-broker in turn-of-the-century New York. De Niro's portrayal—an uncanny, youthful echo of Brando's earlier performance—is both subtle and brilliant. Pacino is equally effective as the increasingly heartless, spiritually bereft mob chief. Although Coppola's razor-sharp attention to production values and character development greatly enhance both scenarios, there is no doubt that these are the two most relentlessly violent selections included in this guide.

1972. 175m. DIR: Francis Ford Coppola. WRIT: Mario Puzo, Francis Ford Coppola. CAST: Al Pacino, Marlon Brando, James Caan, Richard Castellano, Robert Duvall, Sterling Hayward, John Marley, Richard Gates, Diane Keaton.

1974. 200m. DIR: Francis Ford Coppola. WRIT: Mario Puzo, Francis Ford Coppola. CAST: Al Pacino, Robert De Niro, Robert Duvall, Talia Shire, John Cazale, Diane Keaton, Lee Strasberg, G.D. Spradin, Richard Bright.

INVASION OF THE BODY SNATCHERS...

the 1956 original—surely one of the more disturbing sci-fi films ever made—comes highly recommended due to Kevin McCarthy's utterly convincing performance in the leading role. As the story opens, an hysterical McCarthy arrives in San Francisco, raving that his small-town California community has been overtaken by aliens. Doctors are in agreement that this lunatic should be institutionalized posthaste, but with considerable reluctance they first agree to hear his story. The scenario now flashes back in time, to the day when McCarthy has returned from a medical convention to find that many of his neighbors are complaining about family members who have become strangers in their midst. Then the complaints suddenly cease, and McCarthy and girlfriend Dana Wynter agree that something very eerie is taking place. Their confusion changes to abject horror when they finally realize what is happening: the entire town populace is being taken over by cold, emotionless, human-duplicating pods coming from outer space. McCarthy and Wynter run for their lives, but it's a seemingly impossible escape act, since the entire area—even the phone system—is now in the aliens' grip. Films don't get much more tense than this, with director's Don Siegel's fast-paced direction deserving highest honors.

1956. 80m. B&W. DIR: Don Siegel. WRIT: Daniel Mainwaring. CAST: Kevin McCarthy, Dana Wynter, Larry Gates, King Donovan, Carolyn Jones, Whit Bissell.

A KISS BEFORE DYING...

stars Sean Young in dual roles as identical twins, both of whom fall prey to the cold, opportunist Matt Dillon. This manipulative fellow has determined from childhood to leap-frog up the social/economic ladder by marrying into the family of copper magnate Max von Sydow. Having done his research, and done it obsessively well, Dillon kicks off his campaign by pursuing one of von Sydow's twin daughters at the University of Pennsylvania. But when those plans go awkwardly astray, he begins wooing twin number two—

Young again, now as a brunette Manhattan social worker—who also makes the mistake of falling in love with the apparently faultless and sweet-hearted Dillon. The serious problems set in when Young defies the police report claiming her twin committed suicide by launching her own investigation into her sister's death. It's a persistent inquiry which turns up inconvenient witnesses, which in turn obliges Dillon to continue his murderous rampage. Ultimately, of course, the battle for survival will come down to our two principals. One caveat to the scenario is the brief opening sequence, inexplicably dubbed and unnecessarily bloody.

1991. 95m. DIR&WRIT: James Deardon. CAST: Matt Dillon, Sean Young, Max von Sydow, Diane Ladd, James Russo, Martha Gehman.

KLUTE...

is a tense psychological drama co-starring Donald Sutherland as a rural Pennsylvania cop in search of a missing friend, last seen in the environs of New York City. The trail of clues leads the detective to call girl and aspiring actress Jane Fonda, whereupon they join forces, Sutherland protecting her from an increasingly menacing client, while Fonda helps him untangle the mystery relating to his friend's disappearance. The scenario unfolds with effective deliberation, emphasizing mood, character, and the intelligent performances given by our leading players. Of further note is the script's decision to de-glamorize the life of a prostitute, even a 'classy' one. Fonda is allowed to let it all hang out—the fears, the remorse, the loneliness—giving added nuance to the delicate love story which evolves between her and Sutherland.

1971. 114m. DIR: Alan J. Pakula. WRIT: Andy & Dave Lewis. CAST: Donald Sutherland, Jane Fonda, Charles Cioffi, Roy Scheider, Dorothy Tristan, Jean Stapleton.

LIVE WIRE...

stars Pierce Brosnan, who for our money is the foremost male action hero in current cinema, his physical presence and sterling good looks complemented by the intelligence and humor he regularly brings to his performances. In the movie at hand, Brosnan is an FBI terrorist expert who is recruited to help identify a mysterious explosive being exploited by a power-hungry psychopath in Washington D.C. It's in the subplot that Brosnan struts his stuff, as a man still crazy for the wife he is presently separated from, both of them struggling to come to terms with their young son's accidental death. When the couple finally reconcile, the lovemaking sequence is reminiscent of an equally erotic scene between Donald Sutherland and Julie Christie in *Don't Look Now*.

1992. 85m. DIR: Christian Duguay. WRIT: Bart Baker. CAST: Pierce Brosnan, Lisa Eilbacher, Ben Cross, Ron Silver.

MAGIC...

the tale of a ventriloquist's slow descent into madness, marks one of Anthony Hopkins' earlier leading roles. When the story opens, our puppeteer appears to be on the cusp of fame and fortune, agent Burgess Meredith having landed him a regular TV series on a major network. The only caveat is that Hopkins must undergo a complete physical exam before any papers can be signed. Threatened by what such an examination might reveal about his deteriorating mental state, Hopkins and his dummy skip town, hiding out in upstate New York, where by coincidence an old high school crush, unhappily married innkeeper Ann-Margaret, runs a summer resort. But it's autumn, with no tourists or hubby in sight. It would be criminal to divulge any more of the plot, but suffice it to say that a wooden dummy has never seemed so lethally alive. In the mood for a hair-raising psycho-drama? Check this one out!

1978. 106m. DIR: Richard Attenborough. WRIT: William Goldman. CAST: Anthony Hopkins, Ann-Margaret, Burgess Meredith, Ed Lauter.

THE MANCHURIAN CANDIDATE...

opens during the Korean War, as a group of American combatants—including platoon leader Frank Sinatra and play-it-by-the-book sergeant Laurence Harvey—are being led into an ambush by their Korean 'guide.' The soldiers are promptly captured by the North Koreans and flown off to parts unknown. Cut to the States at the end of the war, where Congressional Medal winner Harvey is getting a hero's welcome home, arranged by mother Angela Lansbury for the political advantage it will afford her senator husband James Gregory. But there is considerable mystery surrounding Harvey's alleged battle prowess back in Korea. While his fellow platoon-mates all agree that Harvey was a brave and medal-worthy soldier, they are having trouble remembering exactly what Harvey did to deserve all this adulation. The conundrum deepens when many of the platoon members begin experiencing nightmarish, impenetrable flashbacks of their time in Asia. An increasingly anguished Sinatra finally pays a call on Harvey in New York, hoping the war hero can help him straighten out his own disintegrating life. But the visit reveals a lot more than Sinatra could have expected, whereupon he launches a perilous investigation into the conspiratorial heart of America's political landscape. It is an eerie study of mind control and assassination, with Harvey, Sinatra, Lansbury, and Gregory all delivering stellar performances, heightened by Frankenheimer's mesmerizing camera work. *1962. 126m. B&W. DIR: John Frankenheimer. WRIT: George Axelrod. CAST: Frank Sinatra, Laurence Harvey, Angela Lansbury, Janet Leigh, Henry Silva, James Gregory, Leslie Parrish, John McGiver.*

MISSING...

is vintage Costa-Gavras, a blood-curdling spellbinder based on all-too-true events: General Pinochet's ruthless 1973 Chilean coup. Jack Lemmon stars as the real-life Edward Horman, a conservative American businessman who travels down to Chile in the hopes of finding his missing son, a journalist who has been living in Santiago with wife Sissy Spacek for the last three years. Initially, Lemmon finds himself at constant odds with his daughter-in-law, in particular with her 'paranoid' suspicions that the military might have had something to do with his son's disappearance. But slowly, inexorably, as both American and South American officials continue to stonewall his investigation, Lemmon's eyes are opened to the political inferno going on in his midst, including the fact that his son was probably killed because he knew far too much about America's involvement in the coup. The film is a brilliant fusion of the personal and the political, with co-stars Lemmon and Spacek giving top flight performances. It is, in fact, the compelling and evolving nature of their relationship which stands at the heart of this pulsating scenario. (Lemmon to Spacek, near the movie's finale: "For what it's worth, I think you are one of the most courageous people I have ever met.")

1982. 122m. DIR: Constantin Costa-Gavras. WRIT: Constantin Costa-Gavras, Donald Stewart. CAST: Jack Lemmon, Sissy Spacek, Melanie Mayron, John Shea, David Clennon, Charles Cioffi, Joe Regalbuto.

THE NET...

stars Sandra Bullock as a reclusive computer whiz who unwittingly gains possession of a highly volatile computer disc which puts a killer hot on her trail. She manages to escape the first attempt on her life, but returns from the Bahamas to find that her entire identity—social security number, credit cards, mortgage, the works—has been obliterated via the black magic of modern-day computers. Her new identity, provided courtesy of the villains of the story, is that of a woman wanted for a string of felonies, which means that our desperate heroine can no longer seek assistance from the police. Bullock does an admirable job of playing the isolated, hunted quarry, intrepid and resourceful enough to stay one step ahead of her adversaries right through to the galvanizing finale. An added appeal is comedian Dennis Miller's wryly self-deprecating performance as the ex-boyfriend who is Bullock's only ally.

1996. 118m. DIR: Irwin Winkler. WRIT: John Brancato, Michael Ferris. CAST: Sandra Bullock, Dennis Miller, Jeremy Northam, Diane Baker, Wendy Gazelle.

NIGHT OF THE GENERALS...

a WWII whodunit, is an eerie study of radical psychosis. Omar Sharif stars as the Nazi intelligence officer tracking down the brutal murderer of a prostitute in 1942 Warsaw. The only witness to the crime saw a single detail from the fleeing suspect: his uniform sported a general's insignia. Since there were only three German generals in Warsaw at the time of the homicide—Donald Pleasence, Peter O'Toole, and Charles Gray—the process of elimination must now begin. Two years later, with the original crime still unsolved, we find all four principals in occupied Paris, when and where a second prostitute is similarly slain. Sharif begins his investigation anew, with the additional help of French police detective Philippe Noiret. But a far vaster conspiracy is under way, a group of German generals scheming the murder of Hitler, and it is the failure of this latter plot which indirectly allows the guilty party of the prostitute murders to once again elude arrest. Now we move twenty-two years forward, to 1966 Hamburg, where Police Captain Noiret, who has continued to follow the case in honor of his deceased friend Sharif, at long last tracks down our psychotic. A showdown is at hand. *1967. 148m. DIR: Anatole Litvak. CAST: Omar Sharif, Peter O'Toole, Donald Pleasence, Tom Courtenay, Christopher Plummer, Charles Gray, Philippe Noiret.*

NOT WITHOUT MY DAUGHTER...

a harrowing true-life drama based on Betty Mahmoody's autobiography, stars Sally Field as a Michigan housewife who travels to Iran for a short vacation with her daughter and congenial Iranian-born physician husband Alfred Molina. But conditions have changed dramatically since the good doctor left his homeland; with the ascendency of the Ayatollah, a suffocating conservatism reigns which deprives women of any rights whatsoever. Within this repressive atmosphere, hubby reverts back to his family's reactionary practices and decides his wife and daughter should stay on with him in Iran. When Field objects, beatings and confinement are his method of persuasion, until ultimately conceding she may leave, but only on condition that their daughter remain behind. This proviso being totally unacceptable to our heroine, she has no choice but to attempt the virtually impossible: her and her daughter's escape from Iran with no passport, no money, and minimal knowledge of the language. The fact that we never hear the Muslim viewpoint may be troublesome at times, but it is also the film's undeniable strength. Director Brian Gilbert has fashioned a thriller about a stranger trapped in a *very* strange land, with Field's tour-de-force performance making for compelling viewing throughout.

1990. 116m. DIR: Brian Gilbert. WRIT: David W. Rintels. CAST: Sally Field, Albert Molina, Sheila Rosenthal, Roshan Seth, Sarah Badel.

THE PARALLAX VIEW...

opens with a political assassination and a Warren Report-like investigation which concludes there was only one gunman involved, and no proof whatsoever of a conspiracy. Sound familiar? The scenario now jumps three years forward, when at least eight of the witnesses to the assassination have met untimely deaths. Oregon newspaper reporter Warren Beatty's ex-girlfriend Paula Prentiss is convinced that all the witnesses of the senator's assassination saw some incriminating evidence and for that reason are being systematically eliminated by whatever forces are involved. Beatty remains skeptical until Prentiss herself turns up dead, at which point his own investigation is launched. It's a potent political chiller with obvious parallels to both the Kennedys' and Martin Luther King's assassinations, and boasting a finale which supplies the eeriest moment of all.

1974. 102m. DIR: Alan J. Pakula. WRIT: David Giler, Lorenzo Semple Jr. CAST: Warren Beatty, Hume Cronyn, Paula Prentiss, William Daniels, Kenneth Mars.

PSYCHO...

the 1960 original, is a tough review. What can be said about this black-and-white horror classic which hasn't already been reiterated a thousand times before? Is it the scariest film ever made? You betcha. Also one of the more bizarre? Most definitely. Does Anthony Perkins give his most memorable performance? Without a doubt. Perkins leads the stellar cast as an edgy, bird-like motel proprietor who lives under the despotic sway of his aging, invalid mother. He takes care of Mom, and in return, she apparently keeps him safe from corrupting influences. Then trouble arrives in the form of the attractive Janet Leigh, on the lam from embezzlement charges and staying overnight at the motel. After chatting with Perkins, it would seem that Leigh has decided to set things right by returning the stolen loot. But Perkins' mother intervenes at an unforgettable moment, and there's a mighty mess for Perkins to clean up. Bad goes to worse when Leigh's sister Vera Miles, lover John Gavin, and investigator Martin Balsam all turn up at the hotel, wanting to know what has happened to the missing Leigh. Although the movie sports a pitch black sense of humor, be forewarned that there is more than one abjectly terrifying ambush in store for us viewers. Special mention is due Hitchcock's adroit, exacting direction, and Bernard Herrmann's all-string soundtrack, which is as audibly terrifying as they come.

1960. 109m. B&W. DIR: Alfred Hitchcock. WRIT: Joseph Stefano. CAST: Anthony Perkins, Janet Leigh, Vera Miles, John Gavin, Martin Balsam, John McIntire.

THE RIGHT STUFF...

based on Tom Wolfe's non-fiction book of the same title, tells the oft-riveting story of America's precarious rush into the Space Age. The story opens at Edwards Air Base in 1947, when and where test pilots are flirting with the concept of breaking the Sound Barrier. Certain businessmen are willing to pay big bucks to anyone willing to take the leap into the unknown, but ace pilot Chuck Yeager accepts the risk with no cash payment whatsoever. This ambitious shot at breaking Mach I—flying faster than 750 miles an hour—is the first of many dazzling flight sequences to follow. But Yeager's gutsy accomplishment is left in the dust later that same year, when Russia becomes the first country to successfully launch a rocket into space. Determined to beat the Soviet Union at the PR and 'space game,' our country pushes forward with its own rocket research, with the naked political ambition of sending a man into space before the Russians do the same. And so begins America's astronaut program, wherein a league of military candidates are whittled down to the seven chosen ones, who train, boogie, and spar with the media and scientists alike, in preparation for the country's first manned flights into space. This is an amazingly successful modern-day epic from director Philip Kaufman, sporting excellent performances from a stellar cast which includes Sam Shepard, Ed Harris, Scott Glenn, Dennis Quaid, Fred Ward, and an unforgettable Donald Moffat as President Johnson. Special mention is due the stunning aerospace sequences, great editing which takes advantage of extensive historical footage, and a script which weaves healthy doses of comedy and cynicism into its story of remarkable heroism. An additional plus is the frequent opportunity of observing our story from the astronauts' wives' point of view.

1983. 192m. DIR&WRIT: Philip Kaufman. CAST: Sam Shepard, Scott Glenn, Dennis Quaid, Ed Harris, Fred Ward, Barbara Hershey, Donald Moffat, Kim Stanley, Pamela Reed, Veronica Cartwright.

THE RIVER WILD...

is an exhilarating cinematic outing, thanks to Meryl Streep's bravura performance. The actress spent six months getting into condition for her role, and it shows. At forty-something, she is pure sinew, and her skill with the oars so extraordinary, we have no trouble believing she is the character whom she plays—a sportswoman who was known as an expert white-water rafter in her youth. To celebrate her son's tenth birthday, Streep and workaholic hubby David Strathairn are treating him to a rafting expedition down the Columbia River. Enter Kevin Bacon as a fugitive on the run, and an already rocky family vacation quickly degenerates into a season from hell. The white-water segments are breathtaking, as is the hair-trigger suspense. And the opening scene, with Streep rowing down Boston's serene Charles River at dawn, is a wry overture to the edgy perils to follow.

1994. 108m. DIR: Curtis Hanson. WRIT: Denis O'Neill. CAST: Meryl Streep, Kevin Bacon, David Strathairn, Joseph Mazzello, John C. Reilly.

ROSEMARY'S BABY...

is a gothic horror story that manages to be masterfully spine-tingling with nary a trace of violence, overt or otherwise. Mia Farrow and John Cassavetes co-star as a young married couple who move into a Central Park West apartment house and respond to the friendly overtures of eccentric neighbors Ruth Gordon and Sidney Blackmer. Unfortunately, these two odd-balls turn out to be members of a local coven of witches and warlocks, and without the pregnant Farrow's knowledge they strike a most diabolical bargain with out-of-work actor Cassavetes, promising him the role of a lifetime if he agrees to sign on the dotted line. When Farrow begins suspecting her husband's increasingly erratic behavior has something to do with her unborn child, her tension-filled race toward sanctuary begins. Farrow and Gordon give exceptional performances as the yin and yang at our film's chilling center.

1969. 134m. DIR&WRIT: Roman Polanski. CAST: Mia Farrow, John Cassavetes, Ruth Gordon, Sidney Blackmer, Ralph Bellamy, Maurice Evans, Patsy Kelly, Elisha Cook Jr., Charles Grodin.

SALVADOR...

stands as one of James Woods' more memorable screen turns as real-life photojournalist Richard Boyle, who journeys down to El Salvador in 1980 to document the civil strife unfolding in that country. Surely no one but Oliver Stone, in his directorial debut, would have dared to consider this political morass as the topic for a mainstream movie, or more particularly, to examine the direct links between the incoming Reagan administration and the emerging Salvadorean death squads. With the help of Georges Delerue's pulsating musical score, Woods' amazing leading act, and solid support from James Belushi as Woods' reluctant sidekick, Stone turns this political expose´ into an edge-of-your-seat thriller that's bound to stay with you long after the final credits.

1986. 123m. DIR: Oliver Stone. WRIT: Richard Boyle, Oliver Stone. CAST: James Woods, James Belushi, John Savage, Michael Murphy, Elpidia Carrillo, Cynthia Gibb, Tony Plaña.

THE SHINING...

co-scripted by a woman and directed by the legendary Stanley Kubrick, stars Jack Nicholson at his most maniacal. As the story opens, Jack has accepted a position as winter caretaker at a Colorado Rockies resort, in the hopes it will give him the opportunity to write his first novel. Although he has been warned that the isolation at the 'Overlook Hotel' can be extreme (fierce winter storms frequently cut off the area from civilization), he blithely settles into the handsome, wood-paneled lodge with wife Shelley Duvall and son Danny Lloyd. All seems well and good until Danny's psychic gifts kick in, summoning up horrific visions of past (future?) carnage being wreaked in the hotel. Nicholson is visited by similar visions, which ultimately turn him into a crazed monster hell-bent on killing anyone in his way. Special mention is due Duvall and Lloyd's performances as the cornered victims who fight so tenaciously for their lives. Wendy Carlos' electronic score and John Alcott's sumptuous indoor/outdoor cinematography also add to the thrills.

1980. 146m. DIR: Stanley Kubrick. WRIT: Stanley Kubrick, Diane Johnson. CAST: Jack Nicholson, Shelley Duvall, Danny Lloyd, Scatman Crothers, Barry Nelson, Philip Stone.

SILKWOOD...

scripted by women, is the gripping true-life account of Karen Silkwood's courageous stand against the hierarchy at the Kerr-McGee plutonium plant where she worked. When union organizers warn the facilty's overworked employees that safety precautions at the plant are abysmal, Silkwood takes heed, antagonizing her superiors, and even fellow workers afraid of losing their jobs, by campaigning for a unionized and safer plant. But the moment she goes so far as to pilfer engineering X-rays from her boss' office—doctored X-rays which prove that dangerous shortcuts were allowed during construction—our heroine's fate is sealed. The beauty of this story is that Silkwood is not a saint. She has her shortcomings like the rest of us and stumbles just as often as not. But when circumstances demand an increasingly heroic response, she answers in kind. Despite the film's tendency to telescope its denouement, it stands as high drama, with the customary sterling performance from leading lady Meryl Streep.

1983. 128m. DIR: Mike Nichols. WRIT: Nora Ephron, Alice Arlen. CAST: Meryl Streep, Kurt Russell, Cher, Craig T. Nelson, Diana Scarwid, Fred Ward, Ron Silver.

SOMEONE TO WATCH OVER ME...

is a sexy, moody thriller starring Tom Berenger as a policeman from Queens, New York, happily married to wife Lorraine Bracco when he and two fellow detectives are given an around-the-clock assignment as bodyguards for wealthy Manhattan socialite Mimi Rodgers. The lady witnessed a murder and has agreed to testify against the perpetrator, assuming of course that the cops manage to track down the killer before the killer tracks down our would-be witness. Rodgers, initially a cool customer, gradually warms to her handsome and shy bodyguard, at which point a romance takes wing, with Berenger's wife Bracco waiting anxiously in the wings. Although the film's gripping finale is somewhat contrived, the scenario succeeds due to screenwriter Franklin's decision to give priority to character over plot.

1987. 106m. DIR: Ridley Scott. WRIT: Howard Franklin. CAST: Tom Berenger, Mimi Rodgers, Lorraine Bracco, Jerry Orbach, John Rubinstein, Andreas Katsulas.

STRANGERS ON A TRAIN...

based on Patricia Highsmith's novel, is a tension-filled Hitchcock classic. Farley Granger co-stars as an unhappily married tennis pro whose chance encounter on a train with garrulous oddball Robert Walker is going to change his life, now and forever. After getting acquainted over drinks, Walker learns just enough about Granger's present situation to understand that they have something in common, whereupon he comes up with a most unusual proposition: "Listen, it's so simple. Two fellows meet accidentally, like you and me. No connection between them at all, never saw each other before. Each one has somebody that he'd like to get rid of, so they swap murders. For example: your wife, my father. Crisscross." The advantage of such a 'criss-cross,' of course, is that it provides each of our would-be murderers with a solid alibi for the homicide of someone near and dear. Granger finds the entire scheme repulsive, but when his wife turns up dead, the menacing Walker shows up again, threatening to implicate Granger unless be fulfills his side of the bargain. Among highlights in this suspenseful masterwork is the clever opening sequence, where we become acquainted with the film's antagonists simply by observing two sets of feet heading towards the train station. Among caveats is Laura Elliot's portrayal of Granger's wandering wife, a performance so grating and over the top it's a positive relief to have her dispatched. *1951. 101m. B&W. DIR: Alfred Hitchcock. WRIT: Raymond Chandler, Whitfield Cook, Czenzi Onnonde, Alma Hitchcock. CAST: Farley Granger, Robert Walker, Ruth Roman, Leo G. Carroll, Patricia Hitchcock, Laura Elliot.*

THE STUNT MAN...

stars Peter O'Toole as a megalomaniac film director who has the opportunity to play his favorite power games when fugitive-on-the-lam Steve Railsback stumbles onto his movie set. O'Toole offers him shelter from suspicious nearby cops, and when his stunt man dies attempting a dangerous feat, prevails on Railsback to take the man's place. The understated threat: if our escapee doesn't help this bullying director out of a jam, O'Toole is likely to report him to the police. And so Railsback reluctantly agrees to take on the job and is immediately thrust into the crazy world of filmmaking, while becoming ever more convinced that O'Toole is intent on killing him in order to get the ultimate stunt on film. It's an unnerving exercise in paranoia and manipulation, with O'Toole giving one of his finest screen performances.

1980. 129m. DIR: Richard Rush. WRIT: Lawrence B. Marcus, Richard Rush. CAST: Peter O'Toole, Steve Railsback, Barbara Hershey, Allen Garfield, Alex Rocco, Sharon Farrell.

THE TAKING OF PELHAM ONE TWO THREE...

is a nifty police procedural which boasts a very large and realistic cast of characters, all who join forces to halt catastrophe on the New York subway. As our story opens, four armed thugs hijack a commuter train and take all eighteen passengers hostage in exchange for a million-dollar ransom. Bad goes to worse when the gunmen demand that the cash be authorized by the mayor's office and delivered to them within the hour, or one by one, their hostages will be executed. Manhattan's transit authority works in frantic collaboration with the city's police to beat the deadline, with Walter Matthau taking center stage as a transit detective who coordinates the entire effort. His predictable deadpan humor supplies an eerie, if welcome, juxtaposition to the chilling scenario at hand. Special mention is due David Shire's hair-raising musical score.

1974. 105m. DIR: Joseph Sargent. WRIT: Peter Stone. CAST: Walter Matthau, Robert Shaw, Martin Balsam, Hector Elizondo, Earl Hindman, James Broderick.

THE TENTH MAN...

set in Occupied France during and immediately after WWII, is a measured and character-friendly thriller which will soon have you rooting for the enigmatic coward of the piece. As our story opens, monied lawyer Anthony Hopkins is being imprisoned, having become victim of a random Nazi roundup. Then a German officer is killed by resistance fighters, and in retribution, a Nazi commandant orders one out of every ten captives in this particular stockade to be shot at dawn. Hopkins' group picks lots and Hopkins winds up the loser, destined for the firing squad the following day. But he makes a do-or-die offer to his fellow prisoners, proposing to sign over all of his considerable holdings, including a beautiful country estate, to the family of any man who is willing to be executed in his stead. A young fellow racked with consumption takes up his proposition for the good it will do his poverty-stricken mother and sister. Now the scenario cuts to postwar France to find a destitute Hopkins drawn like a moth to fire to his former estate. As would be expected, it is now the home of the mother and daughter still in deep mourning over the senseless death of their beloved son and brother. For obvious reasons, Hopkins assumes a false identity before gradually working himself into their good graces, becoming both their gardener and their friend. Then our story takes a most unexpected turn. Both Hopkins—and Derek Jacobi as his imposter—give predictably high quality performances. *1988. 100m. DIR: Jack Gold. CAST: Anthony Hopkins, Derek Jacobi, Kristin Scott Thomas, Cyril Cusak, Brenda Bruce, Paul Rodgers.*

THE TERMINATOR...

co-written by a woman, is an intelligently crafted and intense sci-fi option, which offers us a mighty heroine to boot. The story opens in Los Angeles in the year 2029, when the earth has been all-but-destroyed by nuclear holocaust. Sophisticated machines are running the show, and they have decided it's time to rid the planet of whatever pesky human element still remains. The scenario now shifts back to the year 1984, when and where two very different characters—cyborg Arnold Schwarzenegger and mystery man Michael Biehn—materialize out of the future to accomplish opposing assignments here in the past. Our cyborg steals a cache of weapons and a car, then looks up the name 'Sarah Connor' in the phone book. There are three women so named, and this impassive killer promptly dispatches two of them, but not the third, as played by Linda Hamilton, who happens to be out for the evening. Hamilton now takes center stage, ducking into the nearest night spot when she suspects she is being followed. The Terminator hunts her down to the club, but fortunately

for Hamilton, Biehn has gotten to her first, and informs her of her momentous destiny—a fate which will only be fulfilled if she can escape the seemingly all-powerful Terminator's murderous intent. In the leading roles, Schwarzenegger and Hamilton play most worthy opponents.
1984. 108m. DIR: James Cameron. WRIT: James Cameron, Gale Anne Hurd, William Wisher Jr. CAST: Arnold Schwarzenegger, Linda Hamilton, Michael Biehn, Paul Winfield, Lance Henrikson.

THREE DAYS OF THE CONDOR...

stars Robert Redford as one of several CIA data researchers whose primary job is to comb fiction and non-fiction alike in search of international secret codes. One day Redford returns from an unscheduled errand to find his entire group of co-workers brutally murdered by unknown assailants. When he attempts to report the slaughter to his superiors in Central Intelligence, it becomes increasingly apparent that forces *within* the organization arranged the hit and that Redford had been an intended victim as well. The ensuing battle of wits and time pits Redford and unwilling accomplice Faye Dunaway against those who wish to finish the job. This film is both an amazingly successful thriller and an eerie prognostication of the Persian Gulf War.
1975. 118m. DIR: Sydney Pollack. WRIT: David Rayfiel, Lorenzo Semple Jr. CAST: Robert Redford, Faye Dunaway, Cliff Robertson, Max von Sydow, John Houseman, Addison Powell, Walter McGinn, Tina Chen.

TIME AFTER TIME...

opens in Victorian London, where Jack the Ripper is practicing his particularly gruesome brand of butchery on the city's back streets. Coincidentally, scientist/novelist H.G. Wells is about to test out his newly developed time machine for invited guests. But the Ripper gets there first and escapes the police hot on his trail by careening himself into the future. Wells pursues the assassin to 1979 San Francisco in a desperate quest to stop him before any more murders take place. Aside from the ingenious entertainment of observing Wells and the Ripper match acumen and wits, the film offers an amusing view of contemporary America from a nineteenth-century perspective. Malcolm McDowell and David Warner are excellent as, respectively, the scientist and his demonic adversary, and Mary Steenburgen is at her most endearing as Wells' modern-day love.

1979. 112m. DIR&WRIT: Nicholas Meyer. CAST: Malcolm McDowell, Mary Steenburgen, David Warner, Patti D'Arbanville, Charles Cioffi.

12 MONKEYS...

co-scripted by a woman, is a phenomenal sci-fi thriller, dauntingly complex and heartbreakingly tragic. Bruce Willis stars as a captive in a futuristic underground society who is forced to go back in time in order to study the germ warfare apocalypse which wiped out most of the planet's population. The hope is that Willis' investigation into the past—our present—might uncover a means to alter the original catastrophic event. But our time-traveler overshoots the designated year and is thrown into a mental institution where he must convince psychiatrist Madeleine Stowe that he is not delusional, that he truly *is* from the future, and that the planet's fate depends on his being set free. After further misadventures, he finally arrives at the appointed year, only to come face to face with his own implacable destiny. Mind-boggling art direction is aided and abetted by Willis's devastating performance, one which is never marred by his trademark smart-ass one-liners. Special mention is also due Brad Pitt for his best screen performance to date as Willis' hyper-demented asylum mate.

1995. 130m. DIR: Terry Gilliam. WRIT: David & Janet Peoples. CAST: Bruce Willis, Brad Pitt, Madeleine Stowe, Christopher Plummer, Jon Seda, David Morse.

2 DAYS IN THE VALLEY...

teeters so frequently between horror and comedy, it's classification is a tough call. But the film's entertainment value is undeniable. As our story opens, radically spooky James

Spader is finalizing a hit with aging wiseguy Danny Aiello. When circumstances go awry, Aiello is forced to make a narrow escape, whereupon he promptly takes hostage pompous art dealer Greg Cruttwell and his put-upon secretary Glenne Headly. While hiding out at Cruttwell's lavish southern California home, Cruttwell's half-sister Marsha Mason and has-been movie director Paul Mazursky arrive on the scene and become hostages, as well. In the meantime, Spader has discovered that the loot he was after is still back at the scene of the crime and returns to the house to find the place crawling with police, including cops Jeff Daniels and Eric Stolz, who *also* become integral to our plot. Among highlights of this convoluted and multi-character film, there is a pungent scene between fellow 'losers' Aiello and Mazursky, and Stolz's portrayal of a sympathetic cop.
1996. 105m. DIR&WRIT: John Herzfeld. CAST: Danny Aiello, James Spader, Greg Cruttwell, Jeff Daniels, Eric Stolz, Glenne Headly, Teri Hatcher, Charlize Theron, Paul Mazursky, Marsha Mason.

UNDER FIRE...

the story of one man's political awakening, stars Nick Nolte as a hotshot photojournalist doing time covering the 1979 Sandinista revolution. While Nolte's camera documents the guerrillas' attempts to overthrow Anastasio Somoza's harsh military dictatorship, his heart and soul stay safely back at Managua's opulent Hotel Continental with the rest of the international press corps. But that's all about to change, in no small part due to nascent love interest Joanne Cassidy. She plays a public radio reporter who is very much aware of the obscene gap between the luxurious lifestyles of Somoza's upper-class supporters and the poverty-stricken reality of the vast majority of Nicaraguans. With her advocacy, Nolte commits the journalistic sin of losing his 'objectivity,' to the extent of helping out the Sandinista cause by doctoring a photograph of a slain guerrilla leader. This dramatic photo brings TV reporter and anchorman wanna-be Gene Hackman back onto the scene from New York, and our story takes an unexpected turn. Among highlights are convincing contributions from all three leads, and direction from Roger Spottiswoode which successfully captures the feverish last days of Somoza's rule. Of note: the fate of Hackman's character—and its aftermath—is based on true events revolving around ABC correspondent Bill Stewart.

1983. 127m. DIR: Roger Spottiswoode. WRIT: Ron Shelton, Clayton Frohman. CAST: Nick Nolte, Joanne Cassidy, Gene Hackman, Ed Harris, Alma Martinez, Holly Palance.

THE VANISHING...

has been remade in the United States, but we recommend the subtler, far superior Dutch original. A young couple, very much in love, are on an auto excursion through the South of France when the inexplicable occurs; the young woman vanishes without a trace, sending her heartsick boyfriend on an obsessive three-year quest to find out what has happened to her. His persistence reaps its own macabre reward, when he is able to confront the man who orchestrated the disappearing act. This is a psycho-thriller which eschews all the blood and gore for the far more satisfying horrors of crazed obsession. Expect very fine performances from all three leads, particularly Johanna ter Steege, whose character is so sensually charming that despite a relatively short time on screen, her presence resonates throughout.

1988. 107m. In Dutch & French w/English Subtitles. DIR: George Sluizer. WRIT: George Sluizer, Tim Krabbe. CAST: Gene Bervoets, Bernard-Pierre Donnadieu, Johanna ter Steege, Gwen Eckhaus, Bernadette LeSache.

WAIT UNTIL DARK...

co-scripted by a woman, stars Audrey Hepburn as a recently blinded housewife whose husband, Efrem Zimbalist Jr., unwittingly brings home an antique doll stuffed with heroin. When hubby is lured away on a wild goose chase, their Greenwich Village apartment becomes a battleground between one seemingly helpless woman and murderous thug

Alan Arkin. Arkin—convinced that Hepburn is hiding the doll—enlists the aid of two unwilling accomplices, Richard Crenna and Jack Weston, to help him wrench it from her possession. Crenna and Weston may be accomplished con-men, but murder is not to their taste. And just to what extent they are willing to play along with Arkin's increasingly sadistic game is part of the scenario's inherent fascination. One problem for our would-be thieves is that, contrary to their belief, Hepburn has no idea where the doll is located. Then too, she is a lot smarter than they first assumed and has an unexpected ally in the form of the little girl who lives upstairs. Arkin is chilling indeed as the master villain, and Hepburn is totally credible as the terrorized, but cagey victim. The unusually clever screenplay is aided and abetted by Henry Mancini's hypnotic score.

1967. 105m. DIR: Terrence Young. WRIT: Jane & Robert Howard-Carrington. CAST: Audrey Hepburn, Alan Arkin, Jack Weston, Richard Crenna, Efrem Zimbalist Jr.

WARGAMES...

a 'what if' thriller which deftly mixes humor with the horrific, stars Matthew Broderick as a young computer whiz who thinks he's tapped into a new line of video games. In reality, however, he has broken through our country's missile defense system and is challenging NORAD to a game of Global Thermonuclear War. When our electronic genius realizes what he's done and tries to warn the proper authorities of impending catastrophe, Pentagon officials arrest him, and the frightening countdown to Armageddon is launched. It's a spooky look at how we might have—still could?—accidentally trigger WWIII, with Broderick's convincing performance a standout.

1983. 110m. DIR: John Badham. WRIT: Walter Parkes, Lawrence Lasker. CAST: Matthew Broderick, Ally Sheedy, Dabney Coleman, John Wood, Barry Corbin.

WHEN A STRANGER CALLS...

not advised for solo viewing, stars Carol Kane as a babysitter who experiences a night of abject terror when a stranger makes repeated phone calls to the house, asking her "Have you checked on the children?" Well, she *has* checked on the children, thank you, and they are safely tucked in bed. But the phone calls persist, and a panicky Kane seeks the help of local police detective Charles Durning. When Durning finally traces the location of the menacing calls, the news is not good. You take it from here, but 'rest' assured that although there are harrowing scenes in this flick, they chiefly show the result of havoc that's been wreaked. Blood and gore aren't what these screenwriters are after, but high-wire tension, which they deliver in spades.

1979. 97m. DIR: Fred Walton. WRIT: Fred Walton, Steve Feke. CAST: Carol Kane, Charles Durning, Colleen Dewhurst, Tony Beckley, Rachel Roberts.

WITNESS...

co-scripted by a woman, is a classic modern-day thriller which manages to juxtapose the idyllic and the horrific with uncanny genius. Kelly McGillis co-stars as a recently widowed young Amish woman who travels into Philadelphia with her eight-year-old son (Lukas Haas) to visit her sister in Baltimore. But travel plans get seriously waylaid when the young boy inadvertently plays witness to a brutal murder in the Amtrack train station. Police detective Harrison Ford brings the boy and his mother down to headquarters, on the off chance that Lukas can identify the guilty party. The youngster indeed fingers the culprit, in a quietly chilling scene, and suddenly Ford becomes a good cop on the run, forced to seek shelter within the widow's Amish community in rural Pennsylvania. For a brief respite the film now takes a gentle turn, focusing on the Amish lifestyle and the growing attraction between Ford and McGillis, before the brutality of contemporary life, personified by our leading man and the bad guys relentlessly tracking him down, ushers in the intense climax. Among highlights is an exhilarating communal barn-raising, and a suggestive courting dance between our two principals. Special mention is also due the modulated performance from the late Alexander Godunov as the Amish farmer who competes for McGillis' affections, revealing a sadly underused talent.

1985. 112m. DIR: Peter Weir. WRIT: Pamela Wallace, Earl W. Wallace, William Kelly. CAST: Harrison Ford, Kelly McGillis, Lukas Haas, Alexander Godunov, Danny Glover, Josef Sommer, Patti LuPone, Jan Rubes.

THE YEAR OF LIVING DANGEROUSLY...

a visceral political thriller set in 1965 Indonesia, spotlights Linda Hunt's amazing performance as the mysterious dwarf photographer Billy Kwan, a man whose devotion to his poverty-stricken country might unintentionally detonate a powder keg of civil strife. Mel Gibson co-stars as an ambitious Australian radio reporter, one of a small corps of news-starved foreign correspondents hanging out in Jakarta's hotels and bars just prior to the fall of President Sukarno. To scoop his rivals, Gibson relies increasingly on the mysterious Kwan, who arranges exclusive interviews for the Aussie in the belief that he is made of worthier stock than his decadent colleagues. Then British embassy attaché Sigourney Weaver comes sashaying out of that swimming pool and into Gibson's erotic landscape, seriously compromising his one-track, competitive state-of-mind. Romance, revolution, and the possibility of a military takeover combine to make matters very dangerous indeed.

1982. 115m. DIR: Peter Weir. WRIT: Peter Weir, David Williamson, C.J. Kock. CAST: Mel Gibson, Linda Hunt, Sigourney Weaver, Michael Murphy, Bill Kerr, Noel Ferrier, Bembol Roco.

Z...

one of the earlier, and surely one of the finer political thrillers ever made, courtesy of master director Costa-Gavras, is based on the real-life assassination of Greek nationalist Lambrakis.

Art imitating life, the death is first labeled accidental by government officials in charge. But an independent inquest by the young play-it-by-the-book judge Jean-Louis Trintignant uncovers such a labyrinth of right-wing police and political corruption that the government is toppled and the opposition leader becomes premier. The film's depiction of the murder and its follow-up makes for a gripping detective story, which is enhanced by a uniformly superb cast, underscored by Yves Montand's brief, charismatic performance. Among other highlights is Irene Pappas' poignant reaction to her husband's death, and the riotous 'parade of the generals,' as increasingly higher authorities are called onto the carpet by investigator Trintignant. Of note: Mikis Theodorakis' galvanizing musical score became so synonymous with the struggle for democracy in Greece, that the composer was put under house arrest after the advent of the 1967 military coup.

1969. 128m. In French w/English Subtitles. DIR: Constantin Costa-Gavras. WRIT: Jorge Semprun, Constantin Costa-Gavras. CAST: Yves Montand, Jean-Louis Trintignant, Irene Pappas, Charles Denner, Georges Geret, Jacques Perrin.

RAINY DAY
VIDEO FETES

FEMALE DIRECTORS STRUT THEIR STUFF:
BIG – Penny Marshall
DESPERATELY SEEKING SUSAN – Susan Seidelman
MISSISSIPPI MARSALA – Mira Nair
THE PRINCE OF TIDES – Barbra Streisand
TRUE LOVE – Nancy Savoca

WOMEN BREAKING INTO A MAN'S WORLD:
COURAGE UNDER FIRE
HEART LIKE A WHEEL
A LEAGUE OF THEIR OWN
PRIME SUSPECT
YENTL

LOVE *AND* MARRIAGE:
ADAM'S RIB
THE BEST YEARS OF OUR LIVES
FRIENDLY PERSUASION
ON GOLDEN POND
THE THIN MAN

THE TIME MACHINE *ala* HOLLYWOOD:
1930s: THE GRAPES OF WRATH
1940s: THE BEST YEARS OF OUR LIVES
1950s: THE MAN IN THE GRAY FLANNEL SUIT
1960s: THE GRADUATE
1970s: COMING HOME
1980s: THE BIG CHILL
1990s: REALITY BITES

IT'S NEVER TOO LATE— FINDING LOVE IN OUR WISER YEARS:
THE BRIDGES OF MADISON COUNTY
CRAZY FROM THE HEART
INDISCREET
THE RECTOR'S WIFE
THE WASH

GREAT COMEDIENNES ON PARADE:
ANNIE HALL – Diane Keaton
THE AWFUL TRUTH – Irene Dunne
FRENCH KISS – Meg Ryan
HIS GIRL FRIDAY – Rosalind Russell
POSTCARDS FROM THE EDGE - Meryl Streep
PRIVATE BENJAMIN – Goldie Hawn
RUTHLESS PEOPLE – Bette Midler
SOAPDISH – Sally Field

THE NON-SEXIST GORGEOUS HUNKS REVUE (HEY, BUT THESE GUYS CAN ACT!):
AMERICAN GIGOLO – Richard Gere
THE MAMBO KINGS – Armand Assante
MASQUERADE – Rob Lowe
THE MIGHTY QUINN – Denzel Washington
THE RIGHT STUFF – Sam Shepard
THIEF OF HEARTS – Steven Bauer

BERNARD HERRMANN— MAESTRO SUSPENSE COMPOSER:

CAPE FEAR
NORTH BY NORTHWEST
PSYCHO
VERTIGO

THE PEERLESS, BOUNDARY-LESS MERYL STREEP:

A CRY IN THE DARK (Australian)
THE FRENCH LIEUTENANT'S WOMAN (British)
OUT OF AFRICA (Danish)
SOPHIE'S CHOICE (Polish)

SALLY FIELD CONQUERING ALL COMERS:

NORMA RAE (Anti-union corporate greed)
NOT WITHOUT MY DAUGHTER (Iranian fanaticism)
PLACES IN THE HEART (Widowhood & bankruptcy)
STEEL MAGNOLIAS (A beloved daughter's death)

FEMALE BUDDY FLICKS:

ANTONIA'S LINE
THE FIRST WIVES' CLUB
FRIED GREEN TOMATOES
HOW TO MAKE AN AMERICAN QUILT
JUST BETWEEN FRIENDS
THE LONG WALK HOME
MOONLIGHT AND VALENTINO
NINE TO FIVE
PASSION FISH
RICH AND FAMOUS
SISTER ACT
THELMA AND LOUISE
AN UNMARRIED WOMAN
WAITING TO EXHALE
WALKING AND TALKING

INDEX

G

H

I

J

JEAN WARMBOLD, the author of four published mysteries and numerous screenplays, has been a self-acknowledged film buff since first reveling in The Wizard of Oz at age eight. She has viewed and reviewed over 5,000 films before assembling this guide.